Eng.d by A.H. Ritchie

Yours Fraternally
C. T. McClenachan

REVISED AND ENLARGED EDITION.

THE BOOK
OF THE

Ancient and Accepted Scottish Rite

OF

FREEMASONRY:

CONTAINING

INSTRUCTIONS IN ALL THE DEGREES

FROM THE

THIRD TO THE THIRTY-THIRD, AND LAST DEGREE OF THE RITE.

TOGETHER WITH

CEREMONIES OF INAUGURATION, INSTITUTION, INSTALLATION, GRAND VISITATIONS, REFECTIONS, LODGES OF SORROW, ADOPTION, CONSTITUTIONS, GENERAL REGULATIONS, CALENDAR, ETC., ETC., ETC.

BY

CHARLES T. McCLENACHAN, 33°,

THE GRAND MASTER OF CEREMONIES OF THE SUPREME COUNCIL, NORTHERN JURISDICTION, U. S.

Fully Illustrated.

Stone Guild Publishing
Plano, Texas
HTTP://WWW.STONEGUILDPUBLISHING.COM/

2009

Originally Published By:
J. J. LITTLE & CO.
1895

This Edition Copyright © 2008
Stone Guild Publishing, Inc.
Plano, Texas
http://www.stoneguildpublishing.com/

First Paperback Edition 2009

ISBN-13 978-1-60532-041-0
ISBN-10 1-60532-041-2

10 9 8 7 6 5 4 3 2

TO

THOSE GREAT PRINCIPLES

Fraternity and Toleration,

UNITING MAN TO HIS FELLOWS.

EMBRACING ALL THAT PERTAINS

TO

MASONIC BROTHERHOOD;

AND WHICH

INCULCATE ON EARTH THE SUBLIME TEACHINGS

"LOVE OF GOD" AND "LOVE OF NEIGHBOR,"

MAKING THE AFTER-LIFE IN A BRIGHTER WORLD

WORTH LIVING FOR,

THIS VOLUME IS INSCRIBED.

CONTENTS.

	PAGE
Dedication	3
Proem	7
Classification of Degrees	9
History	11
Triple Triangle, Emblematic	22
Introduction to the Ineffable and Sublime Degrees	23
FIRST SERIES—Symbolical Degrees	26
SECOND SERIES—Ineffable Degrees, Prefatory	26
Secret Master	29
Perfect Master	47
Intimate Secretary	61
Provost and Judge	69
Intendant of the Buildings	83
Knights Elect of Nine	95
Knights Elect of Fifteen	105
Sublime Knights Elected	115
Grand Master Architect	125
Royal Arch of Enoch	137
Grand, Elect, Perfect and Sublime Mason	149
THIRD SERIES	179
Prefatory	181
Knight of the East or Sword	183
Prince of Jerusalem	195
FOURTH SERIES	213
Prefatory	215
Knight of the East and West	219
Knight of the Rose-Croix, with attendant ceremonials	243
FIFTH SERIES	285
Prefatory	287
Grand Pontiff	289
Grand Master of all Symbolic Lodges	303
Noachite or Prussian Knight	315
Knight of the Royal Axe	323

CONTENTS.

	PAGE
Chief of the Tabernacle	331
Prince of the Tabernacle	347
Knight of the Brazen Serpent	357
Prince of Mercy	367
Knight Commander of the Temple	385
Knight of the Sun	399
Knight of St. Andrew	417
Sixth Series	435
Prefatory	437
Knight Kadosh	439
Grand Inspector Inquisitor Commander	453
Sublime Prince of the Royal Secret	467
Supreme Council 33d degree, Prefatory	489
Inspector General	491
Appendix to the Grand Constitutions of 1786	493
Powers and Duties of Deputies	497
Ceremony of Inauguration and Constitution of a Lodge of Perfection	501
Ceremonial Degree at the Installation of Officers of the Lodge of Perfection	506
Ceremony of Installation of a Lodge of Perfection	508
Constitution and Installation of a Council of Princes of Jerusalem	516
Installation of Officers of a Sovereign Chapter Rose-Croix,	526
Inauguration of a Consistory of Sublime Princes of the Royal Secret	533
Installation of a Consistory	538
Ceremony of Baptism in the Ancient and Accepted Scottish Rite	555
Grand Visitations—Honors due, etc	577
Forms of Refections, commonly termed Feasts or Banquets	578
Toasts of Obligation at Refections	579
Directions in Drinking Toasts of Obligation	581
Masonic Glossary	582
Councils of Deliberation	584
Discipline	586
Ceremonial for a Lodge of Sorrow	589
Forms of Petition for Membership and Application for Dispensation or Warrant	600
Tableau of Officers of the various Supreme Councils	604
Hebrew Calendar	612

PROEM.

THE Volume now presented to the Masonic public assumes to itself no special originality; but the apparent want of a complete and systematic handbook for the assistance and instruction of those essaying the higher walks of Masonry, in the Ancient and Accepted Scottish Rite, would seem to justify the humble ambition which the Collator of this volume has attempted. His personal experience, extending through a period of years, has taught him the necessity of some complete Monitor whereby the beauty and sublimity of the Rite could be more thoroughly and justly rendered.

Deferring, as he does, with all respect to those who have preceded him in similar efforts, he humbly trusts that if he has not added anything of value, interest, or importance to the beautiful ritual of the Rite, that he may not be accused of detracting from any portion of that solemnity and solid worth which necessarily form the basis of its several Degrees.

If incessant study and a practical familiarity with the exemplification of the work can claim for him any merit, he trusts that this volume may receive favor for the intention which the writers' ambition prompts, and that those who follow in similar paths may rectify such errors as may have been inadvertently committed.

The Collator, in presenting the result of his labors to the public, by no means would claim an approach to perfection; it will doubtless be conceded that in this country, so far as the various degrees have been fully worked, that while replete with beauty, moral and instructive teachings, their *rendering* is still susceptible of elaboration and improvement.

The effort of the Collator has been, in this work, to maintain all the original landmarks of the Rite in their pristine purity, and at the same time to embellish, so far as might be proper, with kindred surroundings, many portions of the work where the original ritual might seem defective.

In performing the self-imposed and pleasing task, which is thus completed, it would be improper to forget the aid that has been attained from the writings of the Illustrious Past Grand Commanders of the Northern Jurisdiction of the United States, and in such portions of this work where the Rituals and Monitors of the Northern and Southern Supreme Councils are the same, much credit is due to the present Grand Commander of the Southern Supreme Council, Albert Pike; and it must appear to the Student, that the Sacred writings have been necessarily drawn upon in this connection, including the Koran, Talmud, Josephus, Herodotus, the Persian Magi, and contemporaneous writings, as also Findel, Addison, and others.

CLASSIFICATION

OF THE

DEGREES OF THE ANCIENT AND ACCEPTED

SCOTTISH RITE.

THERE are Six Series of Degrees in the Order, not including that of Inspector-General, or 33d Degree, and contain in numbers of Degrees the following, respectively, 3, 11, 2,—2, 11, 3, to wit:

FIRST SERIES.

Symbolic Lodge—Symbolic Degrees.

1. Entered Apprentice. 2. Fellow Craft. 3. Master Mason

SECOND SERIES.

Perfection Lodge—Ineffable Degrees.

4. Secret Master.
5. Perfect Master.
6. Intimate Secretary.
7. Provost and Judge.
8. Intendant of the Buildings.
9. Elect of Nine.
10. Knight Elect of Fifteen.
11. Sublime Knight Elected.
12. Grand Master Architect.
13. Royal Arch of Enoch.
14. Grand, Elect, Perfect and Sublime Master Mason.

THIRD SERIES.

Council of Princes—Historical Degrees.

15 Knight of the East or Sword.   16. Prince of Jerusalem

FOURTH SERIES.

Rose-Croix Chapter—Philosophical Degrees.

17. Knight of the East and West.
18. Knight of the Rose-Croix de H-R-D-M.

FIFTH SERIES.

Areopagus—Historical and Philosophical Degrees.

19. Grand Pontiff.
20. Grand Master of all Symbolic Lodges.
21. Noachite, or Prussian Knight.
22. Knight of the Royal Axe.
23. Chief of the Tabernacle.
24. Prince of the Tabernacle.
25. Knight of the Brazen Serpent.
26. Prince of Mercy.
27. Commander of the Temple.
28. Knight of the Sun.
29. Knight of St. Andrew, or Patriarch of the Crusades

SIXTH SERIES.

Consistory—Chivalric Degrees.

30. Knight of Kadosh.
31. Grand Inspector Inquisitor Commander.
32. Sublime Prince of the Royal Secret.

Council—Official and Executive.

33. Inspector-General—33d Degree and Last Grade

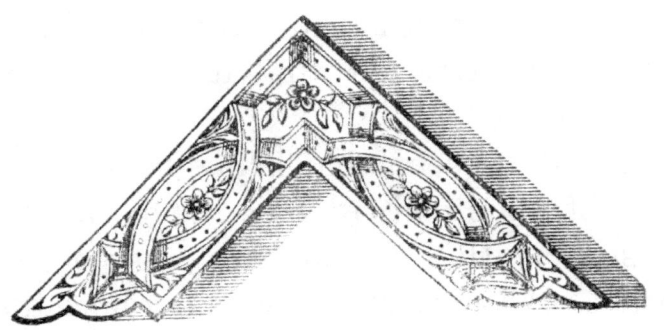

HISTORY
OF THE
ANCIENT AND ACCEPTED SCOTTISH RITE.

THE following pages are not intended to give a full and elaborate history of the Ancient and Accepted Scottish Rite; space cannot be spared in a work intended only as a monitor or handbook for the guidance and instruction of those having an interest in the Rite;—yet it is deemed proper and expedient to insert a brief history for the information of those who might not have the opportunity of searching and examining a subject claiming so much interest.

The antiquity of Freemasonry and its ancient history are evidently involved in fable, and the few authentic historians whose works are extant, have thrown but little light upon the subject. The opinions of those who have written on Freemasonry have differed with regard to its origin as an *organized* institution.

Dr. Robison, who, it is well known, labored to identify Freemasonry with Illuminism, ascribed its origin to the association of Dionysian artificers; Chevalier Ramsay has endeavored to prove that it arose during the Crusades;

Mr. Clinch, that it originated from the institution of Pythagoras; Mr. Barruel, that it is a continuation of the Templars, &c.

Hence it will be seen that it has been allowed, even by the most skeptical, to have been instituted at a period sufficiently remote to entitle it to the appellation of "Ancient;" and we may here dismiss the subject by noting the fact that "its most learned enemies cannot point to the time when Freemasonry *did not exist,* which gives it a fame—a pre-eminence—to which the history of other institutions affords no parallel."

It is not claimed that the Ancient and Accepted Scottish Rite is of extreme antiquity, yet the frosts of time decorate its brow.

Although in a detached form, doubtless some of the degrees had their origin as early as the fourteenth century; yet the Rite, as such, germinated in the latter part of the seventeenth century, and took its distinctive character in the beginning of the eighteenth century.

The late Giles Fonda Yates, a member of the British Archaeological Association, Grand Commander of the Northern Supreme Council of the United States, gave as the result of his research the following:

"The proofs are undeniable that the learning contained in the "Sublime Degrees," was taught long previous to the last century—our M∴ P∴ Brother Dalcho (Rev. Doctor) thinks shortly after the first Crusade. In Prussia, France, and Scotland the principal degrees of our Rite appeared in an organized form in 1713. The unfortunate Lord Derwentwater and his associate English brethren were working in Lodges of Harodim, in 1725, in Paris, when the Grand Lodge of England transmitted to France the Ancient York Constitutions. Many Scotch brethren (adherents of the Pretender, James Stuart) being in France about this time, also cultivated some of the high degrees of our rite."

The opponents of the Ancient Accepted Scottish Rite, such as Findel, and others, assert that the Rite took its origin about the year 1740, from Michael Andrew Ramsay, a native of Scotland, generally known as the "Chevalier Ramsay," who was born at Ayr in 1686, and died in St. Germain-en-laye, in France, in 1743; that from the time of the banishment of the Stuarts from England in 1688, secret alliances had been kept up between Rome and Scotland, the Pretender Stuart having retired in 1719 to Rome; that as these communications became more intimate, the hopes of the Pretender increased; that Ramsay attempted to corrupt the loyalty and fealty of Freemasonry in the Grand Lodge of Scotland, founded in 1736, and being unable so to do, conceived the scheme of assembling and more fully banding together, the faithful adherents of the banished royal family in the higher grades, and thus filling their private coffers; that the Masonic Lodges of France were composed of Scotch conspirators and accomplices of the Jesuits, who had sunk so low they were ready to seize on the abundance of display and effect which were presented; not knowing that the "Masonic titles in our 'Inner East,' like the jewels on our breasts, are not cherished and worn by us for show or aggrandizement, but that they are suggestive of holy truths and self-perfecting duties."

THORY, in the *Acta Latamorum,* says that "Robert Bruce, King of Scotland, under the title of Robert I., created the order of St. Andrew of Chardon, after the battle of Bannockburn, which was fought June 24th, 1314. To this order was afterward united that of Heredon, for the sake of the Scotch Masons, who formed a part of the thirty thousand troops with whom he had fought an army of one hundred thousand Englishmen. King Robert reserved the title of Grand Master to himself and his successors forever, and founded the Royal Grand Lodge of Heredom at Kilwinning."

Dr. Oliver says "this Royal Order afterward confined itself solely to the two degrees of Heredom and Rosycross."

The following is perhaps the more reliable and probable history of the origin of the degrees of the Ancient Accepted Scottish Rite. At or about the period of the Masonic revival and excitement in the early part of the 18th century, there was felt a desire for a deeper research into the arcana of Freemasonry, and a thorough examination of the esoteric doctrines of the Order. The more ardent and brilliant minds of Europe, determining to explore the Kabala, and enticed by so ennobling a study, resolved to establish a superior grade of Masonry, for the exclusive propagation of the Mysteries as yet so little known to them, embracing the Historical, Philosophical, and Chivalric.

With this purpose in view, attempts were made to establish separate and distinct organizations, wherein these sublime truths might be revealed and cultivated.

Nearly all these projects were ephemeral, and were outlived by their projectors, while the "Rite of Perfection," the *germ* of the *organization* of the Ancient and Accepted Scottish Rite—based upon the pure principles of Masonry, and the elucidation of the occult mysteries, containing twenty-five degrees—gradually approached development.

Doubtless the course of the Chevalier Ramsay, in 1740, hastened the consummation of the systematizing and embodying the degrees which had theretofore been for many years detached and unlocated.

Some authorities assert that this Rite of Perfection as an organization was founded in 1753, while others insist that in 1758 certain Masons, styling themselves "Sovereign Princes and Grand Officers of the Grand and Sovereign Lodge of St. John of Jerusalem," founded at Paris a body called "The Council of Emperors of the East and West." This Council has been ordinarily known as the Rite of Perfection, and according to Thory, Ragon, Leveque, Vidal, Ferandie, Clavel, and others, consisted of twenty-five degrees: in 1759 it established a Council of Princes of the Royal Secret at Bordeaux, and from this period began to extend itself.

By the year 1761, the Lodges, Councils, Chapters, and

Consistories of the Rite had increased and extended throughout the continent of Europe; on the 27th of August of that year, Stephen Morin was commissioned Inspector-General for the New World by the Grand Consistory of Princes of the Royal Secret, convened at Paris, under the presidency of Chaillon de Joinville, Substitute General of the Order.

When Inspector-General Morin arrived in America, in accordance with the powers vested by his patent, he appointed Moses Michael Hays a Deputy Inspector General, with the authority to appoint others.

Deputy Inspector Hays appointed Isaac Da Costa Deputy Inspector-General for the State of South Carolina. After the death of Deputy Inspector-General Da Costa, Joseph Myers was appointed his successor.

On the 25th October, 1762, the Grand Masonic Constitutions were finally ratified in Berlin, Prussia, and proclaimed throughout the world for the government of all Lodges, Councils, Chapters, Colleges, and Consistories of the Ancient and Accepted Scottish Rite over the surface of the two hemispheres. In the same year they were transmitted to Inspector-General Stephen Morin, who accepted them.

Deputy Inspector-General Hays appointed Solomon Bush Deputy Inspector-General for Pennsylvania, and Barend M. Spitzer for Georgia, which appointments were confirmed by a Council of Inspectors, convened in Philadelphia, on 15th June, 1781.

On the 1st of May, 1786, the Constitutions of the

Supreme Council of Sovereign Grand Inspectors General of the thirty-third and last degree, were alleged to have been granted at Berlin, Prussia.

No Supreme Councils of Sovereign Grand Inspectors-General were established anywhere in the world till after this date; previously, Deputy Inspectors-General were charged with the powers and duties now vested in such Supreme Councils and the grand bodies under them. In the new constitution this high power was conferred on a Supreme Council of nine brethren in each nation, who possessed all the Masonic prerogatives in their own district, while two Supreme Councils were provided for in the United States of America with equal powers in their respective jurisdictions.

The first Supreme Council ever established under the new constitution of 1786, was that at Charleston, whose jurisdiction extended, constitutionally, over the whole of the United States, until they constituted the Northern Supreme Council. Then the Northern and Southern Jurisdictions were geographically defined.

On the 31st of May, 1801, the Supreme Council of the thirty-third degree for the Southern Jurisdiction of the United States of America, was opened with the high honors of Masonry, by Brothers John Mitchell and Frederick Dalcho, Sovereign Grand Inspectors-General; and in the course of the year the whole number of Grand Inspectors-General was completed agreeably to the Grand Constitutions. The other members of this Council were Emanuel De La Motta, Dr. J. Auld, Dr. James

Moultrie, Abraham Alexander, M. C. Livy, Thomas B. Bowen, and J. De Liebau.

The Supreme Council for the Northern Jurisdiction of the United States, happily progressing as it is at this date (1885), requires no special historic mention in detail. Space would not permit an examination of the trials of the Rite and the various questions that have arisen, all which are now harmoniously adjusted. It is sufficient for the purpose of this brief history to say, that in every respect it has realized all that the earliest founders of the Rite could have hoped for, and its present supporters desire.

On the 20th of December, 1767, Deputy Inspector-General Francken, appointed by Morin, opened and duly constituted a Grand Lodge of Perfection in Albany, State of New York, which is still actively at work.

In 1783, Deputy Inspector-General Hays established a Sublime Grand Lodge of Perfection in Charleston, South Carolina. On the 20th of February, 1788, a Grand Council of Princes of Jerusalem was opened in Charleston by Myers, Spitzer, and A. Forst, Deputy Inspector-General for Virginia.

In the year 1797, a chapter of Rose-Croix De H∴ R∴ D∴ M∴ Knight of the Eagle and Pelican, was instituted in the City of New York. In this year, King Solomon's Lodge of Perfection, at Holmes Hole, Martha's Vineyard, which had been established since 1783 by M. M. Hays and Peleg Clark, surrendered its jurisdiction over the three symbolic degrees to the Grand Lodge of Massachusetts.

In 1802 warrants of constitution were issued for the opening of Sublime Lodges of Perfection in Savannah, Georgia, and many other parts of the United States.

About 1806-7, Consistories of Valiant and Sublime Princes of the Royal Secret were organized in the City of New York, and remained so until the formation of the Supreme Council for the Northern Jurisdiction of the United States.

Attention is again called to the year 1795, when Colonel John Mitchell was appointed by Spitzer a Deputy Inspector-General, in the place of Myers, who had removed; but he was restricted from acting until after Myers' death, which took place in the following year.

After the French Revolution of 1793, the mass of the people became atheists, and with them the great body of Masons; the Bible, as a general thing, was committed to the flames, and sublime Freemasonry fell into disuse; it was not until after the establishment of the Supreme Council at Charleston, in 1801, that the sublime system was revived in France, by the establishment of a Supreme Council at Paris, in 1804, by Count De Grasse, Grand Inspector-General, under authority from the Charleston Council. The Paris Supreme Council still exists.

The Grand Orient of France, which before this held an existence only as a *Symbolic* Grand Lodge of Master Masons," immediately commenced her assumed jurisdiction over all the degrees of the Ancient and Ac

Accepted Scottish Rite; hence a question, which to this day remains in abeyance.

In 1825 a special grant to Brothers Fowler, Bryant, and McGill was issued by the Supreme Council for the Southern Jurisdiction, for the establishment of a Supreme Council, thirty-third degree, in Dublin, Ireland.

Thus from time to time Supreme Councils have been established in almost every nation of the globe.

The following are extracts from the published report of the Southern Supreme Council, on the 4th day of December, 1802:

"On the 21st of January, 1802, a warrant of Constitution passed the seal of the Grand Council of Princes of Jerusalem, for the establishment of a Master Mark Mason's Lodge, in the City of Charleston, South Carolina." "Besides those degrees which are in regular succession, most of the Inspectors are in possession of a number of *detached* degrees, given in different parts of the world; and which they generally communicate, free of expense, to those brethren who are high enough to understand them, such as 'Select Masons of twenty-seven, and the Royal Arch as given under the Constitution of Dublin, six degrees of Maçonnerie d'Adoption, Compagnon Ecossais, le Maître Ecossais, and le Grand Maître Ecossais,' etc., etc., making in the aggregate fifty-three degrees."

As to the Mark and Past Master's degrees, all authority over them was surrendered to the Royal Arch Chapters, at that time springing into existence.

The Royal and Select Masters' Degrees were side or detached degrees of the Ancient and Accepted Scottish Rite. In the Southern States of the Union, the Supreme Council initiated, chartered, and fostered Councils of Royal and Select Masters; and as rapidly as they were self-sustaining, they became independent.

In this wise the Ancient and Accepted Scottish Rite has gradually thrown aside the detached degrees, and rarely confers any, except the grades designated in the regular series. The Rite is in amity with Symbolic Grand Lodges, Grand Chapters, Councils of Royal and Select Masters, and Grand Commanderies,— recognizing no other bodies claiming to be Masonic.

Supreme Councils are the governing power over all Masonry in many nations. A Synoptical History of all the Supreme Councils that have ever existed, with the mode of formation in chronological order, by the Author of this volume, is published in the Proceedings, Supreme Council, Northern Jurisdiction, for 1881, pp. 123-150.

A Congress of the Representatives of eighteen Supreme Councils held at Lausanne, Switzerland, 22d September, 1875, recognized and proclaimed the Constitutions and Statutes of May 1st, 1786, by whomsoever written and promulgated, and promised to maintain and defend with all their power, to preserve and cause to be observed and respected, the territorial jurisdiction of the 22 Supreme Councils named in their schedule, among which were those of the Northern and the Southern Jurisdiction of the U. S.

HISTORY.

This compact still exists in all its integrity. The progress of these regular Supreme Councils is remarkable, and their future, without a shadow, is in the full tide of prosperity. The sublime teachings of the Rite find a ready response in every Masonic heart; fraternal association binds man to his fellow, and the profane world may receive a lesson of wisdom and humanity through a careful observance of its beautiful precepts.

REGULAR SUPREME COUNCILS OF THE WORLD.

Supreme Council.	Orient.	Constituted.
South. Jur. U. S	Charleston	May 31, 1801
France	Paris	Sept. 22, 1804
Spain	Madrid	July 4, 1811
North. Jur. U. S	Boston	Aug. 5, 1813
Belgium	Bruxelles	Mar. 11, 1817
Ireland	Dublin	June 11, 1826
Brazil	Lavradio	1829
Peru	Lima	Nov. 2, 1830
New Granada	Cartajena	1833
England, etc	London	Oct. 26, 1845
Scotland	Edinburgh	1846
Uruguay	Montevideo	1856
Argentine Rep	Buenos Ayres	Sept. 13, 1858
Turin, of Italy	Rome	1858
Colon (Cuba)	Havana	Mar. 25, 1859
Mexico	Mexico	April 28, 1868
Portugal	Lisbon	Oct. 30, 1869
Chili	Valparaiso	May 11, 1870
Central America	Guatemala	Nov. 27, 1870
Greece	Athens	July 24, 1872
Switzerland	Lausanne	Mar. 30, 1873
Canada	St. John	Oct. 16, 1874
Egypt	Cairo	1878
Tunis	Tunis	May 11, 1880

The following Supreme Councils have been formed, but have not received recognition and an exchange of Representation : Dominican Republic, Florence, Hungary, Luxembourg, Turkey, and Venezuela.

These Supreme Councils accomplish the number 30.

Movable Symbolic Transparency for the East,
OF ALL
BODIES WORKING IN THE ANCIENT AND ACCEPTED SCOTTISH RITE.

Movable Slides.—Sun, Moon, Star, Ineffable Name, Corrugated Crimson Plate, with Mica Reflector and Argand Gas-Burner, operating in the triple triangle.

The characters in the interstices are the initials of the nine sacred words.

The Ineffable Tetragrammaton may appropriately be in *Enochian* character.

Additional expressive slides to the above may be used to advantage—such as the sacred words of other Governing Subordinate Bodies.

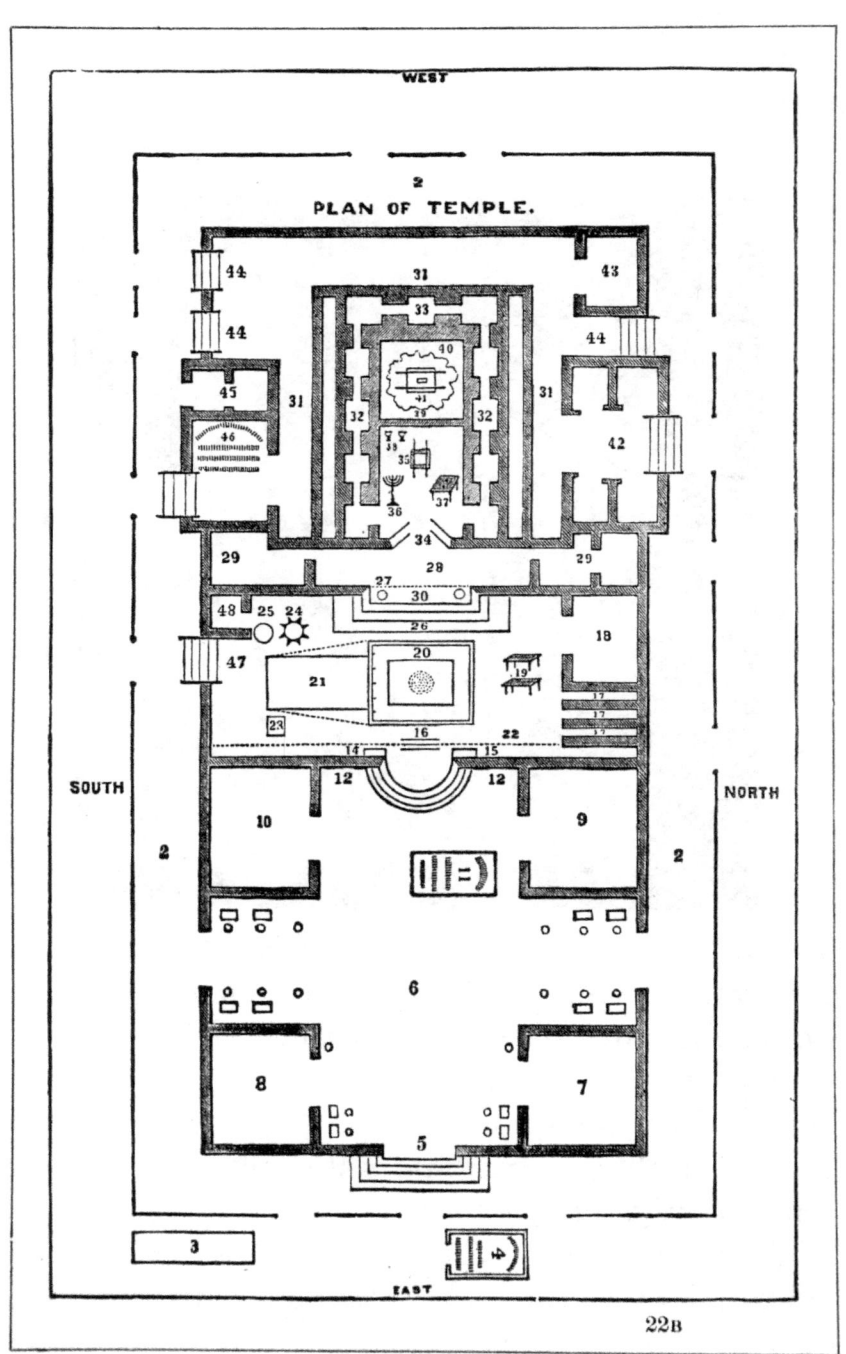

REFERENCES TO PLAN OF TEMPLE.

1. Wall round courts, with 13 openings.
2. The Chel ; space between smaller wall and wall of court.
3. Shops.
4. Small Sanhedrin. Contained 3 rows of 23 men each.
5. Eastern Gate. The chief gate, called "Beautiful." (Acts, iii. 2.)
6. Court of Women, with chests at the entrances for offerings.
7. Chamber of Wood, arranged for each day's use.
8. Chamber of Nazarites, for boiling peace-offerings and burning hair.
9. Chamber of lepers, where they shaved their hair.
10. Chamber of Oil, for the candlestick and flour-offerings.
11. Second Small Sanhedrin. Contained 3 rows of 23 men each.
12. Chambers of Music, under the court, for instruments and vocal practice.
13. Gate of Nicanor, approached by 15 steps.
14. Court of Israel. Length, 187 cubits ; breadth, 11 cubics.
15. Chambers of Vestments and Spicery.
16. Place of Blessing. A landing of 3 steps.
17. Chambers for salt, water, and skins.
18. Slaughter-house.
19. Tables of cleansing.
20. Altar of Burnt-offerings.
21. The Ascent to the Altar, the which it was not permitted to touch.
22. Court of Priests. Length, 135 cubics ; breadth, 11 cubits.
23. Place of Ashes.
24. The Laver and its pedestal.
25. The Draw-well.
26. Steps to the Porch ; $3 + 1 + 2 + 4 + 1 = 11$ steps to the Porch.
27. Two Pillars—Jachin and Boaz.
28. The Porch. In length 70 cubits, in breadth 11 cubits.
29. Chambers of Broken Knives.
30. Veil at entrance of Porch, 20 by 40 cubits.

31. Unoccupied space, called "Circumference" and "The Descent of Rain-water."

32. Chambers round Sanctuary ; 3 tiers, one above the other; total, 38.

33. The Middle Chamber, but not so specially designated. Two tiers high.

34. Door of Sanctuary ; 11 by 20 cubits.

35. Golden Altar of Incense.

36. Candlestick.

37. Golden Table of Shewbread.

38. Two golden Pedestals, on which to temporarily place the blood of the bullock and goat.

39. Two Veils, within the traksin, or partition-wall, which was a cubit in width. The veils did not touch each other by three hand-breadths; hence the separation of the Holy Place from the Holy of Holies.

40. Holy of Holies ; 20 by 20 cubits.

41. Ark, resting on Stone of Foundation.

42. Chamber of Moked (Burning), and chambers for sheep, baking, etc.

43. House of Nitzus, for the guard.

44. Gates.

45. Chambers for supply of water and wood.

46. Chamber of Hewn Stone, for Great Sanhedrin ; 3 rows of 23 men each.

47. Water-gate for the Altar.

48. Upper Chamber of Abtinas. A watch-chamber.

INTRODUCTION.

INEFFABLE AND SUBLIME DEGREES OF THE ANCIENT AND ACCEPTED SCOTTISH RITE.

WHILE the degrees of the Ancient and Accepted Scottish rite commence with the Entered Apprentice, Fellow Craft or Companion, and Master Mason, yet in the United States all authority over these degrees by the Supreme Councils is waived, and they are exclusively administered by the Blue or Symbolic Lodges, working under the jurisdiction of Grand Lodges and the representative system. In other countries, the first three degrees are given in Lodges of Perfection.

It is advisable to confer the first three degrees of the Ancient and Accepted Scottish rite on candidates before further advancement.

The Ineffable degrees begin with the fourth or Secret Master, and conclude with the fourteenth, or degree of Perfection. It is not required that a candidate should be in possession of any other than the Symbolic degrees.

To open a Lodge of Grand, Elect, Perfect, and Sublime Masons, opens all the degrees contained within it;—but a body of any degree may be opened or closed independently.

The order of business in bodies of the rite is as follows:

1. The reading of the records of the previous communication or communications as yet unread and approved. It is judicious at every session that the record be read immediately before closing, that proper corrections, if any, may be made, and before the formal record is made up.

2. Report from the Grand Hospitaller or Almoner of any special case for relief or assistance.

3. Reports of Standing Committees.

4. Reports of Special Committees.

5. Applications for reception or admission to membership.

6. Receptions.

7. Unfinished Business.

8. New Business.

9. Passing the Box of Fraternal Assistance:—no body of the Ancient and Accepted Scottish rite can ever be closed without so doing,—and any member wishing to retire before being called upon by the Grand Hospitaller, must deposit his contribution in the box provided and placed near the seat of the Junior Warden.

The amount collected is under the immediate charge of the Grand Hospitaller or Almoner, and is dispensed by him with the consent of the presiding officer,—first to a worthy distressed brother; or if there be none such, then to some needy and deserving profane: in either case not permitting the recipient to know from what source the relief comes.

INTRODUCTION.

All brethren are required to be clothed with the apron, collar, and jewel of the body in which the degree is open, or that of a higher grade.

It is not essential that *all* the brethren should be clothed in the regalia of the degree being worked at a reception, as this would lead to unnecessary expenditure, accumulation of clothing and depositories. One or more, for exemplification, are recommended, or so many sets as are essential for the proper exhibit of the drama of the degree, and the remainder of the brethren are clothed in the highest grade of the series.

The records of bodies, from the fourth to the thirty-first inclusive, are termed "Engraved Tablets;" those of Consistories and the Supreme Council, "Balustres."

The Battery of *mourning,* is made by the blow being given upon the left fore-arm.

In closing bodies of the Ancient and Accepted rite, the following formula should immediately precede so doing.

The presiding officer asks of his First Assistant if he has any thing further to bring before the body, for the benefit of Masonry in general, of the Ancient and Accepted Scottish rite, or of that body in particular.

If the First Assistant has nothing to offer, the same query is made to the Second Assistant; and if he has nothing to offer, both of the Assistants are directed to make known to the brethren in their respective valleys, that if any one of them has any thing which he desires to offer for the benefit, etc., the floor is tendered to him.

If nothing is offered, the Assistants reply to the presiding officer that silence reigns in their respective valleys.

The following formula is required in the declaration

either of opening or closing an assemblage in the Ancient and Accepted Scottish Rite :

"To the Glory of the Grand Architect of the Universe —in the name and under the auspices of the Supreme Council of Sovereign Grand Inspectors-General of the thirty-third and last degree, for the Northern Masonic Jurisdiction of the United States of America, and by virtue of the authority on me conferred, I declare the works of" etc.

FIRST SERIES.

The symbolic degrees of Entered Apprentice, Fellow Craft or Companion, and Master Mason, are conferred in a Symbolic Lodge in the United States, and reference to them here is not deemed essential.

SECOND SERIES.

THE INEFFABLE DEGREES CONFERRED IN A LODGE OF PERFECTION.

Unless it is expressly stated to the contrary, the officers in a Lodge of any of the Ineffable degrees are as follows:

    1. Thrice Potent Grand Master;
    2. Hiram of Tyre, Deputy Grand Master;
    3. Venerable Senior Grand Warden;
    4. Venerable Junior Grand Warden;
    5. Grand Orator;
    6. Grand Treasurer;

7. Grand Secretary;
8. Grand Keeper of the Seals;
9. Grand Master of Ceremonies;
10. Grand Hospitaller;
11. Grand Captain of the Guard;
12. Grand Organist;
13. Grand Tyler;

and are stationed as designated in the diagram under the title of Degree of Perfection (page 151).

The first four officers of a Lodge of Perfection must be possessed of the 16th grade.

The number of regular members of a Lodge of Perfection does not exceed 27 ; but of late years this ritualistic law has been abrogated.

Beside the festivals of the 24th of June and 27th of December (the two Sts. John's days), the Lodges every year celebrate the building of the first temple of the Grand Architect of the Universe, on the 15th day of Tishri, when "the Prince most ancient and high in degrees shall preside. If the Wardens are the least ancient, their places shall be filled by those most ancient in degrees, whom the T. P. Grand Master shall name;" and the same rule is to be observed with the other officers. The Lodges also observe the 9th day of the 5th month *Ab,* in memory of the destruction of the first temple.

At all receptions, the Grand Orator makes discourses in illustration of the Order, instructs the new brethren, and explains to them the mysteries, and exhorts them to continue their zeal, fervor, and constancy. If he has observed any indiscretion or dispute, he informs the Lodge of it, and takes measures accordingly.

If a brother is a prey to misfortune, it is the duty of every brother to endeavor to alleviate his unhappy situation.

It is the duty of the "Hospitable Brother" to visit all sick brethren, and see that they are well attended to.

If any brother is taken sick, and it shall come to the knowledge of any member, he shall give early advice of it to the Hospitable Brother and to the Lodge, that the necessary succor may be administered.

Should a brother die, all the brethren are expected to attend and assist at his funeral, in the usual manner. It is most proper that the Lodge be then opened in the Perfect Master's degree.

Secrecy in reference to the mysteries, as well as the transactions of the Lodge regarding the character of a brother or applicant, being an indispensable obligation, the T∴ Potent should always, before closing his Lodge, remind the brethren of their duty in this respect, and enforce it in the usual manner and form.

It is the duty of every subordinate body in the Ancient and Accepted Scottish rite to make annual returns to the Supreme Council of its transactions during the year; and its By-Laws, before becoming effective, should be submitted to the Deputy for the State for his approval, and a copy transmitted to the Secretary-General of the Supreme Council, for filing.

In cases of expulsions, a vote of two-thirds of the members present should be required.

FOURTH DEGREE.

Secret Master.

ARGUMENT.

THIS grade, as chronologically arranged, originated with King Solomon, immediately after the assassination of Hiram the builder, and at the time the Temple was but partially constructed.

The King of Israel selected seven of the most worthy and expert brethren, Master Masons, and appointed them special guardians of the Sanctum Sanctorum, and of the sacred furniture of that most Holy Place. They were called Secret Masters, and as in due time they were advanced to higher grades, and thus vacancies were created, others were selected to fill their places. But one guard was on duty at a time, yet seven were selected, and this is termed the mysterious number of this degree, it having many allusions, to the seven cardinal virtues; to happiness, to which our brethren thought there were seven degrees; to the seven stages of life; to the seven laws or principles of Noah, given for the government of his posterity; and to the seven days of the week,—the last having been set apart for the great teaching of this degree, Secrecy and Silence. This degree forms a beautiful introduction to the Ineffable series.

SECRET MASTER.

In the grey dawn of morning, even before the sun rising over Mount Olivet flushed with crimson the walls of the Temple, the chosen few, awe-stricken and grave, had assembled. The light from the seven-branch candlestick in the East was reflected back from the golden floor, from the brazen laver of water, with hyssop and napkins, but fell somberly on the heavy drapings of the sack-cloth on the walls. Amidst the prayers and exhortations, and the solemn chanting of the Levites, the *seven* entered into a mystic bond, and the duty of secrecy and silence was laid upon them. And then the doors of cedar and olive wood heavily carved and gilded were opened, the veils of blue, and purple, and scarlet, and richly embroidered white linen were drawn aside, and the mysteries of the Holy of Holies revealed to them.

None but the Priests and Levites had entered the Sanctum Sanctorum since the Sacred Ark had been brought thither, and now as the Seven Secret Sentinels put off their shoes and washed their feet, and stepped over the golden threshold, they stood in silence blinded with the light that burst upon them. The spreading wings of the Cherubim covered the Ark of the Covenant, but from all sides the walls glittered with gold and precious stones.

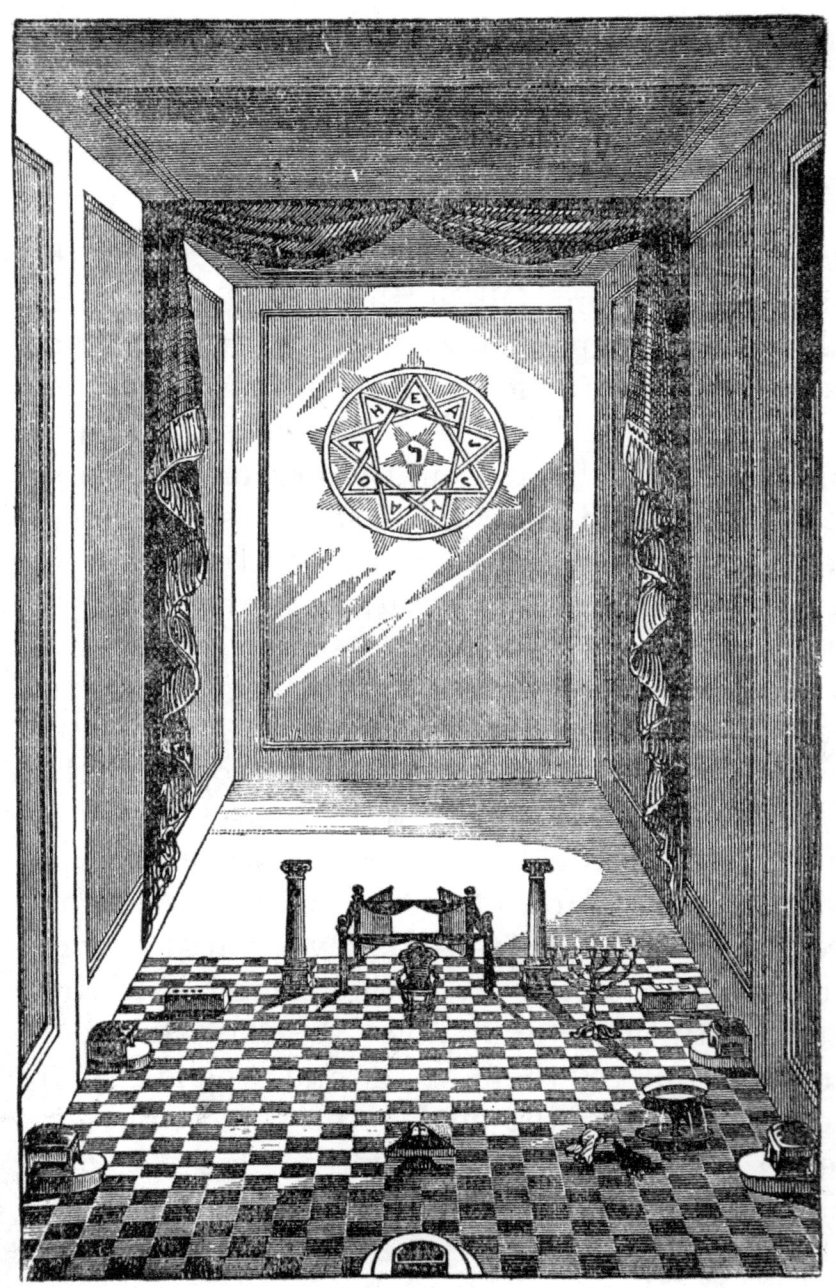

SECRET MASTER.

SECRET MASTER.

THE FOURTH GRADE OF THE ANCIENT AND ACCEPTED SCOTTISH RITE, AND THE FIRST DEGREE OF THE INEFFABLE SERIES.

THE LODGE AND ITS DECORATIONS.

The Lodge of Secret Masters represents the Holy Place or Sanctuary of the Temple; is hung in black, strewed with white tears, and contains the brazen salver of pure water, with napkins and bunch of hyssop, the seven-branch candlestick, which is burning in the East, and which is the only light in the Lodge.

The Sanctuary is separated from the Holy of Holies by a balustrade of white marble and heavy hangings of black. In the balustrade of white marble there is one door of two leaves, made of olive-wood and beautifully ornate. Immediately in front of this entrance are four small columns of white, in quadrangular position, united by rods, from which hangings of four colors, white, blue, purple, and crimson, are suspended: on either side of all these are two brazen columns supporting each a sphere.

Over the East is a large circle, composed of a serpent having its tail in its mouth, enclosing three luminous triangles interlaced, forming nine beams with a blazing star in the centre. In the centre of the star is ׳, and in the interstices of the interlacing triangles, the characters E, A, J, J, Y, A, O, A, H, which are the initials of the nine sacred words.

Within the East is represented the Sanctum Sanctorum of King Solomon's Temple, which afterwards contained the holy ark of the covenant, the ten golden candlesticks, the tablets of the law, the veiled pillar of beauty, the Enochian column, etc.

The jewels of the officers are in crape, as the Lodge is in mourning for the G∴ M∴ Hiram. The furniture is also draped in black.

The altar of perfumes, which is in the Southeast corner of the Sanctuary, during a Reception is burning

SECRET MASTER.

No working-tools are used in this Lodge, for the reason that the labors on the Temple were suspended after the death of Hiram the Builder.

OFFICERS.

The Thrice Potent, who represents King Solomon, in the East.

The Grand Inspector, who represents Adoniram, son of Abda, in the West.

The Treasurer is seated as in Perfection.
The Secretary   "   "   "
The Grand Orator   "   "   "
The Master of Ceremonies is seated as in Perfection.
The Captain of the Guard   "   "   "

The Sentinel, with drawn sword, in front of the small curtains at the entrance to the Holy of Holies.

CLOTHING.

The King, seated in front and to the left of the guarded entrance to the Holy of Holies, is robed in black, bordered with ermine, holding a sceptre and crowned; he wears a wide blue sash from right to left, to which is attached a delta of gold.

On the triangular altar to his left are the apron, collar, gloves, and jewel of the degree, and a white robe; also a wreath of olive and laurel.

The Grand Inspector is seated in the West, wears a white robe and covering, and the apron, collar, gloves, and jewel of the degree, and holding a drawn sword.

All the officers are clothed similar to the Grand Inspector, but having their appropriate jewels, which correspond with those of the same official stations in the degree of Perfection.

Apron*—White, bordered with black, with blue flap. on the flap an eye worked in gold; on the area of the apron, the letter Z within a wreath of olive and laurel.

Collar—Wide white ribbon, edged with black; at the bottom a black rosette, to which is suspended the jewel.

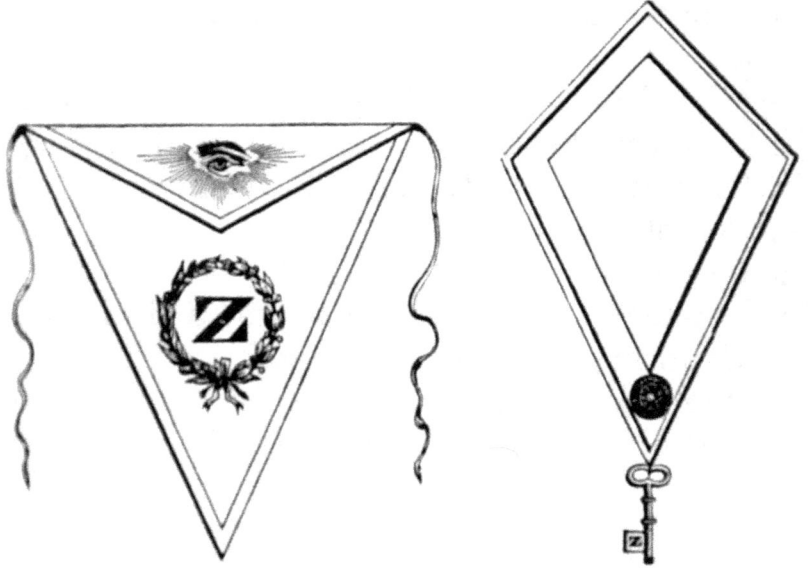

Jewel—An ivory key with the letter Z on the wards.

Gloves—White, with the wristbands bordered with black, and turned over.

Hours of Work—From dawn to close of day.

Battery—••••••• At a Reception given in mourning.

Moral—Secrecy, or Silence and Fidelity.

Symbolic Age—Seven.

All present except the officers are robed in black. During a Reception, the Treasurer's station is vacant, as there can be but seven Secret Masters.

---

* The aprons of the Ineffable degrees are defined in the Northern Jurisdiction as being triangular—those of the Southern Jurisdiction, as square.

SECRET MASTER. 37

OPENING.

∴∴∴∴

*   *   *   *   *

T∴ P∴ What are you taught as a Secret Master?

G∴ I∴ The duty of Secrecy and Silence.

T∴ P∴ What is the hour?

G∴ I∴ The morning star has driven away the shades of night, and the great light begins to gladden our Lodge.

T∴ P∴ As the morning star is the forerunner of the great light which begins to shine on our Lodge, and we are all Secret Masters, it is time to commence our labors.

∴

Whoso draweth nigh to the contemplation of the Ineffable mysteries, should put off the shoes of his worldly conversations; for the place whereon he

stands is holy ground. Set a watch, O Jehovah, before my mouth, and keep thou the door of my lips.

Brother Adoniram, you will give notice, that I am about to open a Lodge of Secret Masters by the sacred number.

* * * * *

RECEPTION.

The candidate is robed in black, etc.

* * * * *

LESSON.

T∴ P∴ The Lord of hosts shall be exalted in judgment, and God that is holy shall be sanctified in righteousness.

Chant. O Lord! have mercy upon us, for thy goodness endureth forever.

G∴ I∴ Woe unto them that draw iniquity with cords of vanity and sin, as it were with a rope.

Chant. O Lord! have mercy, etc.

T∴ P∴ Woe unto them that call evil good, and good evil; that put darkness for light, and light for darkness; that put bitter for sweet, and sweet for bitter.

Chant. O Lord! have mercy, etc.

G∴ I∴ I saw the Lord sitting upon a throne, high and lifted up, and his train filled the temple. Above it stood the seraphim: each one had six wings; with twain he covered his face, with twain he covered his feet, and with twain he did fly.

Chant. O Lord! have mercy, etc.

T∴ P∴ And one cried unto another, saying: Holy, holy, holy, is the Lord of hosts; the whole earth is full of his glory.

Chant. O Lord! have mercy, etc.

G∴ I∴ And the posts of the door moved at the voice of him that spake, and the heavens were filled with smoke.

Chant. O Lord! have mercy, etc.

T∴ P∴ Then said I, Woe is me! for I am undone: because I am a man of unclean lips, for my eyes have seen the King, the Lord of hosts. Then flew one of the seraphim unto me, having a live coal in his hand, which he had taken from off the altar, and he laid it upon my mouth, and said: Lo, this hath touched thy lips; thine iniquity is taken away, and thy sin is purged.

Chant. O Lord! have mercy, etc.

G∴ I∴ Bless the Lord, O my soul; and all that is within me, bless his holy name. Bless the Lord, O my soul, and forget not all his benefits.

Chant. O Lord! have mercy, etc.

T∴ P∴ Who forgiveth all thine iniquities; who healeth all thy diseases; who redeemeth thy life from destruction; who crowneth thee with loving kindness and tender mercies.

Chant. O Lord! have mercy, etc.

G∴ I∴ He hath not dealt with us after our sins; nor rewarded us according to our iniquities. For as the heaven is high above the earth, so great is his mercy towards them that fear him.

Chant. O Lord! have mercy, etc.

T∴ P∴ As for man, his days are but as grass: as a flower of the field, so he flourisheth. For the wind passeth over it, and it is gone; and the place thereof shall know it no more.

PRAYER.

Our Father, who dost rule the heaven and the earth, and all that in them is: Thou Great Supreme, who art the Author of every good and every perfect gift: deign to guide us in our endeavor to combat darkness, and to direct the mind and thoughts of this our brother at the threshold, in the solemn approach to the innermost mysteries of thy holy Temple, where we seek for truth, for the full understanding of the divine lessons contained in thy "Word," and the final attainment of the salvation of the soul immortal.

May this brother feel that the doctrines contained in the new vows he is now about to assume, are worthy of his noblest Masonic thoughts and of his holiest reverence.

Aid us, O Lord! to so instruct him to look within his own heart—that *innermost sanctuary*—that he may prepare to receive the impress of thy Holy Name, which shall be a seal of eternal life.

In thee, O Lord! alone resides the power! To thee be all the glory.   AMEN.

Woe unto those who aspire to that for which they are unfitted.

Woe unto those who assume a burden which they cannot bear.

Woe unto those who assume duties lightly, and afterwards neglect them.

Duty is with us always, inflexible as fate.

In health or sickness, in prosperity or adversity, duty is with us always, exacting as necessity.

It rises with us in the morning, and watches by our pillow at night. In the roar of the city and in the loneliness of the desert, duty is with us always, imperative as destiny.

*   *   *   *   *

T∴ P∴ Whoso draweth nigh to the contemplation of the Ineffable mysteries, let him put off the shoes of his worldly conversation and corrupt affections, for the place whereon he standeth is Holy ground. May we ever remember to keep a watchful eye upon the feet of our affections. Before we approach the house of the Lord, let us seriously consider whether we have taken straight steps in the paths of his commandments, and whether our feet are set in due order and cleansed according to the purifications of the Sanctuary. Let us wash, as it were, in the laver of repentance. Wash you, and make you clean; put away the evil of your doings; acknowledge your iniquities and return unto the Lord, for he will have mercy upon you, and our Elohim will abundantly pardon. Let us incite each other to practise virtue and shun vice. While our feet are prepared for walking in the ways of his commandments, our hands should in like manner be prepared for working in his service.

Saith the father of our ancient Most Potent Grand Master, "I will wash mine hands in innocency, and so will I compass thine altar, O Jehovah." May he who beareth the keys of David be pleased now to open to this brother a door of entrance to the Ineffable degrees. My brother, you have hitherto seen only the thick veil which hides from your view the Sanctum Sanctorum of God's Holy Temple. Your fidelity, zeal, and constancy have won for you the favor you are now about to receive, of viewing some of our treasures and gaining admission into the Secret or Holy place.

*   *   *   *   *

Set a watch, O Jehovah! before my mouth, and keep thou the door of my lips.

Brother Grand Inspector, remove the veil.

*   *   *   *   *

Chant. O Lord! have mercy upon us, for thy goodness endureth forever!

* * * * *

•

In the Ineffable degrees, every lesson taught is connected directly or indirectly with our dearest interest in this or in a future world. The whole system tends to promote the glory of God and the good of mankind. In the symbolic degrees these things are taught generally; in the Ineffable and Sublime degrees, in detail.

Genuine Freemasonry, my brother, is a system of morals, and approaches religion: in fact, such was primitive Freemasonry. Ineffable Freemasonry is practised with an eye single to the improvement of our morals, and a reference to those sublime truths which constituted its principal essence in the earlier ages of the world. It rises above all human institutions, and forms a beautiful auxiliary to the practice of religion. In no place, except in God's Holy Word, are the moral and social virtues enforced by such awful sanctions and decrees.

The degrees upon which you are now entering, are called Ineffable, because they treat of the Ineffable name of the Great Jehovah, and of his Ineffable essence.

* * * * *

O Jehovah! our Adonai, how excellent is thy

name over all the earth! Thy name declares the glory of Elohim. There appears to be power in the name which revealeth secrets.

Freemasonry is an art of great compass and extent. A knowledge of its mysteries is not attained at once, but by degrees. Each degree in Ineffable Masonry is intended to inculcate a moral lesson and the practice of some particular virtue. Advances are made only by much instruction and assiduous application. Each step is progressive, and opens new light and information. According to the progress we make, we limit or extend our inquiries; and in proportion to our capacities, we attain a greater or less degree of perfection.

Freemasonry is an allegorical system. Every doctrine and ceremony has its mystical reference, which is not always apparent at the first blush; so that where the uninformed and weak find only mystery, the true initiate and thoughtful possess food for the employment of the noblest faculties. The true Mason will not rest satisfied with mere ceremonies, which in themselves are cold and heartless, but will study to comprehend their mystical signification. We, as Ineffable Masons, retain and continue to practise these signs and symbols, because we believe they work closer into our hearts than mere words.

*   *   *   *   *

Permit me now, my brother, to receive you as a Secret Master, and give you rank among the Levites.

* * * * *

The laurel, an emblem of victory, is to remind you of the conquest you ought to gain over your passions; the olive, a symbol of peace, which should ever reign among us. With Wisdom, Strength, Prudence, and Fortitude, may you soon obtain the favor of an entrance into the secret vault. It will be your own fault if you are not found worthy, and do not in due time arrive at the sacred place, where, wrapped in divine joy, you may contemplate the pillar of Beauty.

* * * * *

By the rank you now hold among the Levites in the quality of Secret Master, you have become one of the guardians of the Sanctum Sanctorum, and I place you in the number of seven.

The eye upon your apron is to remind you to keep a watchful eye upon the sacred treasures you are set apart to guard, and over the moral conduct of the Craft in general.

Remember, too, that the eye of the Lord is on them that fear him.

* * * * *

Brother Adoniram, it is our order that you cause to be erected a tomb or obelisk, of white and black marble, west-southwest of the Temple, wherein shall be deposited the embalmed remains of our lamented Grand Master H∴ A∴ The white marble shall denote the innocence and purity of our departed Grand Master, and the black the untimely death of him we mourn.

See, therefore, that the solemn duty is speedily executed, and let the obsequies be performed with becoming and imposing ceremonies.

"FREEMASONRY is of heavenly birth; the pillars of Wisdom and Strength support it; its foundation-stone is Virtue; its cement, Charity. Like a rock in the midst of the ocean, it rises above every storm, and bids proud defiance to the raging waves which dash against its base."—G. F. YATES.

FREEMASONRY, in its theoretic and speculative sense, is an acknowledged moral order founded on Charity, the handmaid of Religion, and having for its object the inculcation of divine truths and moral teachings through symbolism.

FIFTH DEGREE.

Perfect Master.

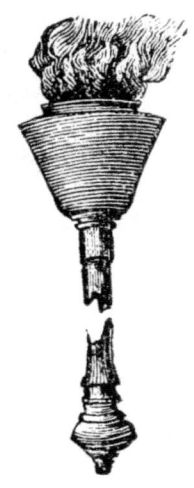

ARGUMENT.

THE solemn ceremonies of the degree of Perfect Master, are intended to represent and recall to mind the grateful tribute of respect we owe to the memory of a departed worthy brother. The examination of the mausoleum—its pronouncement of being perfect—and the advantages we should derive in inculcating the virtues of the deceased—are vividly depicted and impressed upon the initiate.

THE PERFECT-MASTER'S REFRAIN.

Our Ancient Brethren, whelmed in grief,
Lamented their departed Chief,
Let us his pupils long revere
A name to Masonry so dear.
Just Hiram Abif,
Just Hiram Abif.

In mystic rites our Lodge displays
Its sorrows and its fadeless praise.
Long may the sweet acacia bloom
And garlands fresh adorn the tomb
Of Hiram Abif,
Of Hiram Abif.

Look East, look West, its splendors fail,
The lesser lights grow dim and pale,
The glory once reflected there
Now dawns upon a higher sphere.
Blest Hiram Abif,
Blest Hiram Abif.

PERFECT MASTER.

PERFECT MASTER.

THE FIFTH GRADE OF THE ANCIENT AND ACCEPTED SCOTTISH RITE, AND THE SECOND OF THE INEFFABLE SERIES.*

DECORATIONS.

The Lodge is hung with green cloth from eight white columns, four on each side, and equidistant. An altar, draped in black, strewed with tears, is placed in the East at the foot of the throne. In front of the altar is a coffin, draped in black, resting on a bier, with the jewel and apron of Grand Master H∴ A∴

Four lights are placed at each of the cardinal points.

Marks of blood are in the northeast section of the Lodge.

The star in the interlaced triangle of the Secret Master's degree is changed from white to red, so as to throw a lurid light.

---

* Lodges of Sorrow in the Ancient and Accepted rite are usually held in this degree, as see form of ritual in the after part on this work.

TITLES.

1. The Senior Grand Warden is the Master, and represents Adoniram. He is styled Right Worshipful, or Respectable Master, and is clothed as a Prince of Jerusalem. He is seated in the East.

2. The Junior Grand Warden is seated in the West, represents Zabud, and is styled Grand Inspector. He wears a black robe and cap, together with the order and jewel of a Prince of Jerusalem.

3. The Captain of the Guard represents Zerbal, Captain of King Solomon's Guards, and is dressed as a Perfect Master.

4. The Master of Ceremonies represents Stolkin, and is dressed as a Secret Master.

CLOTHING.

Black robe and hood drawn over the head—apron, collar, jewel, and white gloves, bordered with black.

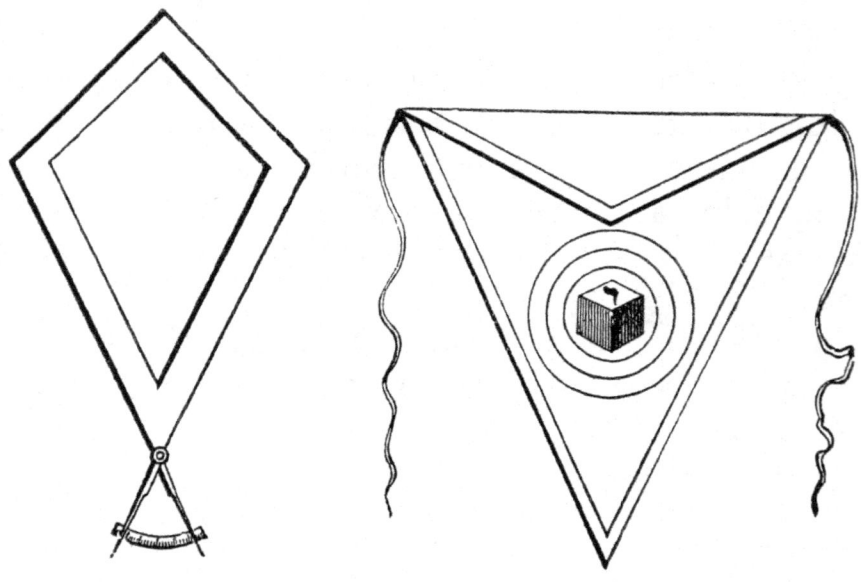

PERFECT MASTER.   53

Apron—White, with a green flap; on the centre is a cubic stone, surrounded by three circles, with the Hebrew letter ׳ in the centre.

Collar—A watered green ribbon, at the end of which is suspended the jewel.

Jewel—A compass open on a segment of a graduated circle at an angle of sixty degrees.

Battery—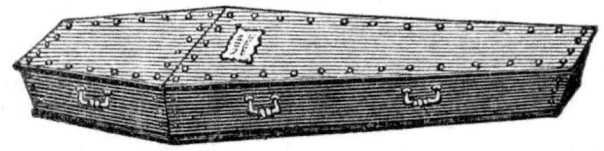 denotes life, death, virtue, and immortality.

Moral—That we should learn to pay due respect to the memory of a deceased worthy brother.

RECEPTION.

ODE.

GREENVILLE.

1. { Come, ye sigh-ing sons of sor-row,
   { Learn from it your fate; to-mor-row,
2. { Once, when full of life, he nev-er
   { Zeal-ous like him be we ev-er,

ODE.

Come, ye sighing sons of sorrow,
    View with me your brother's tomb;
Learn from it your fate—to-morrow
    Death perhaps may seal your doom.

*   *   *   *   *

Sad and solemn flow our numbers,
    While disconsolate we mourn
The loss of him who sweetly slumbers,
    Mould'ring 'neath the silent urn.

*   *   *   *   *

Once, when full of life, he never
    Proved unfaithful to our laws;
Zealous, like him, be we ever,
    To promote the glorious cause.

*   *   *   *   *

To th' exalted power Almighty,
    Softly breathe an ardent prayer—
On his sacred mound tread lightly,
    While we wipe the falling tear.

*   *   *   *   *

PRAYER.

O Almighty and Eternal God! there is no number of thy days or of thy mercies. Thou hast sent us into this world to serve thee, but we wander far from thee in the path of error. Our life is but a span in length, and yet tedious, because of the calamities that enclose us on every side. The days of our pilgrimage are few and evil; our bodies frail; our passions violent and distempered; our understandings weak, and our wills perverse. Look thou upon us, our Father, in mercy and pity. We adore thy majesty, and trust like little children to thine in-finite mercies. Give us patience to live well, and firmness to resist evil, even as our departed brother resisted. Give us, O most merciful Father, faith and confidence in thee; and enable us so to live, that when we come to die we may lie down in the grave like one who composes himself to sleep, and that we may be worthy hereafter to be remembered in the memories of man. Bless us, O God: bless our beloved fraternity throughout the world: may we live and emulate the example of our departed brother; and finally, that we may in this world attain a knowledge of thy truth, and in the world to come. life everlasting. AMEN.

Death regards not those sweet engagements and pleasing intercourses, and those improving joys which are known to Freemasons. Death summons away, in the midst of his day and usefulness, many a beloved brother of our craft. We behold his sun at meridian, and rejoice at its brightness; but alas! it soon sets, and the evening shades of existence close around him forever.

Remember now thy Creator in the days of thy youth, while the evil days come not, nor the years draw nigh when thou shalt say, I have no pleasure in them: while the sun, or the light, or the moon, or the stars, be not darkened, nor the clouds return after the rain. In the day when the keepers of the house shall tremble, and the strong men shall bow themselves, and the grinders cease because they are few, and those that look out of the windows be darkened, and the doors shall be shut in the streets when the sound of the grinding is low, and he shall rise up at the voice of the bird, and all the daughters of music shall be brought low. Also when they shall be afraid of that which is high, and fears shall be in the way, and the almond-tree shall flourish, and the grasshopper shall be a burden, and desire shall fail: because man goeth to his long-home, and the mourners go about the streets: or ever the silver cord be loosed, or the golden bowl be broken, or the pitcher be broken at the fountain, or the wheel broken at the cistern. Then shall the dust return to the earth as it was, and the spirit shall return unto God who gave it.

* * * * *

This ceremony was originally established to commemorate the death of our Grand Master H∴ A∴, whose labors at the building of the first Temple, and whose tragical death, furnish so much of the mystical knowledge of Ancient Craft Masonry. It is retained by us that it may be improved as a lesson

PERFECT MASTER.

both useful and instructive. Let us look forward to brighter scenes, when our deceased brother, who had been smitten down by the resistless hand of death, shall be raised from his prostrate state at the word of our Supreme Grand Master, and admitted to the privilege of the Perfect Lodge above.

HISTORY.

G∴ O∴ Some time after the death of our Grand Master H∴ A∴, King Solomon was informed that the body was found.

*   *   *   *   *

The perpetrators of the horrid deed were not at this time discovered, and it was not certain but that they might have the hardihood and effrontery to mingle with the brethren, and seem to join in the general grief, in order to better conceal their guilt and prevent suspicion. In order to ascertain the truth of the matter, King Solomon caused a general muster of all the workmen to be made.

*   *   *   *   *

Happy to have the poor consciousness of having found the precious remains of so great and so good a man as H∴ A∴, and having an opportunity of paying a just tribute of respect to his memory, he ordered the noble Adoniram, his Grand Inspector, to make suitable arrangements for his interment. The brethren were directed to attend with white gloves and aprons, and he forbade the marks of blood which had been spilled in the Temple to be effaced until the traitors should be discovered and punished.

In the mean while, he directed the noble Adoniram to furnish a plan for a superb tomb or obelisk, of white and black marble, which plan was accepted and the work finished.

*   *   *   *   *

Three days after the funeral ceremonies had been performed, King Solomon repaired with his Court to the Temple, and all the brethren being arranged as at the funeral, he proceeded with his brethren to see and examine the tomb and obelisk, with the inscription thereon. Struck with astonishment and admiration, he raised his eyes and hands to heaven and exclaimed—"It is accomplished and complete!"

SIXTH DEGREE.

Intimate Secretary.

ARGUMENT.

The legend of this degree relates to an incident which occurred in King Solomon's Audience Chamber, upon the supposition of the King of Tyre that a spy or eaves-dropper had been stationed to watch his movements at the time of his complaint that the King of Israel had violated his promise. The life of the supposed spy was demanded, but saved by the intercession of King Solomon, and his zeal and trustworthiness, upon examination, rewarded by his becoming the witness to a new compact.

It is in nowise connected with the degree preceding or succeeding it, and is the mere enactment of an episode occurring pending the period of mourning over the loss of the great builder Hiram.

The ceremony or drama is exciting, and impressive of the lesson intended to be taught, viz.: that we should be ever careful never to offend a brother by prying into his secrets, that the Masonic term eaves-dropping is criminal, and "a soft answer turneth away wrath."

INTIMATE SECRETARY.

THE SIXTH GRADE OF THE ANCIENT AND ACCEPTED SCOTTISH RITE, AND THE THIRD OF THE INEFFABLE SERIES.

THE APARTMENT AND ITS DECORATIONS.

The Lodge-room represents the audience-chamber of King Solomon's Temple. It is hung with black, strewed with silver tears. It has twenty-seven lights, nine toward the East, nine toward the West, and nine toward the South. Upon the table east of the centre of the chamber, are two cross-swords, an hour-glass, a large scroll with seals, a skull, book of the Testimony, and book of the Constitutions.

OFFICERS, AND THEIR COSTUMES.

King Solomon and Hiram, King of Tyre, are styled Thrice Illustrious, and are seated near the East, by the table; the only other officer, the Captain of the Guard—representing Zerbal—is stationed in the West. The two kings are robed as in the Degree of Perfection. The brethren are termed Perfect Masters, and during a reception are stationed without the chamber, as guards, with drawn swords, under the charge of Zerbal.

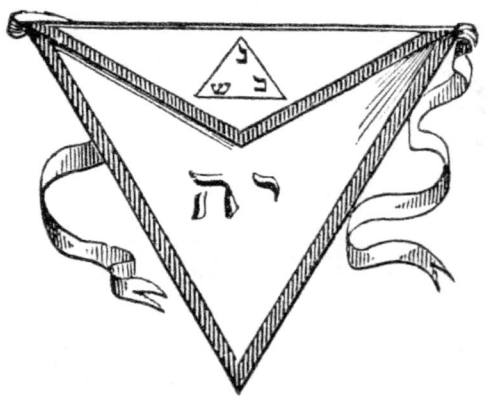 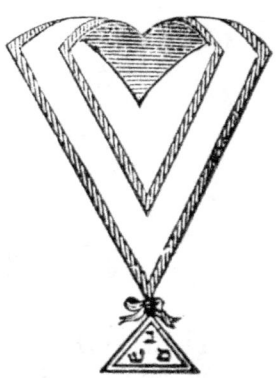

Apron—Triangular, of white lambskin, lined, bordered, and trimmed with bright crimson; on the flap is an equilateral triangle; in the angle of the apex, the letter B (ב), and in the one on the left, N (נ); in the right, Sh (ש); on the centre of the area of the apron, Ih (יה).

Collar—White, bordered and trimmed with crimson, suspended from which is the

Jewel—A golden triangle, similar to that mentioned on the flap of the apron.

Gloves—White, bordered with crimson.

Battery— • •••••• — • thrice repeated.

RECEPTION.

*   *   *   *   *

I honor Joabert for his fidelity and attachment; I gladly acquit him of any intention other than zealous

INTIMATE SECRETARY.

faithfulness. Your friendship, and that of those you govern, I would gladly cultivate; and in accordance with our promise, let the new treaty of alliance be drawn, and Joabert be admitted as our Intimate or Confidential Secretary and Witness, in lieu of our lost friend, whom we now so deeply mourn.

* * * * *

INVESTMENT.

I will now proceed to invest you with the insignia of this degree. The color of your ribbon and apron * * * May you be equally faithful to your engagement but now contracted.

Your Jewel—a solid triangle—is emblematical of law and justice, truth and peace, without which no compact can exist: also of the wisdom, strength, and beauty which should characterize all alliances; and of the three virtues, Faith, Hope, and Charity, or Love. It is also said to be emblematical of those Masons who were present at the opening of the first Lodge of Intimate Secretaries, King Solomon, Hiram, King of Tyre, and Joabert, whom you have represented. It has many allusions, with which a knowledge of our Kabala will make you acquainted.

I also present you with a sword of defence against any attacks which may be made on your integrity and honor as a Mason. As a Confidential Secretary you are intrusted with an especial confidence, and as a full proof of it, we accept you as our Intimate Secretary and a witness to our new alliance.

The room with black hangings, strewed with tears, represents King Solomon's Hall of Audience, to which he was wont to retire to lament the unhappy fate of Hiram Abi. It was in this chamber that King Hiram found him when he came to visit him on the occasion represented at your initiation in this degree. The tears are emblematical of the repentance of Joabert in this chamber, and the grief of Solomon and all true Craftsmen of his day for the loss of Hiram Abi. You will now go to the Grand Orator and learn the history of this degree.

HISTORY.

G∴ O∴ Solomon, in consequence of the treaty established between his ambassadors and Hiram, King of Tyre, solemnly covenanted to furnish a certain number of measures of oil, honey, and wheat, besides the grant of twenty cities, in lieu of the timbers hewn in the forest of Libanus for the building of the Temple, as well as for the stone hewn in the quarries of Tyre. King Hiram went to see the cities so assigned to him, and had the mortification to find them a barren and sandy soil, almost depopulated, and the inhabitants of a rude and uncultivated class, the cities greatly fallen to decay, and that the province in that condition was likely to be a burden rather than an advantage to his treasury. He determined to go in person to Jerusalem and expostulate with Solomon on his breaking the spirit of his promise; while, in truth, it was the intention of

King Solomon, before putting the King of Tyre in possession, to rebuild and adorn the cities, and to change the inhospitable land into cultivated gardens, fields, and meadows.

Arriving at Jerusalem, King Hiram entered the palace, and, without waiting to be announced, went through the court and angrily passed the guard into the audience-chamber, where he found King Solomon alone, mourning over the death of Hiram Abi.

Joabert, the favorite of King Solomon, newly appointed Lieutenant of the Guards—all composed of Perfect Masters—seeing King Hiram enter in such excitement and rage, and not knowing him personally, feared that he intended some violence, and approached the door of the audience-chamber, to be ready to rush in and defend his master if there should be occasion. His zeal and devotion causing him to neglect the precaution which merely curiosity would have observed, he was seen by King Hiram, seized upon by him and dragged into the hall, where he would have been at once slain by the enraged king but for the interference of his own sovereign, who immediately called the guard and ordered them to seize the guilty man and be answerable for his appearance when wanted.

The guards being sent away, King Solomon explained to Hiram that he had intended to rebuild the twenty cities and to furnish the fields with husbandmen before giving them to him: he also assured the king that, of all the favorites and lords of his court, Joabert had always evinced the warmest attachment to his person, and he knew him sufficiently well to be convinced that the indiscretion he had been guilty of was not attributable to the desire to gratify any idle curiosity, but to watch over his safety and interests. He therefore entreated the king to withhold the sentence he had determined to pronounce against him.

The King of Tyre, knowing how gratifying it would be to King Solomon that his favorite should be pardoned, and convinced by the statement of the Captain of the Guard, readily assented, and the two kings renewed their alliance, which was to be perpetual, with mutual promises of fidelity; to which treaty Joabert was selected as the witness or Confidential Secretary—which position had theretofore been filled by the lamented Hiram.

In this you are taught to be zealous and faithful— to be disinterested and benevolent—to act the peacemaker in case of dissensions, disputes, and quarrels among your brethren—and to beware of eavesdropping.

SEVENTH DEGREE.

Provost and Judge.

ARGUMENT.

In accordance with the legend of this degree, King Solomon upon the death of the Grand Master, Hiram, found it necessary to appoint several Judges, in order that justice might be administered among the workmen upon the Temple, their complaints heard, and their disputes decided; for difficulties and disturbances were now more frequent, pending the temporary cessation of work and the period of mourning.

This duty of judgment had devolved upon the lamented Hiram, and his loss caused the appointment of Tito and his associates to listen to and adjust the complaints that might be brought before them.

PROVOST AND JUDGE.

THE SEVENTH DEGREE OF THE ANCIENT AND ACCEPTED SCOTTISH RITE, AND THE FOURTH OF THE INEFFABLE SERIES.

THE APARTMENT AND ITS DECORATIONS.

The apartment represents the middle chamber of King Solomon's Temple, where the records were kept. It is draped with red, and in the East is a blue canopy representing the sky, which is embellished with stars.

Under the centre of the canopy is suspended an ebony box, ornamented with jewels, which contains the records of the tribunal of Provosts and Judges.

In the middle of the chamber hangs an equilateral triangle, in the centre of which is יה; under the triangle is hung an equipoised balance.

The Lodge-room is lighted by five lights—one in each corner and one in the centre of the chamber.

OFFICERS, TITLES, ETC.

Thrice Illustrious—represents Judge Tito, Prince of the Herodim, the oldest of the Provosts and Judges, and is seated in the East.

Senior Warden—represents Adoniram, in the West.

Junior Warden—represents Abda, father of Adoniram, and is also seated in the West.

Orator—represents Josaphat, son of Ahilud, in the South.

Master of Ceremonies—in the North.

Captain of the Guard—in the North.

Sentinel—at the entrance.

The seven officers should be in white robes, and all the other brethren in black robes.

REGALIA, JEWELS, ETC.

Apron—Triangular, white, edged with red; in the middle of the area a pocket, surrounded by five white and red rosettes; on the flap is painted or embroidered a key.

Collar—Red, from which is suspended the

Jewel—A golden key.

Battery—••••-•.

Hour—Break of day—eight, two, and seven.

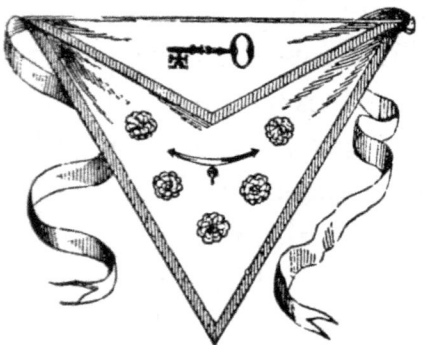

RECEPTION.

* * * * *

The following hymn may be sung in the early part of the reception:

HENRY.

Who never did a slander forge,
    His neighbor's fame to wound,
Nor hearken to a false report
    By malice whispered round.

Who, Vice, in all its pomp and power,
    Can treat with just neglect,
And Piety, though clothed in rags,
    Religiously respect.

Whose soul in wickedness disdains
    His powers to employ,
Whom no rewards can ever bribe
    The guiltless to destroy.

*   *   *   *   *

To render justice and judgment is more acceptable to the Lord than a sacrifice. Ye shall not fear the face of man, for the judgment is God's.

S∴ W∴ Thou shalt provide out of all the people able men, such as fear God: men of truth and haters of injustice, and set them to judge the people at all seasons.

J∴ W∴ Open thy mouth and judge righteously, for he that followeth after righteousness and mercy, findeth life, happiness, and honor.

T∴ I∴ Hear the causes between your brethren, and judge righteously between man and man, and between the citizen and the stranger. Ye shall not respect persons in judgment, but shall listen to the humble as well as to the great.

S∴ W∴ See that ye judge not falsely, nor slay the innocent and the righteous ; and take no gift, for a gift blindeth the wise and perverteth the words of the righteous. Blessed are the peace-makers, for they shall see the Lord.

J∴ W∴ You shall have one manner of law, as well for the stranger as for one of your own country. One ordinance shall be for you and the stranger that sojourneth with you : one law and one custom shall be adjudged for all.

T∴ I∴ Love justice, you that are the judges of the earth. Justice is perpetual and immortal. Oppress not the poor just man, but spare the widow, and honor the ancient gray hairs of the aged. Let not your strength be the law of justice, nor hold that which is feeble to be nothing worth.

*　　　*　　　*　　　*　　　*

Let justice be ever meted out by you; yet let it be tempered with mercy, for as ye judge, so shall ye be judged.

My brother, it is your desire to become a Provost and Judge. Are you aware that he, who would assume that character and would judge and decide between his brethren, must himself be a just and upright man—impartial, cautious, merciful—of pure morals and blameless life and conversation—and that he must, first of all, give judgment against his own faults?

He who would assume the character of Judge is

guilty of a great offence if he does not fully inform himself of the laws and that jurisprudence which he is called on to construe, to apply, to administer, and to enforce—nay, he who ignores his own offences or errors, and punishes the same offences or errors in another, is a false judge and a disloyal Mason.

Let the unjust judge tremble, for God will smite him with the sharp sword of his wrath. Let the unqualified, who usurps the seat of judgment, remember the fate of those who laid their unholy hands upon the ark, and were smitten with God's anger for their presumption.

*   *   *   *   *

Having full confidence, my brother, in your zeal and devotion, I with pleasure receive you as a Provost and Judge over the workmen of the Temple. It gives me joy, my brother, thus to recompense your zeal and attachment to the institution of Masonry. Well assured of your prudence and discretion, we, without hesitation, intrust you with our most important secrets ; and we doubt not that you will discharge all your duties in this grade as you have done in those you have already taken. You have now a twofold duty to perform—as a Judge, to decide all matters of difference that may arise among your brethren ; and as a Provost, to rule over the workmen of the Temple. Be just, impartial, and merciful.

INVESTITURE.

I now invest you with the apron, collar, and jewel of this degree. I decorate you in this quality with this golden key, suspended to a red collar.

Your apron is white, bordered with red, as an emblem of the ardor and zeal of the Masters: the pocket in the middle of the area is intended for the key of the box wherein is contained the plans and records of the tribunal, which key is represented to you by that on the flap. It teaches you to lock carefully up in your heart the secrets of Masonry, and to keep the key ever in your own possession ; and it is especially emblematical of that justice and uprightness that alone can unlock to you the mysteries contained in the higher degrees, and enable you to advance towards perfection. The golden key also opens an urn of gold.

The Lodge represents the middle chamber of King Solomon's Temple.

The triangle is emblematical, here as elsewhere in Masonry, of the Deity, of his omnipotence and omniscience; and it is also emblematical of the three great requisites of a Judge—possessed by him in their perfection and infinitude—*Justice, Equity,* and *Impartiality*. Let that emblem and the balance be ever before your eyes, and remind you of the obligation which you have taken in this degree, of the duties which devolve upon you, of the responsibilities which rest upon you, and which, with God's eye ever fixed upon you, you cannot evade or avoid.

* * * * *

HISTORY.

Orator. It is said that King Solomon, after the death of the Grand Master Hiram, in order that justice might be administered among the workmen upon the Temple, their complaints heard, and their disputes be decided, appointed seven Provosts and Judges to adjust their demands, listen to their complaints, and settle any disputes and differences that might arise among them. He appointed Tito, Prince of Herodim, to be the chief Provost and Judge, Adoniram, and Abda, his father, and four others learned in the law of Moses, to complete the number and constitute the Tribunal. They held their sittings in the middle chamber of the Temple, where the records of the Tribunal were kept, in a box of ebony, studded with precious gems, the key of which was committed to the Provosts or Judges ; and there they considered and adjusted the demands and differences of the workmen, and determined all appeals from the judgment of a single Provost and Judge— administering the same laws to the Phoenician as to the Hebrew, and endeavoring to do entire justice, according to the law of Moses, between man and man.

* * * * *

The necessity for a Court of Judges did not exist until after the death of the Grand Master Hiram, as the number of difficulties and dissensions among the workmen was not so numerous, and judgment was arrived at by the ready decisions of Hiram, which all quietly acquiesced in.

As a Provost and Judge, it is your especial duty to render justice to all, to hear patiently, remember accurately, and weigh carefully the facts and the arguments offered. In our intercourse with others, there are two kinds of injustice : the first, of those who offer an injury; the second, of those who have it in their power to avert an injury from those to whom it is offered, and yet do it not. So active injustice may be done in two ways—by force and by fraud.

Respect not persons in judgment, but listen to the humble as well as to the great. Fear God, for judgment is God's.

While you would administer justice, show mercy. Exhibit the subduing influences of pity, the might of love, the control of mildness, the commanding majesty of that perfect character which mingles grave displeasure with grief and pity for the offender. So brother Masons should treat their fellow Masons who go astray—not with bitterness, nor yet with good-natured easiness nor worldly indifference.

The human heart bows not willingly to what is infirm or wrong in our nature. If it yields to us, it rather yields to what is divine in us. The wickedness of my neighbor will not submit to my wickedness. Therefore deal faithfully, but patiently and tenderly, with evil.

Remember that it becomes not frail and sinful humanity to be vindictive towards even the worst of criminals. Perhaps we owe it solely to a kind Providence having kept from us those temptations, under which we, too, like them, would have fallen.

Finally, as a true Mason and Judge, always remember the injunction : "Thou shalt not respect the person of the poor, nor honor the person of the mighty; but in righteousness shalt thou judge thy neighbor."

Beware of injury to your neighbor. If you have wronged another, you may grieve, repent, and resolutely determine against any such weakness in future; you may, so far as it is possible, make reparation. This is well. The injured party may forgive you, according to the meaning of human language, but the deed is done, and all the powers of Nature, were they to conspire in your behalf, could not make it undone; the consequences to the body, the consequences to the soul, though no man may perceive them, are there—are written in the annals of the past, and must reverberate throughout all time.

Repentance for a wrong done, bears, like every other act, its own fruit—the fruit of purifying the heart and amending the future; but not of effacing the past.

Even the pulsations of the air, once set in motion

by the human voice. cease not to exist with the sounds to which they gave rise; their quickly attenuated force soon becomes inaudible to human ears. But the waves of air thus raised perambulate the surface of earth and ocean; and in less than twenty hours every atom of its atmosphere takes up the altered movement, due to that infinitesimal portion of primitive movement, which has been conveyed to it through countless channels, and which must continue to influence its path throughout its future existence.

The air is one vast library, on whose pages is forever written all that man has ever said or even whispered.

There, in their mutable but unerring characters, mixed with the earliest as well as the latest signs of mortality, stand, forever recorded, vows unredeemed, promises unfulfilled. God reads that book, though we cannot.

So earth, air, and ocean, are the eternal witnesses of the acts that we have done. Every criminal is, by the laws of the Almighty, irrevocably chained to the testimony of his crime. No more fearful punishment to a superior intelligence can be conceived, than to see still in action, with the consciousness that it must continue in action forever, a cause of wrong, put in motion by itself ages before. There is its perpetual, its inevitable punishment, which no repentance can alleviate, and no mercy can remit.

Let us be just, also, in judging of other men's motives.

No man need covet the office of Judge, for, in assuming it, he assumes the most serious and oppressive responsibility.

On all accounts, therefore, let the true Mason never forget the solemn injunction, necessary to be observed at almost every moment of a busy life : "Judge not, lest ye yourselves be judged; for whatsoever judgment ye measure unto others, the same shall in turn be measured unto you."

EIGHTH DEGREE.

Intendant of the Buildings.

ARGUMENT.

THE death of Hiram, the Chief Architect, threw the workmen of the Temple of King Solomon into great confusion; and for a time the construction of the building was stayed, for the want of essential plans and an expert director of the work. The period of mourning having expired, King Solomon, upon consultation, determined to appoint five Superintendents—one for each of the five Departments of Architecture—and under their supervision the building progressed. The ceremony of installing the Superintendents, is in this degree exhibited, instructions given, and lessons of virtue inculcated.

INTENDANT OF THE BUILDINGS.

THE EIGHTH GRADE OF THE ANCIENT AND ACCEPTED SCOTTISH RITE, AND THE FIFTH OF THE INEFFABLE SERIES.

THE APARTMENT AND ITS DECORATIONS.

The apartment represents the middle chamber of King Solomon's Temple, with various symbols of truth and wisdom displayed. The hangings are crimson, with a blue canopy in the East, sprinkled with stars.

The lights are twenty-seven in number, in groups of nine each—each group forming a triple triangle.

The altar is immediately in front of the Master, on which are five other lights. Over the Master is suspended a blazing star, with five points, and in its centre the Hebrew letter J (׳), thrice repeated; this star is surrounded by the triple interlaced triangle.

OFFICERS, TITLES, ETC.

The Lodge consists of five members only, representing the five Chief Architects, who were appointed temporarily, in the place of the lamented Grand Master Hiram.

The Master sits in the East, is termed Thrice Potent, and represents Adoniram, the son of Abda, President of the Board of Architects.

Senior Warden, in the West, represents Joabert, a Phoenician, Chief Artificer in Brass.

Junior Warden, in the South, represents Stolkin, a Hebrew, Chief Carpenter.

Master of Ceremonies, in the North, represents Selec, the Giblemite, Chief Stone-mason.

Captain of the Guard, in the North, represents Gareb, a Hebrew, Chief Worker in Silver and Gold, and Engraver.

During a reception, the Thrice Potent represents King Solomon, and is robed and decorated as in Perfection; the Senior Warden represents Sadoc, the Priest, and is clothed in a white robe and mitre; the Junior Warden represents Ahishar, Governor of the House, and wears a black robe and the collar and apron of the degree.

The brethren sit about the Lodge in the form of a triangle.

REGALIA, JEWELS, ETC.

Apron—Triangular in shape, white, lined with crimson and bordered with green; on the area is depicted a five-pointed star, with the Hebrew J (י), thrice repeated, in the centre, and over that a balance; on the flap is a triangle, with one of the following letters in each angle: ב, א, י (the initials of the words *Ben-khurim, Achar,* and *Jakinah*).

Cordon, or Order—A broad crimson sash, worn from the right shoulder to the left hip; at the point is suspended the Jewel, by a green ribbon.

INTENDANT OF THE BUILDINGS.

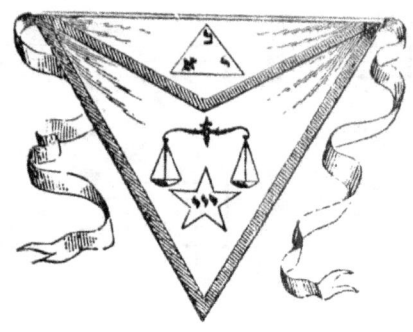 

Jewel—A golden triangle, similar to that described as on the flap of the apron.

Steps—Five grand steps, the heels to a square.

Age—Three times nine—equal to twenty-seven

Battery—• • • • •.

RECEPTION.

* * * * *

ODE.

C.M.   BALERMA.

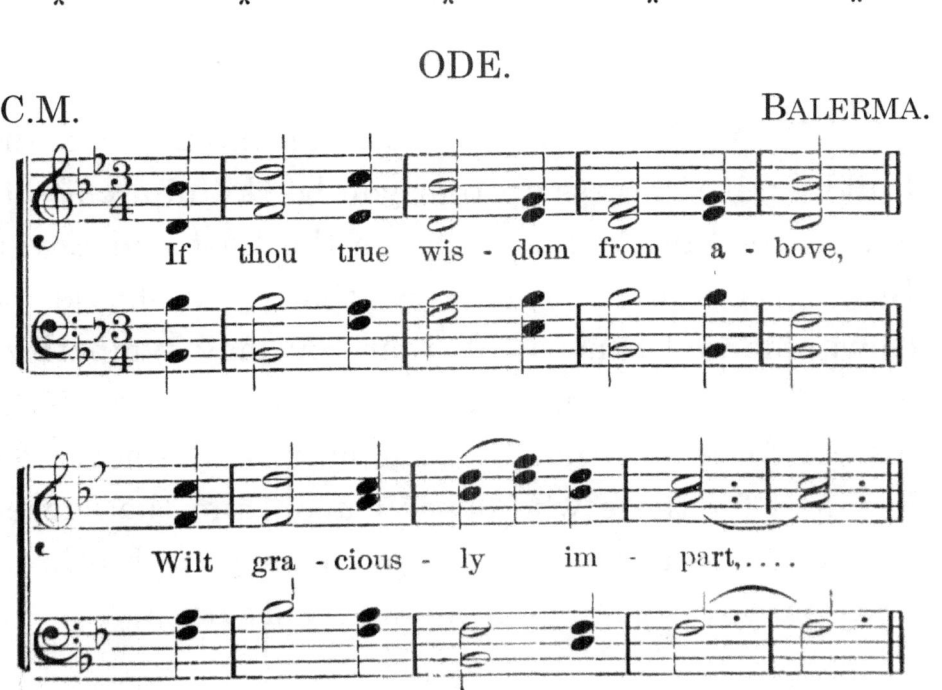

If thou true wisdom from above,
Wilt graciously impart,....

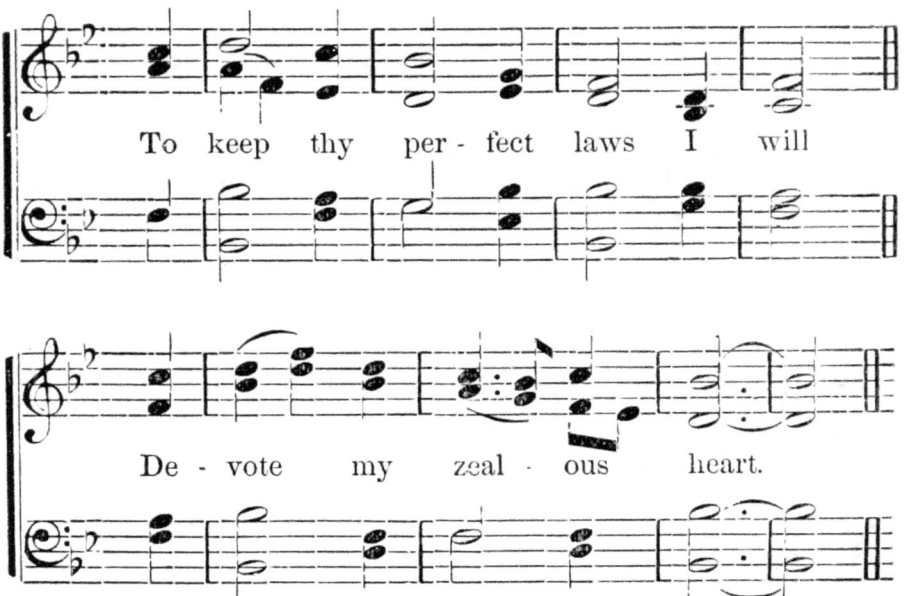

To keep thy perfect laws I will
Devote my zealous heart.

> Direct me in the sacred ways
> To which thy precepts lead,
> Because my chief delight has been
> Thy righteous paths to tread.

T∴ P∴ My Brethren, to become an Intendant of the Building, it is necessary that you be skilful architects and learned in the knowledge of the East and Egypt. But it is equally necessary that you should be charitable and benevolent, that you may sympathize with the laboring man, relieve his necessities, see to his comforts and that of his family, and smooth for him and for those who depend upon him the rugged way of life,—recognizing all men as your brethren, and yourselves as the almoners of God's bounty.

* * * * *

LESSON.

T∴ P∴ I will restore thy judges, as at the first, and thy councillors, as at the beginning; for the light of the righteous shall be established, as the Lord giveth wisdom: out of his mouth cometh understanding and knowledge.

S∴ W∴ Thou shalt not oppress an hired servant, or a laboring man that is poor and needy; on the day when he earns it thou shalt give him his hire, nor shall the sun go down upon it: for he is poor, and it is his life : lest he cry against thee unto the Lord, and God punish thee for this sin.

J∴ W∴ When thou beatest thine olive-trees, thou shalt not go over the boughs again; it shall be for the stranger, the fatherless, and the widow: when thou gatherest the grapes of thy vineyard, thou shalt not glean it afterwards ; it shall be for the stranger, the fatherless, and the widow.

T∴ P∴ If there be among you a poor man, and one unable to work, of thy brethren, within any of thy gates, thou shalt not harden thy heart nor shut thine hand from thy poor brother, but shalt open thy hand unto him, and shalt surely lend him sufficient for his need; for thou art but God's treasurer, to dispense his benefits to the poor.

S∴ W∴ If thy brother be waxen poor, and be compelled to serve thee, thou shalt not rule over him with rigor, but shalt fear thy God. Nor shalt thou discharge those whose labor is their life because thy profits are not large; but thou shalt be God's almoner, for he hath but lent thee all the wealth thou hast, and thou art but his trustee for the poor, the suffering, and the destitute.

*   *   *   *   *

INVESTITURE.

*   *   *   *   *

The battery of five, the five lights on the altar, the five steps, the five-pointed star, and the travel five times about the body of the Lodge, are all emblematical of the first five Chief Architects.

The age is that of a Master Mason (9), multiplied by that of an Entered Apprentice (3), representing that the Architects, or Intendants, were thrice powerful as Masters and Chiefs of Architecture; hence the number of lights in the Lodge.

My brother, I now with pleasure decorate you with a crimson cordon or order, to which is suspended by a green ribbon a triangular plate of gold—the Jewel of the degree. The crimson is emblematical of that zeal which should characterize you as an Intendant of the Building ; and the green, of the hope that you will honor and advance the Craft, and supply, so far as in you lies the power, the place of our late Grand Master Hiram.

I also decorate you with this triangular apron, of

white, lined with crimson and bordered with green. On it you will observe the five-pointed star.

* * * * *

The number five in this degree, my brother, has many allusions, some of which have already been explained to you; it is also to remind us of the five points of fellowship: that we are to go on a brother's errand or to his relief, even barefoot and upon flinty ground; to remember him in our supplications to the Deity; to clasp him to our heart and protect him against misfortune and slander; to uphold him when about to stumble and fall; and to give him prudent, honest, and friendly counsel. Such are the duties you are especially to observe and to teach to others, for they are the first ordinances of Masonry.

* * * * *

HISTORY.

G∴ Or∴ My brother, but little need be said to you of the history of this degree, as it is fully given in the reception. You have on this occasion represented one of the five chief architects appointed by King Solomon to conduct the work upon the Temple, in the place of Hiram, the chief architect, who had been murdered. The king was always desirous of carrying to the highest state of perfection the work he had begun in Jerusalem, and upon the loss of the skilful Hiram, much concern was felt as to whether the original design of the structure could be completed, and, also, as to whether the arrangements that had been projected for ornamentation and decoration would not fail for want of skill and ability on the part of the workmen. Pending these difficulties, on consultation, it was recommended by the High Priest, Sadoc, and Ahishar, Governor of the House, that five artificers, who had been pupils of Hiram, should be placed, as chiefs, over five departments in the construction of the edifice, and that at least the building could proceed, until they could find a Grand Master Architect.

Adoniram, the son of Abda, was selected as the President of the Board of Architects, the others being Joabert, a Phoenician, the chief artificer in brass; Stolkin, a Hebrew, chief carpenter; Selec, the Giblemite, chief stone-mason ; and Gareb, a Hebrew, chief worker in silver and gold, and chief engraver.

King Solomon was well aware that the zeal and abilities of these brethren would be exerted to the utmost in bringing to perfection so glorious a work. In like manner, we expect you to do all in your power to promote the grand design of Masonry, and to bring to perfection the works of this Lodge of Intendants of the Building, exercising and propagating charity and benevolence, educating the poor orphan, comforting the sick and distressed, and providing refuge for the unfortunate.

You have learned in your previous degrees that,

in order to succeed in the great work of erecting a temple not made with hands, and dedicated to the Grand Architect of the Universe, you must emulate the same spirit, the same fortitude and resolution possessed by our Grand Master Hiram—preferring your integrity to your life.

You will still advance toward the light—toward the star blazing in the distance—which is an emblem of the divine truth, given by God to the first men, and preserved amid all the vicissitudes of ages in the traditions and teachings of Masonry. Here, as everywhere in the world, Darkness struggles with Light, and clouds and shadows intervene between you and the truth.

You are now, my brother, a student of the morality of Masonry, with which, we trust, you will become imbued, as for some time you will be exclusively occupied in its study. Step by step you must advance toward perfection in the moral code of Masonry: each Masonic degree is meant to be one of those steps: each is a development of a particular duty, and in the present one you are taught charity and benevolence. With these two virtues, man can best prepare for that future which he hopes for. The law of our being is love of life—this wonderful creation of God—and its interests and adornments, love of the world; not a low and sensual love, not love of wealth, fame, ease, power, and splendor, not low worldliness, but the love of earth as the garden on which the Creator has lavished such miracles of beauty—as the habitation of humanity—the dwelling-place of the wise, the good, the active, and the loving—the place for the exercise of the noblest passions, the loftiest virtues, and the tenderest sympathies: this is the charity or love we would teach in this degree, for God himself is love, and every degree of charity that dwells in us is the participation of the divine nature.

*   *   *   *   *

NINTH DEGREE.

Knights Elect of Nine.

ARGUMENT.

THE three degrees called elect, or Elu—namely, Elect of Nine, Elect of Fifteen, and Sublime Knights Elected—are intimately and essentially connected. They are of an important and interesting nature, the first of the three being established to reward the fidelity and zeal of one of the favorites of the King of Israel, who was the first to detect and bring to justice a certain Craftsman, who, pending the construction of the Temple, had been engaged in an execrable deed.

The great purpose of the degree is to inculcate and illustrate this lesson: That we should be careful how we allow ourselves to be led away by an excess of zeal, even in a good cause, to inflict, as an individual, the punishment justly due for the violation of human or divine laws.

"Free, Ancient and Accepted Scottish Masonry has no ambition to be considered a *Charitable Institution,* in the modern acceptation of that term. In that regard, we are widely different from those secret associations whose chief claim to public consideration is in the assistance they render to the unfortunate poor. However laudable *alms-giving* may be, we are not prepared to accept it with them as a full and complete exercise of all our duties as conveyed in the word *Charity.* Alms-giving is not the full scope of Charity as taught in the old Free Masonic schools of Philosophy. The greatest of the divine virtues given to man is Charity.

"It is that great vital principle of fraternity, of equality, and of liberty, which prompts a man to love his neighbor as himself— it is humble, retiring, hath no shadow of envy, hatred, or malice—it is that love to mankind which prompts us to rush to the rescue of our brethren in adversity, as well as to rejoice with them in their prosperity. In brief, *this* is the substance of all our teachings, and all else is but subsidiary."

Ent∴ Ap∴ Degree, A∴ A∴ S∴ R∴

KNIGHTS ELECT OF NINE.

KNIGHTS ELECT OF NINE.

THE NINTH GRADE OF THE ANCIENT AND ACCEPTED SCOTTISH RITE, AND SIXTH DEGREE OF THE INEFFABLE SERIES.

DECORATIONS, ETC.

The hangings are black, strewed with flames, suspended from eight columns, four on each side. There are nine great lights—eight forming an octagon round the altar, which is in the centre: the other light is placed half-way between the altar and the East. The altar is covered with black, and on it are placed the Book of the Testimony, two cross-swords, and a dagger.

An urn, containing a number of white and black ballots, on the Secretary's desk.

A room representing a cavern.

*   *   *   *   *

TITLES.

The body is styled a Chapter, and consists of nine members, who represent the first Nine Knights Elect. The officers are—

Thrice Potent Master, represents King Solomon;
Senior Inspector, " King Hiram;
Junior Inspector, " Adoniram;
Orator, " Zabud;
Secretary, " Sadoc;
Treasurer, " Josaphat;
Hospitaller, " Ahisar;
Master of Ceremonies, " The Stranger Pharos a poor herdsman;
Captain of the Guard, " Banacas.

CLOTHING.

Apron—White, lined and bordered with black, sprinkled with blood ; in the centre a bloody head held by the hair; on the flap, an arm holding a dagger.

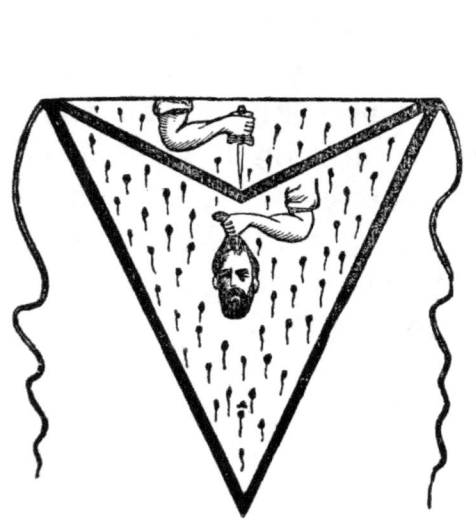

Sash—A broad black watered ribbon, worn from the right shoulder to the left hip; at the lower end nine red rosettes, four on each side, and one at the bottom, from which pendent the

Jewel—A dagger, hilt of gold and blade of silver.

During a reception the Thrice Potent and Senior Inspector wear Royal robes, with crown and sceptre; the Secretary wears robes and mitre of the High Priest.

The Junior Inspector and other officers, robed in black with cowles, and the apron, sash, and jewel of this degree, sit * * * during the working of the degree, with right elbow on the knee and head on the right hand, as if fatigued.

Stranger clothed as a shepherd.

Battery—••••••• – •

The lights are not lighted until the Chapter is opened.

Hour—First hour of night.

Age—Eight and one.

OPENING.

*   *   *   *   *

Q. What are we taught as a Knight Elect of Nine?

A. That we should be careful how we suffer ourselves to be led away by an excess of zeal, even in a good cause, to exercise as individuals the vengeance due for the violation of divine and human laws.

Q. What further does the degree illustrate?

A. The overthrow of ignorance by freedom.

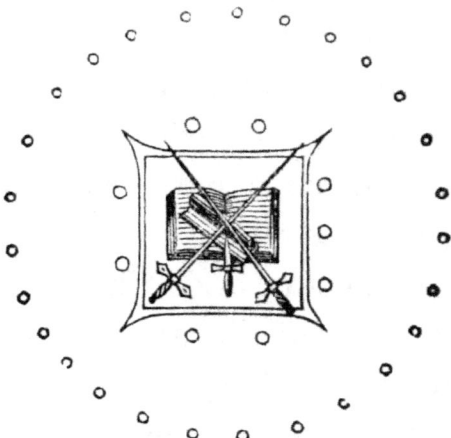

RECEPTION.

*   *   *   *   *

My brother, I now designate and present to you the jewel of this degree. It is the avenging blade, which will be sure to find the perjured and guilty traitor.

I invest you with the other symbols of this degree. * * * This apron and sash denote the melancholy death of our Grand Master H∴ A∴ The bloody arm and red roses, the instrument and the blood shed by the eight and one knights to atone for his death.

*   *   *   *   *

You will now go and salute the Grand Inspector, and then repair to the Grand Orator for the history of this degree.

HISTORY.

G∴ O∴ After the death of the Grand Master, the assassins having made their escape, a great assembly of Masons was convened by King Solomon, to consult as to the best means of discovering and apprehending them. Their deliberations were interrupted by the entrance of a herdsman, who demanded to speak to the king. On being admitted to an interview, he acquainted King Solomon that he had discovered persons concealed in a cave near the coast of Joppa, answering the description given of the traitors ; and he offered to conduct those whom the king should select to the place of their concealment. This being communicated to the Masters, they one and all eagerly requested to be made participators in the vengeance due the assassins. Solomon checked their ardor, declaring that only nine should undertake the task ; and to avoid giving any offence, ordered a selection of nine of the brethren by lot, to accompany the stranger. At the first hour of the night, the favorite of King S∴ and eight others, conducted by the stranger, travelled onward through a rough and dreary country toward the coast of Joppa. On the way, the most ardent of the nine, learning that the murderers were hidden in a cavern not far from where they then were, pressed on ahead, found the cavern, entered it with the shepherd, where, by the dim light of the lamp, he discovered one of the assassins asleep, with a dagger at his feet. Inflamed at the sight, and actuated by an impatient zeal, he immediately seized the dagger and stabbed him, first in the head and then in the heart. The assassin had only time to say "Necum" [pronounced *nay-coom*], or "vengeance is taken," and expired. The avenger then quenched his thirst at the fountain. When the eight arrived at the spot, they asked him what he had done. He replied, "I have slain the assassin of our Grand Master, and have performed a feat for the honor and glory of the Craft, for which I hope to be rewarded." He then severed the head from the body, and taking it in one hand and his dagger in the other, with the eight returned to Jerusalem. In his zeal, however, he hastened into the presence of the king, passing the guards at the entrance. Solomon was at first very much offended that it had been put out of his power to take vengeance in the presence of, and as a warning to, the rest of the workmen, and ordered the guards to put his favorite to death ; but by the intercession of his brethren he was pardoned for his zeal, and they became reconciled. Solomon established the grade of Knights Elect of Nine, and conferred it upon the nine companions.

TENTH DEGREE.

Knights Elect of Fifteen.

ARGUMENT.

THIS degree is a continuation of the series known as the Elu, or Elect degrees, and recounts in detail the mode of the arrest and punishment of the remaining assassins; and reminds us that the unerring eye of Justice will discover the guilty, and they suffer the punishment their crimes deserve. It is intended, morally, to instruct us that ambition and fanaticism, enslavers of mankind, are overthrown and dispelled by the sword of justice and freedom.

KNIGHTS ELECT OF FIFTEEN.

THE TENTH GRADE OF THE ANCIENT AND ACCEPTED SCOTTISH RITE, AND THE SEVENTH DEGREE OF THE INEFFABLE SERIES.

THE CHAPTER—ITS DECORATIONS, ETC.

The hangings are black, sprinkled with red and white tears.

There are fifteen lights, five in the East, and five before each Warden—four forming a square and one in the centre—all of yellow wax.

The altar may be covered with black, strewed with silver tears.

On the altar the Great Lights, Book of Constitutions, two crossed-swords, and two daggers.

OFFICERS, TITLES, ETC.

The Thrice Potent Grand Master, who represents King Solomon.

The Senior Grand Warden represents King Hiram, and sits on his right.

The Junior Grand Warden, in the West, represents Adoniram, the son of Abda.

The Orator represents Zabud, the king's friend.

The Secretary represents Sadoc, the Priest.

The Treasurer represents Josaphat, the son of Ahilud, the Chancellor.

The Hospitaller represents Ahishar, Governor of the House.

The Captain of the Guard represents Zerbal.

The Master of Ceremonies represents the stranger who gave information of the place of concealment of the assassins.

The number of members is regularly fifteen, and no more.

ORNAMENTS AND JEWELS.

The apron is white, lined, edged and fringed with black, and the flap black.

In the middle are painted or embroidered three gates, and over each gate a head impaled on a spike.

The sash is a black ribbon or sash, worn from right to left, on the front of which are painted or embroidered three heads.

The jewel is a dagger, its hilt gold and its blade silver, hanging at the end of the sash.

During a reception the officers are dressed as in the ninth degree.

The age 5 times 3, or. 15 years.

The hour for opening is the sixth hour of the night; the hour for closing is the sixth hour of the day.

Battery— ●●●● —● ●●●● — ●●●●

OPENING.

The fifteen lights are not burning.

*   *   *   *   *

Q. What is the cause to which the Illustrious Elu of the Fifteen are now devoted?

A. That of the oppressed against the oppressor, and of Toleration against Intolerance.

Q. When did the fifteen Elus depart from Jerusalem?

A. On the 15th day of the month Tammuz.

Q. When did they arrive at Gath?

A. On the 18th day of the same month.

Q. What is your age?

A. 5 times 3, or 15 years, complete.

Q. What is the hour?

A. The sixth hour of the night.

Cause, then, the brethren to assemble around the altar, that, renewing our pledges to one another, we may open this Chapter of Illustrious Elus of the Fifteen.

Brethren, you will please assemble around the altar, that this Chapter may be opened in due and ancient form.

*   *   *   *   *

G∴ Or∴ To the cause of every people that struggle against oppression!

J∴ G∴ W∴ To the cause of all who defend Right and Justice against Tyranny!

S∴ G∴ W∴ To the cause of Toleration against Intolerance and Persecution!

T∴ P∴ To the cause of Free Thought, Free Speech, Free Conscience!

All. We devote ourselves, our hands, our hearts, our intellects!

T∴ P∴ Now, henceforward, and forever!

All. Amen!

*   *   *   *   *

T∴ P∴ As these lights shine in this Chapter, so shall the light of freedom illuminate the world.

*   *   *   *   *

S∴ G∴ W∴ As my lights shine in this Chapter, so shall the light of religious and political toleration rise upon the world.

*   *   *   *   *

J∴ G∴ W∴ As my lights shine in this Chapter, so shall the light of education and intelligence yet shine in all the corners of the earth.

T∴ P∴ So mote it be! My brethren, this Chapter is duly opened in due and ancient form.

*   *   *   *   *

RECEPTION.

*   *   *   *   *

The demands of justice remain unsatisfied. Excellent Grand Orator, what saith the law as to him who slayeth his brother?

If any man hate his neighbor, and lie in wait for him, and rise up against him and smite him mortally, that he die, and fleeth into one of the cities of refuge, then the Elders of his city shall send and fetch him thence, and deliver him into the hand of the Avenger of Blood, that he may die. Thine eye shall not pity him, but thou shalt put away the guilt of innocent blood from Israel, that it may go well with thee.

Such is the law ; and the land of Israel is not yet purified of the innocent blood of our brother shed upon the floor of the Temple. One of his assassins has suffered swift punishment, but two remain at large, nor have yet been traced from their retreat in the mountains of Joppa. I fear they have escaped by sea, and are beyond our reach.

Most Potent King, doubt not that the Lord will at length give the two assassins into thy hand.

* * * * *

T∴ P∴ I therefore declare you to be duly invested with the rank and dignity of Illustrious Elu of the Fifteen, which degree I declare to be devoted now and always hereafter to Liberty and Toleration; and I invest you with its collar, apron, and jewel, which need no explanation.

HISTORY.

G∴ O∴ About six months, it is said, after the execution of the assassin, as detailed in the degree of Knights Elect of the Nine, Bengaber, an intendant of King Solomon, in the country of Gath, which was tributary to him, caused diligent inquiry to be made if any person had lately taken shelter in that region who might be supposed to have fled from Jerusalem: he published at the same time an accurate description of the traitors who had made their escape. Shortly afterward he received information that persons answering the description had lately arrived there, and, believing themselves to be perfectly secure, had begun to work in the quarry of Ben-Dekar.

As soon as Solomon was made acquainted with this circumstance, he wrote to Maaka, King of Gath, to assist in apprehending them, and to cause them to be delivered to persons he should appoint to secure them, and have them brought to Jerusalem to receive the punishment due to their crimes.

Solomon then selected fifteen Masters in whom he could place the greatest confidence, and among whom were those nine who had been in the cavern, and sent them with an escort of troops in quest of the villains. Five days were spent in the search, when Zerbal, who bore King Solomon's letter to King Maaka, with Stolkin and another of his companions, discovered them cutting stone in the quarry. They immediately seized them, and, binding them in chains, conducted them to Jerusalem. On their arrival they were imprisoned in the tower of Achizar, and the next morning received the punishment which their crimes deserved.

This degree, my brethren, as you learned by your

reception and obligation, is devoted to the same objects as those of the Elu of the Nine; and also to the cause of the oppressed against the oppressor, and of toleration against intolerance; that is, to the cause of human freedom, corporal and mental, against tyranny exercised over the soul or body.

The assassins of Hiram Abif, whose capture and execution are recounted in this degree, are the symbols of those special enemies of freedom of the body and the soul—Ambition, of which tyranny or despotism is born; and Fanaticism, from which springs intolerance and persecution. To the objects of this degree you have irrevocably consecrated yourself, and whenever in your presence a Chapter of this degree is opened, you will be most impressively reminded of your solemn vows here taken at our altar.

ELEVENTH DEGREE.

Sublime Knights Elected.

ARGUMENT.

THIS, the third of the Elu or Elect Degrees, was intended to emblematically illustrate the reward conferred by King Solomon upon twelve of the Knights Elect of Fifteen who were instrumental in bringing to justice the assassins of the Master Builder Hiram, constituting them Governors over the twelve tribes of Israel,—instructing us that the true and faithful Brother will sooner or later receive his just reward, and morally teaching us to be earnest, honest, and sincere, and to protect the people against illegal impositions and exactions.

SUBLIME KNIGHTS ELECTED.

THE ELEVENTH GRADE OF THE ANCIENT AND ACCEPTED SCOTTISH RITE, AND THE EIGHTH OF THE INEFFABLE SERIES.

THE LODGE—ITS DECORATIONS, ETC.

This Lodge is also called a Chapter, and is decorated like that of the Tenth degree, with the same hangings.

It is lighted, however, by 12 lights, by threes, in the East, West, North, and South—each three forming an equilateral triangle.

OFFICERS, TITLES, ETC.

Same as in the Tenth degree.

The Chapter regularly consists of twelve members only.

CLOTHING, ORNAMENTS, AND JEWELS.

The apron is white, lined, edged and fringed with black, and the flap black. In the middle of the apron is painted or embroidered a flaming heart.

 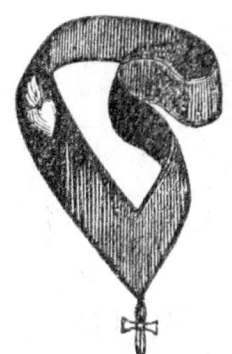

The cordon is a black ribbon, worn from right to left. Over the heart is painted or embroidered upon it a flaming heart; and over that, the words *Vincere aut Mori*.

The altar is uncovered, and supports the four great lights, cross-swords, and two daggers. Points of swords, when on an altar, should always be from the East.

The jewel is a dagger, worn suspended to the sash.

The age is 12 years.

Battery—•••••••••••.

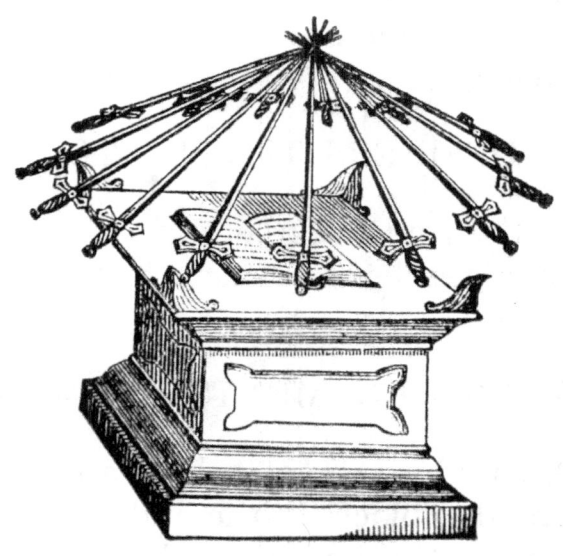

OPENING.

* * * * *

Q. What is your name?
A. Emeth.
Q. What does it signify?
A. A true man—just, fair, sincere, faithful, fearing God.
Q. Where were you received a Prince Emeth, or Elu of the Twelve?
A. In a place representing the audience-chamber of King Solomon.
Q. How many compose a Chapter of Sublime Elu of the Twelve?
A. Twelve or more.

* * * * *

$T\therefore P\therefore$ What does it signify?
A. That my faith cannot be shaken, and my confidence is in God.
Q. What are the characteristics of an Elu of the Twelve?
A. He is frank, fair, sincere, straightforward, reliable, honest, and upright, and thus is Emeth, a true man.
Who were the first Elus of the Twelve?
A. Those whom King Solomon made Princes and Governors in Israel.

* * * * *

G∴ Or∴ That the people among whom we live may be protected against illegal impositions.

J∴ G∴ W∴ That they may be secured in the enjoyment of their political and social rights.

S∴ G∴ W∴ That the burdens of the government may be equally apportioned.

All. We are and will forever remain united.

G∴ Or∴ We will be true unto all men.

J∴ G∴ W∴ We will be frank, honest, and sincere in all things.

S∴ G∴ W∴ We will be earnest in doing that which it may be our duty to do.

T∴ P∴ No man shall repent that he has relied upon our word.

All. And to this we pledge ourselves as Masons and as true men.

*   *   *   *   *

RECEPTION.

*   *   *   *   *

Justice will surely overtake the guilty, and the offence be unerringly followed by its consequences

Freedom of the State can only be attained and perpetuated by instructing the people, by following ignorance into its darkest dens, and there smiting it mortally, without mercy. My brethren, the affairs of the living, too long neglected in our sorrow for the dead and our pursuit of the assassins, now demand our attention. Many complaints have accumulated, and much wrong and oppression is charged to exist.

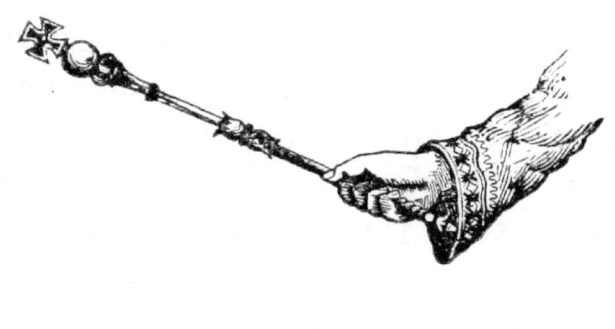

*   *   *   *   *

I will create twelve of the fifteen Knight Elus to be Governors in Israel, with the title of Princes Emeth, giving them in charge the collection of the revenues of my realm, and supreme control, each in his province, as my vicegerents and immediate representatives. They shall, also, when assembled, constitute a Chapter, and a new degree in Masonry be thus created, called the Sublime Elu of the Twelve. And, in order that no one may be offended or mortified, let the twelve be selected by lot.

*   *   *   *   *

My brethren, are you willing to take upon yourselves the duties of Governors in Israel and chiefs over the tribute, with the resolution to discharge those duties faithfully and impartially?

Will you promise to deal honestly and fairly by all men—to know no distinctions of persons—and to see that none are subjected to exaction, extortion, or unjust impositions of burdens?

*　　　　*　　　　*　　　　*　　　　*

T∴ P∴ I invest you, my brother, with the apron, collar, and jewel of this degree ; remember that you wear them as the successor and representative of a Sublime Elu or Prince Emeth of the Court of King Solomon; and that your conduct and conversation must be such as becomes one invested with so high an honor. The flaming hearts are symbols of that zeal and devotedness that ought to animate you, and the motto is your pledge that you will rather die than betray the cause of the people, or be overcome through your own fear or fault.

HISTORY.

G∴ Or∴ The history of this degree is brief. After punishment had been inflicted on the murderers mentioned in the preceding degrees, King Solomon instituted this degree, both as a recompense for the zeal and constancy of the Elus of the Fifteen, who had assisted him to discover them, and also to enable him to elevate other deserving brethren from the lower degrees to those of places in the higher, which had been vacated by their promotion. Twelve of these fifteen he elected Sublime Knights, and made the selection by ballot, that he might give none offence, putting the names of the whole in an urn. The first twelve that were drawn he formed into a Chapter, and gave them command over the twelve tribes. He gave them the name of Emeth, which is a Hebrew word signifying a true man. He exhibited to them the precious things which were deposited in the tabernacle. These, my brother, are the chief objects delineated on our tracing-board, and these you should make the constant subject of your reflections. These last three degrees constitute what are called the "Elu degrees" of the Ancient and Accepted Scottish rite. They elucidate a particular part of the legendary history of Freemasonry, and constitute a peculiar system which is necessarily contained in every rite. In the York rite the Elus are combined into one, and form a part of the third degree. In the French rite they constitute a separate degree, called "Elu," and forming the fourth degree of that rite. In some of the other systems of Masonry the Elus have been divided into numerous degrees, but their purport is always the same—to give details of the detection and punishment, by chosen or elected brethren, of those murderers who first stained the escutcheon of Freemasonry by an atrocious crime.

CLOSING.

* * * * *

T∴ P∴ Brother Senior Grand Warden, what is the hour?

S∴ G∴ W∴ The twelfth hour of the day, Thrice Potent.

T∴ P∴ Then it is time to close this Chapter of Sublime Elu of the Twelve. Cause the brethren to assemble around the altar, that, renewing our pledges to each other, we may close in due and ancient form.

S∴ GV W∴ Brethren, you will please assemble around the altar, and assist the Thrice Potent Grand Master to close this Chapter in due and ancient form.

* * * * *

* * * * *

TWELFTH DEGREE.

Grand Master Architect.

ARGUMENT.

THE degree of Grand Master Architect is alleged to have been established as a school of instruction for the more advanced workmen of the Temple, to assure uniformity in work, vigor in its prosecution, and to reward those more eminent in science and skill. The degree partakes of a scientific nature, in which the rules of architecture and the connection of the liberal arts with Masonry are dwelt upon, and portions of the Fellow Craft or Companion degree are amplified and extensively illustrated. This grade requires of the neophyte that he be thoroughly qualified, intellectually and morally, to be admitted, and instructs him that virtue is as necessary as talents to every Grand Master Architect.

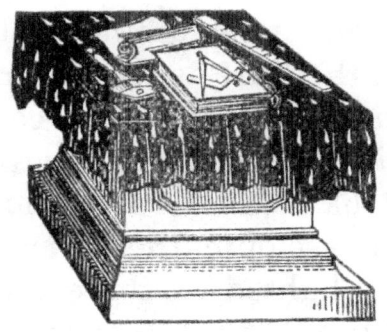

GRAND MASTER ARCHITECT.

THE TWELFTH GRADE OF THE ANCIENT AND ACCEPTED SCOTTISH RITE, AND THE NINTH OF THE INEFFABLE SERIES.

THE CHAPTER–ITS DECORATIONS, ETC.

Bodies of this degree are styled Chapters.
The hangings are white, strewed with crimson flames.
Behind the Master, in the East, are five columns, each of a different order of architecture: Tuscan, Doric, Ionic, Corinthian, and Composite.
In the North is painted the North Star, and a little

below it the seven stars of the Great Bear. In the East, behind the columns, is a luminous star, representing Jupiter rising in the East as the morning star.

Upon the altar, which is in the centre of the room and covered with a black cloth with tears, are the Great Lights, Book of the Constitutions, and on it, all the contents of a case of mathematical instruments.

The Chapter is lighted by three great lights, one in the East, one in the West, and one in the South.

Over the columns, in the East, hangs a triangle, en closing the word אדני.

OFFICERS, TITLES, ETC.

The same as in the three preceding degrees.

CLOTHING, ORNAMENTS, JEWEL, ETC.

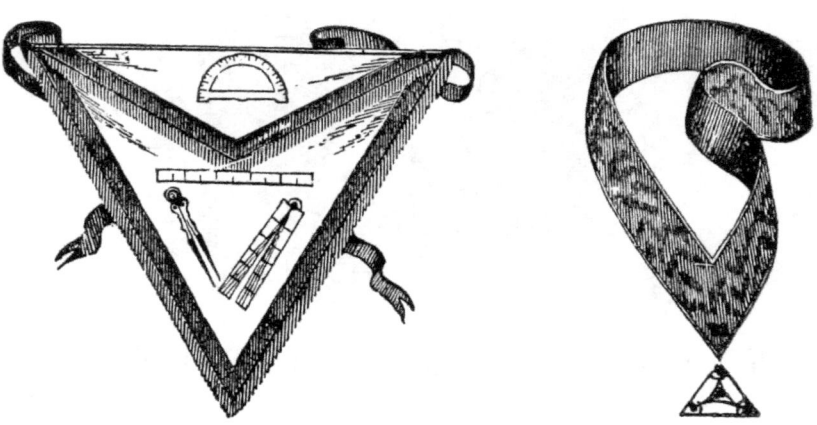

The apron is white, lined and bordered with blue, and fringed with gold. On it are painted or embroidered a protractor on the flap, and in the middle a plain scale, a sector, and the compasses, so arranged as to form a triangle

The cordon is a broad blue watered ribbon, worn from the left shoulder to the right hip.

The jewel is a triangle of gold: on each angle, on one side, is a star enclosed by a semicircle. In the centre, on the same side, is an equilateral triangle, formed by arcs of circles, in the centre of which is the letter א. On the reverse side are five columns, of the different orders of architecture, with the initial letter of

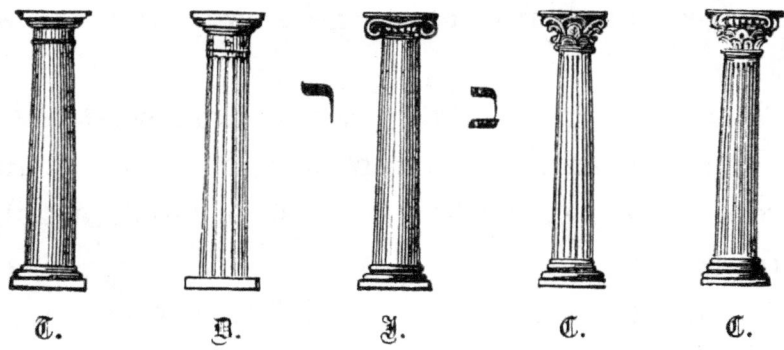

the proper order below each, in old English letters, arranged from left to right, Tuscan, Doric, Ionic, Corinthian, and Composite. Above these columns are a sector and a slide-rule; below them, the three kinds of compasses, the plain scale, and parallel ruler; and between the second and third, and third and fourth columns, are the letters ר - ב (R∴ B∴)

In front of each brother is a small table, and on it a case of instruments, with paper and other articles for drafting.

The age of a Grand Master Architect is the square of 3 x 5, or 45 years.

Battery—•••••—••

OPENING.

In the Opening, the following explanations of the instruments of a Grand Master Architect are given:

Q. What are the instruments of a Grand Master Architect?

A. The different compasses, the parallel ruler, the protractor, the plain scale, the sector and the slide-rule.

Q. What lesson do the different compasses teach us?

A. That life and time constitute but a point in the centre of eternity; while the circle of God's attributes is infinity.

Q. What lesson does the parallel ruler teach us?

A. That we should be consistent, firm, unwavering, and of that equanimity of mind and temper which befits a Mason.

Q. What lesson does the protractor teach us?

A. That we should be upright and sincere, frank in all our dealings, moderate in our professions, and exact and punctual in performance.

Q. What lesson does the plain scale teach us?

A. That we live not only for ourselves, but for others, so as in just and proper measure to serve our-selves, our families, our friends, our neighbors, and our country.

Q. What lesson does the sector teach us?

A. That we should multiply our good deeds, divide that which we can spare of our substance among those who need it more than we, and extract the good that is intended to benefit and bless us from the reverses and calamities of life.

Q. What lesson does the slide-rule teach us?

A. That we should strive to grasp and solve the great problem presented by the Universe and involved in our existence; to know and understand the lofty truths of Philosophy, and to communicate freely of our knowledge unto others.

Q. Where were you received and made a Grand Master Architect?

A. In a place representing the Chamber of Designs, assigned to the Master Khūrūm in King Solomon's Temple.

RECEPTION.

*   *   *   *   *

J∴ G∴ W∴ A wise man will hear and increase in learning, and a man of understanding will attain unto wise counsels ; to understand a proverb, and the interpretation ; the word of the sages and their obscure sayings.

J∴ G∴ W∴ Wisdom preventeth them that covet her, so that she first showeth herself unto them. He that awaketh to seek her shall not labor; for he shall find her sitting at his door. The Lord giveth wisdom;

out of his mouth come knowledge and understanding.

J∴ G∴ W∴ When wisdom entereth into thine heart, and knowledge is pleasant unto thy soul, discretion shall preserve thee, and understanding shall keep thee, and thou shalt understand righteousness, judgment, equity, and every good path.

   *   *   *   *

S∴ G∴ W∴ I wished, and understanding was given me ; and I called upon God, and the spirit of wisdom came upon me, and I preferred her before kingdoms and thrones, and esteemed riches nothing in comparison to her. The Lord by wisdom hath founded the earth ; by understanding hath he established the heavens.

S∴ G∴ W∴ Get wisdom! Exalt her, and she shall promote thee; she shall bring thee to honor, when thou dost embrace her. She shall give to thy head an ornament of grace ; a crown of glory shall she deliver to thee.

  * * * * *

T∴ P∴ No evil can overcome wisdom. She glorifieth her nobility by being conversant with God, and the Lord of all things loveth her. For it is she that teacheth knowledge of God and is the expounder of his works.

T∴ P∴ She knoweth things past, and judgeth things to come. She knoweth the subtleties of speeches, and the solutions of arguments; she knoweth signs and wonders before they be done, and the events of times and ages. By means of her we shall have immortality.

*   *   *   *   *

LECTURE.

It is the true Masonic Light. He who obeys the Masonic law shall find it. The degree which you seek was first conferred upon Adoniram, the son of Abda, when he was appointed Chief Architect of the Temple, and as such the successor of the Master Khūrūm, after having been for a time the chief of the five Intendants of the Building, and after his skill and science as an architect had been thoroughly tested, and he found to be superior to the other four Intendants. It was but the ceremony of his investiture with that office. Afterward it became an honorary degree, conferred first upon the other Intendants, and then upon the Elus, as a mark of honor and distinction. As he advanced, the ancient Freemason ceased to work with the instruments of the laborer, the square, the level, the plumb, and the trowel, and assumed those of the Architect and Geometrician. As he advanced, also, he passed from that branch of geometry and mathematics which occupies itself with the earth, its surface and the things that belong to it, with right lines and angles, and all the figures formed thereby, to the mathematics of the heavens and the spheres. We no longer occupy ourselves with geometry and mathematics as sciences, nor expect of our initiate a knowledge of their problems, or even of their terms. To us the instruments of the geometrician, and all the figures, plane and spherical, drawn by these instruments, have a symbolical meaning. By means of the morality of Masonry, we advance toward its philosophy, and every degree is a step in that direction. If you would succeed to the rank held by Adoniram, you must assume the obligation which it imposes.

*   *   *   *   *

INVESTMENT.

T∴ P∴ I invest you with the apron, collar, and jewel of this degree. Their colors, white and blue, will remind you of what is commonly called symbolic Masonry, or the Blue degrees,—the foundation, but not the completion and perfection of Masonry. Upon the apron and jewel you see the five orders of Architecture, and the instruments of a Grand Master Architect; the symbolic meaning of which you have yet to learn. I now present you with the instruments with which a Grand Master Architect works. Listen, and you shall learn their uses, and of what they are the symbols to us in this degree.

*   *   *   *   *

T∴ P∴ Such are the instruments of a Grand Master Architect, and such the lessons which they teach us. Forget not that you have solemnly sworn to practise all the virtues which they symbolically teach; for thus only can you deserve, how proudly soever you may wear the title of a Grand Master Architect.

HISTORY.

The history of this degree is brief, as its ceremonies are simple. After the murderers of the Master Khūrūm Abai had been discovered, apprehended, tried, and punished, his monument and mausoleum completed, and the matters which concerned the revenue of the realm provided for, King Solomon, to assure uniformity of work and vigor in its prosecution, and to reward the superior and eminent science and skill of Adoniram, the son of Abda, appointed him to be chief Architect of the Temple, with the title of Grand Master Architect, and invested him with that office, as sole successor and representative of the deceased Master Khūrūm Abai, and at the same time made him Grand Master of Masons and the Masonic peer of himself and King Khūrūm of Tsŭr. Afterward the title was conferred upon other Princes of the Jewish court as an honorarium, and thus the degree became established. You have heard what are the lessons taught by the working instruments of a Grand Master Architect, and I shall not now enlarge upon those lessons. The great duties which they inculcate demand much of us, and take for granted our capacity to perform them fully. We hope that we are not mistaken in believing that you possess that capacity, and in expecting that you will be always found equal to the task which you have thus imposed upon yourself.

CLOSING.

* * * * *

S∴ G∴ W∴ The sun has set, and the evening star has risen.

T∴ P∴ The hour of rest has arrived. Give notice to the Grand Masters that this Chapter of Grand Master Architects is about to be closed, that they may aid in so doing.

S∴ G∴ W∴ Brethren in the North, the Thrice Potent Grand Master is about to close this Chapter of Grand Master Architects, and desires your assistance, since the hour of rest has arrived.

* * * * *

THIRTEENTH DEGREE.

Royal Arch of Enoch.

THE ARK OF PHILE.

ARGUMENT.

THIS degree, in fact, forms the climax of Ineffable Masonry; it is the keystone of the arch, and discovers that which is revealed in the succeeding degree of Perfection. It is a most important and interesting grade, and so intimately connected with its successor as to appear like a section of that degree.

The shaded beauties of the sacred words that have been hitherto revealed, and the lessons and virtues that have so gradually been inculcated, in this degree receive a climax, and culminate in the development of the great mystery of Ineffable Masonry.

"The dark clouds and mists that have hitherto veiled the sacred mysteries now begin to be dispelled: the glorious dawn illumines the E∴ with its bright effulgence, and its rays penetrate into dark and hidden places."

ה ו ה י
5 6 5 10 = 26

ה י ח א
5 10 5 1 = 21.

ROYAL ARCH OF ENOCH;

OR,

KNIGHTS OF THE NINTH ARCH.

THE THIRTEENTH GRADE OF THE ANCIENT AND ACCEPTED SCOTTISH RITE, AND THE TENTH DEGREE OF THE INEFFABLE SERIES.

DECORATIONS.

This Chapter of Royal Arch of Solomon represents the audience-chamber of King Solomon. The hangings are alternately red and white.

Lights—Three in the East, three in the West, and three in the South.

OFFICERS.

King Solomon is seated in the East.

Hiram, King of Tyre, is also in the East, on the left of K∴ S∴

Senior Warden represents. Gibulum, and is seated in the West.

Junior Warden represents Stolkin, and is seated in the South.

Treasurer (who represents Joabert), Secretary, Master of Ceremonies, Captain of the Guard, and other officers, stationed as in a Lodge of Perfection.

All Officers and Companions, except the Kings, clothed in black, with apron, collar, and jewel of this degree or of their particular office.

King Solomon wears a yellow robe, purple chasuble, lined with blue, sleeves reaching to the elbows, and rich purple sash, with jewel.

King Hiram of Tyre wears a purple robe, yellow chasuble, and rich purple sash, with jewel.

Apron—Purple silk or velvet, bordered with white; in the centre of the area, the Enochian delta, with rays.

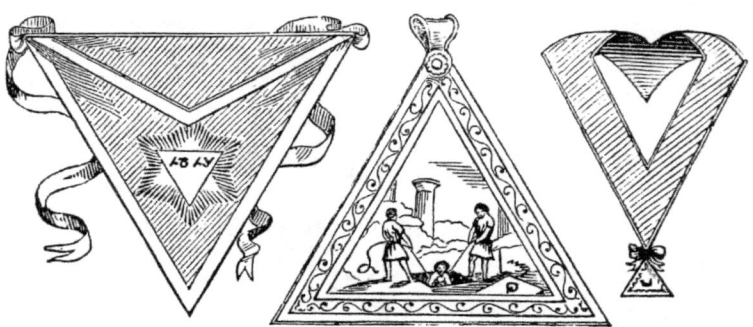

Collar—Purple silk or velvet, and suspended to it the

Jewel—A gold triangle, on which is engraved the delta of Enoch, with rays. On the obverse side of the jewel is a representation of the first three recipients of this degree, two of them lowering the third into the subterranean vault. Around this device, the initials of the words "*Regnante Sapientissimo Salamone, Gibulum, Joabert, et Stolkin invenerunt pretiosissimum Artificum thesaurum subter ruinas Enoch, Anno Mundi 2995.*"

Age—7 times 9=63.

Battery—••• —••• —•••

There should be a separate apartment, without apparent door or window; opening overhead, covered with a trap-door, representing a flat stone with an iron ring to it.

OPENING.

$T\therefore P\therefore$ The Lord is great in Zion. Let all the earth praise him for his great and terrible name, for it is holy.

$S\therefore W\therefore$ Exalt the Lord our God, and worship on his holy hill.

J∴ W∴ He spake from the cloudy pillar and from the fire ; and from the depth cometh forth the riches of secret places.

T∴ P∴ Exalt the Lord our God, for he is holy; and his name, for it is from everlasting to everlasting.

S∴ W∴ What is man, that he should magnify him, or that he should set his heart upon him?

J∴ W∴ We are but of yesterday, and know nothing. Our days are but a shadow: they flee, and we know not.

T∴ P∴ Canst thou, by searching, find out God? Canst thou find out the Almighty to perfection? He is as high as heaven. What canst thou do? He is deeper than hell. What canst thou know?

S∴ W∴ His eyes are upon the ways of man, and he seeth all his doings.

J∴ W∴ O God, let thy work appear unto thy servants, and thy glory unto the children of men!

T∴ P∴ Let the beauty of the Lord be upon us, and establish thou the work of our hands: O Jehovah, establish thou it!

S∴ W∴ I will sing unto the Lord as long as I live; I will sing praises unto my God while I have my being.

J∴ W∴ My meditations of him shall be sweet; I will be glad in the Lord.

T∴ P∴ Mark the perfect man, and behold the upright: for the end of that man is peace. "Mine eyes shall be on the perfect man" saith the Lord.

"The perfect of the land shall dwell with me: they shall walk in my name, and serve me forever." Companions, let us give thanks unto the Lord, who hath given us the treasures of darkness and the hidden riches of secret places.

*   *   *   *   *

PRAYER.

O thou great and eternal Lord God, source of light and of love—thou Sovereign Inspector and Mighty Architect of the wonders of Creation—who from thy throne in the highest heaven in mercy looketh down upon all the dwellers of the earth—lend, we beseech thee, thine ears to the prayers and petitions of thy unworthy servants now assembled in thy presence, to teach the mysteries of that Sublime Edifice which is erected and dedicated to thy Most Holy and Glorious Name. Pour upon us, and all the members of the Mystic Craft throughout the two hemispheres, the rich blessings of thy Providence. Give us strength to overcome temptations, to subdue our passions, and to practise virtue. Fill our hearts with fear without desolation; with confidence without presumption; with piety without illusion; and with joy without licentiousness. Fill our hearts with tender affections for thy divine goodness, and love for our neighbors: make us faithful to our friends and charitable to our enemies. Dispose our hearts, O thou God Eternal! to receive the splendid impressions of Religion and Humanity; our minds, the great lights of Science; and direct our footsteps in the bright paths of virtue.

Let all our actions prove to an admiring world that our lives are sincerely dedicated to Thee, our God, and to the relief of our fellow-creatures. And finally, when we yield up our breath to Thee, the Source of Life, may we, bearing the rich harvest of good actions, be admitted into that Sublime and Eternal Lodge where happiness reigns without alloy, and where, around the throne of the Great Jehovah, we shall sing hallelujahs to his name.

Now unto the King Eternal, Immortal, Invisible, the only Wise God, be the kingdom, power, and glory, forever and ever. Amen!

Omnes. God grant it so may be!

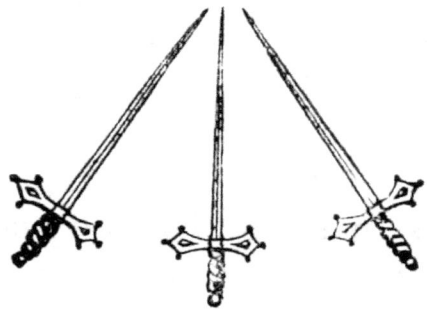

RECEPTION.

*   *   *   *

I shall now invest you with the apron, collar, and jewel of a Knight of the Ninth or Royal Arch.

The color of your apron and collar is purple, and

denotes the royal origin of the degree and the dignity of your station.

The jewel alludes to the delta or golden plate found in the subterranean arch, a more full description of which will be obtained by attending to the history and lecture of the degree.

HISTORY.

G∴ O∴ Companions: this is the history and legend of this degree. Enoch, the son of Jared, was the sixth in descent from Adam. Filled with the love and fear of God, he strove to lead men in the way of honor and duty. In a vision the Deity appeared to him in visible shape, and said to him, "Enoch, thou hast longed to know my true name: arise and follow me, and thou shalt know it."

*   *   *   *   *

Enoch, accepting his vision as an inspiration, journeyed in search of the mountain he had seen in his dream, until, weary of the search, he stopped in the land of Canaan, then already populous with the descendants of Adam, and there employed workmen; and with the help of his son Methuselah, he excavated nine apartments, one above the other, and each roofed with an arch, as he had seen in his dream, the lowest being hewn out of the solid rock. In the crown of each arch he left a narrow aperture, closed with a square stone, and over the upper one he built a modest temple, roofless and of huge unhewn stones, to the Grand Architect of the Universe.

Upon a triangular plate of gold, inlaid with many precious gems, he engraved the ineffable name of God, and sank the plate into one face of a cube of agate.

  *   *   *   *   *

None knew of the deposit of the precious treasure; and, that it might remain undiscovered, and survive the Flood, which it was known to Enoch would soon overwhelm the world in one vast sea of mire, he covered the aperture, and the stone that closed it and the great ring of iron used to raise the stone, with the granite pavement of his primitive temple.

Then, fearing that all knowledge of the arts and sciences would be lost in the universal flood, he built two great columns upon a high hill—one of brass, to resist water, and one of granite, to resist fire. On the granite column was written in hieroglyphics a description of the subterranean apartments; on the one of brass, the rudiments of the arts and sciences.

The granite column was overturned and swept away, and worn to a shapeless mass by the Deluge, but that of brass stood firm, and was found by Noah. Thenceforward the true name of God remained unknown until he said unto Moses in Egypt, when he ordered him to go to Pharaoh, and cause him to send forth the children of Israel out of Egypt: "I am that which I was and shall be: I am the God of thy fathers; the God of Abraham, of Isaac, and of Jacob.

Thus shalt thou say unto the children of Israel, HE WHO IS hath sent me unto you. I am the Lord, that appeared to Abraham, to Isaac, and to Jacob by my name AL-SHEDI, but my name ——— I did not show them."

Moses engraved the ineffable name upon a plate of gold, and deposited it in the ark of the covenant. Moses made the name known to Aaron and Joshua, and afterwards it was made known to the chief priests. The word being composed of consonants only, its true pronunciation was soon lost, but the word still remained in the ark; and in the time of Othniel, in a battle against the King of Syria, those who bore the ark were slain, and the ark fell to the ground. After the battle, the men of Israel, searching for it, were led to it by the roaring of a lion, which, crouching by it, had guarded it, holding the golden key in its mouth. Upon the approach of the High-priest and Levites, he laid down the key, and withdrew. Hence, upon the golden key worn by the treasurer, you see the initials of these words: " *In arc leonis verbum inveni*"—"In the lion's mouth I found the word." This plate of gold was melted down, and made into an image of Dagon by the Philistines, who took it in battle.

David intended to build a temple to God, but bequeathed the enterprise to Solomon, his son, and Solomon selected a place near Jerusalem ; but finding overthrown columns of Enoch's temple, and supposing them to be the ruins of a heathen temple, and not wishing to select a desecrated spot, selected Mount Moriah for the site of his Temple to the true God. Under this temple he built a secret vault, the approach to which was through eight other vaults, all under ground, and to which a long and narrow passage led under the king's palace. In the ninth apartment was placed a twisted column of white marble, on which it was intended to place the ark, and in this apartment he held his private conferences with King Hiram of Tyre and H∴ A∴, they only knowing the way by which it was approached. Solomon proposed to erect a Temple of Justice, and selected as a site the spot where Enoch's temple had stood, and to that end directed that the fallen columns and rubbish should be removed. Gibulum, Joabert, and Stolkin were selected to survey the ground and lay off the foundations.

*   *   *   *   *

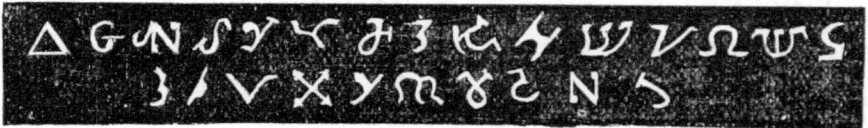

ENOCHIAN ALPHABET.

FOURTEENTH DEGREE

Grand, Elect, Perfect and Sublime Mason.

GRAND ELECT MASON.

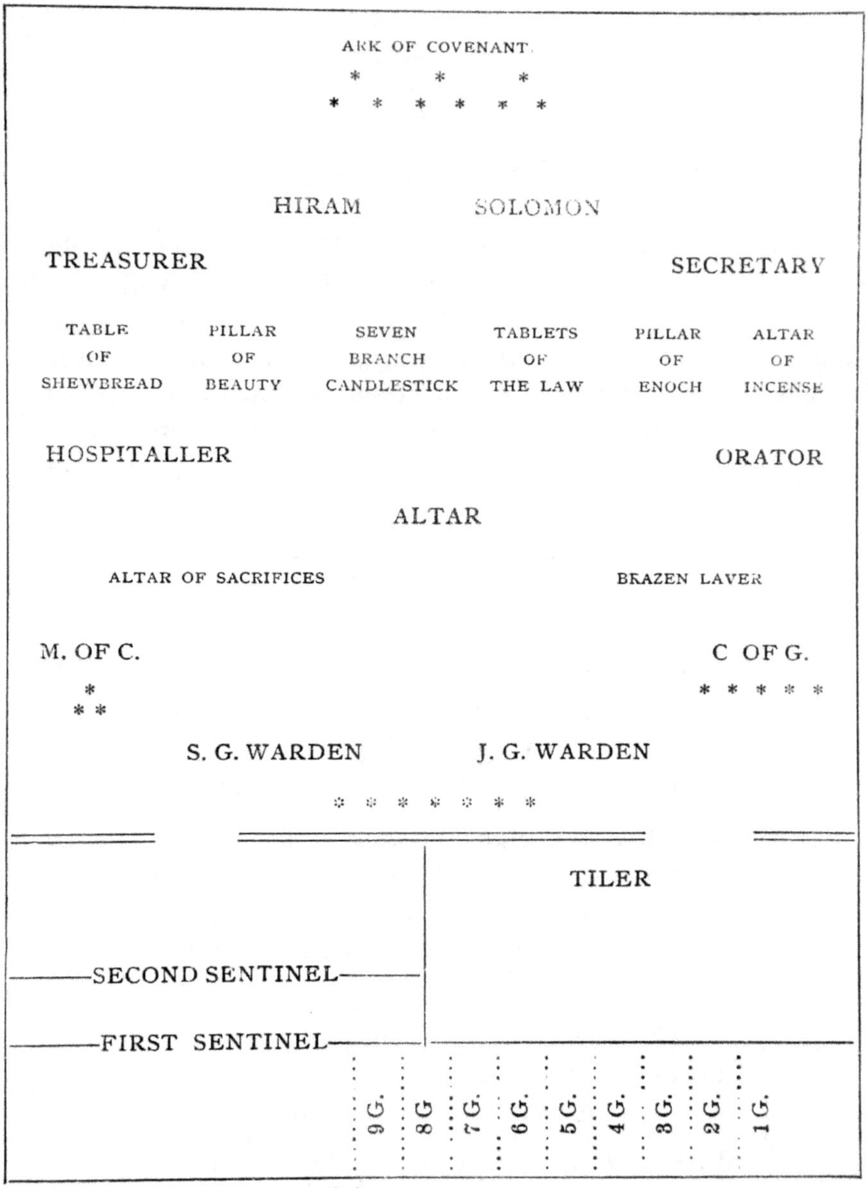

ARK OF COVENANT.
* * *
* * * * *

HIRAM   SOLOMON

TREASURER   SECRETARY

TABLE	PILLAR	SEVEN	TABLETS	PILLAR	ALTAR
OF	OF	BRANCH	OF	OF	OF
SHEWBREAD	BEAUTY	CANDLESTICK	THE LAW	ENOCH	INCENSE

HOSPITALLER   ORATOR

ALTAR

ALTAR OF SACRIFICES   BRAZEN LAVER

M. OF C.   C OF G.
 *   * * * * *
* *

S. G. WARDEN   J. G. WARDEN

* * * * * * *

TILER

———SECOND SENTINEL———
———FIRST SENTINEL———

9 G. 8 G. 7 G. 6 G. 5 G. 4 G. 3 G. 2 G. 1 G.

* * SIGNIFY LIGHTS.

ARGUMENT.

THE Lodge represents the Secret Vault under the Sanctum Sanctorum, in which is the Pillar of Beauty, and on this is placed the Holy four-letter Name. This degree reveals and explains the tetragrammaton, completes the construction of the Holy Temple, and narrates the destruction of both it and the city of Jerusalem, together with the death of Solomon.

TETRAGRAMMATON.

By J F. ADAMS, M. D.

THERE is a word—no mortal tongue
    May dare its mystic sounds combine ;
Nor saint hath breathed, nor prophet sung
    That holiest of the names divine !

Nor may the finger of the scribe
    Presume that hallowed word to write ;
Accursed alike from Israel's tribe
    Were he who dared that name indite !

Yet though no lip nor pen may dare
    That name unspeakable impart,
'Tis ever breathed in secret prayer—
    'Tis ever written on the heart!

With care preserved, the sacred word
    Is erst indeed a blessed dower :
We bow before thy name, O Lord,
    And own its great and marv'lous power !

"*Virtus junxit—Mors non separabit.*"

GRAND, ELECT, PERFECT AND SUBLIME MASON.

THE FOURTEENTH GRADE OF THE ANCIENT AND ACCEPTED SCOTTISH RITE, AND THE ELEVENTH DEGREE OF THE INEFFABLE SERIES.

FORM AND DECORATIONS.

The Lodge should be cubical in form; the brethren (if convenient) sitting about the Lodge so as to form a triangle.

Lights—3, 5, 7, and 9.   3 lights North, in form of a Triangle.
5 lights South, in form of a Pentagon.
7 lights West, in form of a Heptagon.
9 lights East, forming three Equilateral Triangles, in a line.

The Lodge should contain a Pillar of Beauty; the Ark of Alliance; the Seven-Branch Golden Candlestick; a representation of the Burning Bush; the Table of Shewbread; the Altar of Perfumes; the Altar of Sacrifices; the Brazen Salver; the Enochian Pillar; the Golden Urns and Vases; the Gold Delta of Enoch; the Book of the Testimony; the Square and Compasses; the Cubic Stone; the Tables of the Law; the Bread and Wine; the Silver Hod and Golden Trowel; the Silver Plate and Cup.

Pillar of Beauty—Twisted column, pure white marble, about three and a half feet high, on which should be the cube of agate, measuring about six inches on each face, on the upper side of which is the triangular Enochian plate of gold, set in with precious stones, and having on it the Ineffable name

Pillar of Enoch—Marble pieces put together, found in ancient ruins, with Enochian characters upon it.

Brazen Salver—Large brazen basin, containing water on a pedestal three and a half feet high, with ten lavers at its base.

Altar of Sacrifices—Length and breadth equal to one-half the height, with gilded horn on each corner, and covered with gold.

Table of Shewbread—On it twelve loaves of Shewbread, in two piles of six loaves each, and cup with wine.

Altar of Perfumes—On it an urn, with incense burning; size and shape of Altar of Sacrifices.

All the altars should be covered with white cloths.

The Secret, afterward Sacred Vault, is approached by a long narrow passage of nine arches, between which and the Sacred Vault should be a small anteroom; arches dimly lit by one lamp only, hung from the ceiling.

Hangings—Crimson, with pillars at stated intervals.

Burning Bush in the East, behind the Thrice Puissant; in its centre the Ineffable Triangle.

Lightning Boxes, Torches, Thunder-drums, Trumpets, Organ, Gong, etc.

CLOTHING AND DECORATIONS.

OFFICERS.	JEWELS.
1. Thrice Puissant Grand Master,	Crowned Compasses, with blazing sun in the centre.
2. Dep∴ Gr∴ M∴, King of Tyre,	Crowned Compasses, with full moon in the centre.
3. Vener∴ Senior Grand Warden	Gold Trowel.
4. Vener∴ Junior Grand Warden	Sword of Justice.
5. Grand Keeper of the Seals	Ivory Key.
6. Grand Treasurer	Gold Key.
7. Grand Secretary	Gold Pen.
8. Grand Orator	Gold Scroll.
9. Grand Master of Ceremonies	Staff.
10. Grand Captain of the Guard	Spear.
11. Grand Hospitable Brother	Winged Staff.
12. Grand Tyler	Flaming Sword.
13. Grand Organist	Gold Lyre.

The jewels of all the officers are set in gold triangles, and are suspended from collars of white watered silk, having a rosette of white and red at the bottom.

The two Kings in royal robes, with crowns, sceptres, etc.

King Solomon—Yellow robe or mantle, with a blue vestment and an Eastern crown and sceptre.

King of Tyre—Purple robe, with yellow vestment, richly trimmed with fur and gold; Mural crown and sceptre.

Apron—White watered silk, lined with white and bordered with gold, triangular in form, and the Ineffable Delta in the centre.

Collar—White watered silk, bordered with gold, from which is suspended the

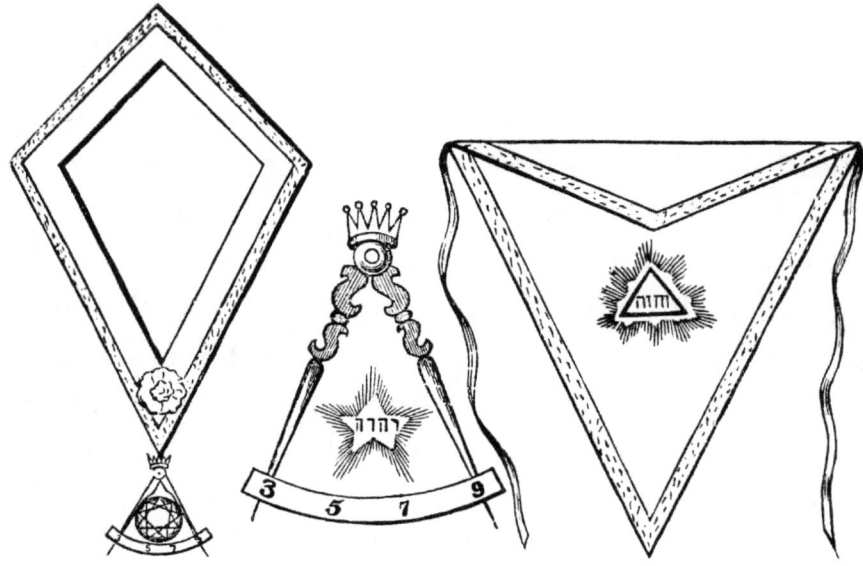

Jewel—Crowned Quadrant, having a golden sun with nine points in the centre; on the reverse is a blazing star; in the centre of the star, the Enochian or Solomonian characters; upon the segment of the circle are engraved, 3, 5, 7, 9.

Ring—Flat band of gold; on the outside a delta, enclosing a ׳; on the inside the following inscription: "Virtue unites, death cannot separate." Also the name of the owner, and date of receiving this degree.

Girdle—Nine colors: blue, red, and yellow, 3; green and purple, 5; white and black, 7; stone and flame color, 9; all interwoven with olive-green.

Gloves—White.

Robes—Black. Caps and swords.

Battery—3,—5,—7,—9.

Age—Square of 9 = 81.

*   *   *   *   *

LESSON FOR OPENING AND CLOSING.

T∴ P∴ The Lord is in his holy Temple; his eyes behold and his eyelids try the children of men.

S∴ W∴ Lord, who shall stand in thy presence, and who shall abide in thy tabernacle?

J∴ W∴ He that walketh uprightly, and worketh righteousness, and speaketh truth in his heart. He that backbiteth not with his tongue, nor doeth evil with his neighbor; but honoreth them that fear the Lord.

T∴ P∴ Who shall ascend into the hill of the Lord, or who shall stand in his holy place?

S∴ W∴ He that hath clean hands and a pure heart ; who hath not lifted up his soul unto vanity, nor sworn deceitfully. He shall receive blessings from the Lord, and righteousness from the God of his salvation.

J∴ W∴ Lift up your heads, O ye gates, and be ye lifted up, ye everlasting doors! and the King of glory shall come in.

T∴ P∴ For now have I chosen and sanctified this house, that my name might be there forever; and mine eyes and my heart shall be therein perpetually.

S∴ W∴ Who is this King of glory?

J∴ W∴ The Lord strong and mighty, the Lord of hosts, our Adonai: he is the King of glory.

T∴ P∴ I will wash my hands in innocency and so will I encompass thine altar, O Jehovah!

S∴ W∴ As for me, I will walk in my integrity. My foot standeth in an even place, and here will I bless the Lord forever.

J∴ W∴ Keep thy tongue from evil, and thy lips from speaking guile: depart from evil, and do good; seek peace, and ensue it. Thus saith the Lord of hosts: Amend your ways and your doings, and I will cause you to dwell in this place forever.

T∴ P∴ But whoso confesseth his sins, and forsaketh them, shall have mercy.

S∴ W∴ Who can say I have made my heart clean—I am pure from sin? For there is not a just man on earth, that doeth good and sinneth not—no, not one.

J∴ W∴ They shall fear the name of the Lord from the west, and his glory from the rising of the sun.

T∴ P∴ From the rising of the sun even unto the going down of the same, my name shall be great among the gentiles; and in every place incense shall be offered, and a pure offering; for my name shall be great among the heathen, saith the Lord of hosts.

S∴ W∴ Sing unto the Lord; sing praises unto his name. Extol him that rideth in the heavens, by his name Jah, and rejoice before him.

J∴ W∴ He discovereth deep things in the darkness, and bringeth to light from the shadow of death.

T∴ P∴ Gather together unto him those that have made a covenant with him by sacrifice, and offer up to him a holy libation with a perfect heart. How excellent is thy loving-kindness and thy righteousness to the upright of heart! for with thee is the foundation of life, and in thy light shall we see the light which shineth more and more unto the perfect day.

PRAYER.

Almighty and Sovereign Grand Architect of the Universe, who, by thy divine power, doth continually search and penetrate the most secret recesses of our hearts, draw near us, we beseech thee, by the sacred fire of thy love. Guide us, by thy unerring hand, in the path of virtue, and by thine adorable presence aid us to keep out all impiety and perverseness.

May the mysterious inscription settle in our minds a true notion of thine unspeakable essence and power, as we preserve the memorials of thy fear. We beseech thee that our thoughts may be engaged, and our hearts set, on the grand work of Perfection; which, when attained, will be an ample reward for all our labor.

Let peace and charity link us together in a pleasing union, and may this Lodge of Grand, Elect, Perfect and Sublime Masons exhibit a faint resemblance of that happiness the elect will enjoy in thy Kingdom forever.

Give us a spirit to refuse the evil and choose the good, that we may not be led astray by those who unworthily assume the title of Grand Elect: may our doings tend to thy glory and our advancement toward Perfection.

May a sweet perfume ascend from the altar of out hearts, and be acceptable to thee, O God, our Adonai! Bless us, O God, and prosper the work of our hands. Keep us through life, and accept us in death. Amen.
Amen. So mote it be.

*   *   *   *   *

RECEPTION.

*   *   *   *   *

And God spake all these words, saying: I am the Lord thy God, which have brought thee out of the land of Egypt, out of the house of bondage.

Thou shalt have no other gods before me.

Thou shalt not make unto thee any graven image or any likeness of any thing that is in heaven above, or that is in the earth beneath, or that is in the waters under the earth: thou shalt not bow down thyself to them, nor serve them: for I the Lord thy God am a jealous God, visiting the iniquity of the fathers upon the children unto the third and fourth generation of them that hate me; and shewing mercy unto thousands of them that love me and keep my commandments.

Thou shalt not take the name of the Lord thy God in vain: for the Lord will not hold him guiltless that taketh his name in vain.

Remember the Sabbath-day to keep it holy. Six days shalt thou labor, and do all thy work: but the seventh day is the Sabbath of the Lord thy God: in it thou shalt not do any work, thou, nor thy son, nor thy daughter, thy man-servant, nor thy maid-servant, nor thy cattle, nor thy stranger that is within thy gates; for in six days the Lord made heaven and earth, the sea and all that in them is, and rested the seventh day: wherefore the Lord blessed the Sabbath-day, and hallowed it.

Honor thy father and thy mother; that thy days may be long upon the land which the Lord thy God hath given thee.

Thou shalt not kill.

Thou shalt not commit adultery.

Thou shalt not steal.

Thou shalt not bear false witness against thy neighbor.

Thou shalt not covet thy neighbor's house, thou shalt not covet thy neighbor's wife, nor his man-servant, nor his maid-servant, nor his ox, nor his ass, nor any thing that is thy neighbor's.

T∴ P∴ Before the altar of a broken and a contrite heart, with the fire of holy zeal, mortify your sins by the hatred thereof. May we all offer up to him on the altar of our hearts a sacrifice of humility and praise, with the fire of fervent charity. From our hearts, too, those altars of incense, may the perfume of our prayers arise for the bestowment of heavenly blessings.

PRAYER.

Almighty and Sovereign Grand Architect of the Universe, thou who ridest in the heavens by thy name Jah, let all the earth keep silence before thee. There is no God like unto thee in the heavens above or in the earth beneath, who keepeth covenant and showeth mercy unto thy servants that walk before thee with all their hearts.

When we draw nigh thy majesty, may we ever preserve the memorials of thy fear, and the indelible character of thine ineffable essence, in our hearts. Oh, purify our hearts, we beseech thee, by the fire of thy holy love, and guide our feet in the way of peace, and in the perfect path which shineth more and more, with a shining light, unto the perfect day. May we all have an interest in that covenant which is well-ordered in all things and sure. May we dwell together in unity, and be all of one mind, having compassion one to another, and love as brethren.

May all Elect Masons, like the Elect of God, put on charity, which is the bond of perfection. May our loins be girt about with the girdle of truth; and finally, having been faithful in all our course, may we be brought to behold the light ineffable, and admitted into that sacred place where the sun shall no more give light by day; neither for brightness shall the moon give light, but the Lord, our Adonai, shall be with us an everlasting light, and our God our glory.

Bless us, and bless the work in which we are engaged; and may the alliance we are about to perfect be eternal. Amen! So mote it be!

*   *   *   *   *

Let me impress you with an ardent zeal for the honor and glory of the Grand Architect of the Universe, to the end that you may always live in his adorable presence, with a head disposed to contrive, a heart to feel, and a hand to execute all those things toward him and your fellow-creatures which are so well pleasing in his sight.

"Behold how good and pleasant it is for brethren to dwell together in unity. It is like the precious ointment on the head, that ran down on the beard, even Aaron's beard, that went down to the skirts of his garments."

Ointment and perfume rejoiceth the heart; so doth the sweetness of a man's friend by hearty counsel. "Let him reprove me: it shall be an excellent oil, which shall not break my head."

"If thy brother be waxen poor and old, and fallen to decay, thou shalt relieve him." Give of thy bread to the hungry, and of thy wine to cheer the heart of the sorrowful; and forget not to pour the oil of consolation into the wounds that sorrow, sickness, or affliction hath rent into the heart of thy fellow-traveller. By kindness and commiseration, fail not to pour the balm of oil and of wine into the bleeding heart. Our labor of duty and love will soon be ended. As the lightning writes its fiery path on the dark cloud and expires, so the race of man, walking amid the surrounding shades of mortality, glitter for a moment through the dark gloom, and vanish from our sight forever.

* * * * *

The holy angels are called "Elect," and with great propriety allusion is made in this degree to the *Shem Hamphorosh,* by which we arrive at the great name of God, which, placed in the shape of a triangle, exhibits this figure:

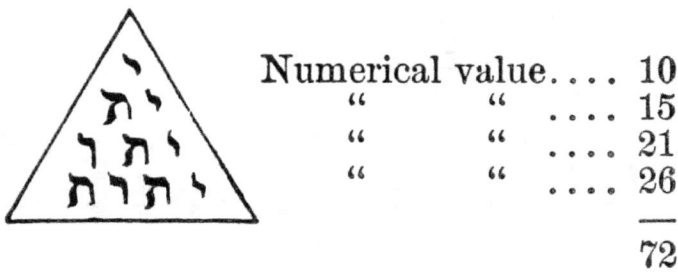

Seventy-two triangles, seventy-two names of Deity, seventy-two attributes, seventy-two angels, and, as the book Zohar asserts, seventy-two steps composing the ladder that Jacob saw in his dream, which the cherubim, seraphim, ophanim, and other holy angels, ascended and descended.

We are further reminded by this book that—"The holy and blessed One raised Enoch from the world to serve him, as it is written, 'for God took him.' God showed him all the repositories of the superior and inferior kingdoms, and he showed him the *tree* (alphabet) of life, respecting which Adam had received his command, its leaves and its branches—we see all in his Book."

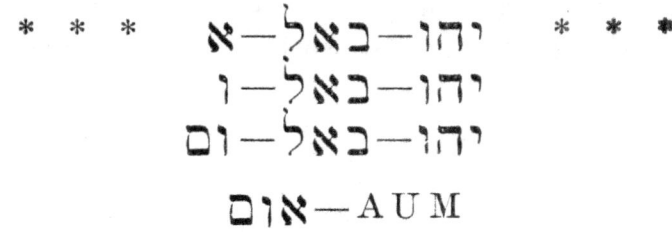

ODE.

Religion builds it, and a beam
From Heaven's own throne—no fitful gleam—
Wraps it in flames, while hand in hand
We round this blazing altar stand.

Let us, as Elect Masons true,
Virtue's eternal league renew;
While celebrating friendship's feast,
Love be our ever welcome guest.

And now in adoration bow
To Him who hears and seals each vow:
Glory to God, who reigns above,
And to our fellow-creatures, love!

INVESTMENT.

I now invest you with the apron, girdle, collar, and jewel of a Grand, Elect, Perfect, and Sublime Mason; and with the greatest pleasure salute you with the title, and grace you with the symbols thereof.

The collar is emblematical of ardent zeal, affection, and charity. The crown upon your jewel is a symbol of the royal origin of the degree. The compass, extended to ninety degrees, denotes the extensive knowledge of the Grand Elect: the sun, in the centre, that our actions should be as open as the full blaze of the noon-day sun, and our charity as diffusive as its beams. This jewel, suspended upon your breast, should make you attentive to your duties, and cause you to walk so as to adorn your station.

The apron, my brother, which you wear, is white, lined with white, and bordered with gold. The white is to remind us of innocence, and of that purity which was required for an entrance to this place: the gold, of wisdom, which should characterize all Grand, Elect, Perfect and Sublime Masons. Its form is supposed to be the true form used by the Perfect Master Mason at the building of the Temple, and alludes to the golden triangle or delta of Enoch, which adorns the centre.

The girdle, which I also invest you with, is the ancient girdle of a Grand, Elect, Perfect and Sublime Mason. It was used of old to bind up and strengthen the body, and enable man to persist in his labors: it is, therefore, an emblem of activity, promptness, and perseverance. The girdle was also used to bind up the garments, and prevent them from flying open and discovering nakedness: it is, therefore, an emblem of charity, the observance of which has laid you under renewed obligations. It was also used for beauty and ornament. Let it be your endeavor to be adorned and rich in the many virtues and qualities which are represented by its various colors.

The colors are arranged according to the mystic numbers of this degree—3, 5, 7, 9.

The three are blue, red, and yellow, by the due mixture of which the primitive colors are all formed.

The five consist of the first three, and green and purple.

The seven consist of the first five, and of white and black.

The nine consist of the first seven, and of stone and flame color.

They are thus explained:

The blue is an emblem of friendship; the red of zeal; the yellow of wisdom, on account of its resemblance to gold. Wisdom, saith the wisest of kings, is far better than fine gold. The green is a beautiful emblem of hope, and of that immortal part of man which never, never dies ; the purple, being a royal color, of dignity and majesty; the white, of purity and innocence; the black, of seriousness and modesty of demeanor. The next color is that of stone, which denotes firmness and durability, and is an emblem of constancy, fidelity, and decision of character—qualities which should be possessed by those who take the degree of Grand Master Architect, and attempt to walk in the footsteps of our Grand Master H∴ A∴; and the flame color, of ardent affection and charity, the peculiar traits of a Grand, Elect. Perfect and Sublime Mason.

The various colors united in this one girdle are expressive of that unity, and the olive interwoven of that peace, which should link us together as brethren. As these various colors shine in your girdle, so let the various virtues they represent shine in your heart and life.

CHARGE.

Thus, my brother, by your meritorious and unblamable conduct, assiduity, constancy, and integrity, you have at last attained the title of Grand, Elect, Perfect and Sublime Mason, which is the summit of Ancient Craft Masonry, and upon your arrival to which I most sincerely congratulate you.

I most earnestly recommend to you the strictest care and circumspection in all your conduct, that the sublime mysteries of this degree be not profaned or disgraced.

As to what remains of completing your knowledge of Ancient Craft Masonry, you will find, by attending to the following history of the degree, and a careful study of its mysteries.

You will now proceed to the Grand Orator, in the South, who will instruct you in the

HISTORY.

G∴ Or∴ My brother, you were informed in the degree of Royal Arch that King Solomon builded a secret vault, the approach to which was through eight other vaults, all under ground, and to which a long and narrow passage led from the palace. The ninth arch or vault was immediately under the Holy of Holies of the Temple. In that apartment King Solomon held his private conferences with King Hiram and Hiram Abiff. After the death of Hiram Abiff, the two kings ceased to visit it, resolving not to do so until they should select one to fill his place; and that, until that time, they would make known the sacred name to no one. After Adoniram, Joabert, and Stolkin had discovered the cube of agate and the mysterious name, and had delivered it to King Solomon, the two kings determined to deposit it in the secret vault, permit the three Masters who discovered it to be present, make known to them the true pronunciation of the ineffable word, constitute the last degree of Ancient Craft Masonry, and term it Grand, Elect, Perfect and Sublime Mason.

The cube of agate was so deposited.

Afterward the twelve Princes of Ameth, the nine Elect, and the Chief Architect were admitted to this degree. The secret vault was thereafter called Sacred Vault, and was originally built by Hiram Abiff, and none but Grand, Elect, Perfect and Sublime Masons knew of its existence, or knew other than the substituted word.

The Temple was completed in the year 3000—six years, six months, and ten days after King Solomon had laid the first corner-stone; and its completion was celebrated with great pomp and splendid magnificence.

Subsequently, while the Temple was being dedicated,

King Solomon conferred this sublime degree on the twenty-five brethren we have mentioned, and in the form you have but now witnessed.

And when the singers and trumpeters were to make one sound in praise and thanks to the Lord, saying, "Praise the Lord, for he is good: his mercy endureth forever;" that the Temple was filled with a cloud, and the name was fully pronounced.

On the second day, an audience was given to all Masons, from the degree of Master to the Royal Arch, and all vacancies were filled.

On the third day, King Solomon devoted his time to advancing and raising Fellow Crafts and Entered Apprentices.

Thus far the wise King of Israel behaved worthy of himself, and gained universal admiration; but in process of time, when he had advanced in years, his understanding became impaired; he grew deaf to the voice of the Lord, and was strangely irregular in his conduct. Proud of having erected an edifice to his Maker, and much intoxicated with his great power, he plunged into all manner of licentiousness and debauchery, and profaned the Temple by offering incense to the idol Moloch, which only should have been offered to the living God. The Grand, Elect, Perfect and Sublime Masons saw this, and were sorely grieved, being fearful that his apostacy would end in some dreadful consequences, and perhaps bring upon them those enemies whom Solomon had vainly and wantonly defied. The people, copying the follies and vices of their king, became proud and idolatrous, neglecting the true worship of God for that of idols.

As an adequate punishment for this defection, God inspired the heart of Nebuchadnezzar, King of Babylon, to take vengeance on the kingdom of Israel. This prince sent an army, with Nebuzaradan, captain of the guards, who entered Judah with fire and sword, took and sacked the city of Jerusalem, razed its walls, and destroyed that superb model of excellence, the Temple. The people were carried away captive to Babylon, and the conquerors carried away with them all the vessels of gold and silver.

This happened four hundred and seventy years, six months, and ten days after the dedication. After the city was taken, and the king's palace and the Temple demolished, some of the Grand Elect Masons bethought themselves of the Sacred Vault and the inestimable treasure it contained. Repairing to the ruins of the Temple at night, they found that the way which led down to the vault had not been discovered, nor the slab of marble which covered it disturbed; but upon it they found the dead body of Galaad, an eminent brother, and Chief of the Levites. He had been intrusted with the custody of the Sacred Vault and the care of the lamps that burned continually.

*   *   *   *   *

Finally, when the time arrived that the Christian

Princes entered into a league to free the Holy Land from the oppression of the infidels, the good and virtuous Masons, anxious for so pious an undertaking offered their services to the confederates, upon condition that they should have a chief of their own election, and whose name was only made known in the hour of battle; which being granted, they accepted their standard and departed.

The valor and fortitude of these Elected Knights were such, that they were admired by, and took the lead of, all the Princes of Jerusalem, who, believing that their mysteries inspired them with courage and fidelity to the cause of virtue and religion, became desirous of being initiated. Upon being found worthy, their desires were complied with, and thus the Royal Art, meeting the approbation of great and good men, became popular and honorable, and was diffused to the worthy throughout these dominions, and thus continued to spread, far and wide, through a succession of ages to the present day.

You will now, my brother, be seated among the Grand Elect.

CLOSING.

*   *   *   *   *

PRAYER.

O Most Holy and Glorious God, thou who dwellest between the Cherubim, and art known in heaven and on earth by thy name Jah; we approach thee with awe and reverence, and implore thy blessing upon us, who know thy great and ineffable name, ere we depart from this sacred place to our several places of abode, and mingle again in the busy scenes and strifes of life. Oh, fill our hearts, we beseech thee, with thy love and fear, that our tongues may speak of thy goodness, and our actions correspond with the lessons taught in this holy place.

Make us steadfast in our obligations to our brethren and in our duty to our fellow-man.

Bless us and prosper us in life, and in death receive us, O Lord, our Adonai! Amen.

Omnes. So mote it be!

ODE.

BREMEN.

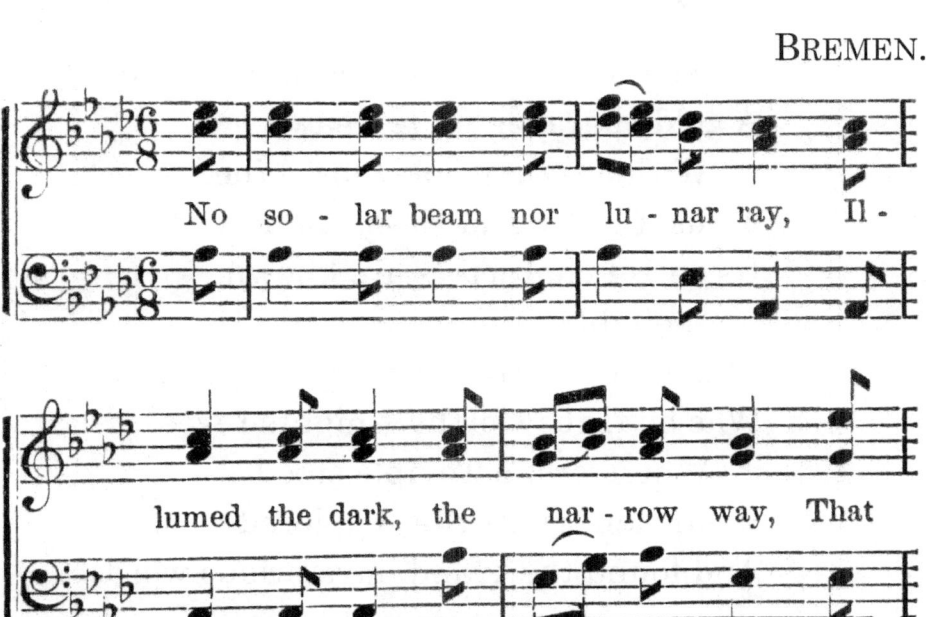

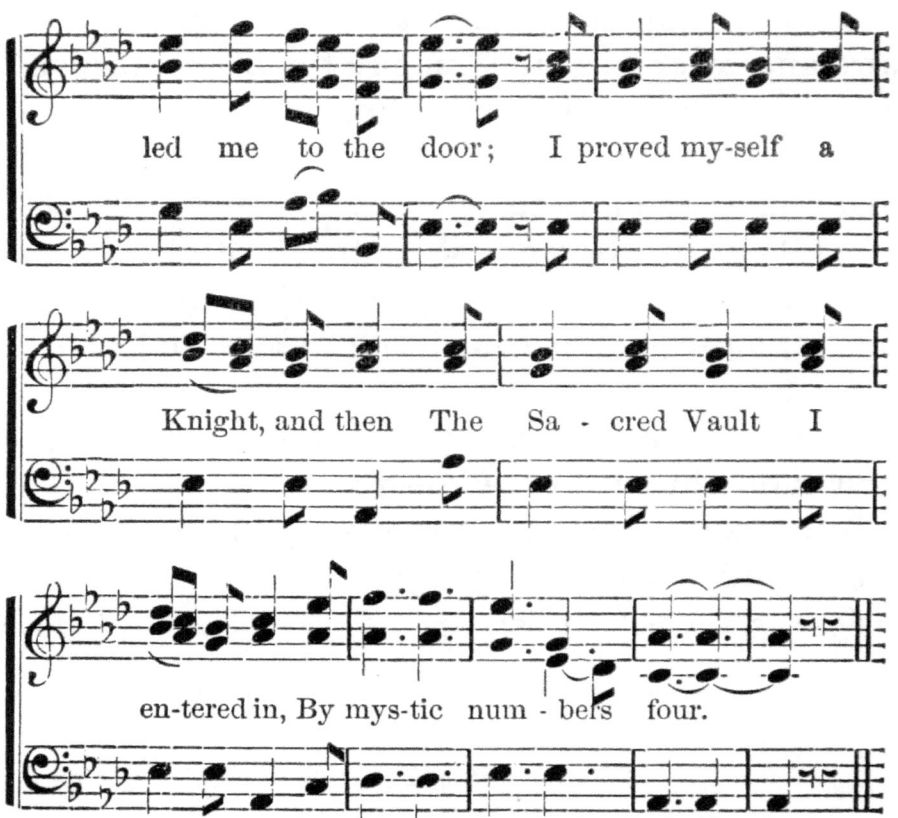

'Twas there, impressed with holy awe,
A gold engraven plate I saw
    With dazzling splendor shine.
To us, the "Grand Elect" alone,
Its secret characters are known,
    Ineffable—divine.
This precious treasure, long concealed,
Was by three worthy Knights revealed
    Where erst a Temple stood.
Its ancient ruins they explored,
And found the grand, mysterious word,
    Made known before the Flood.

Fulfilled was then the promise made,
And Beauty's Pillar soon displayed
   The TREASURE they had found:
Their ardent zeal and piety—
Their dangerous toil and constancy—
   Were with due honors crowned.

Hours like those we all shall prove,
Who, joined in pure and social love,
   Perfection's work pursue.
May the Sublime Grand Architect,
By his unerring laws, direct
   The honored, chosen few.

May all who friendship's feast partake
The good pursue, the bad forsake!
   And may each rite and sign
A happy, lasting influence shed:
The quadrant crowned, the oil, the bread,
   The golden ring, the wine!

Long as I live this ring I'll wear,
Symbol of an alliance dear
   To every brother's heart;
And bless the sacred tie that binds
In virtue's chain; for "virtue joins
   What death can never part."

JEWELS OF A LODGE OF PERFECTION.

T. P. GRAND MASTER.

DEPUTY GRAND MASTER.

SENIOR GRAND WARDEN.

JUNIOR GRAND WARDEN.

TREASURER.

SECRETARY.

ORATOR.

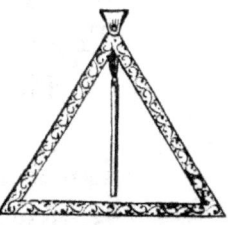
M. CEREMONIES.

CAPTAIN OF GUARD.

HOSPITALLER.

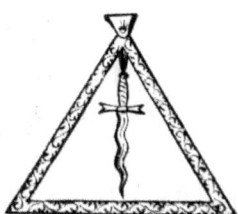
TILER.

THIRD SERIES.

THE

HISTORICAL DEGREES

OF

KNIGHTS OF THE EAST AND SWORD AND PRINCE OF JERUSALEM ARE CONFERRED IN A COUNCIL OF PRINCES OF JERUSALEM, AND RELATE TO THE REBUILDING OF THE SECOND HOLY TEMPLE, UNDER THE AUTHORITY GIVEN BY KING CYRUS AND HIS SUCCESSOR, KING DARIUS.

"The Lord must be one, and his name one."—*Talmud.*

"The Dream is certain; the interpretation thereof sure."—Dan. ii. 47.

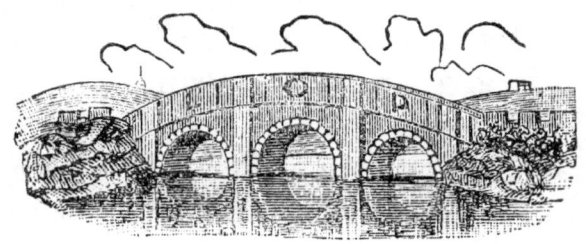

PREFATORY.

The annual meetings of all Councils of Princes of Jerusalem are held on the 20th day of the tenth month— Tebet: stated meetings, at such other times as may suit their convenience. Officers should be elected at every annual meeting, and installed on the 23d day of the eleventh month—Adar—thereafter.

Originally, it was the province of every Council of Princes of Jerusalem to inspect and watch over, with due care and fidelity, Lodges of Perfection, and see that their "*work*" was done in conformity with the regulations and landmarks of the order. This duty of a Council has never been abrogated, but is seldom exercised.

The Grand Feast-day of Princes of Jerusalem shall be celebrated on the 23d day of the eleventh month, Adar, which is the anniversary of the day when thanks were given to the Almighty for the reconstruction of the Temple. Their other Feast-days are as follows:

The 20th day of the tenth month, called Tebet, when "the ambassadors made a triumphant entry into Jerusalem, on their return from Babylon."

The equinoctial days, in the months of March and September, in memory of the Temple having been built twice.

Five members constitute a quorum: a Council can not be opened with a less number.

If a Prince gives another Prince a challenge, he should be excluded forever.

Princes are strictly to observe the rule enforcing justice and good order, and their conduct in life should be irreproachable.

If any member of a Council or Lodge shall be present at, or aid, or assist in giving or receiving any of the sublime or symbolic degrees in a clandestine or irregular manner, contrary to the true intent and meaning of the statutes and regulations of the Supreme Council, or of the constitutions and laws of true Ancient, Free and Accepted Masonry, he subjects himself to expulsion.

A Prince of Jerusalem who visits an inferior Council or Lodge, should present himself clothed with the dress and ornaments of a Prince; and when his approach is announced, the presiding officer sends a Prince of Jerusalem to examine him, and if he reports in his favor, he should be received under the *arch of steel,* and be escorted by four Brethren, and seated on the right hand of the presiding officer. An entry of his name and rank should be made on the engraved tablets, that he may thereafter receive due honors without examination; the same ceremonies should be observed when he retires as when he entered.

Princes have the right of being *covered* in all subordinate Lodges, Chapters, or Councils, and of addressing the Chair without first asking permission.

If at any election of officers, a Prince of Jerusalem solicits votes for himself or any other person, he should be forever expelled.

FIFTEENTH DEGREE.

Knight of the East or Sword.

ARGUMENT.

This degree, which is intimately connected with the one that succeeds it, relates to the Babylonish captivity, which lasted seventy years, the release and return of the 42,360 captives to Jerusalem, and the attempt to build the Second Temple under the direction of Zerubbabel or Sheshbazzar. King Cyrus also permitted the return of the Holy Vessels and Ornaments which had been removed by Nebuzaradan at the time of the destruction of the First Temple.

The return of the captives was contested at the bridge over the river Euphrates, but unsuccessfully; and finally, when laboring to lay the foundation of the Temple, beset on every side by enemies, Zerubbabel ordered that the Masons should work with the sword in one hand and a trowel in the other, that they might be able at any moment to defend themselves from attack.

The Second Temple was forty-six years in construction.

The purpose of the Degree of Knight of the East or Sword is to animate and encourage the Mason to be active in his duties, by presenting in an effective manner some illustrious examples of Humility, Patience, Truth, Wisdom, Chivalric courage and Devotion, as displayed by our ancient Brethren, and also to preserve the remembrance of the events upon which the grade is founded. In this, and the succeeding degree, the initiate appears in a double capacity, as a Craftsman and a Warrior, who must be constantly on the alert, ready either for work or for combat.

KNIGHT OF THE EAST OR SWORD.

THE FIFTEENTH GRADE OF THE A∴ A∴ SCOTTISH RITE,
AND THE FIRST OF THE HISTORICAL SERIES.

APARTMENTS.

A Council of Knights of the East or Sword requires three apartments:
First—Hall of the West.
Second—Hall of the East.
Third—Road from Jerusalem to Persia.

FIRST APARTMENT.

Represents a Grand Lodge of Perfection at Jerusalem. The hall is decorated with red, the furniture in general disorder, and the altars prostrated. The lights are seventy in number, arranged in groups of seven each. A curtain at the East end of the hall conceals a blazing glory.

SECOND APARTMENT.

Represents the interior of the Palace of King Cyrus, and should be decorated according to the usual custom of the Orientals. A throne occupies one end of the hall, with seats for the Minister of State and Counsellors. The room is hung in green. It is brilliantly lighted, by no particular number or arrangement of lights. In the East is a superb throne. In the West are two oriental seats ; in the North and South, seats for the brethren. The Throne is elevated by two steps, and adorned with gold-lace and fringe.

Behind the throne is a transparency representing the dream of Cyrus—to wit, a roaring lion ready to spring upon him; above it a brilliant Glory, surrounded with luminous clouds; and in the centre of the Glory the Ineffable name of God, in Samaritan letters. Out of the clouds an eagle emerges, bearing in his beak a pennant, upon which are the words, "Restore Liberty to the Captives." Below the luminous clouds are Nebuchadnezzar and Belshazzar, loaded with chains, the former on all-fours, eating grass.

IN THE THIRD APARTMENT

A bridge is represented extended over a river, and a rude altar at the end near the first apartment.

OFFICERS IN THE FIRST APARTMENT.

1. Thrice Potent Grand Master.
2. Senior Grand Warden.

KNIGHT OF THE EAST OR SWORD.

3. Junior Grand Warden.
4. Grand Orator.
5. Grand Master of Ceremonies.
6. Grand Captain of the Guards.

All in black robes with their appropriate jewels.

CHARACTERS IN THE SECOND APARTMENT.

1. Cyrus, King of Persia, in royal robes.
2. Grand Master of Cavalry.
3. Grand Master of Infantry.
4. Grand Master of Palace.
5. Grand C. of Guards.
6. Counsellors.

All in appropriate costumes.

Guard, soldiers, &c., with javelins or pikes.

King Cyrus and the Grand Masters of Cavalry Infantry, and of the Palace, wear an order, or broad water-green colored sash, with a green rosette at the bottom, worn from the right shoulder to the left hip.

The green turbans have a golden sun embroidered on the front.

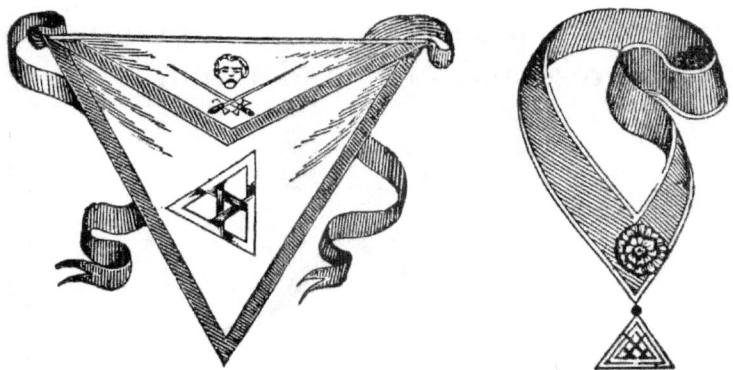

The apron, worn only in the first apartment, is of crimson velvet edged with green; on the flap are embroidered in gold a bleeding head and two swords crossed: in the centre of the apron, three triangles forming a chain with triangular links.

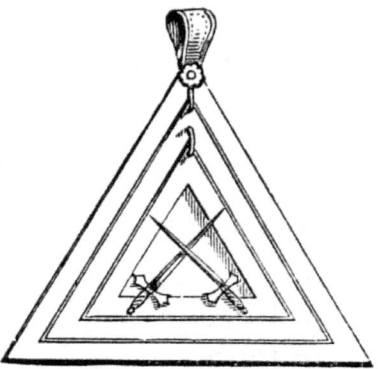

The jewel of gold is three triangles, one within the other, diminishing in size, and enclosing two naked swords crossed, hilts downward, resting on the base of the inner triangle.

The term knight will be added to all titles except the Master's. Each Knight wears a silver trowel with an ebony handle at his right side.

Step—advance boldly by four and one, sword in hand.

Age—ten weeks of years.

Battery—five and two.

Banner of the order—green silk bordered with red: on it are represented a lion and a wolf.

OPENING AND RECEPTION.

The labors in the Council of Princes of Jerusalem being suspended, the members who are to sustain the parts in the second apartment, or Hall of the East, will immediately repair to that apartment and robe themselves, in order that they may be in readiness when Zerubbabel arrives, and will be stationed as follows:

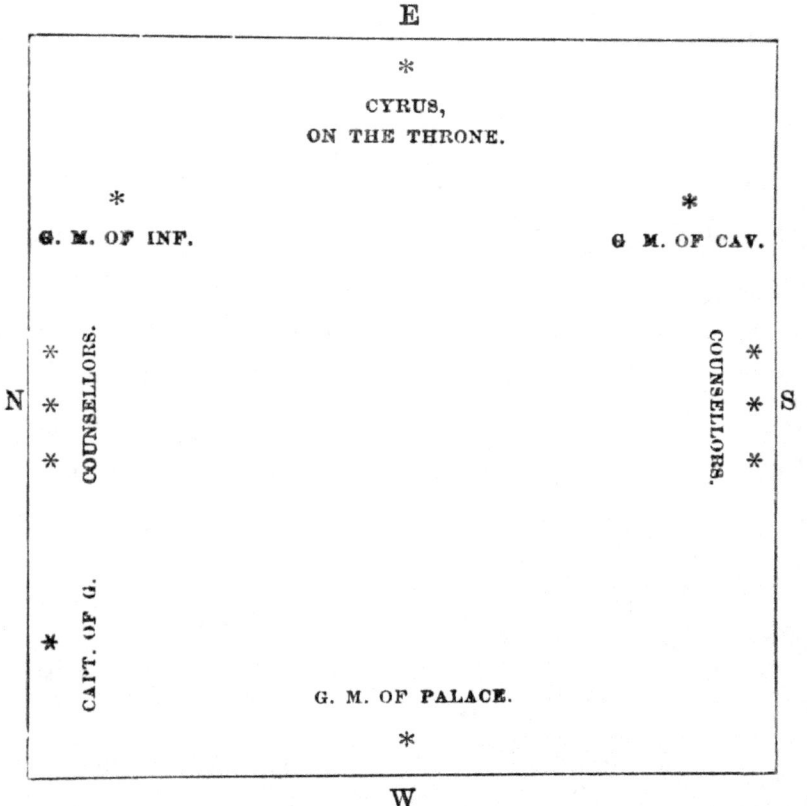

While the second apartment is being prepared, the candidate, who has been clothed with a black robe, is permitted to enter the first apartment without obstruction, where he discovers the brethren engaged in earnest conversation, in groups of two or more.

Previous to admitting the candidate into the Lodge, a copy of the following will be placed in his hands by the Tyler:

Brother—You are summoned to appear this day at a convocation of Grand, Elect, Perfect and Sublime

Masons, at our usual rendezvous. The seventy years of captivity have nearly expired. Cyrus has ascended the throne. We may now be restored to liberty. Come to us. Obey the sign   *   *   *

     *   *   *   *   *

PRAYER BY THE GRAND ORATOR.

O Lord our God, and the God of our fathers! thou didst appoint a stated period for the captivity of thy people in Egypt and Babylon, and thou hast taught us the signs whereby we may learn the approach of our redemption from the long captivity which thy just judgment inflicted upon us. Arise, O Lord! and have mercy upon thy Zion, for the time to favor her, yea, the set time, is come. Stir up the heart of Cyrus, thy servant; for it is written, "The heathen shall fear the name of the Lord, and all the kings of the earth thy glory." Into thy hands we commit our undertaking. From thee alone do we expect success in our endeavors; for vain is the help of man without thee.

Finally, O Lord, we pray thee to incline the hearts of all our brethren to assist in the work on which we this day solicit thy blessing. Amen. So mote it be.

Rise, my brethren! The God of Battles is with us. Our petition has been heard. Let our deliberations to-day be guided by sound discretion. Have faith, my brethren, and success will attend us.

     *   *   *   *   *

God speaketh once—yea, twice—but man perceiveth it not. In a dream—in a vision of the night —when deep sleep falleth upon men, then he openeth the ears of men, and sealeth their instructions.

"An angry lion was about to throw himself upon me and devour me, and, while quaking with fear, I looked for some place of shelter. A splendid light, proceeding from a 'glory,' suddenly dazzled my sight, and I perceived two of my predecessors, Nebuchadnezzar and Balthasar, in the garb of slaves, and loaded with chains. I heard a voice saying to me : 'Loose the bonds of wickedness.' 'Undo the heavy burdens.' 'Let the oppressed go free.' 'Break every yoke.'

"My spirit was troubled, and my sleep fled from me.

*   *   *   *   *

"Thus saith Cyrus, King of Persia: All the kingdoms of the earth hath the Lord God of heaven given me, and he has charged me to build him a house in Jerusalem, in Judea. Who among you are of his people? The Lord his God be with him, and let him go up."

*   *   *   *   *

You see represented, my brethren, the desolation into which has fallen the work of the greatest of Masons; the walls of the Temple demolished, the altar overthrown, the ornaments devastated, and fear and suspicion among the workmen. But at length a change is taking place : our hopes are revived, our chains are broken, our losses are about to be repaired, and our works recommenced. The stones for rebuilding will be taken from the quarries of Tyre, and the wood from the forests of Lebanon, because the second Temple should in all parts be like unto the first, to signify that Masonry is a unity and cannot suffer any material change. You will now visit the outer works and reflect; for of the principal architects of the first Temple, God was the first, Solomon was the second, and Hiram was the third.

   *   *   *   *   *

Knights, the glorious work of rebuilding the Temple is now our object. For you, Zerubbabel and your companions, has been reserved so great a work. The obligation which you have just taken secures its execution. We stand in need of chiefs to guide us, and who, at the same time, will be our defenders.

In the swords with which you are armed, and which you know so well how to preserve, we have the warrant of a successful protection.

Knights, if you consent that Zerubbabel and his associates shall rule the labors of Masonry, building temples and tabernacles in our hearts, and protecting the workmen from their enemies, give the † of assent.

Approach and receive the attributes of your new state, and a knowledge of the mysteries of our reunion.

KNIGHT OF THE EAST OR SWORD.

You have been decorated by King Cyrus with the title of "Knight of the East," and I now decorate you with that of "Knight Mason." This trowel is its symbol. You will work henceforth, Sir Knights, with the trowel in one hand and the sword in the other.

This sash of water-green color must accompany you in all Lodges. It is the mark of knighthood, to which you were admitted by the king, and signifies our hope of being re-established. We have added, in order to preserve the memory of our liberator, this rosette, which is placed at the bottom of the sash.

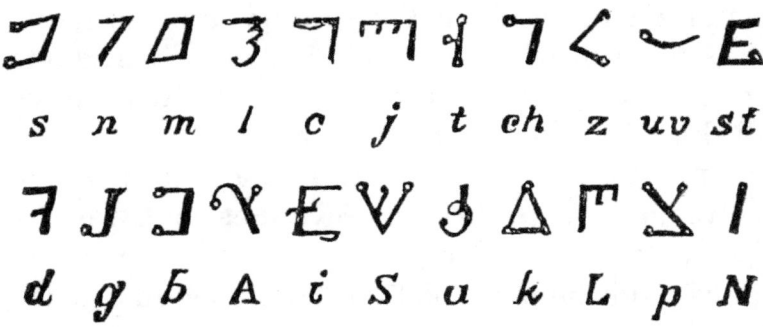

THE WRITING CALLED "PASSING THE RIVER."

DECREE.

Cyrus, The King, to Sysina and Sarabasan.

Sendeth Greeting. Be it known unto you, that I have given leave to all the Jews that are in my dominions, to return into their own Country, and there to rebuild their Capital City, with the Holy Temple at Jerusalem, in the same place where it stood before. I have likewise sent my messenger, Mithridates and Zerubbabel, the Governor of Judea, to superintend the building, and to see it raised sixty cubits upward from the ground and as many over ; the walls to be three rows of polished stones, and one of the wood of the Country, together with an Altar for Sacrifices ; and all this to be done at my charge.

It is my further pleasure that they receive entire to themselves, all the profits and revenues that were formerly enjoyed by their predecessors, and that they have an allowance paid them of 205,500 drachmas, in consideration of beasts for Sacrifices, wine and oil; and 2,500 measures of wheat, in lieu of fine flour, and all this to be raised upon the tribute of Samaria ; that the priests may offer up sacrifices according to the laws and ceremonies of Moses, and pray daily for the King and the Royal family, and for the welfare and happiness of the Persian Empire : and let no man presume to do anything contrary to the tenor of this my royal will and proclamation, upon pain of forfeiting life and estate.

CYRUS.

SIXTEENTH DEGREE.

Prince of Jerusalem

ARGUMENT.

THE Sixteenth Degree, or Prince of Jerusalem, being a continuation of the fifteenth grade, represents historically the troubles and trials of the ancient Masons, in their endeavors to rebuild the Temple; their obtaining permission, and their final success, under the authority and will of Darius, the successor of King Cyrus, in the completion of that noble edifice, in the sixth year of his reign,—which Temple was like unto, if not more magnificent than, the first, built by the great King Solomon. This Temple covered the same ground as the one destroyed by Nebuzaradan, and was furnished with the same precious vessels returned by King Darius from Babylon to the Jews.

The grade of Prince was conferred by King Darius, and ratified and confirmed by the Knight Masons at Jerusalem, as a Masonic acknowledgment to Zerubbabel and his companions for their preservation, and frank averment of Masonic virtues, despite the highest honors tendered by the king.

Formerly, Princes of Jerusalem were entitled to many privileges and prerogatives by virtue of their rank. They had exclusive control over Sublime Freemasonry, from the 4th to the 15th Degree inclusive. Grand Councils of this Grade granted Charters to Lodges of Perfection, and also governed and controlled the symbolic grades of the Scotch Rite, in all countries where no regular Grand Lodge was established. According to the G. Constitutions of 1786, Art. 6, it was provided, "That the power of the Supreme Council shall not interfere with any grade under the 17th," or K. of the E. and W. This power is now exercised by the Supreme Council.

CROWN OF KING DARIUS

PRINCE OF JERUSALEM.

THE SIXTEENTH GRADE OF THE A∴ AND A∴ SCOTTISH RITE, AND THE SECOND DEGREE OF THE HISTORICAL SERIES.

APARTMENTS.

The apartments are four in number: The first represents the Council of the Knights of the East or Sword, when at their labors endeavoring to rebuild the Temple —the furniture being in disorder, the altars overturned, and pieces of masonry lying in confusion in different parts of the room. The platform of the East is concealed by a drop-curtain, the Master presiding at the front of the same.

The second apartment represents the road from Jerusalem to Babylon, and by scenic effects should indicate the open country.

The third apartment is the throne-room of King Darius of Persia. The furniture should be of the most magnificent Oriental kind, draped with green hangings, with golden furniture and aurora-colored trimmings. No Masonic emblems or devices should be seen.

The fourth apartment is the banquet-hall of Darius and should be in keeping with the throne-room.

OFFICERS—FIRST APARTMENT.

1. Most Equitable Sovereign Prince Grand Master, represents Zerubbabel, son of Shealtiel.
2. Grand High Priest Deputy Grand Master, represents Joshua, son of Jozadak.
3. Most Enlightened Senior Grand Warden, represents Seraiah, Prince of Judah.
4. Most Enlightened Junior Grand Warden, represents Mordecai, Prince of Benjamin.
5. Valiant Keeper of Seals, represents Esdras, Prince of the Law.
6. Valiant Grand Treasurer, represents Ananias, Prince of the Temple.
7. Grand Master of Ceremonies, represents Solamiel, Prince of Workmen.
8. Grand Master of Entrances, represents Nehemiah, Prince of the Guards.
9. Grand Tyler.

JEWELS.

All of which are enclosed in squares.

1st Officer—A hand of justice and a mallet, designating Just Ruler.

2d Officer—Circle, surrounding a Delta, designating Eternity of Deity.

3d Officer—Small pillar of strength and shield, designating the Lion of Judah.

4th Officer—Compass on a segment of a circle, designating The Measure of Peace.

5th Officer—Balance in equipoise, designating Justice.

6th Officer—Parallelogram with vase, designating Unbounded Treasure for the Temple.

7th Officer—Trowel and plum, designating conductor of the Works.

8th Officer—Spear, designating Guardian of Secrecy.

9th Officer—Flaming sword, designating Vengeance.

COSTUMES.

The costumes of all the officers, except that of the Grand High Priest, at a reception, are those of Knights of the East or Sword—i. e., black robes with hoods, water-green colored sashes, with rosettes, swords, belts, and trowels. The apron of the fourteenth grade may properly be worn.

The costume of the Grand High Priest consists of a figured tunic of white linen reaching to the feet, over which is worn a purple robe about fifteen inches shorter, upon the border of which are suspended seventy-two small bells, and as many pomegranates, alternating. An ephod is also worn, without sleeves, which extends to the hips, and is gathered in at the waist by a ribbon. A breastplate is also suspended from the neck, nine inches square, containing twelve precious stones, representing the twelve sons of Jacob; and upon it were also the Urim and Thummim—the first of which words is generally rendered "light," and the other "truth, or perfection." Attached to the ephod, and upon each shoulder, is a precious stone. On the one on the right shoulder are the names of the six eldest of the children of Israel, and on the one on the left the names of the six youngest. On the head of the High Priest is a purple or blue linen tiara, to the front of which is attached, by a purple or blue ribbon, a plate of gold, containing the words, "Holy to the Lord," in Hebrew. Sandals should be worn on the feet.

Lights—Seventy in number, representing so many years of trials.

Battery—• ••••

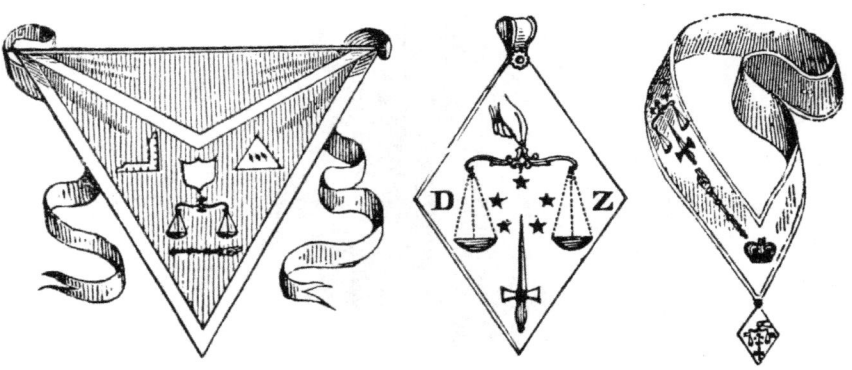

Apron—Crimson, edged with gold, lined with auroracolor. The flap is aurora-color. Painted or embroidered on the area of the apron are a square, a shield, a Delta, a hand of justice, a pair of balances in equipoise, and sometimes a representation of the Temple.

Order—A wide aurora-colored ribbon edged with gold, worn from right shoulder to left hip. Sometimes embroidered in front are, a balance, a hand of justice, a poniard, five stars, and two crowns.

Jewel—A lozenge-shaped mother-of-pearl. Encrusted on it in gold is a hand holding a balance in equipoise: under it a two-edged sword, hilt down, with five stars surrounding the point, the centre one larger than the others, and the letters D and Z in Hebrew, one on the left and the other on the right of the balance.

OFFICERS—THIRD APARTMENT.

1. Darius, King of Persia, son of Hystaspes.
2. The Satrap of Media, father-in-law of the king
3. The Satrap of Assyria.
4. Artaban, Scribe.

Counsellors, Courtiers, Knights, Guards, etc.

COSTUMES.

DARIUS—Long white robe, trimmed richly with purple, and aurichalcan (metallic trimming of gold and copper mixed, esteemed the most precious of metals); over which a long white flowing robe, hanging from the shoulders, and a crown, surmounted with seven spikes, representing the seven conspirators—the front, or seventh spike, taller than the other six. The Order of the King, a horse, neighing, rampant. Over all, a sash of a Prince, which is transferred to the person of Zerubbabel, when created a Prince of Jerusalem.

[Darius conspired, with six other nobles, to destroy Smerdis, who usurped the crown of Persia, after the death of Cambyses. Darius obtained the crown by a species of cunning.]

The Satraps, Counsellors, Knights, etc., appropriately costumed.

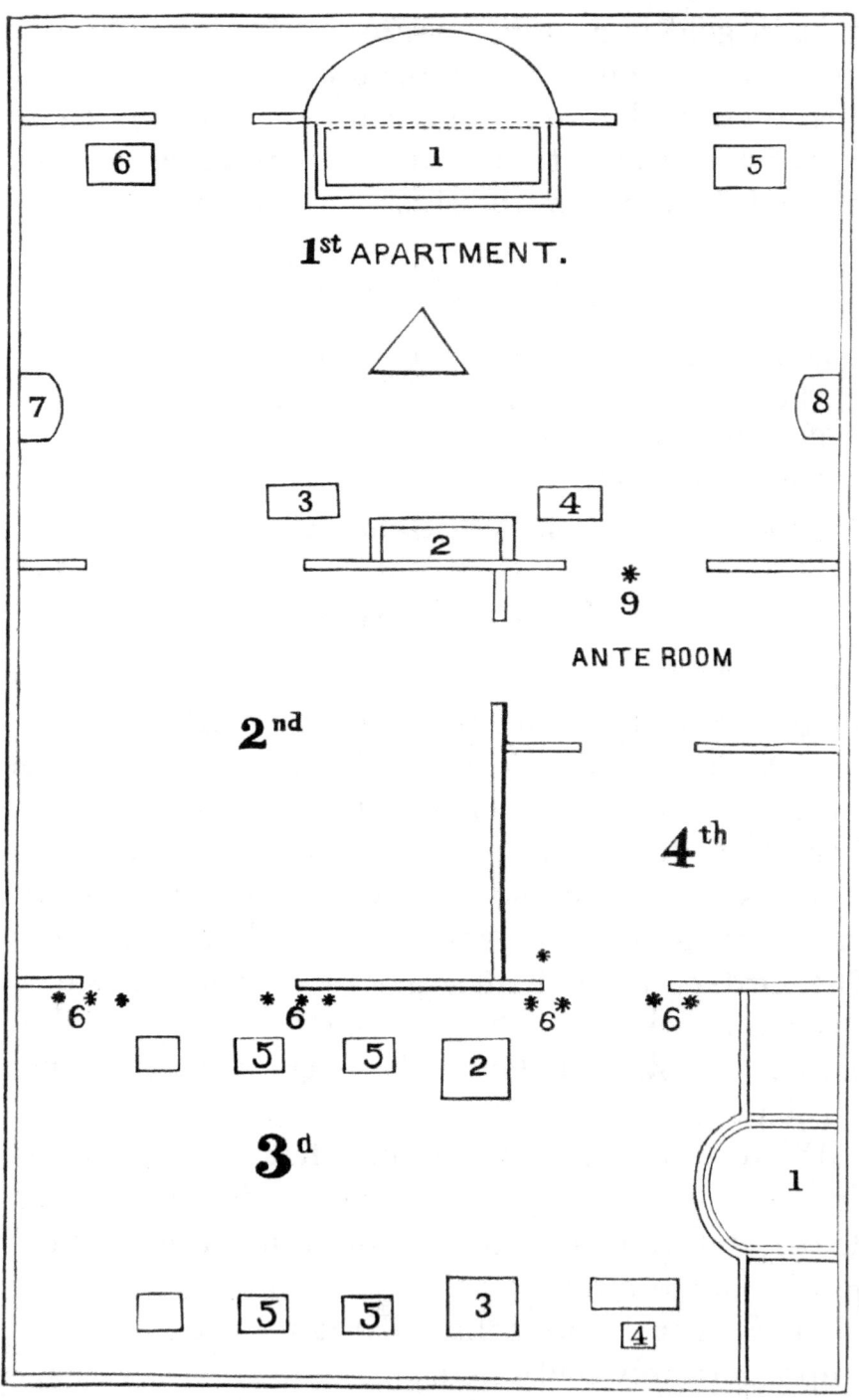

RECEPTION.

*   *   *   *   *

Zer∴ O King, the Masonic people whom I have the honor to govern, wishing to testify to you their joy at the advancement of your august majesty to the throne, have deputed me, with these illustrious Knights, my companions, to tender to you their congratulations on your ascension to the throne of all the East. You have their sincere wishes for your health and happiness.

In consequence of the kindness and benevolence with which you formerly favored me, they have been induced to hope that, in choosing me as their representative, you would be pleased the more graciously to receive what I have to communicate in their behalf; and I myself am happy, while paying you their tribute of respect, to have the opportunity to acquit myself also of what is due to our former friendship.

Darius. Zerubbabel, your people have not misjudged. They could not have selected an agent to act for them that could possibly have been more acceptable to me than thou art.

We notice with pleasure that you have not forgotten our ancient ties of affection and friendship; and Darius will not, on his part, forget those ties which were dear to him while yet in private life.

Your arrival among us is very opportune, to enable you to participate in the feast we give this day to the grandees of our kingdom, and to this we invite you and your associates. Previous to which we wish you to pronounce your opinion on a certain question that shall be propounded for discussion.

Satrap of Assyria, do you state the question, and the reward we have promised to him who shall answer it in the most satisfactory manner.

Sat∴ of A∴ The King of Kings, wishing to dispense his favors with a liberal hand, has deigned to promise the second place near his august majesty, the privilege of being clothed in purple, wearing a golden baldric, and being seated on a golden throne, to him who shall be able in the most satisfactory manner to resolve the question : "What is that which holds the most powerful sway over mortals?"

Can it be possible that a question like this can for one moment be a subject of doubt or deliberation to any one who adverts to thee, thou Son of the Sun? You have this day, composing your court, one hundred and twenty-seven potentates of the most distant nations. Peace and war are in your hands. The life and death of your subjects depend upon your will. A word from your lips is a decree to all the earth. All we possess belongs to thee. Our very persons are yours. The universal world has no master but you. There cannot be a more puissant, than Darius, King of all the East—Sovereign of Sovereigns Therefore I say, "The King Darius."

* * * * *

Sat∴ of M∴. What remains for me to say, O King? Shall I dare to differ in opinion from the Satrap of Assyria, who has received the plaudits of your whole court? He contends there is nothing greater than yourself. O King! I acknowledge your greatness— the eclat of your name, the splendor of your throne, the magnitude of your power, and the grandeur of your riches.

But greater than all this is the empire of Beauty! This softens the heart of the most ferocious, gains over judges the most severe, and triumphs over masters the most imperious. Deprived of fortune, it needs it not. If devoid of worldly rank and dignity, it rises above all. All stations of life are subject to it. The power of the gods of the earth, though respected and feared, is as nothing in comparison with the power of Beauty.

The will of sovereign rulers often depends upon its caprice. What was my daughter Apame? Without wealth or rank, before her beauty elevated her to the nuptial bed of Darius. To-day this great Prince rules over you. In her turn, she reigns over him. He wills what she desires—he does what she approves. Does she rejoice, he is pleased. Is she melancholy, he is afflicted. She is the soul that gives the impress and the bias to all his movements. From her he learns to find something more interesting than kingly greatness. She sees him at her feet, and he voluntarily submits all his imperial glory to her beauty Therefore I say, "Beauty."

*   *   *   *   *

Zer∴ What is this, O Darius, I hear in your court? Is it already corrupted by flattery and effeminacy? Reject! reject with indignation those sentiments of yourself that have just been uttered. Strength and power reside in kings. Beauty has its influence, but it is the mark of wisdom to acknowledge the empire of Truth. Truth is omnipotent—greater than any transitory throne—more endurable than any frail decaying beauty. These are both of short duration but truth lives forever.

The power of kings, as well as that of beauty, is subject to the revolutions of chance. Truth changes never—always pure, always simple. It is the essence of the Grand Architect of the universe. It is the tie of all treaties. It is the motive of every just action, the basis of all laws, the seal of sovereign majesty, the object of every good man's search. We love those who demonstrate it, and detest those who conceal it. Lying disguises it, and, by borrowing its appearance, furnishes the best proof and clearest avowal of its superiority. Considerations more powerful than human, O King, induce me thus to dare to speak to you in its favor, in opposition to the too flattering sentiments which might have seduced you from the true path. You are yourself, great Prince, I am sure, about to confirm by your decision the empire of Truth.

Darius. Yes, Zerubbabel; come, and by receiving

the reward so justly due you, cause to shine forth the triumph of truth. Receive this order.

* * * * *

The highest reward we can bestow upon you will not be commensurate with your deserts for having saved us from this snare of corruption. We are infinitely indebted, besides the recompense offered, and in order to attach nearer to our person so precious a friend as thou art, Zerubbabel, we tender you, this moment, the office of Grand Master of our House.

Zer∴ Sovereign of Sovereigns, for the favors which you lavish on me, I have not words to express my heartfelt gratitude; but the will of Him who regulates the destinies of all men, does not permit me to be the master of my own destiny. I am irrevocably bound to the fortunes of my people whom I conduct; and the accomplishment of the decrees of heaven, relative to the re-edification of God's holy Temple, will not allow me to accept what you are so willing to do for me this day.

* * * * *

DECREE.

Darius, King of Kings, Sovereign of Sovereigns, to Saraboyan, Grand Master of the Army, and to our other Grand Officers, and to our people beyond the river, Greeting:

Zerubbabel and the Deputies of the Jews, having brought their complaints of the troubles with which you harass them, in their efforts to reconstruct their Temple and city, which Cyrus, of glorious memory, had permitted them to build, we write this letter; commanding you, as soon as you receive it, without fail to second, with all your zeal and our authority, the execution of the work.

If any one dare to impeach these our commands, or in any way hinder the execution of them, we order you to crucify him, and to confiscate his property for the use of the holy Temple.

As a mark of our confidence in Zerubbabel, we create him Sovereign Prince of Jerusalem, and on the Knights that accompanied him in his embassy we confer the rank and title of Princes, with such powers as he shall establish on them; and we grant him full power and authority to install Princes, and elevate to the dignity of Princes of the Cities those whom he may see fit, and deem worthy and capable.

We delegate to him plenary authority, and we declare the Temple, and the workmen employed on it, to be free from all imposts from us.

Thus we will and order. Done at our Castle of Ecbatam, the 20th day of the month Tebet, in the year of the world 3483, in the year of Cyrus the fifteenth, and of our reign the second.

[SEAL.]   DARIUS.

*   *   *   *   *

You have already been invested, Illustrious Prince, with the sash adopted by the Masonic Princes, in token of their golden memory of the unbounded liberality of Darius, King of Persia, to the oppressed Jews. May its aurora-color, with the early dawn.

daily bring to your mind the beauties of lasting friendship for your fellow Princes, against whom you never can combat, and in whose favor, as well as in your own, you have assumed new vows. It is suspended from the right shoulder to the left hip. The apron of this grade is triangular, and in rich keeping with the sash. The area is crimson, in token of the sufferings of the Jews from the Samaritans, when building the second Temple: the trimmings and triangular flap aurora-color, for like reasons as mentioned in describing the sash. Upon the area of the apron are wrought, in gold, a representation of the second Temple and precious vessels.

The jewel is made of mother-of-pearl, in the form of a lozenge, having incrusted upon it, in gold and silver, a balance at equipoise, on either side of which is a D and a Z in Hebrew : beneath the centre of the scale, a dagger with point up ; resting on which is a star, with two smaller stars on either side thereof. The mother-of-pearl denotes purity; the scales, justice ; the dagger, vengeance; the five stars, Zerubbabel and his four companions.

*   *   *   *   *

HISTORY.

Knights and Princes, I deem it unnecessary to narrate to you an extended history of this degree. Like the preceding one, the ceremony is so replete with the incidents relating to the history of the re-edification of the Temple, that little need be added.

The first fourteen degrees of Ineffable Masonry have reference to the construction of the first Temple, the demolition of it by Nebuzaradan, under the authority of Nebuchadnezzar and Balthasar, and the conveying to Babylon of all the precious vessels and material; also, the driving into the fastnesses of the mountains and the uncultivated country all Masons of whatever grade.

The fifteenth and sixteenth degrees have direct reference to the reconstruction of the Temple by Zerubbabel; first, by permission of Cyrus, King of Persia—as exemplified in the fifteenth degree—and then more completely by the sanction of his successor, King Darius, who (with Artaxerxes) made every effort to restore the Temple in its beauty, and to refurnish it with the precious vessels taken from the first edifice.

After the sacking of Jerusalem, and the destruction of King Solomon's Temple, the Masons remained captives and exiles for seventy years, during all which period they kept faithfully their promise to rebuild the Temple of their God, by preserving some portions of the holy furniture and holding Masonic Lodges. Shortly subsequent to obtaining permission of King Cyrus to reconstruct the edifice, and while the foundation was not yet complete, Cyrus died. Great apathy and indifference, in consequence, existed among the brethren, more especially as they were the subjects of hatred by the various tribes of Samaritans and Syrians, who constantly harassed them; and they were compelled, if they continued their work at all, to labor with the sword in one hand and the trowel in the other. In the second year of the reign of King Darius, however, the High Priest succeeded in arousing a spirit of industry, and obtaining the consent of Zerubbabel to again make application for protection and liberty to rebuild the Temple.

Darius, or Darayavuste, in the Persian part of the great triangular inscription at Behestun, on the frontier of ancient Media, reigned 485 years B. C. He was 29 years old when he ascended the throne, and reigned 36 years.

The friendship of Darius for Zerubbabel, in his younger days, gave opportunity for the pressure of the suit of the Jews; and by the power of truth—as exhibited in the striking incident in the ceremony—permission in its amplest form was obtained from the king, and Zerubbabel created a Prince: which honor was confirmed by the Jews, and made a Masonic grade of distinction.

*   *   *   *   *

TRIUMPHAL CHORUS.

AIR.—"Suoni la tromba."

RAISE the glad voices of triumph,
    No longer shall tyrants enslave us ;
    Lo ! he is coming to save us,
        Judah's lion to save.
Crown him with garlands of laurel,
    Clothe him in raiment of honor,
    Welcome to Salem our Brother,
        Zerubbabel the brave.
Huzza ! warmly we welcome our brother,
    Zerubbabel the brave.

Welcome the day of rebuilding;
    The Chief of whom we honor shall lead us.
    The prayers of the righteous shall aid us ;
        Once more is Judah free.
And on the mountain so holy
    Our Temple shall raise to the Lord.
    In Zion his name be adored !
        To Him bend the knee.
Hosanna ! In Zion our God be adored;
    To Him bend the knee.

Glory to God in the highest!
    He leads us from bondage and night,
    He brings us to freedom and light,
        His name shall be adored.
And on the bells of the horses
    Shall be written in letters of gold
    The Prophetical phrase as of old,
        "Holiness to the Lord!"
Hosanna ! once more we will sing as of old
    "Holiness to the Lord !"

FOURTH SERIES.

THE

PHILOSOPHICAL DEGREES

OF

KNIGHT OF THE EAST AND WEST, AND KNIGHT OF THE EAGLE AND PELICAN OR ROSE-CROSS, ARE CONFERRED IN A ROSE-CROIX CHAPTER, AND RELATE TO THE BUILDING OF THE THIRD TEMPLE—"ONE NOT MADE WITH HANDS"—WITHIN THE HEART OF MAN.

"Benam yesdam bakshaishgher dadar."
"In the *name* of the most merciful just God."
Persian Magi.

In all bodies of the Ancient and Accepted Scottish Rite, brethren who have attained the degree of Grand, Elect, Perfect and Sublime Mason, are entitled to, and should of right, be covered, except when a degree is being worked; at which time all should conform, and lend their endeavors to aiding in the effectiveness of the drama, by robing and costuming accordingly.

The following engraving designates the most appropriate, convenient, and economical form of covering, it being light, composed of four sides, purple, with movable joints, in order that it can be pressed flat—fillet of crimson, and crowning-button of white velvet.

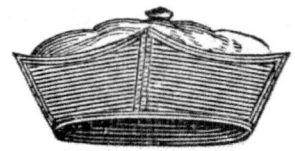

"He who discovereth secrets is a traitor; and he who keeps his tongue, keeps his soul."—King Solomon.

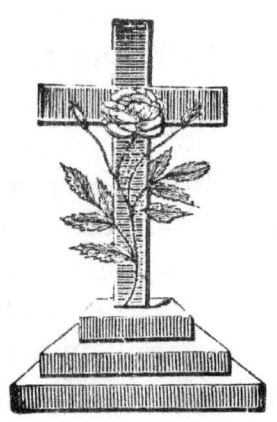

PREFATORY.

BODIES of these degrees are styled "*Sovereign Chapters*" The diploma of a Knight Rose-Croix is called a *Brief*. All written documents are called *Engraved Columns*. The following are the articles for the general government of Knights Rose-Croix:

ART. 1.—The principal festival of the Rose-Croix Knights is held on Thursday preceding Good Friday. It is incumbent on all Chapters to assemble on that day; and if a Knight should be where there is no Chapter, he is to observe the time in communion of spirit with all Knights around the globe.

ART. 2.—S∴ P∴ of Rose-Croix are styled Knights Princes, and Perfect Masons of H-R-D-M.

ART. 3.—The Princes have the right of presiding in all Lodges working under the A∴ and A∴ rite; and if the chair is refused them, they take their place at the right of the Master: if this honor is not offered them, they may seat themselves on the floor in the N∴ E∴ of the Lodge in token of humility, when the works will at once cease.

ART. 4.—All Princes of Rose-Croix are forbidden any Chapter or Lodge, without the jewel or order belonging to this degree; and they should never sign any Masonic document without affixing their quality to their name, and dating it "from the Orient of Herodim."

ART. 5.—When a Knight visits a Chapter not his own, he places himself in humility; but the M∴ W∴ may cause him to take a place by his side in the E∴

A Knight Rose-Croix is not to be tyled when he presents himself for admission into a Lodge. He should therefore have a special brief evidencing his rank.

ART. 6.—A regular Chapter must meet at least five times in a year; that is, Ash-Wednesday, Thursday before Easter, Good Friday, Easter Sunday, Ascension Day, and Christmas. They should also join with their brethren in the observance of St. John's days.

ART. 7.—If a Knight of Rose-Croix, being alone, hears of another Knight sojourning, not over three leagues from him, he should invite him to participate in the observance of Holy Thursday; in which case they meet each other half-way.

ART. 8.—No Chapter can be opened unless five Knights be present. The minutes must be signed by at least three of the Knights present.

ART. 9.—A Knight of Rose-Croix must be charitable. He must relieve the indigent, visit the sick and the prisons. No Chapter should be held without a collection for the poor. The Sovereign is the Treasurer of this fund, as necessity may require.

ART. 10.—Duels between Knights are strictly forbidden, under the most severe penalties.

ART. 11.—A Knight of Rose-Croix is bound by his honor to the service of his God, his government, and his country, to the last drop of his blood.

ART. 12.—No Knight of Rose-Croix can refuse to attend the Chapter when summoned, unless sick,—when he shall present his reasons to the Chapter.

ART. 13. The Chapter must be lighted with white or yellow wax candles, or pure olive-oil.

ART. 14.—No discussions foreign to the business of the Chapter can be allowed. Calumny, satire, and personal remarks are ever to be avoided as crimes.

ART. 15.—The grade of S∴ P∴ R∴ Croix de H∴ should never be conferred without the most scrupulous inquiries and circumspection as to the moral, religious, and other *necessary* qualifications of the applicant.

ART. 16.—No document can be valid unless signed by the Sovereign Secretary, and sealed by the Keeper of the Seals.

ART. 17.—The officers must be elected annually on Holy Thursday, and immediately enter on their duties. The retiring officers should be prepared to hand their books, accounts, and funds to their successors on that day.

ART. 18.—No serving brother can be admitted in any Chapter. The two brethren last received must act in that capacity.

ART. 19.—If a Knight of Rose-Croix dies, all the Knights must participate in the funeral ceremonies, and wearing under their coats, if they cannot openly display them without scandal, the order and jewel of the grade. Great care must be taken that the deceased is buried with his collar.

ART. 20.—A Knight at his admission adopts as his own some characteristic, the choice of which is left to himself, as Fortitude, Toleration, &c., but expressed in Latin, as Eques a Fortitudine, &c. Those of the first three officers and Master of Ceremonies are always the same—Knights of Wisdom, of Strength, of Beauty, of Alarm.

ART. 21.—A Knight R. Croix, in writing his name, writes the consonants only; and an unequal number, if there be more than two. To his name may be appended this mark ✠ red ink.

SEVENTEENTH DEGREE.

Knights of the East and West.

ARGUMENT.

THE Seventeenth degree of the Rite Ancient and Accepted, is the first of the series of Modern or Accepted degrees, as used in contradistinction to the term Ancient. It may also be designated, the first of the Philosophic degrees.

The Word is again lost, and, figuratively, the third Temple—in the heart of man—is to be built and dedicated to the God of Truth. The revelations made in the ceremony of initiation cannot be fully understood in this degree, as they are introductory to the succeeding degree of Rose-Croix, in which *mysterium consummatum est.*

When the Knights and Princes united to conquer the Holy Land, they took an oath to spend, if necessary, the last drop of their blood to establish the true religion of the Most High God. Peace having been made, they could not practically fulfil their vows, and therefore, on returning to their respective countries, they resolved to do in theory what they could not do in practice. They took the name of Princes of Jerusalem and Knights of the East and West, in memory of the place where this Order was first instituted, and because their doctrines came from East and West. They have, ever since their first establishment, adhered to their customs and forms of reception. In the year 1118, the first Knights of the Order, to the number of eleven, took their vows between the hands of Armelfo Guavi Mundos, Prince and Patriarch of Jerusalem, who hailed from the province of Amiens, in France.

KNIGHTS OF THE EAST AND WEST.

THE SEVENTEENTH GRADE OF THE ANCIENT AND ACCEPTED SCOTTISH RITE, AND THE FIRST DEGREE OF THE PHILOSOPHICAL SERIES.

APARTMENTS AND DECORATIONS.

But one spacious apartment, beside the Preparation room, is needed. It should be in the form of a heptagon, hung with crimson, sprinkled with stars of gold. In each angle is a square column, on the capitals of which—beginning at the southeast and going round by the southwest, in regular succession—are the initials respectively of the following words: Beauty, Divinity,

Wisdom, Power, Honor, Glory, Force; and on the bases of these columns are the initials respectively of the words Friendship, Union, Resignation, Discretion, Fidelity, Prudence, and Temperance. On each column is a brilliant light.

In the East is an altar upon a canopied platform, to which you ascend by seven steps, supported or upheld by four lions, having between them a cherubimic figure with six wings and four heads, representing respectively the heads of a lion, an ox, a man, and an eagle.

In front of the altar is a throne, always vacant, and a footstool.

The seat of the Master is at the foot of the platform, in front, and over the seat hangs a two-edged sword, surrounded by seven stars.

In the East are displayed the Sun and Moon.

In the West are two thrones, raised three steps each, for the two Wardens.

Around the room are twenty-four seats richly decorated.

An assembly of Knights of the East and West is called a Preceptory, and is composed of twenty-four members.

On the right of the Master is a small table, having on it a ewer, napkins, and vase of perfumed oil.

On the altar is a silver basin with perfumed water, a chafingdish with live coals, and a large Book, sealed with seven great seals of green wax, at least two inches in diameter, attached to red ribbons that, at the other end, pass through holes in one lid, being slightly attached to it by a drop of wax, so as to be easily separated, leaving the seals whole.

The tracing-board of the degree is a heptagon, embraced within a circle, the upper portion forming a rainbow. At the angles of the heptagon, on the outside, are the initials of the seven words which are on the capitals of the columns of the degree (B. D. W. P. H. G. F.); at the angles on the inside are the initials of the seven words which are on the base of the columns, (F. U. R. D. F. P T.) Near the centre of the heptagon is the figure of a man in a long white robe, with a golden girdle round his waist, and standing on a section of the globe: hair and beard white as snow: his right hand extended, holding seven stars surrounding the˙: his head encircled by a glory emanating from a

Delta: a two-edged flaming sword in his mouth. Around him stand seven golden candlesticks, with candles burning; and over each of these, one of the letters E. S. P. T. S. P. L., the initials of the names of the seven Churches—Ephesus, Smyrna, Pergamos, Thyatira, Sardis, Philadelphia, Laodicea. The Sun and Moon are also depicted, and the basin and chafingdish.

OFFICERS.

Venerable Master, represents John the Baptist.
Zealous Brother Senior Warden.
Zealous Brother Junior Warden.
Faithful Brother Treasurer.
Faithful Brother Secretary.
Faithful Brother Lecturer.
Faithful Brother Examiner.
Faithful Brother Senior Deacon.
Faithful Brother Junior Deacon.
Faithful Brother Outer Guard.
Faithful Brother Inner Guard.

All brethren are termed Faithful, and represent the disciples of John the Baptist

CLOTHING, ETC.

All are clothed in long white robes, with a red cross on the breast, circlets of gold upon their heads (coronet-shaped), and gold belts.

Apron—Yellow satin, triangular in shape, lined with crimson and bordered with gold; on the flap a two-edged sword, and in the centre of the area a tetractys.

Order—Broad white ribbon, worn from right to left,

and crossed by a broad black one from left to right—from the latter is suspended the

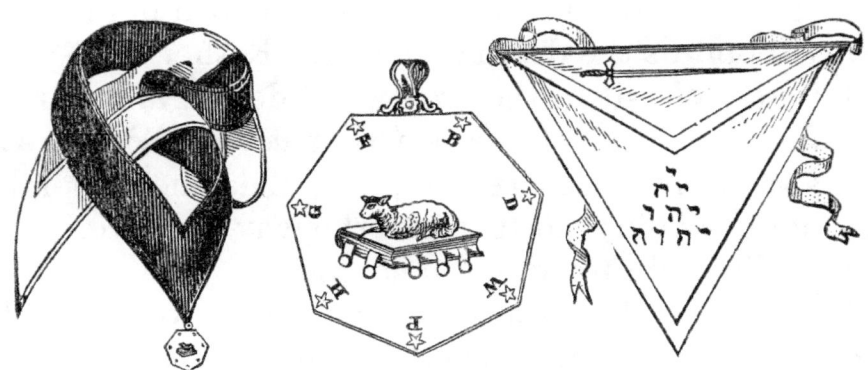

Jewel—Heptagonal medal of gold and silver. On one side are engraved the same letters as are on the capitals of the columns, with a star over each: in the centre, a lamb lying on the Book of the Seven Seals: on the obverse side, two swords crossed, with points up, the hilts resting on an even balance: in the corners, the initials of the seven Churches.

Battery—•••••—•

OPENING.

*   *   *   *   *

PRAYER.

(With responses.)

V∴ M∴ Hear us, our Father, God of the ancient patriarchs, whom they adored on the plains of Chaldea!

Response. Be gracious unto us, O God.

V∴ M∴ We wander in the desert in darkness—we turn to the East and look for the promised light.

Res. Send us the dawn of day, our Father.

V∴ M∴ We sit in the shadow of death, and our feet tread the margin of the sea that covers Sodom. Our tents whiten the desert upon its sterile shore. Send us thy light to guide our feet into the way of peace.

Res. Thy light to be the life of men.

V∴ M∴ Send us the new law of love for which the world pines and languishes. Make war and bloodshed to cease among the nations, and heartburnings among the faithful to be no more.

Res. Help us to love one another.

V∴ M∴ Save us from our enemies, and from the hand of all that hate us. Help us to serve thee without fear all the days of our life.

Res. Amen. So mote it be. Amen.

Soft music upon the organ during the above prayer and responses. The following hymn will then be sung.

HYMN.

TWEED.

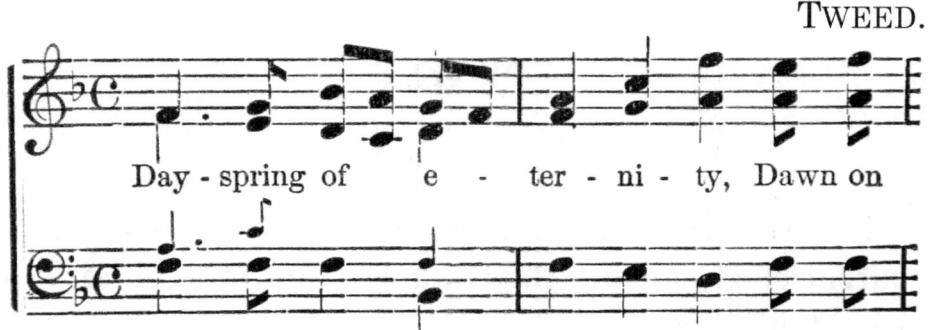

peace and joy, All the pow'rs of wrong de - stroy.

V∴ M∴ The first faint blush of dawn dims the light of the morning star, and this preceptory is about to be opened.

Music soft and low during the following.

V∴ M∴ The glittering seven fade in the north, and the day cometh.

J∴ W∴ Ye shall keep my Sabbaths, and reverence my sanctuary.

S∴ W∴ Ye shall obey my judgments, and keep my statutes.

V∴ M∴ Ye shall not profane the name of your God.

J∴ W∴ Ye shall love and venerate, every man, his father and mother.

S∴ W∴ Ye shall not glean your vineyards, nor gather every grape, nor wholly reap the corners of your fields, but leave something for the poor and the stranger.

V∴ M∴ Nor steal, nor deal falsely, nor lie one with another.

J∴ W∴ Nor defraud nor despoil your neighbors

S∴ W∴ Nor go up and down as tale-bearers among the people.

V∴ M∴ Thou shalt not hate thy brother in thy heart, nor suffer thy neighbor to go astray for want of warning.

J∴ W∴ Ye shall rise up respectfully before the hoary head, and honor the presence of the aged man, and fear your God.

S∴ W∴ Ye shall not vex the stranger in your land; for ye were strangers in the land of Egypt. These are the statutes and judgments of the Lord your God.

RECEPTION.

The candidate is subjected to an examination the most strict in regard to the (*Pista* or) pledges he has given in the degrees of Ancient Craft Masonry: also as to his proficiency in the Kabala of those degrees.

*   *   *   *   *

(Ceremonies of purification and sanctification are here introduced.

V∴ M∴ (* * *) He that hath an ear, let him hear what the Spirit saith unto the churches: To him that overcometh will I give to eat of the Tree of Life which is in the midst of the Paradise of God.

S∴ W∴ (* * *) He that hath an ear, let him hear what the Spirit hath said unto the churches: He that overcometh shall not be hurt of the second death.

J∴ W∴ (* * *) He that hath an ear to hear, let him hear what the Spirit saith unto the churches: To him that overcometh will I give to eat of the hidden manna, and I will give him a white stone, and on the stone a new name written, which no man shall know but him that shall receive it.

V∴ M∴ (* * *) He that overcometh, and laboreth in my service unto the end, to him will I give power over the nations, and his influence shall control and guide them; and I will give him the morning star.

S∴ W∴ (* * *) He that overcometh shall be clothed in robes of white, and I will not erase his name from the Book of Life, but I will own him as mine before our Father and all his angels.

J∴ W∴ (* * *) Him that overcometh will I make a pillar in the Temple of our God, and he shall remain there forever; and I will write upon him the name of God, and the name of the city of God—the New Jerusalem—and mine own new name.

V∴ M∴ (* * *) To him that overcometh will I grant to sit with me near my throne, even as I also overcame and am seated with my Father. Be zealous, therefore and repent.

*   *   *   *   *

KEIGHTS OF THE EAST AND WEST.

HYMN.

L. M.   DR. MARTIN LUTHER.

From East to West, o'er land and sea,

Where broth-ers meet, and friends a-gree;

Let in-cense rise from hearts sin-cere,

The dear-est off-'ring gath-ered here.

Our trust reposed on God alone,
Who ne'er will contrite hearts disown;
Our faith shall mark that holy light,
Whose beams our dearest joys unite.

Light comes from God. When clouds and darkness are around us, we should implore his aid. Let us do so, my brethren.

PRAYER.

Our Father, who, when darkness brooded upon the vast chaos, and the universe lay a confused mass of struggling forces, without form and void, didst move upon it, and saidst, "Let there be light!" and light was; thou who didst set the light against the darkness, and calledst the one Day and the other Night; thou who didst set the lesser and the greater lights in heaven, enable this candidate to find the light he seeketh. Let the dawn of the new day arise to him, and shine upon the clouds of error, and cause the darkness of ignorance to flee away and be seen no more forever. Amen.

Omnes. Amen! amen!

V∴ M∴ And amen!

*   *   *   *   *

The living know that they shall die, but the dead know not anything; neither have they any more a reward, for the memory of them is forgotten: also their love, and their hatred, and their envy is now perished; neither have they any more a portion forever in anything done under the sun.

S∴ W∴ Remember now thy Creator in the days of thy youth, while the evil days come not, nor the years draw nigh when thou shalt say, I have no pleasure in them; while the sun, or the light, or the moon, or the stars be not darkened, nor the clouds return after the rain.

V∴ M∴ In the day when the limbs are not yet trembling with age, nor the head bowed with sorrow, nor the eyes dim with weeping; before thou goest to thy long home, and the mourners go about the streets; before the silver cord is loosened, and the golden bowl is broken, and the pitcher shivered at the spring, and the wheel shattered at the cistern; before the dust returns to the earth as it was, and the spirit to God who gave it.

CHANT.

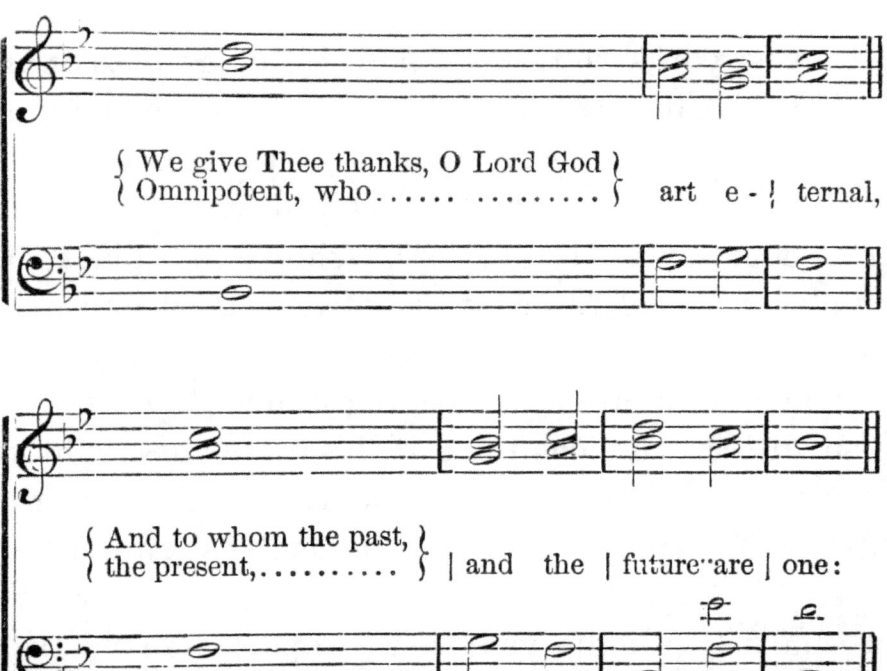

INVESTITURE.

I invest you with the apron of this degree: its color is emblematical of the dawn; its shape, of the Deity and of justice; the Tetractys upon it, of the universe, with the Deity in its centre. I invest you with the order of this degree: its two colors, white and black, are emblematical of the contest between good and evil. I invest you with the jewel of this degree: its heptagonal shape will be explained hereafter, as also will the devices upon it; its materials, gold and silver, symbolize the sun and the moon, the great lights of day and night—themselves emblems of strength and beauty, the two pillars at the threshold of Masonry. In the year 1127 Pope Honorius II., at the request of Stephen, a Patriarch of Jerusalem, ordained the Knights should be clothed in white; to which Pope Eugenius III. added a red cross, to be worn on the breast.

I finally present you with this coronet, in token of your present rank in Masonry. Remember that it, like the other insignia of the Ancient and Accepted Rite, is honorable only so long as it is worn with honor. On the brow of the dishonest, the dissipated, the vicious, or the base, honors undeserved are the extremest disgrace. See, therefore, that you wear it worthily and well.

HYMN.

HALLENBECK.

Truth dawns up-on the hu-man soul, And er-ror dis-ap-pears; No long-er darkness hath con-trol O'er wea-ried, length-ened years.

No longer for men's sorrow groan,
    Their sins, their shame, their tears,
But still and stately past God's throne
    March onward, banish fears.

The sun is radiant in the sky,
    The earth in regal state
Waits but the Hallelujah cry
    That opes the holy gate.

LECTURE.

My brother, this *Preceptory* is in the form of a heptagon, hung with crimson, and sprinkled with stars of gold. In each angle is a column, on the capitals of which, beginning at the southeast and going round by the southwest in regular succession, are the initials respectively of the words Beauty, Divinity, Wisdom, Power, Honor, Glory, and Force—the seven mystic characters of the heptagon, signifying:

Beauty, to adorn our works.

Divinity, to study which is one of our principal aims.

Wisdom, to invent and work.

Power, to punish and confound the calumnies of wicked brethren and the profane.

Honor is an indispensable quality in a Freemason, to labor with respectability.

Glory, that the true Freemason is an equal to the prince or potentate.

Force, which is necessary to support and maintain us.

On the bases of the columns you will observe the initials of the seven qualities which should be possessed by brethren of this grade:

FRIENDSHIP,   UNION,   RESIGNATION,
DISCRETION,   FIDELITY,   PRUDENCE,
                   TEMPERANCE.

Friendship is a virtue which ought to reign among the brethren.

Union is the foundation of our society.

Resignation to the regulations and decrees of the order without murmuring.

Discretion, that as a Mason you should be on your guard and never suffer yourself to be surprised in relation to our mysteries.

Fidelity, to observe all your engagements.

Prudence, to conduct yourself so that the profane, though jealous, may never be able to censure your conduct.

Temperance, to always avoid every excess which may tend to injure the soul or body.

The seven vices which all good and true Freemasons will ever strive to avoid are:

HATRED,   PRIDE,   DISCORD,
INDISCRETION,   PERFIDY,   RASHNESS,
                   CALUMNY.

Hatred injures all the fine feelings of the heart.

Discord is contrary to the very principle of society

Pride prevents the exercise of humility.

Indiscretion is fatal to Freemasonry.

Perfidy should be execrated by every honest man.

Rashness leads into unpleasant and difficult dilemmas.

Calumny, the worst of all, should be shunned as a vice which saps the very foundations of friendship and society.

The *Book of the Seven Seals,* which only one can open, is Masonically explained as representing a Lodge or Council of Masons, which the all-puissant alone has the right or power to convene or open.

The breaking of the *first seal* displayed a bow, arrows, and crown, signifying that the orders of this Preceptory should be executed with as much promptness and exactitude as an arrow sent from a bow, and be received with as much submission as if they came from a crowned head.

The *second seal* displayed the sword, denoting that this Preceptory and the order in general is always armed for its defence and to punish the guilty.

The *third seal* revealed the balance—the symbol that Masonry should always act with justice in all her ministrations.

The *fourth seal* produced the skull, which is the representative of that brother who has caused himself to be excluded from the Lodge or Preceptory.

The *fifth seal* displayed a white cloth stained with blood, invoking us that we should not hesitate if necessary, to spill our blood in the defence or in the promotion of the cause of Freemasonry.

The *sixth seal* when opened caused the sun to be darkened and the moon to be changed to blood, as a representation of the power of Supreme Councils to interdict the works of inferior bodies, when irregular, until they shall have acknowledged their error and submitted to the rules and regulations of the Craft.

The *seventh seal* when broken was followed by silence, broken by the successive blasts of the seven trumpets, signifying that Freemasonry is extended over the surface of the earth on the wings of the wind and fame, and supports itself with honor. The perfume from the altar represents the good odor of virtue, and denotes that the life of a good Freemason should be free from all reproach and perfumed by a good report.

Your Masonic age is very ancient, and you are termed a Patmian, as coming from Patmos.

The seven golden candlesticks denote the seven churches—to wit, Ephesus, Smyrna, Pergamos, Thyatira, Sardis, Philadelphia, Laodicea.

The *two-edged sword* pendent in the East has been explained when referring to the opening of the second seal, and that none, not even the Ven∴ Master, is exempt from the exercise of judgment and justice.

The Ven∴ Master represents John the Baptist, and

the twenty-four seats the twenty-four elders or disciples, who were Esseneans.

HISTORY.

Lecturer. This, my brother, is the first of the Philosophical degrees of the Ancient and Accepted Rite, and the beginning of a course of instruction which will fully unvail the heart and inner mysteries of Masonry. Do not despair because you have often seemed on the point of attaining the inmost light, and have as often been disappointed. In all time truth has been hidden under symbols, and often under a succession of allegories—where vail after vail had to be penetrated before the true light was reached and the essential truth stood revealed.

We are about to approach those ancient religions which once ruled the minds of men, and whose ruins encumber the plains of the great Past, as the broken columns of Palmyra and Tadmor lie bleaching on the sands of the desert. They rise before us—those old, strange, mysterious creeds and faiths—shrouded in the mists of antiquity, and stalk dimly and undefinedly along the line that divides time from eternity; and forms of strange, wild, startling beauty mingle in the vast throng of figures, with shapes monstrous. grotesque, and hideous.

The religion taught by Moses, which, like the laws of Egypt, enunciated the principle of exclusion, borrowed at every period of its existence from all the creeds with which it came in contact. While by the study of the learned and wise, it enriched itself with the most admirable principles of the religions of Egypt and Asia, it was changed in the wanderings of the people, by everything that was impure or seductive in the pagan manners and superstitions. It was one thing in the time of Aaron and Moses, another in that of David and Solomon, and still another in that of Daniel and Philo.

At the time when John the Baptist made his appearance in the desert, near the shores of the Dead Sea, all the old philosophical and religious systems were approximating to each other, while the philosophers of Greece, all (except the disciples of Epicurus) more or less Platonicians, seized eagerly upon the beliefs and doctrines of the East. The Jews and Egyptians, before then the most exclusive of all people, yielded to that eclectism which prevailed among their masters, the Greeks and Romans. It was held by a vast number, even during the preachings of Paul, that the writings of the Apostles were incomplete, that they contained only the germs of another doctrine, which must receive from the hands of philosophy not only the systematic arrangement which was wanting, but all the developments which lay concealed therein—mysteries handed down from generation to generation in esoteric tradition.

*   *   *   *   *

NO∴ P∴ D∴ V∴ D∴ M∴—A French abbreviation, signifying "Do not forget your Masonic Regalia."

Chain of Flowers.—The Masonic nomenclature for a wreath of flowers, in like manner as a *Chain of Union,* signifies the forming a circle by the brethren taking hold of hands, as in the case when the password is communicated, or the banquet-song is sung.

The *Clepsydra,* or Hour-glass, may at all times be properly placed in the East.

The term *Essoine,* in the Ancient and Accepted Scottish Rite, signifies the inability of a brother to assist at a communication, and informs the body thereof.

Louveton, Louveteau, Louvetine, Lewton—all signify a Mason's son.

∴ THESE three points or dots distinguish Masonic abbreviations.

Various attempts have been made to explain their origin; they are said to allude to the three lesser lights; or, as they were first introduced by French Masons, they may refer to the situation of the three principal officers of the Lodge in the French Rite, where the Master sits in the East and the two Wardens in the West.

They are alleged by others to be inverted, and thus to allude to the initial name of Deity as represented in the original of the Hebrew forming the *triune circles of eternity,* thus: ∵ ▽ hence, (the Hebrew yod).

EIGHTEENTH DEGREE.

Knight of the Rose Croix.

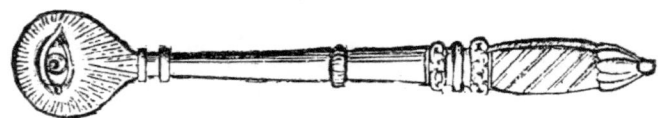

ARGUMENT.

THE Novice is still in search of the Truth and the lost Word he journeys for a period of years, learning the three virtues which are to guide him: from a place of horror and gloom, merges, at the appointed time, the sacred initials, giving glory to Masonry and light and life to the world.

This degree, like the one preceding it, is philosophical. The end of all philosophy is to free the mind from those encumbrances which hinder its progress toward perfection, and to raise it to the contemplation of immutable Truth and the knowledge of divine and spiritual objects. This effect must be produced by easy steps, lest the mind, hitherto conversant only with sensible things, should revolt at the change.

Knight of the Eagle and Pelican is one of the titles applied to a Rose-Croix H-R-D-M Freemason; yet that degree is not strictly an order of knighthood, in the commonly received sense of the term.

In these degrees, it is readily perceivable that we have now fully entered upon a long course of instruction into all the mysteries of the esoteric doctrine.

There are a number of Rose-Croix degrees differing in a measure from each other in the work and in their teachings. The Alchemical or Hermetic Masons taught a different degree in all respects from the so-called *Christian* Rose-Croix; and they again a different one from the universal, tolerant, and more acceptable grade. The following words of one of the most eminent students of Masonry, and an ardent admirer of the A∴ and A∴ Rite, may be quoted here.

"If anywhere brethren of a particular religious belief have been excluded from this degree, it merely shows how gravely the plans and purposes of Masonry may be misunderstood; for whenever the door of any one degree is closed against him who believes in one God and the soul's immortality, on account of the other tenets of his faith, that degree is no longer Masonry, which is universal, but some other thing, that is exclusive, and accordingly intolerant. Each degree erects a platform on which the Israelite, the Mahommedan, and the Christian may stand side by side and hand in hand, as brethren." Whatever your religion, your birth-place, or your language, you are among brethren. One language is spoken in common, the language of the Scottish Rite of Masonry, which speaks directly to the heart.

ECCLESIASTES XII.

"Remember now thy Creator in the days of thy youth."

REMEMBER thy Creator
    While the pulse of youth beats high;
While the evil days come not,
    Nor the weary years draw nigh,
When man can find no pleasure
    In the hollow things of earth,
And the heart turns sick and sad,
    From the jarring sound of mirth.

Ere the light of stars is darkened,
    Ere the glorious sun grows dim,
And the bitter cup of sorrow
    Is filling to the brim;
When the grinder's song is low,
    And the wailing mourners come,
Marching in the death-procession,
    As man goeth to his home.

Ere the golden bowl be broken,
    Or the silver cord unwound,
The pitcher shattered, at the well
    The broken wheel be found.
In the day when keepers tremble,
    And the strong men bow the knee,
Then shall dust to dust return,
    And to God the spirit flee.

KNIGHT OF THE ROSE CROIX,

PERFECT PRINCE DE H-R-D-M, KNIGHT OF THE EAGLE AND PELICAN.

THE EIGHTEENTH GRADE OF THE A∴ AND A∴ SCOTTISH RITE, AND THE SECOND DEGREE OF THE PHILOSOPHICAL SERIES.

APARTMENTS.

The ceremony of Reception of a Knight of the Eagle and Pelican requires properly four apartments, as follows.

FIRST APARTMENT.

The first apartment is hung in black, spread with white tears; and is lighted simply by the taper of the Most Wise, the two lights on the throne, and the dim light of three transparencies.

Three columns, of the Doric, Ionic, and Corinthian orders of architecture respectively, about five feet in height, are appropriately placed in the Chapter, and support on their capitals transparent inscriptions of the three virtues, one on each, which should be removed when the Chapter is closed.

The canopy in the East is black, bordered with white fringe; on the platform below it is the irregular throne of the Chapter, surmounted by three crosses, the centre one most prominent, with a full-blown white rose upon it: on either side thereof is a candlestick with a yellow wax candle lighted. Both throne and crosses are to be concealed by two black curtains coming together before them, and which are opened at the appointed time.

The Most Wise Master has before him a small low table covered with black, and on it, lighted, one wax candle, a Book of the Testimony, a compass and square, and a triple triangle; also the regalia for the candidate. By the table is a low black seat or ottoman. The furniture and properties are in disorder. A ewer, with water and napkins, should be placed in the South.

SECOND APARTMENT.

The second apartment should represent two small apartments, the one leading imperceptibly into the other. The one labyrinthian, with ascending and descending steps, interlacing each other; the other * * *

THIRD APARTMENT.

A small apartment draped or painted black, called the "Chamber of Reflection," in which is a rude chair and table; on the latter, a skull and cross-bones and an ancient-shaped dim-burning lamp, also a Book of the Testimony.

FOURTH APARTMENT.

Which may very properly and advantageously be represented by a judicious rearrangement of the first apartment. All the furniture and properties are in order, perfect harmony and accord exist, for the Word is found; the room should therefore be decorated in an

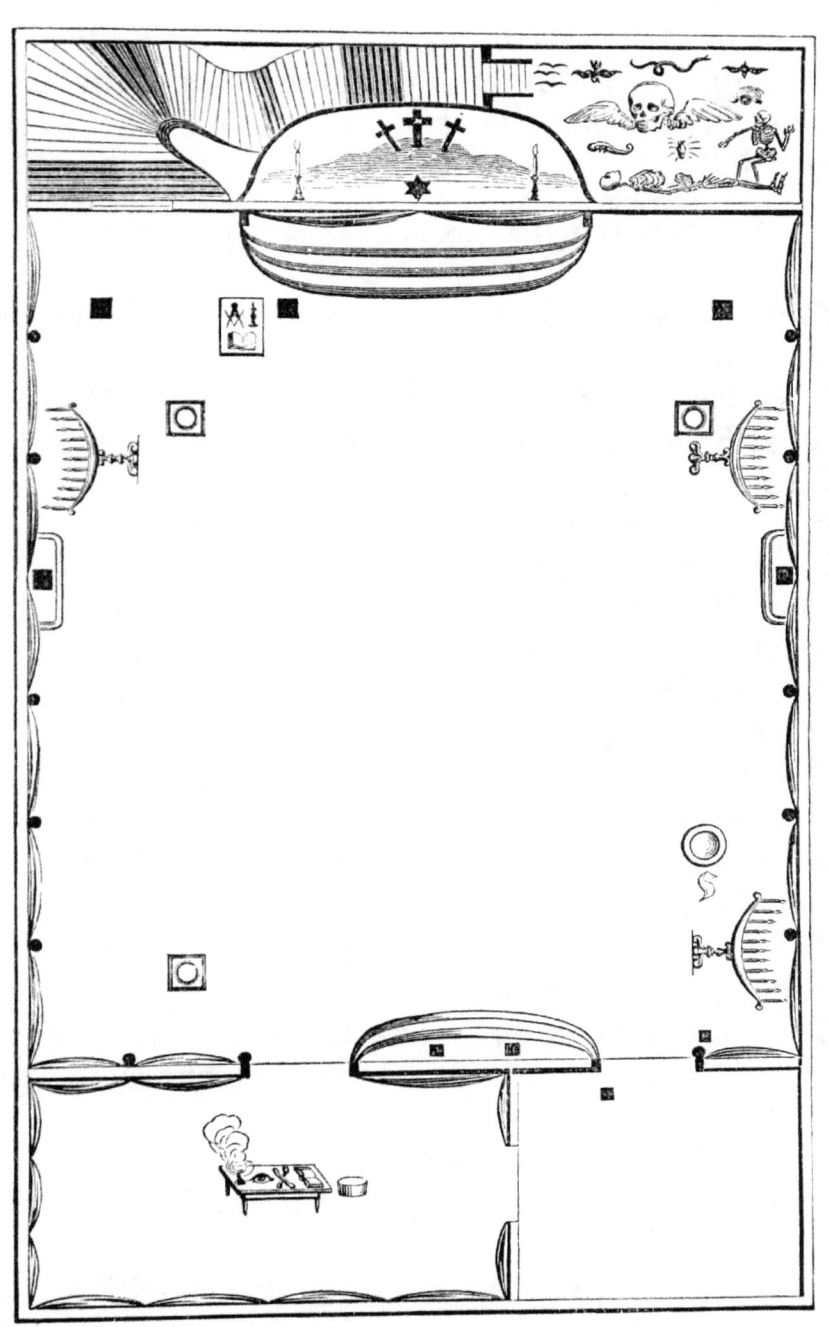

appropriate and dazzlingly magnificent manner. The thirty-three lights, composed of three candelabra of eleven branches each, with yellow wax candles, must now shine forth in their brilliancy, and the blazing star with six beams is seen in the East. The hangings are red.

OFFICERS, AND THEIR JEWELS.

Most Wise and Perfect Master, or Most Wise Tirshatha.
Most Excellent and Perfect Knight Senior Warden.
Most Excellent and Perfect Knight Junior Warden.
Most Perfect Knight Orator.
Most Perfect Knight Master of Ceremonies.
Most Perfect Knight Secretary.
Most Perfect Knight Treasurer.
Most Perfect Knight Guardian of the Tower.

All brethren are addressed as Respectable and Perfect Knights.

The Most Wise wears on his breast a flaming star of silver, with seven points: in the centre the letter I, in gold; around it the initials F. H. C.: his characteristic is *Wisdom*.

The Senior Warden wears a triangle: his characteristic is *Strength*.

The Junior Warden wears a square and compass—the one fastened on the other: his characteristic is *Beauty*.

These Jewels are used in addition to the Grand Jewel, which is worn by all the Knights.

CLOTHING AND DECORATIONS.

The Knights should be dressed in black or dark clothes, and wear over the same a chasuble of white cloth bordered with black ribbon or wool, one inch wide The chasuble has a black cross both before and behind— extending its entire length—made of wide ribbon or other material; it is lined with white, and should be worn only in the first apartment. Over all is worn from right to left a black watered SASH, bordered with crimson, three inches wide, in the middle of which, and where it crosses the breast, is a small red ribbon cross; near the bottom, two inches from the rosette, is also a small red ribbon cross; at the bottom is a small red rosette, and over it one smaller of a black color: from the lower rosette hangs a small gold cross.

Apron.—Of white leather or satin, bordered with red, as is also the flap. There are three red rosettes arranged in triangular form around the apron. On the area is a representation of a red passion cross, seven inches long; and on the flap a death's head and crossbones, either painted or embroidered.

Grand Jewel—Is an open compass, its points resting on a quarter circle. Between the legs of the compass is a cross, reaching from the head of the compass down to the quarter circle; on the cross is an opened rose; at the foot of the cross, on one side is an eagle with wings extended against the points of the compass, head downwards; on the obverse side is a pelican, tearing its breast to feed with blood its young, seven in number, in a nest under it; on the head of the compass on each

OBVERSE.

REVERSE.

side of it is an antique crown with seven points; on the quarter circle, on one side is engraved the hieroglyphical characteristic of the Knight, and on the other side the cabalistic letters of the degree. * * * * *

The compass and are of the circle of the Jewel should be composed of gold, and the eagle and pelican of silver. This Jewel should be worn suspended to a black watered COLLAR, three inches wide, bordered with crimson; there should be three crimson ribbon crosses on it—one on each side, and one at the point above the crimson rosette at the bottom.

All the jewels when worn in the first apartment should be covered with black crape.

In the centre of this first apartment at a reception, there is a confused mass, representing the debris of an edifice in ruins, composed of broken columns, chapiters, and every species of Masonic emblems. If anything is placed upon the two side crosses in the East, it must be a human skull and two thigh-bones crossed.

KNIGHT OF THE ROSE CROIX.

The Banner of the Rose-Croix, hanging in the East to the left of the M∴ W∴, is a square piece of white satin, lightly sprinkled with crimson, edged with a gold fringe, upon which is embroidered or painted the side of the jewel representing the "Pelican," with the words "Lux E Tenebris" above the pelican, and the words "Faith, Hope, Charity" below, painted in gold on a ribbon.

Visitors are expected to salute the M∴ W∴ and the two Wardens, with their swords; then facing the East, return their swords and give the sign of recognition to each of the same officers; again face the East and stand under the sign of G∴ S∴—the Knights of the Chapter remaining standing at salute. At the close of the welcome by the M∴ W∴, the swords will be sheathed, the Battery given, and with the sign the acclamation. A visitor may then respond to the M∴ W∴ Such visitors as are entitled may then be conducted to the East.

The title "Perfect" is not used among the Knights in the first apartment.

In the fourth apartment the collar and sash are turned, presenting the same appearance; except where it was black it should be crimson, and where it was crimson it should be black.

When a candidate is admitted he is called a probationer or novice: when fully received he becomes a neophyte, or one newly born.

The *crux ansata* in the East should be of gold. The labors are supposed never to close, and when a Chapter is about to work, it is said the labors are resumed.

The labors begin when the Word is lost, and are suspended when the Word is recovered.

A novice must be subjected to three ballots.

Battery—●●●●●●—●

RECEPTION.

* * * * *

The stars have disappeared, the light of the sun and moon is obscured, and darkness has fallen upon the face of the earth.

* * * * *

My brother, you are still engaged as a Mason in search of light and truth; of which search, the many journeys you have made in the different degrees are symbolical. But your search is not for the truth of any particular creed or religion—that search would be in vain, for what is truth to one is not truth to another: often by argument and evidence, but almost always by the accidents of birth, education, and circumstances, our religious belief is formed; and argument and testimony strike the mind of man, when arrived at his religious creed and faith, only to glance off and leave no impression.

Our symbols and ceremonies envelop the great primitive truths, known to the first men that lived: with whatever particular meaning they may have—peculiar, or believed to be peculiar, to particular creeds, and differing, as the faith differs of those who receive them—we have nothing to do.

We are about to conduct you through certain forms and ceremonies, to display to you certain symbols and emblems; we do not give you in advance their interpretation, but only indicate to you their general tendency; we place the thread in your hands that will guide you through the labyrinth; it is for you to apply and interpret the symbols and ceremonies of the degree in such manner as may seem to you truest and most appropriate.

A vast multitude of men believe that the Redeemer of man has already appeared upon the earth: many believe he was a man; many, the Son of God; and many, the Deity incarnate: a vaster multitude still wait for the Redeemer: each will apply our symbols and ceremonies according to his faith.

* * * * *

PRAYER.

Great and dread Being, Father, who wast, when beside thee there were time and space alone; a single thought of whom shaped itself into an universe of suns and worlds, and infinite myriads upon myriads of living creatures; eternal as time and infinite as space; to whom all the past and all the future now is and ever will be present; thou by whom no creature that lives is forgotten or unregarded, look with favor upon us and upon this our brother; deign to bless him, to protect him, and make his labors fortunate; watch over him; illuminate his mind with wisdom, that he may understand our symbols; and teach him to trust in thee. Amen!

* * * * *

Faith is the substance of things hoped for, the evidence of things not seen.

By faith Abraham, when he was tried, offered his only-begotten son.

By faith the children of Israel forsook Egypt, not fearing the wrath of the king; by faith, they passed through the Red Sea as by dry land, which the Egyptians essaying to do, were drowned.

By faith the walls of Jericho fell down, after they were compassed about seven days.

Faith subdueth kingdoms, worketh righteousness, obtaineth promises, stoppeth the mouths of lions.

>By *faith,* a steady course we steer
>   Through ruffling storms and swelling seas;
>By *faith,* we pass the vale of tears
>   Safe and secure, though oft distressed;
>By *faith,* subdue the king of fears,
>   And go rejoicing to our rest.

*   *   *   *   *

Blessed is the man that trusteth in the Lord, and whose hope the Lord is: for he shall be as a tree planted by the waters, and that spreadeth out her roots by the river. She shall not wither when the heat cometh, but her leaf shall be green; and she shall not be careful in the year of drought, neither shall she cease from yielding fruit.

The hope of the righteous shall be gladness, but the expectation of the wicked shall perish.

The wicked is driven away in his wickedness, but the righteous hath hope in his death.

> The *hope* of heaven our spirits cheer;
>   No more we grieve for sorrows past,
> Nor any future conflict fear,
>   So we may safe arrive at last.
>
> O Lord, on thee our hopes we stay
>   To lead us on to thine abode,
> Assured thy love will far o'erpay
>   The hardest labors of the road.

*   *   *   *

Though I speak with the tongues of men and of angels, and have not charity, I am become as sounding brass and a tinkling cymbal.

Though I bestow all my goods to feed the poor, and give my body to be burned, and have not charity, it profiteth me nothing.

Charity suffereth long, and is kind.

Charity envieth not.

Charity vaunteth not itself—is not puffed up.

Charity never faileth.

> Blest is the man whose softening heart
>   Feels all another's pain,
> To whom the supplicating eye
>   Is never turned in vain.

To him protection shall be shown,
   And mercy from above
Descend on those who thus fulfil
   The Mason's law of love.

And now abideth Faith, Hope, and Charity, these three, but the greatest of these is Charity.

Hosanna in the highest! on earth peace and goodwill toward men.

HYMN.

Aletta.

Grateful notes and numbers bring, While the name of God we sing. Holy, Holy, Lord our God, Be thy perfect name adored.

> Men on earth, and saints above,
> Sing the great Redeemer's love.
> Lord, thy mercies never fail:
> Hail! Celestial Goodness, hail!

* * * * *

CHARGE

By virtue of the powers with which I am invested by the Supreme Council, and by the consent of these Knights, my brothers and equals, I do admit and receive and constitute you a Perfect Prince Freemason of H-R-D-M, Knight of the Eagle and Pelican, under the distinctive title of Rose-Croix, now and forever, henceforth, to enjoy all the prerogatives attached to this grade.

My Brother, virtue and humility are the foundations of this degree; henceforward be you, therefore, virtuous, modest, and unpresuming; mark our guiding star of prudence, and so live that you may not disgrace or dishonor the name that you have earned, the characteristic to which you are entitled, and the jewel which you will hereafter wear.

LECTURE.

My Brother, each of us makes such application to his own faith and creed, of the symbols and ceremonies of this degree, as seems to him proper. With these special interpretations we have nothing to do—

like the legend of our Grand Master Hiram, in which some see figured the condemnation and sufferings of Christ; others, those of the unfortunate Grand Master of the Templars; others, those of the first Charles; and others still, the annual descent of the sun at its winter solstice to the regions of darkness—the basis of many an ancient legend: in no other way could Masonry possess its universality—that character which has ever been peculiar to it from its origin, and which enabled two kings, worshippers of a different Deity, to sit together as Grand Masters while the walls of the first Temple arose; and the men of Gebal, who bowed down to the Phoenician gods, to work by the side of the Hebrews, to whom those gods were an abomination.

* * * * *

Pythagoras said: "God is neither the object of sense nor subject to passion, but invisible, only intelligible, and supremely intelligent. In his body he is like the light, and in his soul he resembles Truth. He is the universal Spirit that pervades and diffuses itself over all nature. All beings receive their life from him. There is but one only God, who is not, as some are apt to imagine, seated above the world, beyond the orb of the universe; but being himself all in all, he sees all the beings that fill his immensity: the only Principle, the Light of heaven, the Father of all.

"He produces everything, he orders and disposes

everything; he is the Reason, the Life, and the Motion of all being!"

* * * * *

The peculiar cipher of this degree is subject to your use. The Feast of Bread and Wine is to us the symbol of fraternity and affection, and of that perfect union which must ever exist among Knights of the Rose-Croix.

Masonry has a mission to perform, with her traditions reaching to the earliest times, and her symbols dating further back than even the monumental history of Egypt extends. She invites all men of all religions to enlist under her banners, and to war against evil, ignorance, and wrong. You are now her knight, and to her service your sword is consecrated: may you prove a worthy soldier in a worthy cause, and may the great and Supreme Architect be always with you, and bless you with life everlasting.

ANTHEM.

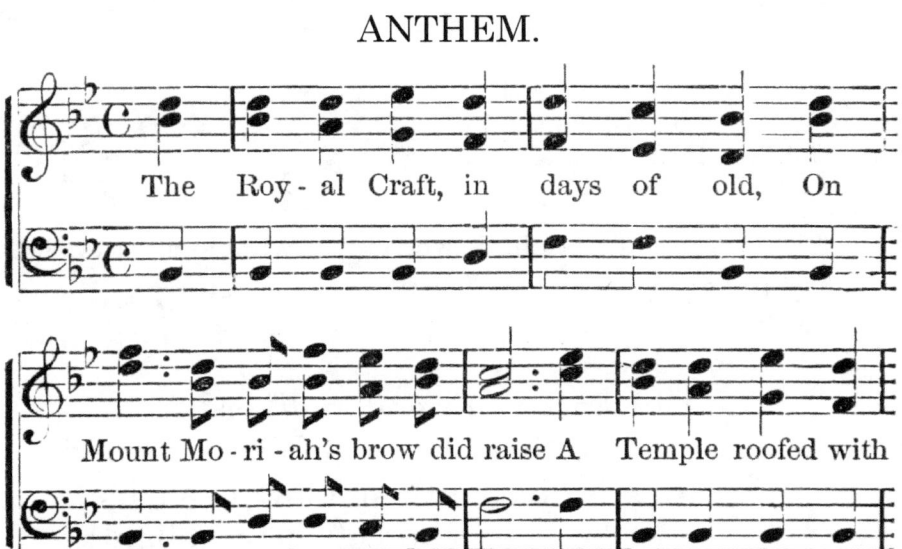

The Roy-al Craft, in days of old, On Mount Mo-ri-ah's brow did raise A Temple roofed with

Our Father, Friend and Lord divine,
  Rend thou the vail of passion's night!
In all souls truth and love enshrine!
  Robe every child of earth in light!

KNIGHT OF THE ROSE CROIX.

That all of Adam's erring seed
    May cease from strife, and fruitful toil
To every clime and every creed
    Bring peace and plenty, wine and oil!

And when these Temples, framed by thee—
    Our bodies—ope their portals wide,
And our imprisoned spirits flee
    To seek what thou dost wisely hide;

Free and Accepted may we prove,
    When angels bring us near to thee,
Prepared, in thy Grand Lodge above,
    To take our last Sublime Degree.

ORDINARY.

CEREMONY OF THE TABLE.

To the glory of the Grand Architect of the Universe; in the name and under the auspices of the Supreme Council and Sovereign Chiefs of Exalted Masonry, and by virtue of the authority on me conferred, I call this Chapter from labor to refreshment.

This Chapter is now called to refreshment. Before we part, let us eat together the bread earned by our labors, and thank our heavenly Father for furnishing us with the means for sustaining life. Brother Master of Ceremonies, visit the avenues.

    *   *   *   *   *

Sovereign Creator of all things and source of light and life, who providest for all our necessities, bless the nourishment for the body we are about to take, and make it to give us strength to labor for thy glory and the advancment of all the great interests of humanity. Amen.

Take; eat, and give to the hungry!   *   *
Take; drink, and give to the thirsty!   *   *

Peace be with you, my brethren, and remain with you always. Remember that your duty is, not to be better than your brethren, but to be better than yourselves; that the more you have, the more you owe to those who need assistance. The Peace of our Master be with you always.

*   *   *   *   *

NOTE.—This Ceremony is a manifestation of fraternal love, as inculcated by Masonic philosophy. Rose-Croix Knights after the benediction silently disperse, and the Chapter remains at refreshment until regularly convened or called by the Most Wise. Thus a Rose-Croix Chapter is seldom if ever closed, as the Table Ceremony is indispensable whenever there is a call to refreshment, which should be at every assembling.

While the Knights quietly disperse, the following may appropriately be sung by the Choir.

HYMN.

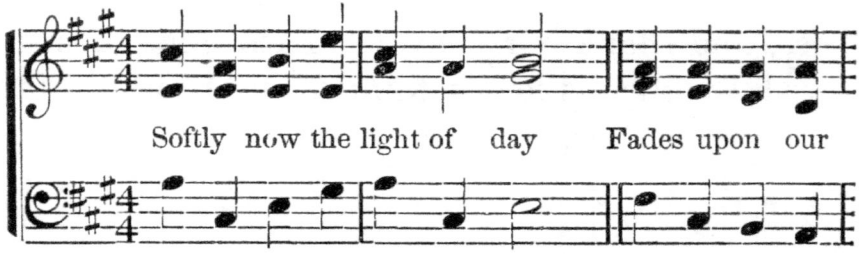

KNIGHT OF THE ROSE CROIX.

sight a-way; Free from care, from la-bor free.

Lord, we would com-mune with thee.

Soon for us the light of day
Shall forever pass away;
Then, from care and sorrow free,
Take us, Lord, to dwell with thee.

HOLY THURSDAY, OR MAUNDAY THURSDAY

DECORATIONS, ETC.

A stated meeting of all Chapters Rose-Croix is held on Thursday before Easter: this meeting is indispensable.

If a Rose-Croix Knight be necessarily alone, he must, in spirit at least, feast that day with his brethren.

A wreath must be placed upon the cross in the East.

The Pelican feeding its young should be prominently displayed in the Chapter-room upon a white column.

Two additional yellow wax candles should be burning on the irregular throne in the East.

The three columns, Faith, Hope, and Charity, should be displayed in position.

The silver salver with Passover-bread and goblet of white wine should also be provided.

The altar should be plain and hung with black, with the Book of Constitutions, and a square, compass, and *Crux ansata* of gold upon it. On the *Crux ansata* should be enamelled the letters —∴ —∴ —∴ —∴

A little in front of the Master, on his right and left, are two triangular columns, draped in white, five feet in height. Upon each is a triangular transparency, on one side of which is a word. This word, on the column on his right, is I—— on that on his left, I——. In the West, a little in front of the Wardens, on the right and left, are two columns, precisely alike, each with a similar transparency. On that upon the right is the word R——, and on that upon the left, the word N——. Each transparency turns upon a pivot, so that the words (until then concealed) may be displayed at the proper moment, which will not transpire until Easter Sunday.

On this most solemn festival, a young lamb, roasted. is to be eaten at the feast. It must be white, without spot or blemish, and killed with a single blow of a knife. One of the brethren must prepare it; and the head and feet must be cut off, and burned as an offering. At the repast, each must eat a piece. If a brother be travelling, and meet another brother on the road, they are obliged to go to some convenient place to perform this duty. This particular repast is styled the *Mystic Banquet*.

On Holy Thursday, in the rear of the East will be depicted the following scene. The Celestial Vault studded with stars; the sun absent, and the moon obscured with clouds. In the extreme East, among the clouds, an Eagle hovers. In the centre of the scene is the representation of a mountain, on the summit of which is a cubical stone, and on that a crimson rose. Around the mountain, below, hang clouds and darkness; and further to the West, at its base, are all the ancient working-tools of Masonry, in fragments, with the two mystic columns prostrated, and each broken in two. The words *Wisdom, Strength,* and *Beauty* will be displayed on a ribbon over this scene.

The above general arrangement of the Chapter-room will remain until Easter Sunday.

CEREMONY—HOLY THURSDAY.

*   *   *   *   *

M∴ W∴ This Chapter is now called to refreshment. Before we part, let us eat together the bread earned by our labors, and thank our Heavenly Father for furnishing us with the means for sustaining life.

(●)

B∴ M∴ of Cer∴, visit the avenues, and see if there be any brother, or even any of the profane, who suffer from hunger or thirst: if there be, bring him in, for whoever he may be, he is our brother, and we will freely divide with him our bread and wine.

(● ● ●)

Brothers and Knights, let us assemble around the

altar of fraternal love, joyfully strengthening the tie which binds our hearts together.

(In silence and order, the Knights follow the M∴ W∴ to table.

INVOCATION.

Sovereign Creator of all things, and source of life and light, who providest for all our necessities, bless the nourishment for the body we are about to take, and make it to give us strength to labor for thy glory and the advancement of all the great interests of humanity. Amen!

BRIEF OF ADDRESS.

From time immemorial, man has plighted his faith and confidence in his fellow-man by drinking from the same cup and eating from the same loaf.

Among Eastern nations at the present day has this method of solemnizing a pledge been retained. We learn from history, and our fathers of the Masonic faith, that in the ancient mysteries of Judea and Egypt, the newly initiated were presented with bread and wine as a symbol of the new life they were about entering upon, and that they were henceforth to be devoted to the laws of truth, and knowledge of their rights and duties.

This ceremony is noted as having been practised in the mysteries of Judea and Eleusis, in their initiation to what they called the degree of Perfection.

The Hebrews acquired the custom from the Egyptians,

and celebrated their feasts of the Spring full moon, with bread and wine.

With us it is simply a manifestation of fraternal love, as inculcated by Charity and Masonic philosophy.

The solemn feast of the Rose-Croix Knights is held this day, and commemorates the feast of the Passover, observed by the Jews.

Respectable and Perfect Knights, the feast of which we are about to partake is thus ordered:

"On the 10th of the month of Nisan, they shall take to them every man a lamb, a lamb for a house; and if the household be too little for the lamb, let him and his neighbors next unto his house take it, according to the number of the souls. Your lamb shall be without blemish, a male of the first year... and ye shall keep it up until the 14th day of the same month, and the whole assembly of the congregation of Israel shall kill it in the evening: and they shall eat the flesh in that night, roasted with fire, and ye shall let nothing of it remain until the morning, nor break any bone of it; and that which remaineth of it until the morning, ye shall burn with fire.

"And thus shall ye eat it: with your loins girded, your shoes upon your feet, and your staff in your hand; and ye shall eat in haste; it is the Lord's Passover. And this day shall be unto you for a memorial, and ye shall keep it as a feast to the Lord throughout your generations, a feast by an ordinance forever."

This feast, and the bread and wine of which we partake, are to us symbols of fraternity and brotherly affection, and of that perfect union that must ever subsist among Brother Knights of the Rose-Croix.

Thus, Brother Knights, are we assembled, solemnly and fraternally pledging ourselves one to another in brotherly love, in the presence of the angels and of that great Intelligence that surrounds us in our every action.

We belong to no creed or school, but to universality, where Truth is the base and Morality the handmaid: we are Knights of Masonry, and to her service our swords are consecrated: may we prove worthy soldiers in a worthy cause.

*   *   *   *

The Most Wise then takes two cakes whole of the Passover-bread, and a broken one, in his hand together, and breaks the upper cake; but he must not eat thereof till he breaks a piece off the broken one; then saying * * * gives a piece of each to every one at the table. Both pieces are eaten together. After this commences the general feast of the lamb and white wine.

*   *   *   *   *

The Ceremony of Extinguishing the Lights will then proceed.

CEREMONY OF EXTINGUISHING THE LIGHTS.

This ceremony takes place on every Thursday before Easter, after the Table Ceremony, and begins the moment the "Word" is returned to the Most Wise, and when all have resumed their positions.

At the West end of the table is a candelabra with seven branches of unequal size, so as to form a triangle, the middle branch making the top of the triangle. In each a yellow wax candle must be burning. All being around the table, at a sign from the Most Wise, the officers in reverse order proceed to perform their allotted tasks.

*   *   *   *   *

Behold, the Emancipator of mankind, the friend of the poor and destitute, the comforter, who, covering with the mantle of his *word* the nakedness of the lowest among the low, has introduced them into the Banquet-room of Immortality, there to enjoy the seat which has been from all eternity prepared for them by the Father.

Guests of one day, and disinherited the next! the friend is dead, the benefactor is no more! Woe unto us! Woe unto us! Woe unto us! Error triumphs, Truth has disappeared, ignorance has extinguished the light of philosophy.

*   *   *   *   *

Thy fate is sealed, thou must die! and thy Knights will not be there to defend thee. Pray unto our Father to guide us in the arduous path of life, so that, when the last hour shall have come, we may rise to the bosom of our only friend, contemplate his beaming countenance, and enjoy forever the sublime lessons which he, no doubt, delivers to the pure beings who surround him.

"Love ye each other."

Close, as in the Table Ceremony, with the Benediction.

EASTER SUNDAY.

DECORATIONS, ETC.

On Easter Sunday the altar will be splendidly decorated, and hung with white and crimson, and strewed with flowers and garlands, as in fact should be the entire room; the altar should also have upon it the Book of Constitutions, etc., as on the occasion of Holy Thursday; the words on the columns should be displayed; and the representation in the East should be changed to the following:—The whole East represents the sun and moon shining in a clear sky, glittering with stars. In the extreme East is seen in the sky a cross surrounded by a glory, and by a bright cloud, in which appear the heads of seven angels; on the cross is a white rose in full bloom, and in its centre the letter ▪. In the centre of the scene is the representation of a mountain, on the summit of which is a blazing star, with seven luminous points, and in the centre of that is also the letter. In the north is an eagle, hovering in the air; the square, compasses, trowel, and other Masonic emblems are scattered about, as also the cubical stone. The words *Faith, Hope, Charity,* and *Truth* will be displayed on a ribbon over this scene

KNIGHT OF THE ROSE CROIX.

CEREMONY—EASTER SUNDAY.

*   *   *   *   *

Proceed as on Holy Thursday till the time for the ADDRESS, which may be delivered by the Most Wise, Orator, or such Brother Knight as may be selected for the special occasion.

The Address should be brief, and explanatory of the joyful feast about to be partaken of, and at which greater license is given than on the Feast of Holy Thursday.

The feast is not confined to any particular class of food, nor to white wine.

The following hymn of praise may succeed the Address:

HYMN.

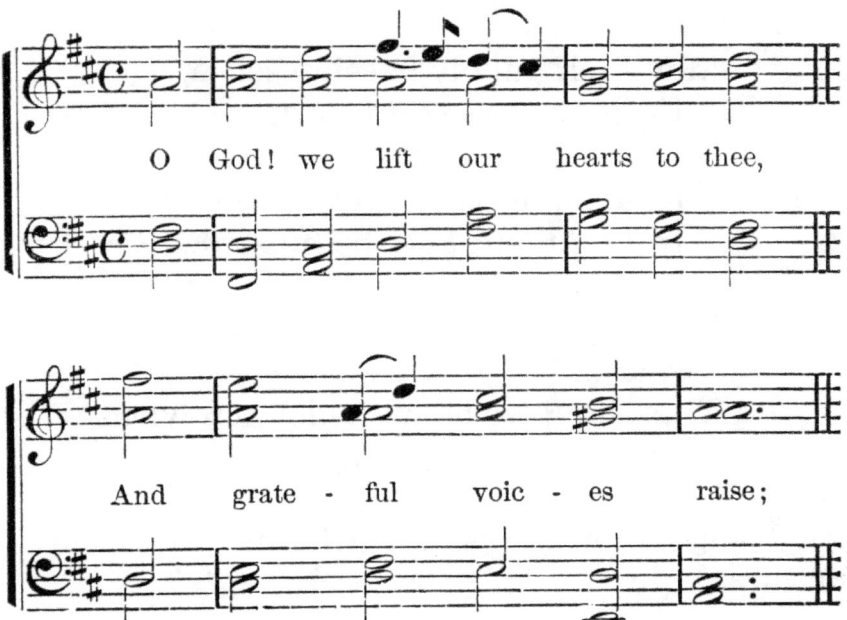

O God! we lift our hearts to thee,
And grate-ful voic-es raise;

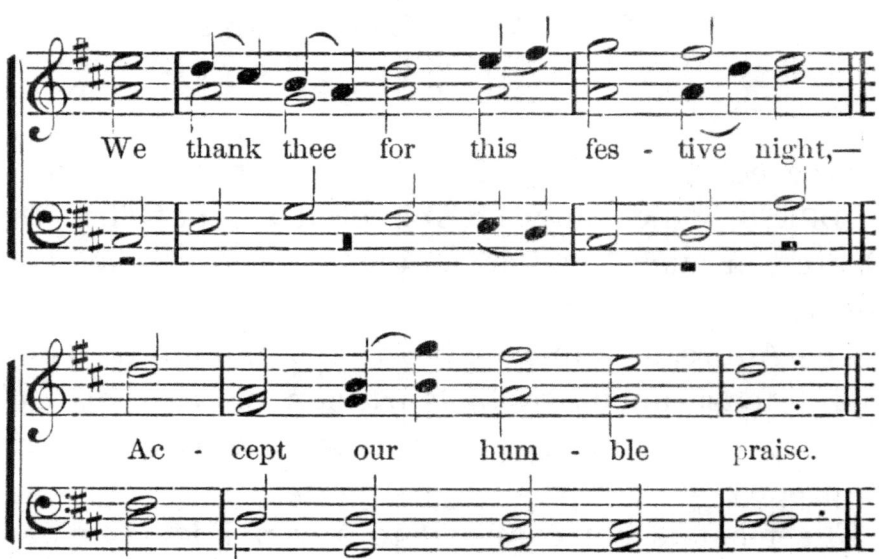

We thank thee for this fes-tive night,—
Ac-cept our hum-ble praise.

Here may our souls delight to bless
 The God of truth and grace,
Who crowns our labors with success,
 Among the rising race!

May each unholy passion cease,
 Each evil thought be crushed,

Each anxious care that mars our peace
 In *Faith* and *Love* be hushed.

Oh! may we all in *Truth* abound,
 And *Charity* pursue;
Thus shall we be with glory crowned,
 And love as angels do.

All being in readiness, the following ceremony *must* transpire:

CEREMONY OF RE-LIGHTING ON EASTER SUNDAY.

This ceremony takes place immediately after the Ceremony of the Table. As in the Ceremony of Extinguishing the Lights, it begins as soon as the "Word" has been returned to the Most Wise. Each Knight is then at his post, and the music has stopped.

The table is arranged as in the Ceremony of Extinguishing the Lights; the yellow wax candles have remained unlit since the previous Thursday.

The Knights being round the table, at a signal from the Most Wise, the officers in reverse order discharge their several duties.

*   *   *   *   *

We have at last re-entered the Banquet-room, and we resume therein the seat which our Father had provided for us.

Immortal guests, no power can henceforth deprive us of our inheritance! Glory unto our Father! Glory unto our Father! Glory unto our Father! Love and Liberty give light and life to philosophy.

Truth reappears.

Proceed then, my brethren; think and act upon your own responsibility. You are now of age! Now you are redeemed! You have your own life in charge, now and forever! The Master shall ever follow you on the way! He will be your witness, your helper! He will aid your weakness and extend his hand to you in the hour of peril! The doors of the Infinite are opened unto you.

Close, as in the Table Ceremony, with the Benediction.

FUNERAL CEREMONY.

DECORATIONS OF THE CHAPTER.—ROSE-CROIX.

The throne, altar, and seat of the officers must be hung with black. In the place formerly occupied by the deceased, there must be a chair covered with black cloth, strewed with tears, and an escutcheon of the Scotch Rite colors, upon which is written the name of the deceased. The escutcheon is surmounted with a death's head resting on two thigh-bones crossed. The collar of the highest degree possessed by the deceased, surrounds the escutcheon. At the lower extremity of the escutcheon hangs the jewel of the order, and behind it is a sword across its scabbard, the point downward.

The walls of the Chapter are strewed with black garlands. The coffin is placed in the centre, and upon it the regalia of the deceased, whose feet shall be turned toward the west. The candlesticks, three in number, are black, surrounded with black crape, and bearing eleven lights each.

Between the coffin and the West there must be a triangular pyramid. On the first side is the All-seeing eye of Providence, within the circle formed by a serpent biting its tail; on the second, a death's head, over which is a butterfly; and on the third, a Genius, holding in the right hand a torch reversed and extinguished, and in the left, a torch erect, burning.

Before the Altar is an antique tripod surrounded with black crape, on which is a vessel containing perfumed alcohol; on each side, a basket of flowers on a truncated column; on the opposite side, the banner of the Chapter, with a knot of black crape. Above the coffin is a sepulchral lamp; and near the tripod, pans of incense and perfumes. There should be an organ in the West: a vessel filled with water, another filled with wine, and a third one filled with milk, are located respectively in the east, west, and south of the coffin; a vessel for ablutions in the north; and in the hands of the Master of Ceremonies, a torch for the Most Wise.

At the East end of the Chapter there should be a kind of representation of the Elysian Fields, with abundance of flowers, verdure, and light, all of which are concealed by a thick black curtain, which is drawn aside at the moment of departure for the last resting place.

CEREMONY.

The labors of the Chapter are resumed in the usual manner, observing to make the mourning battery.

The Most Wise will then address the Chapter on the ceremony of the day, and the merits of the deceased.

 * * * * *

M∴ W∴ Sir Knight Mas∴ of Cer∴, engrave on the columns of this Sovereign Chapter, that on the ———— —day of ——————, in the vulgar era, the soul of our beloved brother, Sir Knight ———— ————, has returned to his Father, and that we have intrusted his mortal coil to the earth.

 * * * * *

PRAYER.

M∴ W∴ O Grand Architect of the Universe! Almighty God! All live and breathe in thee! For thee, light and darkness are but one! Thou seest us at our death as thou hast seen us at our birth, and, like the manifestations of life, the secrets of the grave are known to thee; in both states we are in thy presence! May our beloved brother forever dwell with thee as he has dwelt with us! May his death teach us how to die, and be unto us a preparation for that immortality which we hope to enjoy in thy bosom. Amen.

 * * * * *

INVOCATION.

M∴ W∴ O thou merciful Father, whose supreme wisdom has put an end to our present life, and who, by the admirable providence of thy designs, hast decreed the cessation of the pangs and sorrows of suffering virtue, the deliverance of the oppressed and the terror of the iniquitous; thy infinite power has combined all things with a view that nothing should perish, and that our bodies, like our souls, should escape annihilation. Oh! thanks to thee for the feeling with which this consoling idea inspires us; for it soothes the regret which the sight of this coffin awakens within our hearts ! May the immortal soul of our brother enjoy peace and happiness, and those pure ecstasies to which his assiduous labors in the cause of light and truth have entitled him.

*   *   *   *   *

Perfect Knight, our Brother ——— ——— hears not our call. As this torch, he once lived and gave light, and he was a guide unto all seeking for light; but like it, a breath has extinguished his life and sunk him into the dark bosom of death. It is in vain that we call his name in these precincts. He is no more! No more shall we hear his voice! Let us then pay the last tribute of our respect to his memory, and from the eternal bourne wherein he now travels, may he be conscious of our sorrow.

* * * * *

Knights, the gloomy colors covering these walls and our attributes, the dull silence which dwells in that coffin, the sorrow which prevails in our hearts, and these dismal trophies of death, may remind us that from the very bosom of corruption arise the perfumes and joys of life! Death is but the initiation of eternal life; a pure conscience fears it not.

* * * * *

HYMN.

Cease, ye mourners, cease to lan-guish O'er the graves of those ye love; Pain and death, and night and anguish, En-ter not the world a-bove.

While in darkness ye are straying,
    Lonely in the deep'ning shade,
Glory's brightest beams are playing
    Round the immortal spirit's head.

Cease, ye mourners, cease to languish
    O'er the graves of those ye love:
Far removed from pain and anguish,
    They are chanting hymns above.

Light and grace at once deriving
    From the hand of God on high,
In his glorious presence shining,
    They shall never, never die.

    *   *   *   *

Let the strength which for thee was once derived from the vegetable kingdom, return to its source, and with thy mortal remains, to that material life which so beautifully expounds the wise designs of our Almighty Father.

    *   *   *   *   *

May death purify thee! May the waters of charity wash off all thy faults; and, in presence of this grave wherein thou restest, may we remember thy virtues only.

    *   *   *   *   *

Oh! thou, who art now freed from all the snares of duplicity, flattery, intolerance, hypocrisy, and falsehood, may truth shine for thee in all its glory, and reconcile thee to the errors and falterings of humanity!

* * * * *

May the soul of our brother return to its celestial abode, as the perfume of this incense rises toward heaven! May the Grand Architect receive it in his Eternal Chapter, and bestow upon it the reward in store for the righteous.

* * * * *

M∴ W∴ My brothers, it is now the hour to carry our brother to his grave: let us follow, in silence, his coffin to the last resting-place. Weep ye not as those who have not Hope, for when, according to the laws of nature, our last hour shall have chimed, we shall follow him to meet beyond the grave, and rise from darkness to light.

* * * * *

HYMN.

Solo Voice.   DR. H. S. CUTLER.

On thy bo-som, mighty Lord,

KNIGHT OF THE ROSE CROIX. 283

As we pass the vale of death,
   Round us throw the arm of love:
When we yield this fleeting breath,
   Bear us to thy Lodge above—
In the "house not made with hands,"
   Compassed round with angel bands.

In the resurrection morn,
   Raise us with thine own right hand.
Freed from envy and from scorn,
   Bring us to the better land—
Where from labor brethren cease,
Share refreshment, dwell in peace.

FIFTH SERIES.

THE

HISTORICAL AND PHILOSOPHICAL DEGREES

OF

GRAND PONTIFF, G∴ MASTER OF SYMBOLIC LODGES, NOACHITE OR PRUSSIAN KNIGHT, KNIGHT OF THE ROYAL AXE, CHIEF OF THE TABERNACLE, PRINCE OF THE TABERNACLE, KNIGHT OF THE BRAZEN SERPENT, PRINCE OF MERCY, COMMANDER OF THE TEMPLE, KNIGHT OF THE SUN, AND KNIGHT OF ST. ANDREW OR PATRIARCH OF THE CRUSADES, ARE CONFERRED IN AN AREOPAGUS OF KNIGHTS KADOSCH, OR BY THE IMMEDIATE SANCTION OF A CONSISTORY.

"Go forth to battle, and employ your substance and your persons for the advancement of God's religion. Verily, God loveth those who fight for his religion in battle array, as though they were a well compacted building."—*Koran.*

"THE exterior world, like a great book, gives us intelligible and truthful readings of Nature's laws, leading us to look through Nature up to Nature's God.

"The Lodge is a symbol of the world extending from East to West, from North to South, from the depth of the Earth to the Celestial heavens. In the East the rising Sun, the grand source of light and heat, shines in the Lodge as the unwearied ruler and guide of our working-hours, the symbol of his Creator's power and watchful care; while the Moon, the resplendent orb of night, with her attendant stars, reflects the greater glories of divine munificence, diffusing light and harmony in our pathway to *Truth, Liberty,* and *Fraternity.*

"The *Union Cord* with *Love Knots,* which runs around the Lodge upon the architrave, is indicative of the Mystic-tie which unites us in the bonds of a happy Fraternity, telling of full, generous love to 'Fellow-man.'"

Fel∴ Craft Deg∴ A∴ A∴ S∴ R∴

PREFATORY.

The Eleven degrees of the Areopagus, conferred under the authority of the Chapter of Knights Kadosch, and which form the fifth series of the A∴ A∴ Scottish Rite, most beautifully unfold the errors and frailties of humanity, and most thoroughly instruct us how to overcome them and advance toward that perfect state hoped for by mortality. We still proceed in the construction of the Third Temple as initiated in the degrees of the Rose-Croix, and with the hope and endeavor to make the world a Temple fit for the dwelling-place of the G∴ A∴ of the Universe.

The laws governing the Consistory rule and control in the Areopagus.

No Rose-Croix Knight should attempt to enter upon this series, unless he has fully made up his mind to calmly, thoroughly, and with the best of his intellect, study to fully comprehend its teachings and follow its revelations, deductions, and analogies to a complete issue, for otherwise he is treading upon dangerous ground.

With the Areopagus ends all instruction in the A∴ A∴ Scottish Rite; what follows is practical, and is intended as the summing up of all Masonry.

Let the Historical and Philosophical degrees of the Areopagus be well heeded.

The novitiate, before embarking in them, should be warned to take due heed of these culminating degrees of *Universal Religion*.

RITUAL HYMN

IN THE

GRECIAN MYSTERIES.

THOU God of Heaven and Hell, of land and sea! Whose thunders dread the Olympus shake, And whom the Genii fear, and Demons serve! The Fates, stern and unbending for all else, Obey thy sovereign will. Of all that live, Immortal One, Thou art the sire. When wrathful thou dost speak, the entire world Doth quake, the unchained winds in fury swell The sea, and fearful darkness gathers round The earth, and fiery storms do plow the vast Expanse above! Yet art thou wise and kind; That mighty law, which rules the stars, comes forth From Thee; and aye before thy golden throne, Unwearied stand those holy ones who do Thy will, and bear thy gifts to man. The bright And glorious spring, adorned with brilliant hues, And crowned with new-born flowers, and winter swathed In shining bands of ice, are, by thy will Created. All do come from Thee,—springs, flowers, Summer's joys, and autumn's golden fruit,—To Thee, and Thee alone, we owe them all.

NINETEENTH DEGREE.

Grand Pontiff.

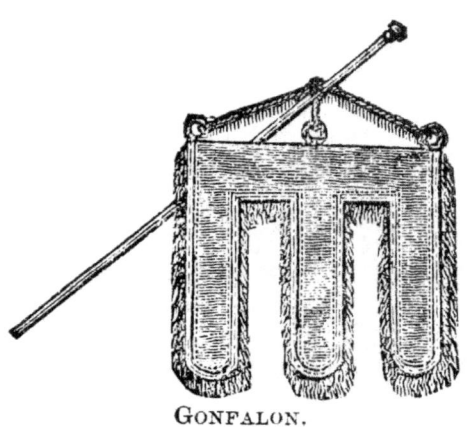
GONFALON.

ARGUMENT.

IN entering upon a new series or division of the degrees of the Ancient and Accepted Rite, we are still in pursuit of good, and laboring for the destruction of evil,—following the same laws as those laid down in the two preceding degrees, and taking another bold step toward the purification of our own souls, and sowing, for others to reap fruits of eternal happiness.

This degree is founded upon certain apocalyptic mysteries relating to the New Jerusalem; it rests upon the three characteristic virtues taught in the Eighteenth degree, and proclaims the Alpha and Omega.

GRAND PONTIFF;

OR,

SUBLIME SCOTCH MASON.

THE NINETEENTH GRADE OF THE ANCIENT AND ACCEPTED SCOTTISH RITE, AND THE FIRST DEGREE OF THE HISTORICAL AND PHILOSOPHICAL SERIES.

APARTMENTS.

The apartments are two, beside the Preparation Room.

THE FIRST APARTMENT

is styled the Chapter Room, and is hung with blue hangings, sprinkled with stars of gold; it is lighted from the East by the triple interlaced triangle, with the sun in the centre, in full blaze.

Behind the curtain that conceals the platform in the East should be a fine representation, by scenic effect, of the New Jerusalem—a square city, suspended in the clouds, and represented as descending from the heavens to the earth by slowly unrolling or lowering the same. The city is represented surrounded by a halo; it has twelve gates of pearl—three on each side—and at each gate an angel, with a name written on his crown, which are the names of the twelve tribes of the children of

Israel. Through the city flows a river, on either side of which is a flourishing tree, bearing twelve fruits, answering to the twelve precious stones in the Grand Pontiff's breastplate.

Under this movable painting is a representation of the city of Jerusalem in ruins; and in it a serpent, with three heads, in chains, as if about to be crushed by the descending celestial city.

An empty salver is stationed in the centre of the Chapter-room.

THE SECOND APARTMENT

is a plain dark room, with a portion divided off by a dropped curtain; in the room, a single chair.

OFFICERS, AND THEIR DECORATIONS.

Thrice Potent (wearing a breastplate with twelve precious stones).
Warden.
Orator.
Senior Deacon.
Junior Deacon.
Master of Ceremonies.
Captain of the Guard.

All the officers and Grand Pontiffs wear long white robes; as also a *fillet* of sky-blue satin round the forehead, having twelve golden stars embroidered thereon.

Order—A broad crimson sash, edged with white, with twelve silver stars on the front of the same, and worn from the left shoulder to the right hip.

Jewel—A golden parallelogram, with the Greek Alpha on one side and the Omega on the other.

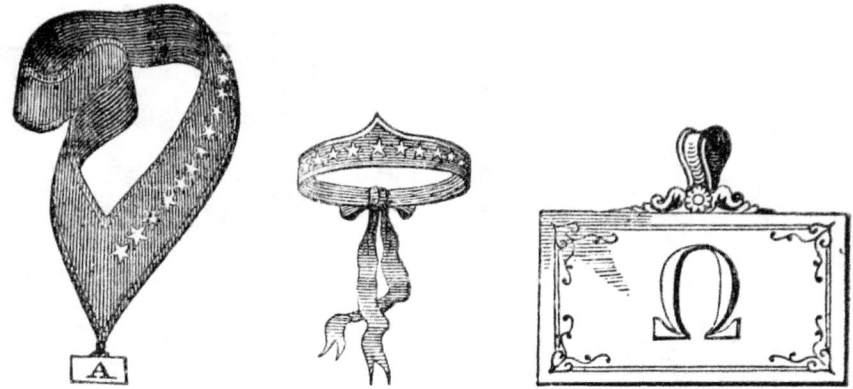

The Grand Pontiffs style each other "Faithful" or "True Brothers."

Battery—• • • • • • • • • • •

The following is the arrangement of the Chapter at the commencement of a

RECEPTION.

The Chapter-room is hung in black, and the altars are draped; all the brethren are robed in black; the sun is turned to blood.

   *   *   *   *   *

HYMN.

HANDEL.

No longer for men's sorrow groan—
  Their sin, their shame, their tears—
But still and stately past God's throne
  March onward—banish fears.
The sun is radiant in the sky,

  The earth, in regal state,
Waits but the "Hallelujah" cry
  That opes the Holy Gate;

And ancient time waits but the Light
    That lifts the fearful pall;
Then sin no more the world shall blight,
    And Good shall conquer all.

    *   *   *   *   *

PRAYER.

T∴ P∴ O thou dread, eternal, and most merciful Being, who alone canst aid thy servants in their mighty task of battling against the evils of this world, in expelling *ignorance* and *intolerance*—hear our prayer.

Seven Breth∴ Hear our prayer.

T∴ P∴ Thou who dost ever listen to the breathing, burning prayer of justice and of truth, guide thine erring children in the paths of righteousness, and teach them to shun all *injustice* and *superstition*—oh! hear our prayer.

Seven Breth∴ Hear our prayer.

T∴ P∴ We humbly pray thee, that thou wilt also imbue our hearts with the true light, that dark *ingratitude, indolence,* and *intemperance* may find no shelter there; that the hallowed spirit of our Maker may hold dominion over our souls, while instructing others; that they may be in like manner imbued with the Holy Spirit, and may successfully struggle against the demons of darkness and perdition. Against all such, Father of light and life, hear our prayer.

Seven Breth∴ Hear our prayer.

T∴ P∴ Heavenly Father, in the earnestness of our prayer, let now this awful embodiment of woe and the emblem of foul evils pass from us, for we know without prayer we cannot drive from our hearts those demons of the soul's destruction.

Change, O heavenly Father, change the spirit within us! Teach us what is good! teach us thyself, and may we understand! Let evil give place to good, as we now pledge our vows henceforth, as true and devoted Pontiffs, to devote ourselves, our hearts and hands, to the cause of truth and justice as against all the evils of the world. In this, our vow, hear our prayer.

Seven Breth∴ Hear our prayer.

T∴ P∴ And now, unto the Great Jehovah be all praise, and honor, and glory; and may we all say, Amen.

Seven Breth∴ Amen.

*   *   *   *   *

The Chapter is now arranged with the blue hangings and stars of gold; the sun is changed to its bright appearance; and the curtain in the East is drawn aside, displaying a large gold cross with a white rose upon it, placed on a prominence on the staging.

*   *   *   *   *

GRAND PONTIFF.

HYMN.

Unto God all praise be given,
Sin and sorrow forth are driven;
Celestial goodness fills our soul,
And Truth alone our hearts control.

Pontiffs, clad in white array,
   Seek to journey in thy way;
While virtues guide their erring feet,
   And mirrored Truth their prayers repeat.

Life-giving Cross can now be placed
   With virtues, knights have ever graced,
Within the East, the source of light,
   While paeans are sung by angels bright.

PRAYER.

O Heavenly Father, source of all intelligence and goodness, we appear before thee clothed in white garments, symbolic of the purity of our hearts, and of that beneficence and virtue we would crave from an all-merciful Providence—grant our prayer.

Omnes. Grant our prayer.

T∴ P∴ Give us *Faith,* that we shall see the New Jerusalem, that we may receive thy commendation for our works, and join in singing with the innumerable throng that surrounds thy throne, Holy, holy, holy is the Lord God of Sabaoth!

Omnes. Grant our prayer.

T∴ P∴ Give us *Hope* for the salvation of the soul, and aid us in the struggle for the perfection of our intelligence, and in the advancement of man toward a true understanding of thy will.

Omnes. Grant our prayer.

T∴ P∴ Fill our souls with the love of God and of a just appreciation of our fellow-man. May the immensity of thy love, and thy care even of the falling sparrow, imbue our hearts with never-failing *Charity.*

Omnes. Grant our prayer.

T∴ P∴ By the Mystic Rose and Cross, by the power of thy Word, as thou art the Alpha and Omega, grant us wisdom and the exercise of justice, and fill our hearts with gratitude to our Maker for all his goodness to us.

Omnes. Grant our prayer.

* * * * *

INVESTITURE.

This Robe of white linen with which I now invest you is emblematical of that equity and purity which should characterize one who is consecrated to the service of Truth; and reminds us also of the vesture of the one hundred forty and four thousand who refused to wear the mark of the beast on their foreheads; for it is so written, They shall walk with me in white, for they are worthy; he that overcometh, the same shall be clothed in white raiment, and I will not blot out his name out of the Book of Life, but I will confess his name before my Father and before his angels.

This Cordon of crimson, bordered with white, teaches you that the zeal and ardor of a Knight and Pontiff ought to be set off by the greatest purity of morals and perfect charity and beneficence: the twelve stars upon it, and upon the fillet, allude to the twelve gates of the new city.

This Fillet is the peculiar emblem of your Pontificate; and as the slightest contact with earth will soil its spotless purity, remember that so the least indiscretion will soil the exalted character you have now voluntarily assumed.

Receive this Jewel, and let the letters upon it—the first and last of the Greek and Hebrew alphabets—remind you of him who was from the beginning, and ever shall be—the Alpha and the Omega, the First and the Last—on whose promises we rely with perfect confidence; in whose mercy and goodness we implicitly trust, and for the fulfilment of whose wise purposes we are content to wait.

*   *   *   *   *

LECTURE.

O. My brother, the true Mason labors for the benefit of those who come after him, as well as for the advancement and improvement of his race. That is a poor ambition which contains itself within the limits of a single life. All men who deserve to live desire to survive their funerals, and to live afterward in the good that they have done mankind, rather than in the marble of men's memories. Most men desire to leave some work behind them that may outlast their own day and generation: that is an instinctive impulse given by God, and is often found in the rudest human heart—the surest proof of the soul's immortality and of the fundamental difference between men and the wisest brutes. To plant the tree that, after we are dead, shall shelter our children, is as natural as to love the shade of those our fathers planted. The rudest unlettered husbandman, painfully conscious of his own inferiority, will toil and stint himself, to be enabled to educate his child, that he may walk in a higher sphere of usefulness in this world.

*   *   *   *   *

We build slowly and destroy swiftly. Our ancient brethren who built the temples at Jerusalem, with myriad blows felled, hewed, and squared the cedars, and quarried the stones, and carved the intricate ornaments which were to compose the temple: by stone after stone, with the combined efforts and long toil of Apprentices, Fellow Crafts, and Masters, the walls arose; slowly the roof was framed and fashioned; and many years elapsed before at length the building stood finished, all fit and ready for the worship of God, gorgeous in the sunny splendors of Palestine. So they were built. A single motion of the arm of a rude, barbarous Assyrian, or drunken Roman or legionary Goth of Titus, moved by a senseless impulse of the brutal will, flung in the blazing brand; and with no further human agency, a few short hours sufficed to consume and melt the temple to a smoking mass of black and unsightly ruin.

Be patient, therefore, my brother, and wait. The issues are with God, to do if right belongs to us.

Therefore faint not, my brother, nor be weary in well-doing; be not discouraged at men's apathy, nor disgusted with their follies, nor tired of their indifference. Care not for returns and results, but see only what there is to do, and do it, leaving the result to God.

Sworn Knight of Justice, Truth, and Tolerance—good Knight and true—Grand Pontiff—be patient, and work.

The hour is accomplished.

Transmutation from Gnostic Talisman to Masonic Symbols.

"FREEMASONRY is a moral order, instituted by virtuous men, with the praiseworthy design of recalling to our remembrance the most sublime truths in the midst of the most innocent and social pleasures, founded on liberality, brotherly love, and charity."—ARNOLD'S *Dutch Dictionary*.

"WITH the exception of Christianity, I know of no other institution in which benevolence so pure, and philanthropy so disinterested, are taught in obedience to the command of God; nor where, but in the gospel, the social and moral duties are enforced by such awful sanctions as in the Lodges of the brotherhood."

REV. DR. DALCHO.

TWENTIETH DEGREE.

Grand Master of all Symbolic Lodges.

ARGUMENT.

The duties, powers and privileges of a Master in opening and closing a Lodge and conducting the work are herein defined. The right of supervision over subordinates, the personal representation of specific virtues, the definition of titles, etc., are also herein designated; and the true position and relationship of the officers to each other are given.

Further, that the right to govern in a Lodge is not only that acquired by a formal selection through the suffrages of the brethren, and a subsequent installation, but by the power of Masonic intelligence attained through patient labor and the study of Masonic law, and of the true understanding and ability to teach the tenets, doctrines, and symbolic legends of the Order. Exemplification is given in brief, but much important instruction of the true manner of conferring degrees in the Ancient and Accepted Scottish Rite is impressed upon the candidate ; and he is charged, as a Master of all Symbolic Lodges, to preserve Masonry in its primitive purity.

GRAND MASTER OF ALL SYMBOLIC LODGES;

OR,

MASTER AD VITAM.

THE TWENTIETH GRADE OF THE ANCIENT AND ACCEPTED SCOTTISH RITE, AND THE SECOND DEGREE OF THE HISTORICAL AND PHILOSOPHICAL SERIES.

THE APARTMENT, AND ITS DECORATIONS.

But one apartment is needed, and the assembly is styled a Lodge; the hangings are blue and gold. In the East is a throne, ascended by nine steps, and is surmounted by a canopy. Over the East, lighting the Lodge, is a glory surrounding a triangle, in the centre of which are the words "*Fiat lux*." In the centre of the room is the triangular altar, on which rest a Bible, Square, Compass, Sword, and Mallet. The altar has three columns about it, forming a triangle, on which are these words: on that in the East, "TRUTH;" on that in the West, "JUSTICE;" on that in the South, "TOLERATION."

The rough and smooth ashlars and working-tools of a Symbolic Lodge are disposed about the apartment. The Lodge is lighted by nine lights of yellow wax, in a candlestick with nine branches, placed between the altar and the South; the lights are arranged in three triangles, one within the other.

OFFICERS, ETC.

Venerable Grand Master is stationed in the East.
Senior Warden " " West.
Junior Warden " " South.
Orator " " North.
Treasurer is stationed as in a Symbolic Lodge.
Secretary " " "
Senior Deacon " " "
Junior Deacon " " "

Hospitaller is stationed to the left of Senior Warden.

A Lodge cannot be opened with less than nine members.

The brethren are sometimes termed Grand Masters.

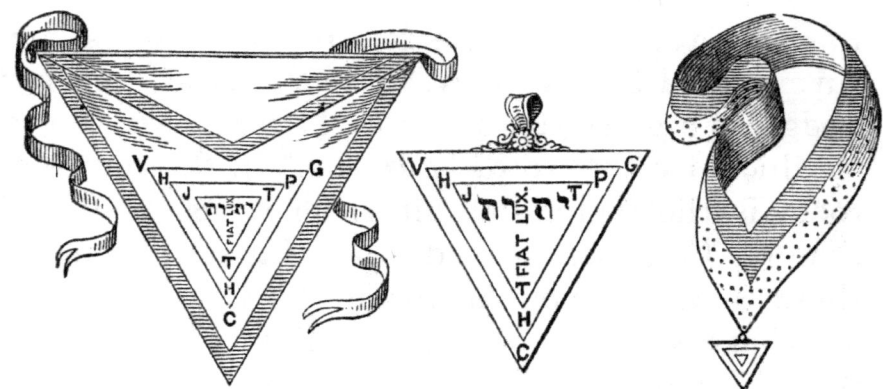

Apron—Yellow, bordered and lined with blue; in the centre of the area are three equilateral triangles, one within the other, with the initial letters of the nine great lights in the corners, arranged as follows: At the apex of the outer triangle, the letter C; at the right-hand corner above, G; at the left-hand corner, V; at the apex of the middle triangle, H; and at the right and left hand corners, P and H; at the apex of the inner triangle, the letter T, and at the right and left hand corners, T and J. In the centre of the inner triangle is the Tetragrammaton, and across it, from below upward, the words "*Fiat lux.*"

Cordon—A broad sash of yellow and blue, passing from the left shoulder to the right hip.

Jewel—Of gold; upon it the triangles, letters, and words, as upon the area of the Apron.

Battery—• •—•.

RECEPTION.

*   *   *   *   *

INVESTITURE.

The Apron, my brother, with which I now invest you, is triangular in shape, as indeed are all the aprons used in this Order. It is unnecessary to state to you that its form relates to the fourth great light, which reminds us of the Deity and his attributes; the yellow relates to the superiority of the grade, while the blue border and lining is the emblem of Truth, which encompasses it; the triple triangle on the area exhibits the threefold power of God, and their angles the nine great lights, with the initial letter of each in the respective corners; the Tetragrammaton, crossed by the words, "*Fiat lux,*" in the centre of the triangle, needs no explanation.

The Cordon is yellow and blue, for reasons already set forth in describing the apron.

The Jewel, also, is described by the representation on the area of the apron.

*   *   *   *   *

I now present you with this Gavel, as a symbol of a Grand Master of all Symbolic Lodges of our Order: remembering you are a Master *Ad Vitam,* or for life—that is, during your mortal existence and your correct Masonic deportment in life—you are entitled to assume the gavel in all Symbolic Lodges of the Ancient and Accepted Rite, providing there are none present superior to you in rank; but never fail to keep in mind the three requisites of a Master —Toleration, Justice, and Truth. As the presiding officer of a Lodge, it will be your particular duty to dispense light and knowledge to the brethren. That duty is not performed—nor is that which the old charges require, that, at opening and closing, the Master shall give, or cause to be given a lecture, or part of a lecture, for the instruction of the brethren —by asking and receiving the answers to three or four merely formal and trivial questions. On the contrary, that duty is far higher and more important; and it behooves the Master to be prepared to perform it. Nor should any one accept the office of Master, until, by acquaintance and familiarity with the history, morals, and philosophy of Masonry, he is fitted to enlighten and instruct his brethren. That you may ever remember that duty, you will now, under the direction of the Senior Warden, proceed symbolically to perform it, by restoring to us the splendor of our nine great lights in Masonry.

*   *   *   *   *

LECTURE.

The true Mason, my brother, is a practical philosopher, who, under religious emblems, in all ages adopted by wisdom, builds, upon plans traced by nature and reason, the moral edifice of knowledge. Masonry and Philosophy, without being one and the same thing, have the same object, and propose to themselves the same end—the worship of the Great Architect of the Universe.

As Grand Master of all Symbolic Lodges, it is your especial duty to aid in restoring Masonry to its primitive purity.

You have become an instructor. Masonry long wandered in error. Instead of improving, it degenerated from its primitive simplicity. Less than two hundred years ago its organization was simple and altogether moral; its emblems, allegories, and ceremonies easy to be understood.

*   *   *   *   *

Innovators and inventors overturned that primitive simplicity. Ignorance engaged in the work of making degrees, and trifles, and gewgaws, and pretended mysteries, absurd or hideous, usurped the place of Masonic truth Oaths, out of all proportion with their object, shocked the candidate, and then became ridiculous, and were wholly disregarded. Acolytes were exposed to tests, and compelled to perform acts, which, if real, would have been abominable, but being mere chimeras, were preposterous, and excited contempt. Eight hundred degrees of one kind and another were invented. Infidelity, Hermeticism, Jesuitry, were taught under the mask of Masonry. The rituals of the regular Orders, copied and imitated by ignorant men, became nonsensical and trivial. Candidates were made to degrade themselves, and to submit to insults not tolerable to a man of spirit and honor. It has even been seriously questioned whether, notwithstanding the beautiful order and systematic arrangement of the degrees in the Ancient and Accepted rite—free as they are from all incongruities, and perfect as the lessons are in the teachings of the various virtues—the number might not advantageously have been reduced, and thus Masonry have been simplified.

In the heterogeneous mass of over eight hundred degrees called Masonry, was found Judaism and chivalry, superstition and philosophy, philanthropy and insane hatred, a pure morality and unjust and illegal revenge, strongly mated, and standing hand in hand within the temples of peace and concord; and the whole system was one grotesque commingling of incongruous things and fine conceptions, overlaid and disfigured by absurdities engendered by ignorance, fanaticism, and senseless mysticism.

And empty and sterile pomp, with lofty titles arbitrarily assumed, and to which the inventors had not condescended to attach any explanation that should acquit them of the folly of assuming temporal rank, power, and titles of nobility, made the world laugh and the initiate feel ashamed.

Some titles we retain; but they have with us meanings entirely consistent with the spirit of equality which is the foundation and peremptory law of its being—of all Masonry. The Knight, with us, is he who devotes his hand, his heart, his brain to the science of Masonry, and professes himself the sworn soldier of Truth. The Prince is he who aims to be chief *(princeps)*—first or leader—among his equals, in virtue and good deeds. The Sovereign is he who, one of an order whose members are all sovereigns, is supreme only because the law and constitutions are so which he administers, and by which he, like every brother, is governed. The titles, Puissant, Potent, Wise, and Venerable, indicate that power of virtue, intelligence, and wisdom, which those ought to strive to attain who are placed in high office by the suffrages of their brethren; and all our other titles and designations have an esoteric meaning, consistent with modesty and equality, and which those who receive them should fully understand.

As Master of a Lodge, it is your duty to instruct your brethren that the degrees are all so many constant lessons, teaching the lofty qualifications which are required of those who claim them, and not merely idle gewgaws, worn in ridiculous imitation of the times when the nobles and priests were masters, and the people slaves; and that in all true Masonry, the Knight, the Pontiff, the Prince, and the Sovereign are but the first among their equals; and the Cordon, the Clothing, and the Jewel, but symbols and emblems of the virtues required of all good Masons.

As Master of a Lodge, you will be exceedingly careful that no candidate, in any degree, be required to submit to any degradation whatever, as has been too much the custom in some of the degrees; and take it as a certain and inflexible rule, to which there is no exception, that Masonry requires of no man anything to which a knight and gentleman cannot honorably, and without feeling outraged or humiliated, submit.

The degrees of the Ancient and Accepted rite form a connected system of moral, religious, and philosophical instruction: sectarian of no creed, it has been deemed not improper to use the old allegories based on occurrences detailed in the Hebrew and Christian books, and drawn from the ancient mysteries of Egypt, Persia, Greece, India, the Druids, and the Essenes, as vehicles to communicate the great Masonic truths—as it has used the legends of the Crusades and the ceremonies of the order of knighthood.

The Ancient and Accepted rite of Masonry has now become, what Masonry at first was meant to be —a teacher of great truths, inspired by an upright and enlightened reason, a firm and constant wisdom, and an affectionate and liberal philanthropy.

We teach the truth of none of the legends we recite. They are to us but parables and allegories, involving and enveloping Masonic instruction, and vehicles of useful and interesting information. They teach us wisdom, and the folly of endeavoring to explain to ourselves that which we are not capable of understanding: we reproduce the speculations of the Philosophers, the Kabbalists, the Mystagogues, and the Gnostics. Every one being at liberty to apply our symbols and emblems as he thinks most consistent with truth and reason, and with his own faith, we give them such an interpretation only as may be accepted by all. Our degrees may be conferred in France or Turkey; at Pekin, Ispahan, Rome, or Geneva; upon the subject of an absolute government or the citizen of a free State; upon sectarian or theist. To honor the Deity, to regard all men as our brethren and equally beloved by the Supreme Creator of the universe, and to make himself useful to society and himself by his labor, are its teachings to its initiate in all the degrees.

* * * * * *

"Oh! that Temple of God, from the House of the Past,
    Shineth down o'er the centuried years;
And my heart, through the veil of the mysteries vast,
    The voice of King Solomon hears,
Asking me, with the sign of a Master—
    Why my soul no Temple rears!
With the Three Great Lights ever shining above,
    And the tools of my craft at hand—
Why I build no fabric of prayerful love,
    With the arch of a lifetime spann'd;
And the wings of embracing cherubs,
    Overbrooding its altars grand!

"Oh! the House of the Lord that Our Lives might raise
    How it gleams from our fair Youth-time:
How its manifold arches and architraves blaze
    Through the wilderness dust of our Prime—
Yet our years, when they moulder to ashes,
    Behold but its wrecks sublime!
For the House that we build in a lifetime's length,
    From the midst of our worldly din,
Hath no Jachin and Boaz, established in strength,
    And no Holy of Holies within;
And we bear up no Ark of the Covenant,
    From out of our Desert of Zin.

* * * * *

"Oh! the Cedars of Lebanon grow at our door,
    And the quarry is sunk at our gate;
And the ships out of Ophir, with golden ore,
    For our summoning mandate wait;
And the Word of a Master Mason
    May the House of our Soul create!
While the Day hath light let the light be used,
    For no man shall the Night control!
"Or ever the silver cord be loosed,
    'Or broken the golden bowl,'
May we build King Solomon's Temple
    In the true Masonic Soul!"

TWENTY-FIRST DEGREE.

Noachite, or Prussian Knight.

ARGUMENT.

WHOSOEVER hath been wronged by the great, or oppressed by the powerful; whosoever hath been unjustly accused, or his household outraged; whosoever hath fallen into the hands of corrupt judges; whosoever hath suffered by bribery or extortion; let him come freely forward and prefer his complaint, and right shall be done him by the Grand Chapter of Prussian Knights, from whose judgment there is no appeal;—coming from the North and the South, the East and the West, to hear the complaints of the oppressed, judge the guilty, and teach men how to be free.

As Knight and Mason, it is our bounden duty to shield and protect the innocent, as it is to assist the distressed; and that, while rendering justice, we remember our vows, believing all guiltless until convicted; and yet, while it is the obligation that formally makes a Mason, a violation of that vow by an overt guilty or wilful act dissolves the knot of our alliance, and, without the form of trial, we cease to be of the Brotherhood.

Whatever be our rank, if we wilfully err, we have no claims upon a brother or the Order, either in sustaining us in that error —whatever may be its advantages—or in relieving us from its consequences.

NOACHITE, OR PRUSSIAN KNIGHT.

THE TWENTY-FIRST GRADE OF THE ANCIENT AND ACCEPTED SCOTTISH RITE, AND THE THIRD DEGREE OF THE HISTORICAL AND PHILOSOPHICAL SERIES.

THE CHAPTER—ITS DECORATIONS, ETC.

Bodies of this degree are styled GRAND CHAPTERS.

A Grand Chapter must be held in a retired place, on the night of the full moon, in each lunar month. The place is lighted by a large window or opening, so arranged as to admit the rays of the moon, the only light allowed, at as early an hour of the night as practicable.

The presiding officer sits facing the moonlight. He is styled "Lieutenant Commander." The Commander is unknown to the members. The other officers are—the Warden of the North, the Warden of the South, the Orator, styled "Knight of Eloquence," the Secretary, styled "Knight of the Chancery," the Treasurer, styled "Knight of the Finances," the Master of Ceremonies, the Warder, who acts as Captain of the Guards, and the Standard Bearer, who stands at the right hand of the Lieutenant Commander. The Knights are styled "Prussian Knight-Masons."

The *dress* is entirely black, except the gloves and apron; with sword and spurs.

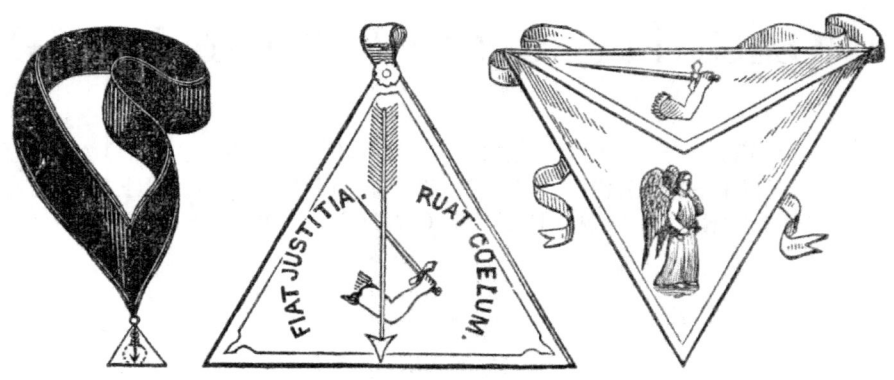

The *order* is a broad black ribbon, worn from right to left; and the *jewel* is a golden triangle traversed by an arrow, point downward, suspended from the collar. On the jewel is an arm upraised, holding a naked sword, and around it the motto, "FIAT JUSTITIA, RUAT CŒLUM." The *apron* and *gloves* are yellow.

On the upper part of the apron is an arm, naked and upraised, holding a naked sword; and under it a human figure, erect, with wings, the forefinger of his right hand on his lips, and the other arm hanging by his side, holding a key in the left hand—being the Egyptian figure of Silence.

The blazonry of this degree is: 1st. *Azure,* a moon *argent,* surrounded with stars *or;* 2d. *Sable,* an equilateral triangle traversed by an arrow *or.*

The statutes of the Order forbid holding a Table Lodge.

Battery—• • •

RECEPTION.

* * * * *

Dost thou agree and promise that thou wilt be just and righteous, and in all things strive to emulate that Patriarch from whom we take the name of Noachites; who, alone with his family, was found worthy to be saved, when God destroyed mankind with the Deluge?

Dost thou promise that thou wilt be neither haughty nor vain-glorious; nor obsequious to the great, nor insolent to thy inferiors?

Dost thou promise that thou wilt be humble and contrite before the Deity; and ever bear in mind the fate of Phaleg and his followers, who endeavored to build a tower whereby they might climb beyond the reach of another Deluge, and defy the omnipotence of God?

Dost thou promise, as a member of this Tribunal, to give righteous judgment only, against all persons whomsoever; to be impartial between the high and the low; to be cautious and slow to determine, and prompt to execute; to smite the oppressor and the wrong-doer, and protect the widow, the orphan, the poor, and the helpless; to be swayed neither by bribe nor fear, nor favor nor affection; and still to temper justice with mercy, remembering that there is no man who doth not err and sin?

* * * * *

HISTORY.

The Knights of this Order originally united themselves together in the times of the Crusades; when, in consequence of the general disorder that prevailed all over Europe, and the multitude of estates and titles left to be disputed, wrong and violence went unrebuked, and became superior to the law. Composed at first of a few Masons, who had learned the rules of justice from the teachings of the Order, they exerted only a moral influence, owing to the purity of their lives and the justice of their opinions. They called themselves Noachite Masons; because they strove to imitate the primeval justice and purity of the beloved Patriarch. Finding that where their influence was most needed, mere advice and exhortation, addressed to the rude Barons and haughty rapacious priesthood, had no effect, they assumed the power to enforce performance of their judgments; and through the common people and a multitude of the poorer Knights who had found the benefit of their protection, and who revered their justice, they found a ready means of compelling obedience and inflicting punishment. Their number was limited, and their persons unknown. They met always at night, when the moon was full; and the more perfectly to remain unknown, allowed no light but hers.

Lest their own members should become haughty and vain-glorious on account of the mysterious power they possessed, they inculcated humility, and incessantly reminded each other of that haughtiness and pride which led the descendants of Noah to erect the Tower of Babel; and of the miseries of Phaleg, who suggested the idea of its building, and who therefor condemned himself to a rigorous penitence, and buried himself in the vast solitudes of Northern Germany, in what is now the kingdom of Prussia, where he is said to have builded a temple in the shape of a Delta, and therein to have passed his life, imploring the mercy of God.

The Order, in several parts of Germany, was popularly known as the Holy Vehme, and even kings trembled at its judgments. It continued to exercise its vast powers until law and civilization rendered them no longer necessary; but the Order still continued to exist, deciding Masonic controversies only and inflicting no other than Masonic punishments. As it continued more particularly to flourish in Prussia, the members took the name of Prussian Knights.

The Chapters of this degree are no longer tribunals to try and punish for offences committed without the limits of Masonry. They claim no jurisdiction except between their own members, and exercise none between those of the inferior degrees, except by their consent. And in all their judgments it is their rule and duty to judge of other men's motives and actions by the same rules by which they judge their own; to believe others equally as honest in their views as themselves; and to find for the conduct of others the same excuses that they find for their own; for this alone is justice. And they prove their humility by their tolerance; which causes them to believe that their opinions are as likely to be erroneous as the opinions of others to the contrary, and that the Deity alone knows what is truth.

They meet only on the nights of the full moon, and allow no other light than hers, because such was the ancient custom of the Order, derived from the mysteries of Ceres and the old worship of Isis. In the heavenly host they admire the work of the Supreme Creator, and the universal laws of harmony and motion—the first two laws that emanated from God.

TWENTY-SECOND DEGREE.

Knight of the Royal Axe.

ARGUMENT.

THE object held in view in the degree of Knight of the Royal Axe, is to teach all men that labor is honorable, and that we should strive to improve the condition of the toiling millions. We are all workmen in our several vocations, whether in actual labor, preparing plans for the laborers, or studying the calculations of Philosophy, the advancement of civilization and knowledge, the destruction of ignorance and barbarism.

KNIGHT OF THE ROYAL AXE;
OR,
PRINCE OF LIBANUS.
THE TWENTY-SECOND GRADE OF THE ANCIENT AND ACCEPTED SCOTTISH RITE, AND THE FOURTH DEGREE OF THE HISTORICAL AND PHILOSOPHICAL SERIES.

LODGES, OFFICERS, DECORATIONS, ETC.

Bodies of this degree are styled Colleges. There are two apartments. The first is a plain room, of moderate dimensions, without any fixed number of lights, and prepared to represent a workshop on Mount Lebanon. The second is hung with red, and lighted by 36 lights, arranged by sixes, and each six by twos. It represents the Council-room of the Round Table. In the centre of the room is such a table, around which the brethren sit. The altar is in the East, and upon it are an open Bible, the square and Compasses, and an Axe.

The officers are a Chief Prince, who is styled "Thrice Puissant," a Senior and a Junior Grand Warden, a Master of Ceremonies, and Captain of the Guard.

The *order* is a broad, rainbow-colored ribbon, worn as a collar. It may be worn as a sash, from right to left, and is lined with purple. The jewel, suspended to the collar, is an axe and handle of gold. On the top or end of the handle are the letters נ and ש; on one side of the handle, ל, and on the other צ; on one side of the blade א ב ר ז נ and ע; and on the other, ב א מ י ה ש.

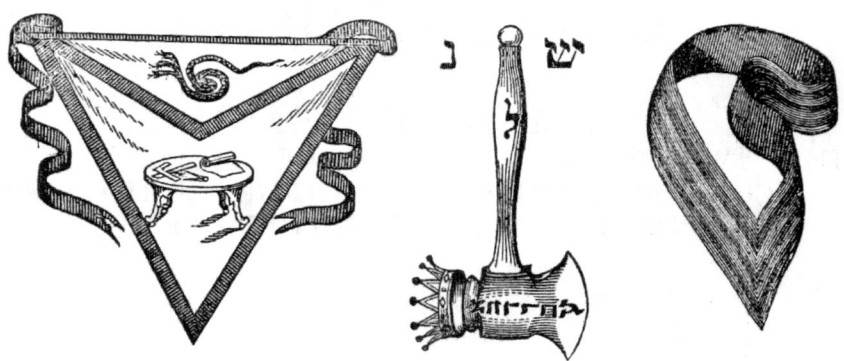

The letters on the top are the initials of the names of Noah and Solomon; those on the handle, of Libanus and Tsidun; those on one side of the blade, of Adoniram, Cyrus, Darius, Zerubbabel, Nehemiah, and Ezra; and those on the other side, of Shem, Kham, Yapheth, Moses, Ahaliab, and Betselal.

The *apron* is white, lined and bordered with purple. On the middle a round table is embroidered, on which are mathematical instruments, and plans unrolled. On the flap is a serpent with three heads.

The *tracing-board* is a view of the mountains and forests of Lebanon, the summit of the mountain covered with snow; and of the Temple erected of its cedars and pines. It is in the form of an axe.

In the workshop the Senior Warden presides, and is styled "Master Carpenter." He and all the brethren wear frocks or blouses and aprons.

There is no particular alarm or battery in the workshop.

Battery—●●—●●—●●

OPENING.

* * * * *

PRAYER.

Thou who didst create the universe, and hast builded it in infinite magnificence, as thou art infinite in skill and wisdom, bless us in our daily labors, and prosper the work of our hands! Teach us and all men that labor is honorable! Improve the condition of the toiling millions! Teach the rich and the haughty compassion for those over whom they have control; and hasten the coming of the day when all men shall acknowledge the great truth, that to work well in our appointed sphere is the most acceptable prayer that man can offer up to thee. Amen!

RECEPTION.

* * * * *

HISTORY.

The Tsidunians or Phoenicians were ever ready to aid the Israelites in their holy enterprises. The tie between them was the mysteries, into which the principal persons of both nations were initiated; Moses having necessarily received them in Egypt, before he could marry the daughter of a priest of On. These mysteries, modified by Solomon, or perhaps at an earlier day by Joshua, or even Moses, to suit the genius and manners of the Jewish people, became Masonry, such as it was practised at the building of the Temple, and such as it has in part come down to us. Khūrūm, King of Tsur, in Phoenicia, and Khūrūm Abai, also a Phoenician and not a Jew, were likewise initiates; and hence the intimate connection between them and Solomon, as Masons. The people of Tsidun, a city of Phoenicia, were employed by Noah to cut cedars on Mount Libanus, of which to build the ark, under the superintendence of Japhet. His descendants repeopled Tsidun and Phoenicia, and procured and furnished the cedar from Lebanon to build the Ark of the Covenant; and at a later day his posterity, under Adon Khūrūm, cut in the same forests cedars for King Solomon; and at a time still later, they felled timber on the same mountains to construct the second temple.

Upon the same mountain they established Colleges of Artificers, like those in Etruria, and afterward at Rome; from which latter many deduce Masonry. But the Etrurians, who emigrated from Assyria to Egypt and afterward to Etruria—better known as the Hyksos, from Resen on the Tigris, or as the Shepherd Kings—carried with them the same mysteries, which went also with them into Phoenicia; and the Etrurian and Roman Colleges were in all respects like those of Mount Libanus. These artificers everywhere adored the Grand Architect of the

Universe, and had their signs and words by which to recognize each other. Solomon himself, whose wisdom necessarily gave him a true idea of the dignity of labor, built a palace on the mountain, to which he often repaired to inspect the progress of the work. The names of the Patriarchs who were the inspectors and conductors of the workmen on the mountain at different periods, are preserved in our passwords. The institution of Colleges upon Mount Libanus was perpetuated by the Druses, from whom the Crusaders obtained a knowledge of this degree.

When God in His eternal council conceived the thought of Man's creation, He called to Him the three ministers that continually waited upon the throne—Justice, Truth, and Mercy—and thus addressed them: 'Shall we make Man?' Justice answered: 'O God, make him not, for he will trample on Thy laws;' and Truth also answered: 'O God, make him not, for he will pollute Thy sanctuaries.' But Mercy, dropping on her knees and looking up through her tears, exclaimed: 'O my God, make him and I will watch over him with my care through the dark and dreary paths he will have to tread.' And God made Man, and said to him: 'O Man, thou art the child of Mercy—go and deal with thy brother.'"

COMMANDING COLORS OF THE VARIOUS SERIES OF DEGREES.

1st Series	—	Symbolic Degrees, 3d	—	Field, flag, and pennon, Blue			
2d	"	Ineffable	"	14th	"	"	Crimson.
3d	"	Historic	"	16th	"	"	Light green or Orange.
4th	"	Philosophic	"	18th	"	"	White sprinkled with Crimson.
5th	"	Historic and Philosophic Degrees,		29th—Field,			Purple.
6th	"	Chivalric		"	32d	"	White & Black.
Inspector-General,					33d	"	White.

All expulsions from the Rite by the Supreme Council or Ballustres of Offence, are *"published in red letter,"* and distributed to whom it may concern.

The *Book of Gold* contains the full record of the Supreme Council, and is sealed to all except members of the Council.

TWENTY-THIRD DEGREE.

―――――

Chief of the Tabernacle

ARGUMENT.

THIS degree is intimately connected with, and is preliminary to, that which immediately follows, called Prince of the Tabernacle. The form of the Tabernacle is distinctly defined, and the old sacerdotal ceremonies of the ancient temples described and portrayed, with useful explanation and instruction.

Unholy sacrilege and presumptuous interference with sacred ceremonies are forbidden and punished; and only those with hearts divested of all impurity, are commended in the performance of holy rites.

CHIEF OF THE TABERNACLE.

THE TWENTY-THIRD GRADE OF THE ANCIENT AND ACCEPTED SCOTTISH RITE, AND THE FIFTH DEGREE OF THE HISTORICAL AND PHILOSOPHICAL SERIES.

THE LODGE—ITS DECORATIONS, ETC.

Lodges in this degree are styled Courts.

The hangings are white, supported by red and black columns, by twos, placed at intervals, according to the taste of the architect. The Court represents an encampment of the Twelve Tribes, in the desert, near Sinai. The standards of the tribes, made after the following model,

are planted around the Court near the walls, in the following order:

In the East, that of Judah: the color of the standard being crimson, in stripes or waves; and the device a Lion, couchant, between a crown and sceptre.

Next to Judah, on the side toward the North, that of Issachar: color of the standard, greenish yellow; device, an Ass, couchant, between two burdens or packs.

Next to Judah, on the side toward the South, that of Zebulon: color, light green, and device a Ship.

Next toward the South, that of Simeon: color yellow; device, a naked Sword.

In the South, that of Reuben: color a brilliant crimson; device, a Man.

Next to Reuben, on the side toward the West, that of Gad: color, bluish green; device, a field covered with Stars.

Next toward the West, that of Manasseh: color variegated, like agate; device, a Vine running over a wall.

In the West, that of Ephraim: color variegated, like opal; device, a Bull.

Next toward the North, that of Benjamin: color, violet; device, a Wolf.

Next toward the North, that of Asher: color, blue; device, a Tree in full leaf.

In the North, that of Dan: color, that of the goldstone; device, an Eagle, holding a serpent in his beak.

Next to Dan, toward the East, that of Naphtali: color, bluish green; device, a female Deer running at speed.

In the centre of the Lodge is a representation, reduced in size, of the Tabernacle of Moses, described in Exodus,

Chapters 26 and 36, as nearly accurate as circumstances and the means of the Court will allow.

First comes the Court of the Tabernacle, which was a rectangular enclosure, 150 feet long from East to West (if the cubit be taken to have been 18 inches), and 75 feet wide, from North to South. It was formed (except the gate or entrance) by curtains of white linen, 7½ feet high, supported by pillars of acacia-wood, set in brass sockets, and with hooks and fillets of silver. There were of these pillars, 20 on the North side, 20 in the South, and 10 in the West. On the East, the white curtains on each side of the entrance measured 22½ feet, and were supported by three pillars on each side. The gate itself was 30 feet wide, formed by curtains of tapestry, of blue, scarlet, purple, and white linen thread, wrought with admirable skill in needlework.

Within the Court, the Tabernacle משכן, *Mishkan,* was set. It was a double tent, the foregoing word particularly applying to the inner curtains, and אהל *Ahel,* to the outer curtains of goat's hair. The Tabernacle is also termed מקדש *Mikdash,* or Sanctuary. It was constructed of curtains, woven of fine thread, of white linen, blue, purple, and scarlet, embroidered with cherubim.

The length of each curtain was twenty-three cubits or forty-two feet, and each was six feet in width. They were ten in number; and five of them were coupled or sewed together in one piece, and five in another; and these two were so arranged that they could be fastened together along their edges, by fifty loops on one edge of each, and fifty hooks of gold; so that "it should become one Tabernacle."

Over this Tabernacle was a Tent [אהל, *Ahel*] or cover, of cloth of goats' hair, composed of eleven curtains, each thirty cubits or forty-five feet long, and six feet wide. Of these, five were coupled together in one piece, and six in another; and the two pieces were so arranged, with fifty loops on one edge of each, and fifty hooks of brass, that they could be fastened together, "that it might be one."

*   *   *   *   *

No description of the shape of the tent is given; but in the East, and especially in Arabia, customs and fashions have not changed ; and a tent is now what it was in the days of Moses. Those now used in Arabia are of this model,

of an oblong shape, and eight or ten feet high in the middle. They vary in size, and have accordingly a greater or less number of poles to support them—from three to nine. And it is usual for one large tent to be divided into two or more apartments by curtains, for the different portions of the family.

The tents of the Bedaweens are not conical, as they are often represented in pictures, but have a roof edged with drop-curtains, or such curtains as might be made from the dark tanned skins of goats, hung around the eaves.

Below is a drawing of a Bedaween tent.

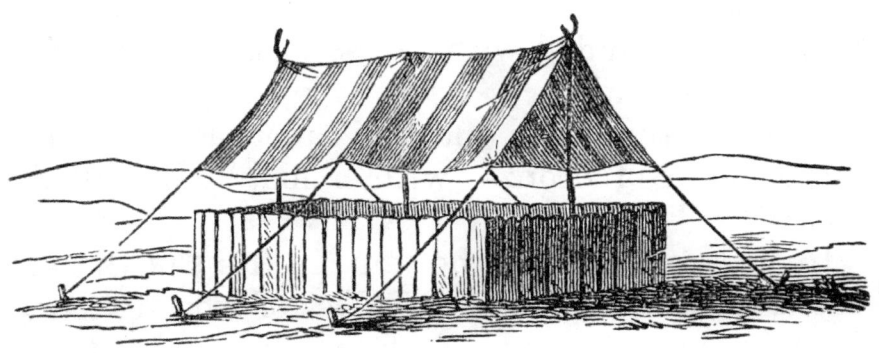

Thus the Tabernacle in the Court-room should represent a tent, oblong in shape, stretched upon a frame of poles and forks, one pole in the middle serving as a ridge-pole. Over this, hanging to the floor, on the North and South sides, and the rear or West, and seaching on top, on each side, to and over the ridgepole, should be two curtains, joining together by hooks and loops in the middle of the rear, of white, blue, scarlet, and purple linen or cotton thread woven together, and embroidered with cherubim, or animals with the bodies of lions, the feet of oxen, the faces of men, and the wings of eagles. Over this should be similar curtains of gray woollen stuff; and on top, as a covering, red morocco, and over that, tanned leather.

The hanging curtain at the mouth of the tent, and

the vail dividing the Tabernacle into two parts, should be as above described; as also should the enclosure of the Court, if not the fence.

The furniture of the Court is as follows:

In front of, and perhaps ten feet from the entrance of the Tabernacle, is the altar of sacrifice, made of white wood, hollow, and plated on top with brass. It is to be four and a half feet high, and seven and a half feet square, with projections in the shape of tongues of flame (called horns in the Bible) at each corner, standing upright. It is made to be carried by staves of light wood, banded with brass, passing through rings in two of the sides.

Between this altar and the Tabernacle is a laver or large basin of bronze, with a foot to it, filled with water.

In the front part of the tent, in front of the vail, on the North side, is the Table of the Presence or Shewbread. It is made of white wood, and is three and a half feet long, one and a half feet broad, and two and one-fourth feet high, the top covered with plates of brass, gilded, and with a gilded rim or border round its edge on the top. Below the top is a strip of wood four inches wide, with a similar rim or border round its lower edge. A little lower down, at equal distances from the top, is a ring, gold-plated, on each leg, through which gilded staves pass to carry it.

On this table are twelve small loaves of wheat bread, in two piles of six each, sprinkled with frankincense and salt; and a large bowl of pure wine.

On the south side of the tent, opposite the table, is the candelabrum, gilded, representing pure gold. It consists of an ornamented base, of a shaft rising out of it, and six arms, coming out by threes from two opposite sides of the shaft, each two arms equidistant from the central shaft, forming a semicircle, and all being in one line, and of equal height or level on top. On the summit of the central shaft, and on those of the six arms, are lamps, not candles, all in globular shades, but the central one being much the largest. These lamps are to be fed with pure olive-oil.

Before the middle of the vail, and in the outer part of the tent, is the altar of incense, eighteen inches square and three feet high, with flames or horns of brass at each corner, the top covered with a plate of yellow metal, imitating gold, with a rim of the same round it, and two gold rings on each of two opposite sides, below the rim, for gilded staves or rods to pass through, by which to carry it.

In the centre of the inner portion of the tent (the קרש קשים *Kadosh Kadoshim,* or Holy of Holies,) stands the Ark of the Covenant, of wood, three and three-fourth feet long, two and one-fourth feet broad, and two and one-fourth feet high, with short feet at each corner. It is plated within and without with brass, so as to appear like pure gold, and has round its upper edge a rim or cornice, gilded to represent gold. On the two longer sides, at the corners, are four brass rings, to receive the staves of wood, gilded, by which it is carried.

On the Ark is a lid, called the Expiatory (or Mercy-Seat), as long and wide as the Ark, and representing solid gold. At each end is, also, as of solid gold, a cherub, or winged figure of a female, each with two wings long enough to meet half-way between them, higher than their heads. Their heads should be bent down as though looking upon the Expiatory.

On the altar of incense are the roll of the Book of

the Law and a poniard; and on the Book of the Law, the Square and Compasses.

The presiding officer sits in the East, represents Aaron, and is styled "Most Excellent High Priest." The Wardens sit in the West, and represent his two sons, Eleazar and Ithamar, and are styled "Excellent Priests." The Orator, Secretary, and Treasurer sit on the East of the Tabernacle, the Master of Ceremonies on the West of it, the Captain of Guards on the South of it, and the Sentinel on the North. The other officers and members sit on the North, South, and West of it. All except the first three officers are styled "Worthy Levites."

The presiding officer wears a robe or gown, of pure white linen, reaching to the feet, fitting close to the body, with loose sleeves coming as low as the elbows—covering the shoulders, and closed round the neck. This is girded to the body, just under the breast, by a girdle four fingers broad, wound round and round the body from the breasts to the navel, and the ends hanging down to the ankles. The robe is embroidered with needlework, in different colors; and the girdle is of loosely woven white cotton, embroidered with flowers of blue, scarlet, and purple. Over the robe or gown is the "robe of the Ephod," an Egyptian tunic of blue stuff, woven in one piece, with an aperture for the neck in the middle of it, and apertures for the arms; without sleeves, large and loose, and reaching to the knees. Round the hem, at the bottom, is a fringe of blue, scarlet, and purple tassels, in the form of pomegranates, with a small gilded bell between each two; this is also tied round with a girdle, white, embroidered with blue, scarlet, and purple, and gold interwoven.

He wears also the Ephod, a short cloak with sleeves, of gold, blue, purple, scarlet, and fine linen thread, embroidered richly, and covering the shoulders, by shoulder pieces that unite the back and front parts, which are separate. On each shoulder of it is an agate, set in gold, and each having upon it six names of the tribes, according to precedence of birth. This Ephod has strings, that go out from each side, and tie to the body.

He also wears the breastplate or gorget, ten inches square, of the same sort of cloth as the Ephod, doubled so as to form a kind of pouch, to hold the Aurim and Themim. On its outside are twelve precious stones, in four rows, as they are named in Exodus xviii. 17—20; on each side of which is engraved the name of one of the tribes. This is fastened to the front of the Ephod by means of dark blue ribbons, tied in four rings of gold at the corners of the breastplate, and four that meet them on the ephod itself. The rings at the upper corners are on the inside of the breastplate, but those below are outside. There are also two other rings of gold, larger, at the upper corners, on the outside, from which cords of twisted gold-thread reach and fasten to the agates on the shoulders. And it is further fastened by a sash or girdle, of the same stuff as itself, to which the lower side is attached, and which is tied in front of the body, and hangs down to the lower edge of the Ephod.

The Urim or Aurim, and Thummim or Themim, carried in the pouch or breastplate, are small images of sapphire (or blue stone), of Re and Thmei, Light and Truth, in a sitting posture, each holding the tau cross.

The bonnet is a turban of fine white linen, circular, covering half the head, something like a crown, of thick linen swathes doubled round many times, and sewed together, surrounded by a linen cover, to hide the seams of the swathes. The mitre of the High-Priest is this turban, with another above it, of swathes of blue, embroidered, so that the whole is conical in shape. In front of the turban, on the forehead, is a plate of gold, extending from one ear to the other, fastened by strings tied behind, and also by a blue ribbon attached to the mitre; on which is engraved the inscription:

קרש ליהוה

KADOSH L'IHOH, "HOLY TO THE LORD!"

The two Wardens wear the same dress in all respects, except the breastplate, and the mitre, instead of which they wear the bonnet or turban of white linen.

The High-Priest and Wardens wear no apron. The other officers and members wear a white apron, lined with scarlet, and bordered with red, blue, and purple ribbons. In the middle is painted or embroidered the golden candelabrum with seven lights.

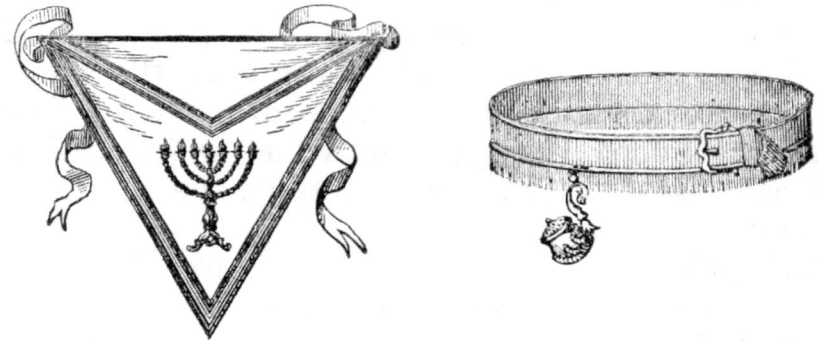

They also wear a red leather belt, fringed along the lower edge with gold, and edged with gold; from which hangs a small silver censer, or ornamented cup, with a long handle, the end whereof, on which the cup sits, is shaped like an open hand. This is also the form of the jewel of the degree.

For receptions there is also a dark apartment, with an altar in the centre, on which are placed a feeble light and three skulls. In front of the altar is a skeleton.

Battery—••—••—••—•.

RECEPTION.

* * * * *

1. Thus shalt thou say to the house of Jacob, and tell the children of Israel: Ye have seen what I did unto the Mitzrayim, and how I bare you on the wings of eagles, and brought you unto myself.

2. Now, therefore, if you will obey my voice indeed, and keep my covenant, then ye shall be a peculiar treasure unto me, above all people; for all the earth is mine.

3. And ye shall be unto me a kingdom of priests, and a holy nation. These are the words which thou shalt speak unto the children of Israel.

* * * * *

INVOCATION.

H∴ P∴ O mighty and inscrutable Being, for whose very self there is no name whatever, and even the ineffable word expresses a limitation of thy infinite essence! of whom all the deities of all the nations are but personifications of single attributes: we bow down unto thee as the simple absolute existence, that with a thought didst from thyself utter all the worlds! Eternal Father, of whose thought the universe is but a mode! Unchangeable! Coeval with time, and coextensive with space! whose laws of harmony, that thy will is, rule all the movements of the suns and worlds! Thou art the all: in thee all things exist. O guide and guard us, and lead us safely toward thee, that we faint not by the wayside, nor wander into the darkness like lost children. Amen. *All.* So mote it be!

*　　*　　*　　*　　*

LECTURE.

H∴ P∴ I accept and receive you, my brother, as a Levite and Chief of the Tabernacle, and consecrate and devote you henceforth to the service of the children of light; and I now invest you with the belt, jewel, and apron of this degree. The jewel, or censer of silver, is ever to remind you to offer up unceasingly to God the incense of good deeds and charitable actions, dictated by a pure and upright heart.

Josephus tells that the mixture of materials in the curtains of the Tabernacle, and the clothing of the priests, was not without design. "It served," he says, "as a symbol of the universe. For the scarlet seemed emblematical of fire; the fine linen, of the earth; the blue, of the air; and the purple, of the sea; two of them being thus compared for their color: the fine linen and the purple on account of their origin, as the earth produces the one, and the sea the other."

To us, in this degree, the white of the apron, its principal and chief color, is symbolical of the infinite beneficence of God; the blue, of his profound and perfect wisdom; the crimson, of his glory; and the purple, of his power.

The candelabrum with seven branches, upon the apron, wrought in gold, represents to us, as it represented to the ancient Hebrews, what were known in the earlier ages as the seven planets, or principal heavenly bodies: the Sun in the middle, with Mars, Jupiter, and Saturn on one side, and Venus, Mercury, and the Moon on the other. It also represents the seven archangels whom the Hebrews assigned to the government of those planets; Zerakhi-al, the Dawn, or Rising of God, to the Sun; Auri-al, the Light of God, to Mars; Gabari-al, the Strength of God, to Jupiter: Mayak-al, the Semblance of God, to Saturn; Khamali-al, the Mercy of God, to Venus; Raph-al, the Healing of God, to Mercury; and Tsaph-al, the Messenger of God, to the Moon: of whom Mayak-al, or Michael, was represented with the head of a lion; Auri-al, or Auriel, with that of an ox; Raph-al, or Raphael, with a human head and the body of a serpent; and Gabari-al, or Gabriel, with that of an eagle; and all of the seven being attributes and manifestations of Al, the great Semitic Nature-God of the ancient Patriarchs; as to whom, and these planets, and angels, and their connection with Masonry, you will be more fully instructed as you advance.

The number 7 is the sacred number in all theogonies and in all symbolisms. It is the spirit, assisted by all the elementary powers; the soul, served by nature; the Holy Empire (*Sanctum Regnum*), spoken of in the clavicules of Solomon. It reappears everywhere in the Hebrew writings and in the Apocalypse; and here, particularly, in the seven lamps of the candelabrum. Under the symbols of the seven planets which it represents, the ancients figured the seven virtues so peculiarly Masonic:

Faith, that aspiration toward the infinite, was represented by the Sun; Hope by the Moon; Charity, by Venus; Force (or Fortitude), always victor over rage and anger, by Mars; Prudence, by Mercury; Temperance, by Saturn; and Justice, by Jupiter (Tsaduc, the Just), conqueror of the Titans.

The world, the ancients believed, is governed by seven secondary causes; and these are the universal forces designated by Moses under the plural name Elohim, The Gods. These forces, analogous and contrary the one to the other, by their counter-action produce the equilibrium, and regulate the movements of the spheres. The Hebrews called them the Seven Great Archangels. The seven planets correspond with the seven colors of the prism, and the seven notes of the musical octave. The seven sacraments are also referred to in this great universal number of the Master Mason.

*   *   *   *   *

TWENTY-FOURTH DEGREE.

Prince of the Tabernacle

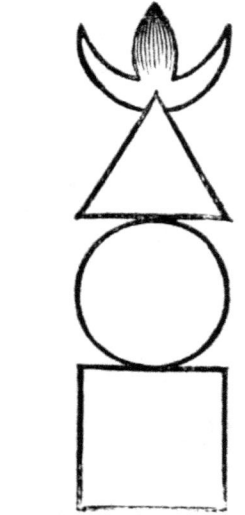

PERFECTED CREATION.

THE PRELIMINARY TRIALS OF EARTH, WATER, FIRE, AIR, ETHER.

ARGUMENT.

The degree of Prince of the Tabernacle illustrates the ceremonies of the Priests in the ancient Temples, and explains the esoteric meaning of their many avocations in equipping the Temple and sustaining their various sacerdotal duties. This degree is most intimately connected with, and should be considered a continuation of, that of the Chief of the Tabernacle. The especial duties of a Prince of the Tabernacle are to labor incessantly for the glory of God, the honor of his country, and the happiness of his brethren; to offer up thanks and prayers to the Deity in lieu of sacrifices of flesh and blood.

PRINCE OF THE TABERNACLE.

THE TWENTY-FOURTH GRADE OF THE ANCIENT AND ACCEPTED SCOTTISH RITE, AND THE SIXTH DEGREE OF THE HISTORICAL AND PHILOSOPHICAL SERIES.

THE COURT—ITS DECORATIONS, ETC.

The Hall consists of two apartments. The first, which is the smaller, adjoins the second, and is called the Vestibule, where the brethren clothe themselves. It is furnished at all points like a Master Mason's Lodge, except that instead of a printed Bible, a roll of parchment, representing the Book of the Law, lies on the altar, upon the Book of Constitutions; and that the letter ʼ is suspended in the East, instead of the G.

The second apartment is furnished in every respect like the principal apartment in the 23d degree, with these additions:

In the East is suspended the Pentagram, or Blazing Star, in the following shape, of vermilion, illuminated as a transparency:

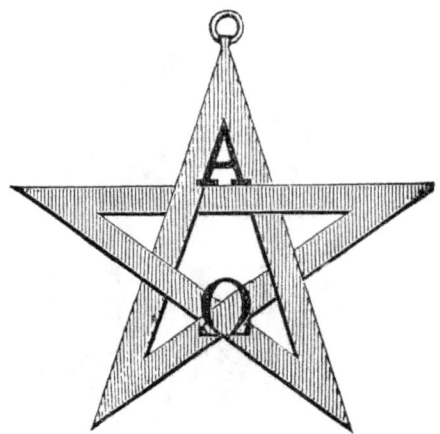

There are two sets of hangings around the room, one red and the other black.

On the table of shew-bread, in the Tabernacle, is a silver vessel containing perfumed oil.

OFFICERS AND CLOTHING.

The Assemblage is styled "The Court." The presiding officer represents Moses, and is styled "Most Puissant Leader." He sits in the East. Near him, on his right, is the second officer, who represents Eleazar, the High-Priest, the son of Aaron. He is styled "Most Excellent High-Priest," and wears the full-dress of his office, as described in the 23d degree. On the left of the Leader sits the third officer, clothed as the Priests in that degree, and representing Ithamar, the son of Aaron. He is styled "Excellent Priest."

The Orator represents the Puissant Prince Eliasaph, the son of Lael, of the house of Gershon, and sits in the West.

The Secretary represents the Puissant Prince Eliazaphan, the son of Uzziel, of the house of Kohath, and pits to the south of the Tabernacle.

The Treasurer represents the Puissant Prince Zuriel, the son of Abihael, of the house of Merari, and sits to the north of the Tabernacle.

The Expert represents Aholiab, and sits to the right of the Leader, in front.

The Assistant Expert represents Bezeleel, and sits to the right of the Orator, in front.

The Grand Master of Ceremonies represents Caleb, the son of Jephunneh, and sits facing the Leader in front of the Tabernacle.

The Grand Captain of the Guards represents Joshua, the son of Nun, and sits on the right side of the Tabernacle, facing the East.

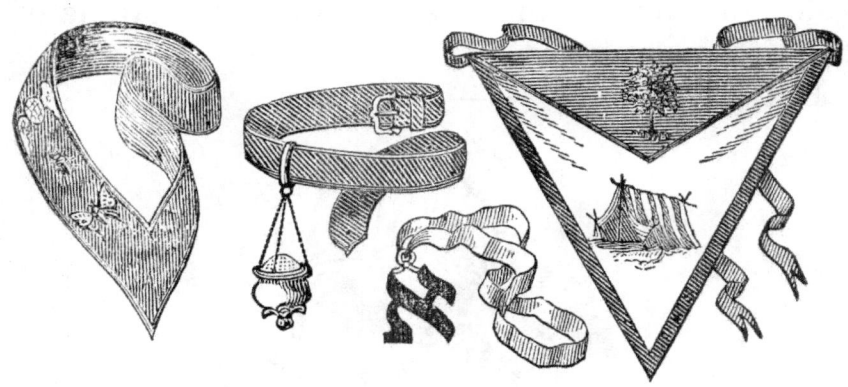

All the officers, except the Leader and Wardens, and all the other members, are styled "Levites;" and these officers and members all wear a turban of white muslin; a broad, watered scarlet ribbon, worn from right to left; a girdle of red leather, fringed below with gold, and edged with gold-lace, from which girdle a small silver censer is suspended. (*See 23d degree.*)

On the front of the ribbon are embroidered, in gold, a winged globe, and under it a scarabæus, under which is a brilliant butterfly; all symbols of immortality.

The *apron,* which is not worn by the first three officers, is of white lambskin, lined with scarlet, bordered with light green, and the flap with light blue. In the middle of the apron is printed a representation of an Arabian tent, in gold; and on the flap a representation of a myrtle-tree, of violet color.

The *jewel* is the letter א, suspended from a short collar of narrow, watered, violet-colored ribbon.

The Most Puissant Leader wears a tunic of blue silk, its collar decorated with rays of gold representing a glory, and the body of it sprinkled with stars of gold. On his head he wears the white turban, with a purple band round the forehead, embroidered with stars of gold; and also surmounted by a small triangle of gold, the apex downward.

Battery—••—••—••—•.

RECEPTION.

* * * * *

My brother, the initiate is he who possesses the lamp, the cloak, and the staff.

The lamp is reason enlightened by science; the cloak is liberty, or the full and entire possession of one's self, which isolates the sage from the currents of instinct; and the staff is the assistance of the occult and eternal forces of nature.

The lamp lights the past, the present, and the future, which are the three sides of the triangle. It burns with a threefold flame; the cloak is in three folds; and the staff is divided into three parts.

This number, nine, is that of the reflexes of the Deity, and expresses the divine idea in all its abstract power. Hence it is sacred in Masonry. For that it was that Hermes made it the number of initiation; because the initiate reigns over superstition, and by superstition, and can walk alone in the darkness, supported as he is upon his staff, wrapped in his cloak, and lighted by his lamp.

Reason has been given unto all men; but all do not know how to use it. That is a science that must be learned. Liberty is offered to all; but all have not the power to be free. That is a right which we must conquer. Force is within the reach of all men; but all men do not know how to lean upon it. That is a power of which one must possess himself.

These are to us, in this degree, the three great lights on the east, west, and south of the altar.

To attain the Holy Empire, that is to say, the science and power of the Magi, four things are indispensable: an *intellect* enlightened by study; an *audacity* which nothing checks; a *will* that nothing can conquer; and a *discretion* that nothing can corrupt or intoxicate. To Know, to Dare, to Will, to be Silent—these are the four words of the Magus, written in the four symbolic forms of the sphynx.

*   *   *   *   *

All the phenomena of nature depend on one single immutable law, represented by that symbolic form, the cube; and this furnished the Hebrews with all the mysteries of the divine tetragram.

Take care that thou dost not mistake the shadow for the reality. In everything, the vulgar habitually do so. They turn from the light, and wonder at the obscurity which they themselves project.

Listen and learn. Interpret our symbols for yourself. In every rough ashlar of marble is hidden the perfect cube. One is the symbol, the other its meaning. The sun and moon in our lodges are the truth, and the reflection of the truth in doctrine. Allegory, the mother of all dogmas, is the substitution of the impression for the seal, of the shadow for the reality. It is the falsehood of the truth, and the truth of the falsehood.

A dogma is not invented; a truth is veiled and a shadow produced, to suit weak eyes. The initiator is not an impostor, but a revealer—that is, in the original meaning of the word, one who veils anew. He is the creator of a new shadow.

The work of God is the book of God. For the letters to appear, there must needs be two colors on the page. Search and discover. You are about to be taught by symbols. Forget not the universal law of equilibrium. The ancients, in their evocations, always erected two altars, and sacrificed two victims, one black and one white; and the Priest, holding in one hand the sword, and in the other the rod, had to have one foot naked and the other shod.

Prepare, now, for admission to the inner mysteries.

* * * * *

M∴ P∴ My brethren, the power of darkness has prevailed over the prince of light. The earth mourns, and is wrinkled with frost. The leaves drop from the trees; snow shrouds the mountains, and cold winds sweep over the shuddering skies. All nature laments; and we share the common sorrow. Excellent Senior Warden, let prayers be offered up in the tabernacle for the return of light and the reascension of the Sun, and of that moral and spiritual light of which he is the type.

S∴ W∴ Most Puissant, all the nations of the earth do fast and pray. Our ancient taskmasters on the banks of the Nile mourn for Osiris. The Chaldeans lament for Bel, and the Phoenicians for Thammuz. The Phrygian women clash their cymbals and weep for Atys; on the Syrian hills and over the Etruscan plains the virgins lament for Dionusos; while far in India the Brahmans pray for the return of Cama; and in Persia the Magi predict the resurrection of Mithras. The dead will rise again, as the wheat grows from the grain; and all the world will then rejoice.

M∴ P∴ We, like our ancient masters, mourn Osiris—the type to us of the sun, of light, of life. The scorpion and the serpent rule the winter waves, on which the frail ark tosses that contains his body. Weep, my brethren, for Osiris! Weep for light lost, and life departed, and the good and beautiful oppressed by evil! Man hath fallen from his first estate, and is lost, as the sun hath sunken into the icy arms of winter. Weep for Osiris, type of the good, the true, the beautiful! How shall his body be recovered from the embraces of the hungry sea; and earth again be gladdened by his presence?

* * * * *

Brethren, behold a new Priest of the Tabernacle, to be instructed and prepared to fulfil all his duties as a Prince of well-doers in this frail Tabernacle of life, that he may be raised on the great day of account, a shining monument of God's glory, in the tabernacle of eternity.

TWENTY-FIFTH DEGREE.

Knight of the Brazen Serpent.

ARGUMENT.

THE Degree of Knight of the Brazen Serpent relates to the time when the camp of the Israelites was pitched at Punon, on the eastern side of the mountains of Hor, Seir, or Edom, in Arabia Petræa, on the confines of Idumæa, after the death of Aaron, when the new moon occurred at the vernal equinox, in the fortieth year of the wandering of the children of Israel in the desert.

The duties of a Knight of the Brazen Serpent are: To purify the soul of its alloy of earthliness, that through the gate of Capricorn and the seven spheres it may at length ascend to its eternal home beyond the stars; and also to perpetuate the great truths enveloped in the symbols and allegories of the ancient mysteries.

FAITH!

KNIGHT OF THE BRAZEN SERPENT.

THE TWENTY-FIFTH GRADE OF THE ANCIENT AND ACCEPTED SCOTTISH RITE, AND THE SEVENTH DEGREE OF THE HISTORICAL AND PHILOSOPHICAL SERIES.

THE LODGE—ITS DECORATIONS, ETC.

The Lodge, in this degree, is styled the Council.

The camp, standards, and tabernacle with its court, are as in the two preceding degrees. In the East is a transparency on which is painted a cross, with a serpent coiled round it and over the arms.

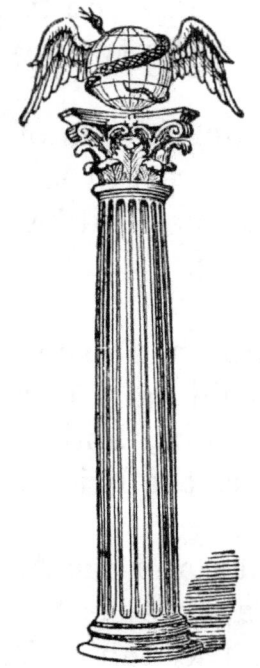
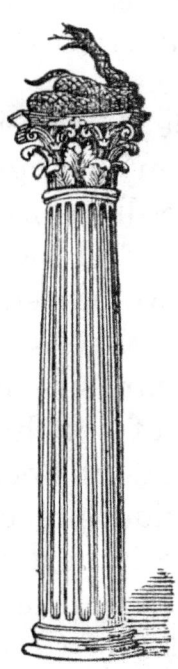

On the right of the presiding officer is a short column, on which is a winged globe encircled by a serpent. On the left of the Senior Warden and right of the Junior Warden are similar columns, on each of which is a serpent or basilisk, his body coiled in folds, and his head and neck erect above the folds. The globe and all the serpents are gilded.

The presiding officer represents Moses, and is styled "Most Puissant Leader." The Senior Warden, sitting in the West, on the left, represents Joshua, the son of Nun; and the Junior Warden, in the West, on the right, represents Caleb, the son of Yephanah. The former is styled "Most Valiant Captain of the Host;" and the latter, "Illustrious Chief Prince of the Tribes." The Orator sits on the right of the Most Puissant Leader, represents Eleazar, the son of Aaron, and is styled "Most Excellent High-Priest." He wears the full dress of the High-Priest, as prescribed in the two preceding degrees.

The Secretary represents Ithamar, the son of Aaron, sits on the right of the presiding officer, at the side of the hall, a little to the front, and is styled "Excellent Scribe." He wears the Priest's dress, as prescribed in the two preceding degrees.

The Treasurer represents Phinehas, the son of Eleazar, sits on the left of the presiding officer, at the side of the hall, a little to the front, and is styled "Excellent Recorder." He also wears the Priest's dress, as before prescribed.

The Expert sits on the south side, and the Assistant Expert on the north side of the Tabernacle; the Grand Master of Ceremonies in front of the Senior Warden, and the Grand Captain of the Guard near the door of entrance. These brethren are all styled "Respectable;" and the other members are addressed as "Brother and Knight A," or "B."

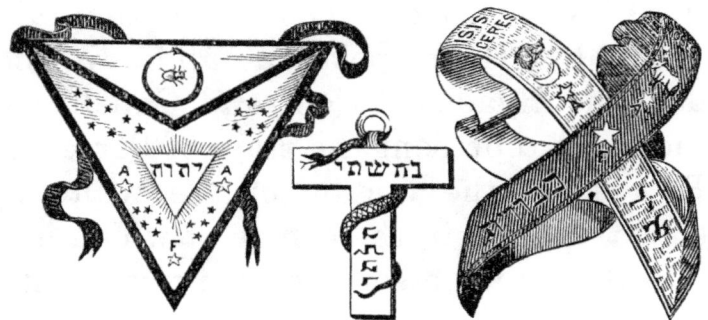

The *order* is a crimson ribbon, on which are depicted the words, one under the other, Osiris, Ormuzd, Osarsiph, Moses; and under them a bull, with a disk, surmounted by a crescent between his horns. This is worn from left to right; and across it, from right to left, is worn a broad, white, watered ribbon, on which are the words Isis, Ceres, over a dog's head and a crescent. On the right breast, on the left breast, and at the crossing of these orders, is a star of gold. Under that on the right breast is the letter A [for Aldebaran]; under that on the left breast the letter A [for Antares]; and under that at the crossing of the orders, the letter F [for Fomalhaut]. On the crimson cordon is the word גבורה [Gevurah—Valor]; and on the white, און [Aun—Virtus], meaning active energy or generative power, and passive energy or capacity to produce.

The *jewel* is a tau cross, of gold, surmounted by a circle — the Crux Ansata—round which a serpent is entwined. On the upright part of the cross is engraved the word הלתי [HoLaTaI, he has suffered or been wounded], and on the arms the word נחשתן [NeChuSh TaN, the Brazen Serpent].

The *apron* is white, lined and edged with black; the white side spotted with golden stars, and the black side with silver ones. Those on the white side represent, by their position and distances, the Pleiades, the Hyades, Orion, and Capella. Those on the black side represent the stars of Perseus, Scorpio, and Bootes. In the middle of the white side is a triangle in a glory, in the centre of which is the word יהוה. On the flap is a serpent in a circle, with his tail in his mouth, and in the centre of the circle so formed a scarabæus or beetle. Over this is a star of gold, with the letter R [Regulus] over it; on the right side of the apron another, with the letter A [Aldebaran] over it; on the left side another, with the letter A [Antares] over it; and at the bottom of the apron another, with the letter F [Fomalhaut] over it.

Battery—• • • • •- • •- •

RECEPTION.

*   *   *   *   *

So much of the truth as it is given to mortals to know, is within the reach of those alone whose intellects are unclouded by passion or excess. To attain it, to comprehend the delicate distinctions of the thought in which the truth is embodied, the intellect, like a keen instrument of the finest steel, must be able to dissect the thought, and distinguish one from the other its invisible nerves. The edge of the instrument is blunted by the indulgence of the sensual appetites, or of the intemperate passions of the soul

Therefore it is that the sages have always required of those who sought to scale the heights of philosophy a preparatory discipline, of long-continued temperance and self-restraint; and fasting is enjoined, as well as prayer.

If thy intellect is dull and coarse by nature, or clouded and confused by indulgence, the symbolisms of the Kabala will have no meaning to thee; and we shall address thee in a foreign tongue.

Thus it is that true Masonry has always been, and always must be, confined to a few; since to the mass its truths are foolishness and valueless.

*   *   *   *   *

Most Puissant Leader, the soul of the people was discouraged, because of the way, journeying from Mount Hor, by the way of the Red Sea, to compass the land of Edom; and they spake against Adonai and against thee, saying: "Why hath Al-Shadai and his servant Moses brought us up out of Egypt, to die in the wilderness? There is no bread nor any water, and our souls loathe this light manna. We go to and fro these forty years; and as Aaron died in the desert, so also shall we all die here. Let us put trust in Adonai no longer; but let us call on the great gods Amun and Astarte, Osiris and Isis, to deliver us from this misery." And as they cried aloud on them, lo! Adonai sent fiery serpents among them, by whom much people hath died. And those that remain have repented and said unto me: "Put chains upon thy neck in token of our penitence, and go unto Moses our leader, and beseech him to pray unto Adonai that he take away the serpents from us;" and I have done as they desired.

* * * * *

My brother, life is a war, in which one must prove his soldiership, in order to rise in rank. Force is not given. It has to be seized.

He only is worthy of initiation in the profounder mysteries who has overcome the fear of death, and is ready to hazard his life when the welfare of his country or the interests of humanity require it; and to die even an ignoble death, if thereby the people may be benefited.

* * * * *

I have prayed for the people, and Adonai hath said unto me: "Make thee an image of a venomous springing serpent, and set it upon a pole; and it shall come to pass that every one that is bitten, when he looketh upon it, shall live."

* * * * *

The plague of serpents is stayed; and as they have fled to their caves, so the celestial serpent flees, with the scorpion, before the glittering stars of Orion. The great festival of the vernal equinox approaches, and it is time to prepare ourselves by purification for the Passover. Light will soon prevail once more over darkness; and the pulses of life again beat in the bosom of the earth, long chilled by the wintry frosts.

*   *   *   *   *

Let the brazen cross and the serpent be borne before the congregation, and be forever a symbol of Faith, by the dying out whereof in the hearts of nations, they fall into decay; and lest the knowledge of its true symbolic meaning should in time be lost, and the people hereafter imagine it to be something divine, and worship it, we will perpetuate the remembrance of this day's events, and the true meaning of this and our other symbols, and of the fables of Osiris and Ormuzd, and Typhon and Ahriman, as the last degree of those sacred mysteries which Joseph, the son of Jacob, like myself, learned from the Egyptians, and which I have taught to you; such as our forefathers practised on the plains of Chaldæa.

*   *   *   *   *

The Father sends fiery serpents to sting and slay his children. Yet he commands us to forgive those who trespass against us. And this law is not the mandate of his will, but the expression of his nature. Who will explain this great mystery?

Below, upon the earth, the serpent is the minister of death. Its image, lifted on high, heals and restores life.

The first sages who sought for the cause of causes saw good and evil in the world; they observed the shadow and the light; they compared winter with spring, old age with youth, life with death, and said: "The first cause is beneficent and cruel. It gives life and destroys."

"Are there, then, *two* contrary principles—a good and an evil?" cried the disciples of Manes.

No! the two principles of the universal equilibrium are not contrary to each other, though in apparent opposition; for it is a single wisdom that opposes them one to the other.

The good is on the right, the evil on the left; but the supreme good is above both, and makes the evil subserve the triumph of the good, and the good serve for the reparation of the evil.

*   *   *   *   *

Wherefore this first cause has always revealed itself by the cross;—the cross, that *one* composed of *two,* each of the two divided, so that they constitute four;—the cross, that key of the mysteries of India and Egypt, the tau of the patriarchs, the divine symbol of Osiris, the stauros of the Gnostics, the keystone of the Temple, the symbol of occult Masonry;—the cross, that central point of junction of the right angles of four infinite triangles; the four-in-one of the divine tetragram.

*   *   *   *   *

TWENTY-SIXTH DEGREE.

Prince of Mercy.

ARGUMENT

WHEN Domitian was emperor of Rome, in the night of persecution, when danger and death hung on their footsteps, the Christian Masons met in the Catacombs,—an assemblage of whom is represented in this Degree of Princes of Mercy, who were representatives of the *faithful* by means of the *Triple Covenant,* the points of which were—that made with Noah when God set his bow in the heavens; that made with Abraham, for him and his descendants; and that made with all the earth, that the day should come when light, truth, and happiness should be victorious over darkness, error, and misery.

The assemblages generally met to celebrate the Mysteries in the great Temple of Elephanta; then in the secret chambers of that of Bouddha at Salsette; in the roofless fanes of Persia, in the forest temples of the Druids, in the pyramids of Memphis, in the vaults of Crete and Samothrace, in the great temple of Eleusis, under the Holy of Holies at Jerusalem, and in the Catacombs under Rome.

PRINCE OF MERCY;

OR,

SCOTTISH TRINITARIAN.

THE TWENTY-SIXTH GRADE OF THE ANCIENT AND ACCEPTED SCOTTISH RITE, AND THE EIGHTH DEGREE OF THE HISTORICAL AND PHILOSOPHICAL SERIES.

DECORATIONS, ETC.

Bodies of this degree are styled Chapters. The hangings are green, supported by nine columns, alternately white and red; upon each of which is a chandelier, holding nine lights. The canopy over the throne is green, white, and red; and before the throne is a table, covered with a cloth of the same colors. Over the throne hangs a triple interlaced triangle of broad bars, two of which are white, and one black; and in its centre the letter '. Instead of a gavel, the presiding officer uses an arrow, the plume of which is red on one side and green on the other, the spear white, and the point gilded.

By the altar is a statue or statuette of white marble, the naked figure of a virgin. Over it is a drapery of

thin white gauze. This represents Truth, and is the palladium of the Order of Princes of Mercy.

The altar, placed in the centre of the room, is of a triangular shape, each side measuring 18 inches, and its height being 36 inches. The top is a plate, like gold, on which, formed of different colored stones, is the word יהוה; and under that a passion cross, on either side of which, above the arms, are the Greek letters I͂C.... X͂C. At each corner is a flame of brass.

PRINCE OF MERCY.

The presiding officer is styled "Most Excellent Chief Prince."

The Wardens, "Excellent Senior Warden," and "Excellent Junior Warden."

The Expert and Assistant Expert are styled "Respectable Senior and Junior Deacons."

The Captain of the Guards is styled "Valiant Guard of the Palladium;" and the Tiler, "Captain of the Guard."

The other officers are styled "Venerable."

The Chief Prince wears a tricolored tunic, green, white, and red, and a crown with nine points. The other members wear white tunics. All wear the Order, which is a broad tricolored ribbon, green, white, and red, worn from right to left.

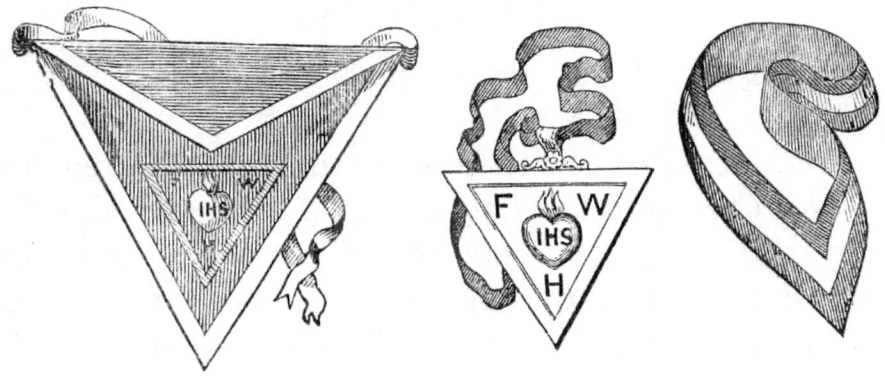

The *apron* is scarlet, with a wide border of white. In the centre is an equilateral triangle, the bars forming the sides of which are green. In the centre of this are the emblems on the jewel, embroidered in gold. The flap is sky-blue.

The *jewel* is an equilateral triangle, of bars of gold, with a flaming heart of gold in the centre. On the heart are the letters I∴ H∴ S∴ and on the respective sides of the triangle, W∴ on the right, F∴ on the left, and H∴ at the bottom. This jewel is suspended from a small collar of narrow, watered, purple ribbon, and hangs on the breast.

The March is 3 equal steps, the first taken with the left foot.

The Order is, standing, the right hand on the right hip.

The age is 9 by 9, or 81.

The Tessera, or mark, given to the initiate, is a small fish, of ivory or mother-of-pearl, on one side of which is the word יהוה, and on the other ⊤ ⊥ ⊗ ‖ ⊏

Battery—•••—•••—••—•••—•••—•

RECEPTION.

*   *   *   *   *

M∴ E∴ Listen to the ancient dogmas and teachings.

Or. Thus said the holy books of ancient India: There are three supreme gods, the three forms and aspects of the first, the supreme, single, invisible God, cause of all phenomena, and soul of the world: and these three, the powers of *creation, preservation,* and *destruction,* distinct in persons, are but one God, the triple form of the Supreme, the word A∴ U∴ M∴, first utterance of the Eternal.

J∴ W∴ Said the ancient Hindoos: Chrishna, the second person of the Trimourti, born of a royal virgin, without sin, descended into hell, arose again, and ascended to heaven. He will appear again at the end of the world, will become man, and mounted on a white horse, with a sword glittering like a comet, will traverse the world and destroy the guilty. The great serpent shall consume the universe; but the seeds of creation shall be preserved in the lotus; and a new creation shall commence.

S∴ W∴ Above all existences, said the ancient Bouddhists, is the spirit, universal, indestructible, who during incalculable time preserves all that is, and remains in repose, until the laws of destiny oblige him to create new worlds. From him flow the Bouddhas, each a trinity of intelligence, law, and unison, each a Redeemer. The stars shall salute him at his nativity, and all mankind unite in orisons to God.

M∴ E∴ From the supreme divinity and ancient unlimited time, said the old Persians, emanated the pure light. He will in the fourth age create Sosiosch the Saviour, who shall prepare the human race for the general resurrection.

Or∴ Mithra, it was said in the ancient Sabean Mysteries, is the Grand Architect of the universe himself, appearing in visible shape, the spirit of the sun and light, the eye of Ormuzd. He is three and one; for his essence illuminates, warms, and makes fruitful at once. He is the incarnate mediator, bringing back souls to God.

J∴ W∴ The Supreme God Alfader, said our ancient brethren the Druids, is eternal. He made heaven, earth, and air, and men, and gave to men immortal souls.

S∴ W∴ Amun-Re, said the ancient Egyptians, the uncreated, is the Supreme Triad, father, mother, and son, from whom the long chain of Triads descends to the incarnations in human form. Osiris, final conqueror of Typhon, shall sit in judgment on all the dead, and pronounce the final sentence, on each according to his deserts.

M∴ E∴ He, said the Hebrew Kabalists, is the Supreme, the hidden lamp, whereof is no cognition. He is found to have three heads, contained in one head. Wisdom is the father, and intelligence the mother, and from them flows truth. These three are—Chochmah, wisdom; Binah, the mother of understanding; and Daath, intellectual cognition.

Or∴ Again, hear ye! In the beginning was the Word, and the Word was with God, and the Word was God: all things were made by him: in him was life, and that life was the light of mankind; the true light, which lighteth every man that cometh into the world. And the Word became incarnate, and dwelt among men, and they beheld his glory, the glory of the first-born of the Father. Thus said the ancient Christian Masons; and they said also: There are three that bear record in heaven; the Father, the Word, and the Holy Spirit, and these three are one.

* * * * *

J∴ W∴ Thus in all ages the golden threads of truth have gleamed in the woof of error. Fortunate the Mason who, by the light of wisdom, the true Masonic light, second emanation from the Deity, can discern the golden threads, God's hieroglyphics, written when time began; and read them aright, as they were read by our ancient brethren in the early ages!

S∴ W∴ Thus in all ages the word of God, his thought, not uttered in a voice audible to mortal ears, has spoken in the souls of men, and taught them the great truths of reason, philosophy, and religion. Fortunate the Mason to whom that word, the Deity manifest, is audible, intelligible, significant; God's thought, that made the stars and all that is, and the great laws of harmony and motion!

M∴ E∴ Thus in all ages rosy gleams of light, piercing the dark clouds of error, have taught mankind that truth and light, perfect and glorious, linger below the horizon, in time to rise to fill God's universe with light and glory, at the dawn of his promised day. Fortunate the Mason, who with firm faith and hope accepts these struggling rays that gild the clouds, as ample evidence that in God's good time his dawn of day will come, and be eternal.

CHANT.

*   *   *   *   *

You have assumed the name of Constans, and thus profess yourself firm, intrepid, and persevering. This Lodge represents a Lodge of Christian Masons held at night, in the gloomy catacombs under Rome, in the time of the persecuting Emperor Domitian; and you represent a Catechumen who, having attained the second degree of the Essenian and early Christian Mysteries, sought by receiving the third and last degree to become one of the faithful or the elect. Whatever your faith, you at least believe, as they did, in the unity and providence of God.

*   *   *   *   *

PRAYER.

Infinitely Illustrious and Supreme Father, infinitely various of counsel, who consumest all things, and again thyself reproducest and repairest them; who directest the ineffable harmonies that are the law of the boundless universe! Universal Parent of eternally successive being; who art everywhere present; of whose essence are justice, mercy, and goodness; author of life and soul, of all that moves; aid us to keep thy commandments and perform our duties! Keep us from the slippery descents of vice, and help us to stand firm in the ways of duty! Support and strengthen this our brother, and all Masons everywhere! Fill our souls with love for thee! Save us from persecutors; teach us and all our brethren to be tolerant of error, the common lot of man; and send our life a happy, blameless end!

All. Our Father who art in heaven, hallowed be thy name, etc. Amen! So mote it be.

M∴ E∴ My brother, you have ascended too high

in Masonry to be longer subjected to physical tests and trials, or you would again in this degree have represented the Fellow Craft, or Companion, advancing toward the Master's degree.

In the early days of Christianity, there was an initiation like those of the Pagans. Persons were admitted on special conditions only. To arrive at a complete knowledge of the doctrine, they had to pass three degrees of instruction. The initiates were consequently divided into three classes: the first, auditors, the second, catechumens, and the third the faithful. The auditors were novices, prepared by ceremonies and instruction to receive the dogmas of Christianity. A portion of these dogmas was made known to the Catechumens; who, after particular purifications, received baptism, or the initiation of the *theogenesis* (divine generation); but in the grand mysteries of that religion, the incarnation, nativity, passion, and resurrection of Christ, none were initiated but the faithful. These doctrines, and the celebration of the holy sacraments, particularly the Eucharist, were kept with profound secrecy.

*   *   *   *   *

To avoid persecution, the early Christians were compelled to use great precaution, and to hold meetings of the faithful [of the household of faith] in private places, under concealment by darkness. They assembled in the night, and they guarded against the intrusion of false brethren and profane persons spies, who might cause their arrest During the early persecutions they took refuge in the vast catacombs which stretched for miles in every direction under the city of Rome, and are supposed to have been of Etruscan origin. There, amid labyrinthine windings, deep caverns, hidden chambers, chapels and tombs, the persecuted fugitives found refuge, and there they performed the ceremonies of the mysteries.

They conversed together figuratively, and by the use of symbols; and those who were initiated were bound by solemn promise not to disclose or even converse about the secrets of the mysteries, except with such as had received them under the same sanction.

*   *   *   *   *

This then is the history of the sufferings of Jesus Christ, and its Masonic application as made by the Christian Mason. Some of the ceremonies of the first three degrees, which, whatever your faith, may not be uninteresting to you, since you are in no wise required to receive them as correct, are as follows:

*   *   *   *   *

M∴ E∴ Behold, the darkness is past, and the true light now shineth. My brother, you have before this been brought to light in Masonry, when the Worshipful Master, with the aid of the brethren, first made you a Mason. You have been taught to believe in the true God. You have passed through degrees intended to remind you of the Essenian and Hebrew mysteries; and in this you have heard described those practised by the first Christians. As you were not required to profess a belief in the tenets of the Essenes or the Pharisees, so neither here are you required to believe in the divine mission or character of Jesus of Nazareth. We shadow forth the secret discipline of the early Christians, as we do the other Mysteries, as the diverse and often eccentric forms in which Masonry has developed itself in the different ages of the world. Masonically, we know not whether you be Christian, Jew, or Moslem. If you be Christian, you will see in this degree a Christian ceremony; and so you have the right to interpret it. Your brethren will respect your faith, as they have a right to demand that you shall respect theirs. If you be not a Christian, you will see in it a mere historical allegory, symbolizing great truths, acknowledged alike by you and them.

While you were veiled in darkness, you heard repeated by the voice of the great past its most ancient doctrines. No one has the right to object, if the Christian Mason sees foreshadowed in Chrishna and Sosiosch, in Mithras and Osiris, the divine Word, that, as he believes, became man, and died upon the cross to redeem a fallen race. Nor can he object if others see in the Word that was in the beginning with God, and that was God, only the logos of Plato and Philo, or the uttered thought or first emanation of light, or the reason, of the great, silent, uncreated Deity, believed in and adored by all.

We do not undervalue the importance of any truth. We utter no word that can be deemed irreverent by any one of any faith. We do not tell the Moslem that it is only important for him to believe that there is but one God, and wholly unessential whether Mahomet was his prophet. We do not tell the Hebrew that the Messiah, whom he expects, was born in Bethlehem nearly two thousand years ago; and as little do we tell the Christian that Jesus of Nazareth was but a man, or his history the revival of an older legend. To do either is beyond our jurisdiction. Masonry, of no one age, belongs to all time; of no one religion, it finds its great truths in all.

Masonry is a worship; but one in which all civilized men can unite. It trusts in God, and hopes; it believes, like a child, and is humble. It draws no sword to compel others to adopt its belief, or to be happy with its hopes. And it waits with patience to understand the mysteries of nature hereafter.

The greatest mysteries in the universe are those which are ever going on around us; so trite and common to us that we never note them or reflect upon them. There are other forces in the universe than those that are mechanical.

Here are two minute seeds, not much unlike in appearance, and two of larger size. Hand them to Chemistry, which tells us how combustion goes on in the lungs, and plants are fed with phosphorus and carbon, and the alkalies and silex. Let it decompose them, analyze them, torture them in all the ways it knows. The net result of each is a little sugar, a little fibrin, a little water—carbon, potassium, sodium, and the like—one cares not to know what.

We hide them in the ground; and the slight rains moisten them, and the sun shines upon them, and little slender shoots spring up and grow; and what a miracle is the mere growth! the force, the power, the capacity, by which the little feeble shoot, that a small worm can nip off with a single snap of its mandibles, extracts from the earth and air and water the different elements with which it increases in stature, and rises imperceptibly toward the sky!

One grows to be a slender, feeble stalk, like an ordinary weed; another a strong bush, armed with thorns, and sturdy enough to bid defiance to the winds; the third a tender tree, subject to be blighted by the frost, and looked down upon by all the forest; while another spreads its rugged arms abroad, and cares for neither frost nor ice, nor the snows that for months lie heaped around its roots.

But lo! out of the brown foul earth, and colorless invisible air, and limpid rain-water, the chemistry of the seeds has extracted colors—four different shades of green, that paint the leaves, which put forth in the spring upon our plant, our shrub, and our trees. Later still come the flowers—the vivid colors of the rose, the beautiful brilliance of the carnation, the modest blush of the apple, and the splendid white of the orange. Whence come these colors? By what process of chemistry are they extracted from the carbon, the phosphorus, and the lime? Is it any greater miracle to make something out of nothing?

Pluck the flowers. Inhale the delicious perfumes, each perfect and all delicious. Whence have they come? By what combination of acids and alkalies could the chemist produce them?

And the fruit—the ruddy apple and the golden orange—the texture and fabric how totally different! the taste how entirely dissimilar!—the perfume of each distinct from its flower, and from the other. Whence the taste and this new perfume? The same earth and air and water have been made to furnish a different taste to each fruit, a different perfume not only to each fruit, but to each fruit and its own flower.

Is it any more a problem whence come thought and will and perception, and all the phenomena of the mind, than this, whence come the colors, the perfumes, the taste of the fruit and flower?

And lo! in each fruit new seeds, each gifted with the same wondrous power of reproduction—each with the same wondrous *forces* wrapped up in it to be again in turn evolved;—forces, that had lived three thousand years in the grain of wheat found in the wrappings of an Egyptian mummy; forces, of which learning, and science, and wisdom know no more than they do of the nature and laws of action of God. What can *we* know of the nature, and how can *we* understand the powers and mode of operation, of the human soul, when the glossy leaves, the pearl-white flower, and the golden fruit of the orange are miracles wholly beyond our comprehension?

We but hide our ignorance in a cloud of words; and the words too often are mere combinations of sounds without any meaning.

What force draws the needle toward the north? What force moves the muscle that raises the arm, when the will determines it shall rise? Whence comes the *will* itself? Is it spontaneous—a first cause, or an effect? These too are miracles, inexplicable as the creation, or the self-existence of God.

*   *   *   *   *

On being now again brought to light, you see upon the altar before you the luminous delta, with three equal sides, in all ages the representation of Deity, the trinity of wisdom, power, and harmony; and upon it the ineffable name, and the cross, in all time the emblem of eternity.

*   *   *   *   *

M∴ E∴ My brother, the colors of this degree are green, red, and white. They symbolize the Masonic trinity. The green is an emblem of the infinite wisdom; the red, of the supreme energy, force, or power; and the white, produced by mingling all the colors, of the divine harmony.

On the three sides of the jewel you see the letters W∴ F∴ and H∴—the initials of the words Wisdom, Force, and Harmony; and on the inflamed heart in the centre, three letters which the Christian Mason reads as the initials of the phrase, Jesus Hominum Salvator; but which you are at liberty to read S∴ I∴ H∴— Sapientia, Imperium, Harmonia—Wisdom, Power, and Harmony.

Perhaps you suspect that there is still remaining behind an inner meaning of the word "Trinity," connecting itself with your title of Scottish Trinitarian. It may be so. Masonry discloses its secrets cautiously, and never makes the whole truth known at once.

* * * * *

CROWN OF VENUS URANIA. ISIAN HEAD-DRESS AND MAIYA'S HOLY SIGN.

TWENTY-SEVENTH DEGREE.

Knight Commander of the Temple.

ARGUMENT.

THE degree of Knight Commander of the Temple is sometimes called Teutonic Knight of the House of St. Mary of Jerusalem. The Order originated at the siege of St. Jean d'Acre, when tents were made for the sick and wounded of the sails of the ships; and while they fought the infidel Saladin by day, and nursed the sick and wounded soldiers by night, the Knights engaged themselves to guard the city of Jerusalem against the Saracens; to protect Christendom; to succor and assist the feeble and oppressed, and to defend the innocent. Their five excellent qualities were Humility, Temperance, Chastity, Generosity, and Honor; and they practised all the Masonic virtues. This is the first *strictly* chivalric degree of the Ancient and Accepted Scottish rite.

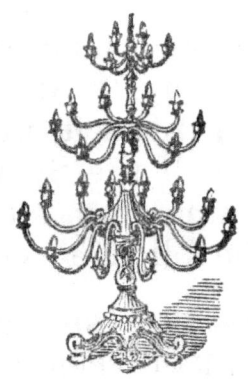

KNIGHT COMMANDER OF THE TEMPLE.

THE TWENTY-SEVENTH GRADE OF THE ANCIENT AND ACCEPTED SCOTTISH RITE, AND THE NINTH DEGREE OF THE HISTORICAL AND PHILOSOPHICAL SERIES

LODGES, FURNITURE, ETC.

Bodies of this chivalric degree are styled Chapters. The hangings are scarlet, with black columns at intervals, on each of which is an arm or branch, holding a light. The hangings and columns are so arranged as to make the shape of the Chapter a circle.

The canopy and throne are of scarlet, sprinkled with black tears.

In front of the East is a candelabrum, with three circles of lights, one above the other. In the lowest circle are *twelve* lights; in the middle one *nine;* and in the upper one *six*.

In the centre of the room is a very large round table, on which are five lamps, with globular shades of ground glass, arranged in the shape of a passion-cross, the vertical shaft extending East and West, the head of the cross to the East. These lamps must be fed with olive oil. On this table is a crucifix, a copy of the Pentateuch in Hebrew, a crown or garland of laurel, a sword and large key, crossed, an apron and pair of gloves of the degree; and scattered upon it, in no particular order, all the working tools of the Symbolic Lodge. Around this table all the Commanders sit.

In the West are the following sentences:

"IN MANY WORDS THOU SHALT NOT AVOID SIN."
"LIFE AND DEATH ARE DISPENSED BY THE TONGUE."

OFFICERS AND TITLES.

The Sovereign Grand Commander of the Supreme Council of the 33d degree is the Grand Master of the Order. The Commander-in-Chief of the Consistory in which the Chapter is held is the Provincial Grand Master.

The presiding officer of a Chapter is styled "Commander in Chief," with the title of "Eminent." The Senior Warden is styled "Marshal;" and the Junior Warden, "Turcopilier;" the Orator, "Hospitaller;" the Master of Ceremonies, "Draper;" the Secretary, "Chancellor;" the Treasurer, "Seneschal;" the Expert and Assistant Expert, "First," and "Second Lieutenant;" and a "Captain of the Guard." In addressing each, the words "Brother Knight" are prefixed to his official title. The Tiler is styled "Sentinel." There is also a "Chaplain."

The Eminent Commander sits on the east side of the table; the Marshal and Turcopilier on the West side, the latter on the right of the former; the Hospitaller on the south side; the Draper on the north; the Secretary on the left of the Eminent Commander, half way between him and the Hospitaller; and the Treasurer on the right of the Eminent Commander, half way between him and the Draper; the First Lieutenant on the right of the Hospitaller; the Second Lieutenant on the left of the Draper; and the Captain of the Guard on the right of the Junior Warden. The Chaplain sits on the right of the Eminent Commander.

DRESS, DECORATIONS, ETC.

The *apron* is of scarlet-colored lambskin, lined and edged with black. The flap is white, and on it is a Teutonic Cross (described as a cross potent sable, charged with another cross double potent *or,* surcharged with an escutcheon of the Empire, the principal cross surmounted by a chief *azure, semée* of France). Thus:

In the middle of the apron is a key, in black, and round it, embroidered in green of the proper shade, a garland or wreath of laurel.

The *gloves* are white, lined, edged, and embroidered with red.

The *order* is of white watered ribbon, edged with red, worn as a collar (*en camail*), at the bottom of which the jewel hangs. On each side of the collar is embroidered in black and gold the Teutonic Cross.

A *sash* is worn across the body, from right to left being a broad watered scarlet ribbon, edged with black, at the end of which hangs a gold cross of the Order.

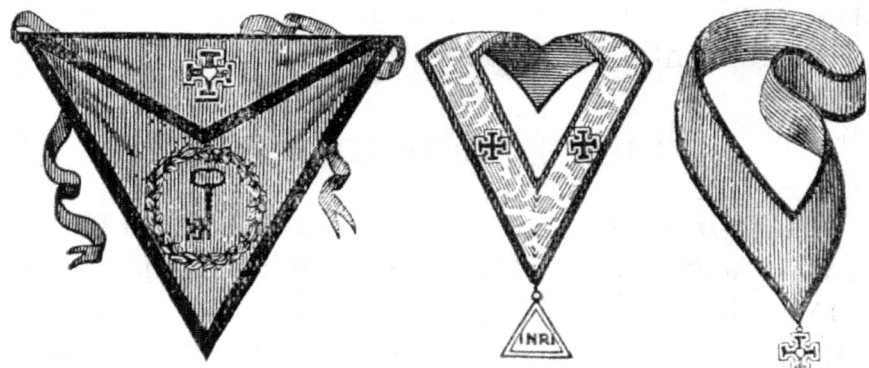

The *jewel* is a triangle of gold, on which is enamelled the word INRI.

The hilt of the sword is in the shape of a cross, and gilt. The scabbard and sword-belt are black.

Under these decorations, each wears a tunic of white woollen stuff, reaching to the mid-thigh; and over all a Knight's mantle of scarlet velvet, reaching nearly to the ground, lined with white silk. On the breast of the tunic is embroidered a Teutonic Cross, as above described; and on the right side of the mantle a passion-cross, in black.

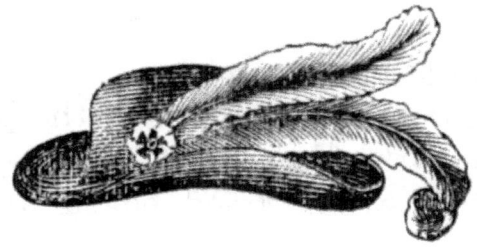

The *hat* is broad-brimmed, with red plumes, and a black and white cockade.

A gilt spur is worn on each heel.

Battery—••••–•••–••.

KNIGHT COMMANDER OF THE TEMPLE. 391

RECEPTION.

* * * * *

The following dirge is sung in the adjoining apartment.

DIRGE.

Solemnly..   BRO. HENRY TUCKER.

O Mason, who dost sleep away
Life's brief, uncertain, stormy day;
We all must die, we all must die, And death is ever drawing nigh.

The Brother Terrible on high
With sonorous voice to all will cry.
    "We all must die! We all must die!
    "Judgment is ever drawing nigh.

"Assemble, Masons, one and all!
"Rise in the body at my call!"
    We all must die! We all must die!
    And heaven, we trust, is drawing nigh!

       Repeat the last two lines.

    *   *   *   *   *

Those who formerly entered this Order consecrated themselves to the service of the sick and suffering, were constantly employed in works of mercy, and devoted themselves to the service and defence of the Christian faith. They were no longer allowed to act for themselves; but on the contrary were obliged absolutely to renounce their own will and pleasure, and implicitly to comply with that of their superiors. The change of circumstances and manners make this strictness to be no longer required; but you will contract with us an analogous engagement.

    *   *   *   *   *

E. C. By my authority and power as Commander-in-chief of this Chapter, and in the name of the Grand Master of the Order, I hereby constitute, create, and dub thee a Knight Commander of the Temple. Be true, devout, and brave! Arise, A. B., no longer a serving brother, but a Knight; and may glory and good fortune attend you!

Receive now the five trophies of this degree.

I crown you with this garland of laurel. This especially is meant to crown your good works, done to the Order, the Lodges, and your brethren; and to encourage you to persevere.

I present you with the apron and gloves, the collar, sash, and jewel of the Order. The colors of these decorations are white, red, and black. For whom this latter color, the emblem of sorrow and mourning, is worn, you will know at a proper time.

I present you with the sword of a Knight, to enable you to maintain the rights of Masonry and of men, and to punish their enemies and tyrants. If in that contest you should fall, you will have fulfilled the noblest destiny of a Knight and gentleman.

I present you with the spurs of a Knight. As

you have worn them worthily, so may you wear them with honor! God forbid that for any act of base unworthiness you should ever be deprived of them!

I present you with the pallium or mantle of the Order. This cross is the sign of the Order, which we command you constantly to wear.

Take this sign in the name of God, for the increase of faith, the defence of the Order, and the service of the poor. We place this cross upon your breast, my brother, that you may love it with all your heart; and may your right hand ever fight in its defence and for its preservation, as the symbol of knightly Masonry.

* * * * *

HISTORY.

When St. Jean d'Acre, the ancient Ptolemais, on the southern side of which was Mount Carmel, was besieged by the Christian forces, for nearly two years, under Guy of Lusignan, King of Jerusalem, Conrad, Marquis of Montferrat, and other princes and leaders from every country in Europe,—and especially by Henry VI. of Germany, son of Frederich Barbarossa, joined, near the end of the siege, by Philip Augustus of France and Richard Coeur de Lion of England,—they were long afflicted with famine, until they ate the flesh of horses with joy, and even the intestines sold for ten sous; men of high rank, and the sons of great men, greedily devoured grass; the starving fought together like dogs for the little bread baked at the ovens; they gnawed the bones that had already been gnawed by the dogs; and noblemen, ashamed to *beg,* were known to *steal* bread.

*   *   *   *   *

Sickness, also, caused by the rains and the intense heat, decimated the Christian forces. The wounded German soldiers, whom none of the others understood, could not make known their sickness nor their necessities. Certain German nobles from the cities of Bremen and Lubec, who had arrived at Acre by sea, moved by the miseries of their countrymen, took the sails of their ships, and made them a large tent, in which for a time they placed the wounded Germans, and tended them with great kindness. Forty nobles of the same nation united with them, and established a kind of hospital in the midst of the camp; and this noble and charitable association, like the Knights of the Temple and of St. John of Jerusalem, soon and insensibly became a new Hospitaller and Military Order. This was in the year 1191. In 1192, Pope Celestin III., at the request of the Emperor Henry VI., solemnly approved of the Order, by his bull of the 23d of February. He prescribed, as regulations for the new Knights, those of St. Augustine; and for special statutes, in all that regarded the poor and the sick, those of the Hospitallers of St. John; in regard to military discipline.

the regulations of the Templars. This new Order exclusively composed of Germans, was styled "The Order of Teutonic Knights of the House of St. Mary of Jerusalem;" as the Templars were styled, "of the House of the Temple at Jerusalem."

A great number of noblemen, who had followed that Prince (Frederic of Suabia, second son of the Emperor) to Acre as volunteers, some actuated by religious enthusiasm, and some by the desire of glory, joined the soldiers of the Temple and of the Hospital, or engaged in attending on the wounded and caring for the sick of their nation. This was the origin of the Teutonic Order, the first branch of that of the Templars.

The chiefs, desiring to advance these pious gentlemen and to gratify the German nation, proposed to them the institution of a new Order of Chivalry, to be at once hospitaller and military. Forty German lords, distinguished by their nobility and feats of arms, agreed to these, and became the founders and original members of the Order. On entering the Order, they bound themselves by the three solemn vows, and also obliged themselves to serve the poor, in imitation of the Hospitallers, and to follow the claustral and military discipline of the Templars, in peace as well as in war.

Their title of Knights of the House of St. Mary of Jerusalem was given them, because while the city of Jerusalem was under the government of the Latin Christians, a German had erected there, at his own expense, a hospital and oratory for the sick of his nation, under the protection of, and dedicated to, the Virgin Mary.

* * * * *

To distinguish this Order from the other two, they adopted the black cross. It is ordinarily said that they also adopted the white mantle; but about the year 1210, the Templars of Palestine complained to Pope Innocent, that after they had received from the Holy See the white mantle as the distinctive dress of their Order, the Teutonic Knights, and especially those of St. Jean d'Acre, had assumed to wear it. Innocent wrote to the latter, and to their Grand Master, Herman Bart, a gentleman of Holstein, and directed that, in order to avoid all occasion for jealousy or quarrel, they should content themselves with their ordinary dress, and leave the white color to the Templars; and at the same time he ordered the Patriarch of Jerusalem to see to it that the Teutonic Knights should follow their first custom, and to censure, and so compel them to do it, if necessary.

It is true that they paid little regard to the mandate of the Pope, and soon adopted the white mantle again; but it was not their primitive dress; and therefore we, in this degree, wear a different color.

The leading objects of the three great military orders were the same.

The Teutonic Knights soon rivalled the other orders in numbers and influence.

* * * * *

In the year 1226, most of the Teutonic Knights went from the Holy Land to Prussia; the people of which were still idolaters, waging cruel war against their Christian neighbors, murdering priests at the foot of the altar, and employing the sacred vessels for profane uses.

* * * * *

For many years the Teutonic Knights held Prussia as a fief depending on the crown of Poland.

After the Order of the Temple had been "suppressed, extinguished, and abolished," in the year 1312, by the papal bull of the 6th May of that year, by which all persons were forbidden to enter the Order, or to assume the name of Templars, or to wear their dress, under pain of excommunication, an extension of the same, in the same year, adjudged all the property and estates of the Templars to the Knights of Rhodes (of St. John, or the Hospitallers, afterward Knights of Malta), except such as were in the realms of Spain, and without prejudice to the right of any kings, princes, or lords to any property of the Order in other countries.

A Knight Commander of the Temple should have five excellent qualities, which are represented by the five lights that form the symbolic cross upon our table,—Humility, Temperance, Chastity, Generosity, and Honor.

TWENTY-EIGHTH DEGREE.

Knight of the Sun.

ARGUMENT.

THERE is but one God, uncreated, eternal, infinite, and inaccessible: that the soul of man is immortal, and his existent life but a point in the centre of eternity: that harmony is in equilibrium, and equilibrium subsists by the analogy of contraries: that analogy is the key of all the secrets of nature, and the sole reason of being of all revelations: and, finally, that the *Absolute* is REASON, which exists through itself: that evil, and wrong, and misery are the necessary discords that unite with the concords of the universe to make one great harmony forever. Such is the argument of this the last philosophical degree of the Ancient and Accepted Scottish Rite; its doctrine is derived from the Kabala, and is the same as that of the Hermetic philosophers who wrote on Alchemy.

Nature is revelation, and the light of truth shines everywhere in the world. Magism was made for kings and priests alone. He who dreads to lose his own ideas, and fears new truths, and is not disposed to doubt everything, rather than admit anything at random, should not seek to learn the teachings of this degree, for they will be useless and dangerous to him; he will misunderstand them and be troubled by them, and yet be more troubled should he chance to comprehend them.

He who prefers anything to reason, truth, and justice, whose will is uncertain and wavering, who is alarmed by logic and the naked truth, should not rashly engage in the pursuit of the high sciences; but once on the road, he must reach the goal or perish; to doubt is to become insane, to halt is to fall, to go back is to precipitate one's self into an abyss.

Sancta Sanctis! **The holy things for the holy!**

400A

Temple of the Sun at Nineveh.

"SANCTO . SANCO . SEMONI . DEO . FIDIO . SACRUM."

IN the Veda there are only three deities : * Dyaus in heaven, Indra in the sky, and Agni on the earth. Dyaus, Indra, Agni, however, are but manifestations in the Sun, the bright Sky, and the Fire derived from the solar light. In the Vedic hymns, we find perpetual allusion to the sun with his life-bestowing rays. The Persians, the Assyrians, the Chaldeans, all worship the sun.

Sun worship was introduced into the mysteries not as a material idolatry, but as the means of expressing an idea of restoration to life from death, drawn from the daily reappearance in the east of the solar orb after its nightly disappearance in the west.

"The Sun is the symbol of sovereignty, the hieroglyphic of royalty ; it doth signify absolute authority."

Sol is the fire of heaven which lights the generative fires of earth, the genial parent who renews in its season all nature, and gives fertility to both animal and vegetable creation, and which, therefore, came to be worshipped as the giver of procreative power.

As men are, so will their ideas of God be ; each one, according to his cultivation and idiosyncrasies, projects on his mental canvas the highest ideal of the Illimitable of which he is capable. Had man worshipped nought less noble and elevating than the Sun he would have done well ; for he could adore nothing greater save the Supreme Creator of the Sun.

* Sometimes Parganya (Atharva-veda, xii. 1. 12.)

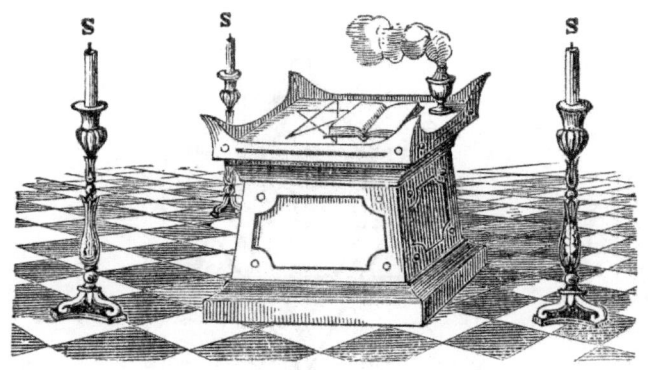

"SOLI SANCTISSIMO SACRUM"—SACRED TO THE MOST HOLY SUN.

KNIGHT OF THE SUN:

OR,

PRINCE ADEPT.

THE TWENTY-EIGHTH GRADE OF THE ANCIENT AND ACCEPTED SCOTTISH RITE, AND THE TENTH DEGREE OF THE HISTORICAL AND PHILOSOPHICAL SERIES.

"Lux e Tenebris."

COUNCIL-CHAMBER—ITS FURNITURE, ETC.

Bodies of this degree are styled Councils. Each Council consists of not less than ten members.

The hangings of the Council-Chamber should represent the open country—mountains, plains, forests, and fields.

The chamber is lighted by a single light. This is a great globe, suspended in the South, and represents the sun. The only additional light is from the transparencies.

In the East is suspended a transparency, displaying the sign of the Macrocosm or of the Seal of Solomon, the interlaced triangles, one white and the other black.

Above the transparency in the East are, in gilded letters, the words *Lux e Tenebris*.

In the West is suspended a transparency, displaying the sign of the Microcosm or the Pentagram, traced on white with lines of vermilion, and with a single point upward, thus:

In the South is a painting of the Temple of Solomon. At the entrance to it, to which an ascent by seven steps is represented, is painted a man, holding in his arms a white lamb, between the columns Jachin and Boaz.

In each corner of the chamber is suspended, about six

feet above the floor, an equilateral triangle; its three sides colored respectively *white, black,* and *red,* and each side measuring about eighteen inches, thus:

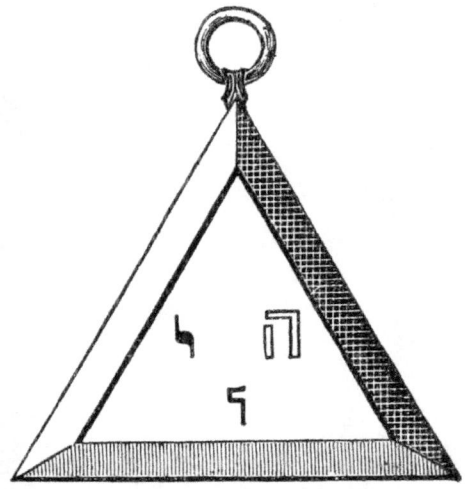

In the North is a transparency, on which the following figure appears:

"The understanding of the occult is the knowledge of the equilibrium."—Sohar, Book I., Siphra de Zeniutha.

On the right of the presiding officer, in the East, on a gilt pedestal, is a *caduceus,* gilded; the upper part of it a *cross,* surmounted by a *globe*—two *serpents* twining around the caduceus, their heads rising above the cross.

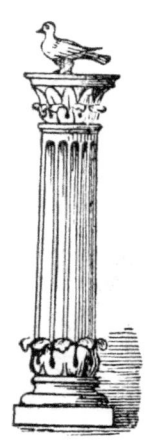 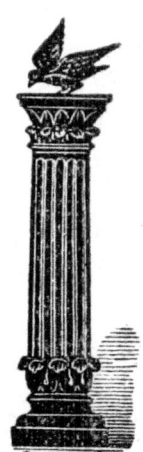

On the right of the officer in the West, on a white pedestal, is a white *dove,* its wings folded; and on his left, on a black pedestal, a black *raven,* its wings extended, as if just alighting.

On the east, west, and south of the altar, in the centre of the chamber, are three candlesticks, the candles not burning; and over each candlestick the letter S.

The ceiling of the chamber should represent the heavens, with the crescent moon in the West; the principal planets, and the stars in the constellations Taurus and Orion, and those near the pole-star.

The altar is square, with a gilded horn or flame at each corner. On it is a plate of white marble, upon which is inlaid in gold the pentagram. Upon this lies the book of constitutions open, and near it a censer.

CFFICERS—THEIR STATIONS, CLOTHING, ETC.

The presiding officer is styled "Father Adam." He sits in the East, clothed in a saffron-colored robe, and

KNIGHT OF THE SUN.

with head covered. In his right hand he holds a sceptre, its handle gilded, and on the top a globe of gold. His jewel is a sun of gold, suspended by a chain of gold, worn round the neck. The reverse side of the jewel is a hemisphere of gold, showing the northern half of the ecliptic and zodiac, with the signs from Taurus to Libra inclusive.

When the degree is conferred, no jewel or apron is worn.

There is but one Warden. He sits in the West, and is called "Brother Truth." He wears a rose-colored robe, and bears a white rod, at the end of which is an eye of gold. His jewel is like that of the Master.

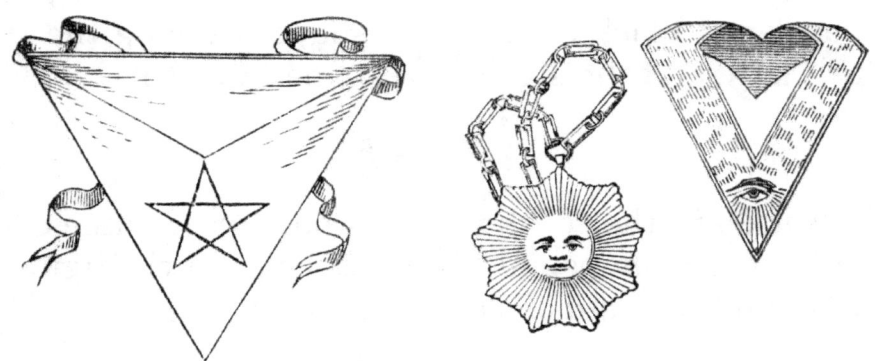

The *order* of the degree is also worn by each of these officers. It is a broad, white, watered ribbon, worn as a collar. On the right side is an eye of gold.

The *apron* is of pure white lambskin, with no edging or ornament except the pentagram, which is traced on the middle of it with vermilion.

There are seven other officers, who are styled, collectively, "The Seven Malakoth" (מלאכות, *Kings, Envoys, Angels*), and, separately, "the first, second, third," etc., מל אך, *Malak,* or, "Brothers Gabriel,

Auriel, Michael, Raphael, Zarakhiel, Hamaliel, and Tsaphiel." The first is called "*Malak Malakoth*."

These officers wear robes of a bright flame-color, with the cordon of the degree, and for a jewel a seven-pointed star of gold. They wear also the apron. The jewel may be suspended from the collar.

These officers are stationed thus:

Gabriel sits in the northeast, having on his right his banner, square in shape, of crimson silk, having upon it the figure of an eagle, and the sign of the planet Jupiter.

Michael, in the southeast, having on his right his banner of black silk, of like shape, bearing the figure of a lion, and the sign of the planet Saturn.

Auriel, in the southwest, his banner of flame-colored silk, of like shape, on his right, bearing the figure of a bull, and the sign of the planet Mars.

Raphael, in the northwest, his banner of green silk, of like shape, on his right, bearing the figure of a man, and the sign of the planet Mercury.

Zarakhiel, in front of Father Adam, his banner of purple silk, of like shape, on his right, bearing the sign of the Sun.

Tsaphiel, in front of Brother Truth, his banner of white silk, of like shape, on his right, bearing the sign of the Moon.

☽

And Hamaliel, in the South, his banner of blue silk, of like shape, on his right, bearing the sign of the planet Venus.

♀

Gabriel wears also bracelets of pure tin; Michael, of lead; Auriel, of steel; Raphael, of hollow glass, partly filled with quicksilver; Zarakhiel, of gold; Tsaphiel of silver; and Hamaliel, of polished copper. The banners of Michael, Gabriel, Auriel, and Hamaliel are fringed with silver; those of the others with gold.

The other members of the Council are termed Aralim (plural of Aral, אראל, Lion of God; hero). They wear the collar and apron, but no robe. Their jewel is a five-pointed star, suspended by a flame-colored ribbon on the left breast.

Of these brethren, one acts as Herald, one as Expert, one as Tiler.

Battery—•••–••••.

OPENING.

The following is the beautiful and expressive prayer used in the opening of this sublimely philosophical degree.

PRAYER.

O uncreated reason, spirit of light and wisdom, whose breath gives and withdraws the form of everything! The universe is thy utterance and revelation. Thou, before whom the life of beings is a shadow that changes, and a vapor that passes away! Thou breathest forth, and the endless spaces are peopled; thou drawest breath, and all that went forth from thee return to thee again. Unending movement, in eternal permanence! we adore and worship thee with awe and reverence. We praise and bless thee in the changing empire of created light, of shadows, of reflections, and of images; and we incessantly aspire toward thy immovable and imperishable splendor. Let the ray of thy intelligence and the warmth of thy love reach unto us! Then what is movable will be fixed, the shadow become a body, the dream a thought. Incline us, O Spirit of Spirits! to obey thy will! Help us, O Eternal Soul of Souls! to perform our duties! O imperishable breath of life, O mouth that givest and takest away the existence of all beings, in the flow and reflow of thy eternal word, which is the divine ocean of movement and of truth, make our efforts to do good effectual, and let the light of thy divine truth shine in the souls of all mankind! Amen!

RECEPTION.

But little of the immense amount of instruction contained in the degree of *Knight of the Sun* can be given in a manual of the rite; the degree is voluminous, and the monitorial parts are extensive, and it is deemed more appropriate that they should be laid before the student and neophyte directly from the ritual in the hands of the Commander-in-chief of the Consistory. The following points are however inscribed.

*   *   *   *   *

1. Science is preserved by silence, and perpetuated by initiation. The law of silence is absolute and inviolable, only with respect to the unitiated multitude. Science makes use of symbols; but for its transmission, language also is indispensable; wherefore the sages must sometimes speak.

— But when they speak, they do so, not to *disclose* or to *explain,* but to lead others to *seek for* and *find* the truths of Science and the meaning of the symbols.

*   *   *   *   *

2. The Hermetic Masters said, "Make gold potable, and you will have the universal medicine." By this they meant to say, appropriate truth to your use, let it be the spring from which you shall drink all your days, and you will have in yourselves the immortality of the sages. We are the authors of

our own destinies; and God does not save us without our co-operation.

— Death *is not,* for the sage. It is a phantom which the ignorance and weakness of the multitude make horrible.

— Change is the evidence of movement, and movement reveals *life* alone. Even the body would not be decomposed if **it** were dead. All the atoms that compose it retain life, and move to free themselves. The spirit is not the first to be disengaged, that it may live no longer. Can thought and love die, when the basest matter does not?

— If change should be called death, we die and are born again every day; for every day our forms change. Let us fear, then, to go out from and rend our garments, but let us not dread to lay them aside when the hour for rest comes!

* * * * *

3. The divine light, that outshining of the supreme reason or word of the Deity, "which lighteth every man that cometh into the world," has not been altogether wanting to the devout of any creed. The permanent revelation, one and universal, is written in visible nature, is explained by reason, and completed by the wise analogies of faith.

— Faith has in all ages been the lever whereby to move the world.

* * * * *

4. There is no invisible world. There are only different degrees of perfection in the organs.

— The body is the gross representation, and, as it were, the temporary envelope of the soul.

— The soul can perceive, by itself, and without the intervention of the bodily organs, by means of its sensibility and lucidity, the things, whether spiritual or corporeal, that exist in the universe.

— There is no void in nature; all is peopled.

— There is no real death in nature; all is living.

* * * * *

5. What we call death is change. The supreme reason, being unchangeable, is therefore imperishable. Thoughts, once uttered, are immortal. Is the source or spring from which they flow less immortal than they? How could the thoughts exist, if the soul from which they emanated were to cease to be? Could the universe, the uttered thoughts of God, continue still to exist if he no longer were?

* * * * *

6. Nature is the primary, consistent, and certain revelation or unveiling of God. It is his utterance, word, and speech. Whether he speaks to us through a man, must depend, even at first, on human testimony, and afterward on hearsay or tradition. But in and by his work we *know* the Deity, even as we know the mind of another man, and his thoughts, by his acts and words. We can no more be face to face

with the soul of another man than we can with God.

* * * * *

7. Analogy is the last word of science, and the first of faith.

— Harmony is in equilibrium; and equilibrium subsists by the analogy of contraries.

— The absolute unity is the supreme and last reason of things. This reason can neither be one person or three persons: it is one reason, and *the* reason, surpassing and transcendent.

* * * * *

—Religions seem to be written in heaven and in all nature. That ought to be so; for the *work* of God is the *book* of God, and in what he writes we ought to see the expression of his thought, and consequently of his being; since we conceive of him only as the supreme thought.

* * * * *

In the West, over the Warden, you behold the holy and mysterious pentagram, the sign of the microcosm, or universe, called in the Gnostic schools "The blazing star," the sign of intellectual omnipotence and autocracy, which has been partially explained to you heretofore. It represents what is called in the Kabala microprosopos, being in some sort a human figure, with the four limbs, and a point representing the head. It is the universe contained within the Deity.

It is a sign ancient as history and more than history; and the complete understanding of it is the key of the two worlds. It is the absolute philosophy and natural science.

All the mysteries of Magism, all the symbols of the gnosis, all the figures of the occult philosophy, all the kabalistic keys of prophecy, are summed up in the sign of the pentagram, the greatest and most potent of all signs.

The white *dove* and black *raven* in the West represent the two principles of Zoroaster and Manes, good and evil, light and darkness; and the fourth and fifth sephiroth of the Kabala, the mercy or benignity, and the justice or severity of the Deity.

*   *   *   *   *

The candidate in the ancient initiations surrendered without reservation his life and liberty to the Masters of the Temples of Thebes or of Memphis; he advanced resolutely amid innumerable terrors, that might well lead him to suppose that it was intended to take life. He passed through fire, swam torrents of dark and foaming water, was suspended by frail ropes over bottomless gulfs. Was this not blind obedience, in the fullest sense of the word? To surrender one's liberty for the moment, in order to attain a glorious emancipation, is not this the most perfect exercise of liberty itself? This is what those

NEOPHYTE PASSING THROUGH THE GREATER EGYPTIAN MYSTERIES.

have had to do, what those have always done, who have aspired to the Holy Empire of magical omnipotence. The disciples of Pythagoras imposed on themselves a complete speechlessness for many years; and even the followers of Epicurus only learned the sovereignty of pleasure, by a self-imposed sobriety and calculated temperance. Life is a warfare, in which one must prove himself a man, to ascend in rank. Force is not given: it must be seized.

* * * * *

If the sacred Scriptures are inspired, God himself has told us that *he* makes good and creates evil.

It is owing to human vanity that no man has ever dared to reason with common sense on this subject. Man pursues, tortures, and kills the most innocent animals, birds, and fishes, to gratify his appetite, or for mere pleasure. He crushes thousands of insects without a thought of wrong; nay, he destroys, as does every other animal, myriads of animalcalæ and infusoria daily, unconsciously, and without being able to avoid it. Throughout the whole scale of animal creation, one creature lives by devouring another, and every step taken, or movement made, or breath drawn by each, crushes out life. Pain and sickness, calamity and death, are the lot of all created beings.

* * * * *

The world teems everywhere with life, and is peopled with innumerable myriads of beings sensitive to pain. It was not created for man alone; and it is not only precisely what the divine and perfect wisdom intended, but it is all that a material world, peopled by beings with material bodies, could by possibility be. The millennium on this earth is the real Utopia, fabulous and impossible, of visionary dreamers. Man is what the Deity meant he should be—imperfect, feeble, fallible, liable to err, and sensitive to pain, but capable of improvement and progression, and of a heroism that can smile at agony, be content with destitution, preserve an equal mind under the lash of injustice, and without unmanly fear await the approach of death and count the pulses of his life. The man who can do this has attained the equilibrium of faith and reason, and may claim to be called Magus, Prince, Adept, and Knight of the Sun.

TWENTY-NINTH DEGREE.

Knight of St. Andrew.

ARGUMENT.

The degree of Knight of St. Andrew is intended to inculcate equality—representing the poor knight equal to the monarch; and exhibits the requisites of knighthood—protection to the defence-less and innocent, the possession of virtue, patience, and firmness; and represents the Knight as the exponent of truth, and one alike without fear and without reproach.

The Cross of St. Andrew, in heraldry, is termed the Cross Saltire, emblem of suffering and humility. Tradition says that St. Andrew was crucified on the 30th of November, on a cross of that form

The beautiful Masonic doctrine of Toleration is exemplified in this, the last of the instructive degrees of the Historical and Philosophical Series.

The lecture of this degree is inserted in this volume, and is a fitting climax to the theory of *Universal Religion*.

KNIGHT OF ST. ANDREW;

OR,

PATRIARCH OF THE CRUSADES.

THE TWENTY-NINTH GRADE OF THE ANCIENT AND ACCEPTED SCOTTISH RITE, AND THE ELEVENTH DEGREE OF THE HISTORICAL AND PHILOSOPHICAL SERIES.

APARTMENTS, AND THEIR DECORATIONS, ETC.

Two apartments are necessary, beside the preparation-room.

THE FIRST APARTMENT.

The hangings are crimson, supported by white columns; seats of the Master and Wardens, crimson, with gilt ornaments, while those of all the other knights are blue.

In each corner of the Chapter-room is a St. Andrew's Cross; and nine lights, by threes, are on the East, West, and South sides of the altar, in the centre of the room. During a reception this hall represents the court of Salah-eddin (Saladin), the great Sultan of Egypt and

Syria. No Masonic emblems appear. A parchment Koran lies on a table in front of the throne, and Saracenic standards, displaying the Crescent, stand near the seats of the Grand Master and the Wardens. The Chapter-room at this time is hung with green and gold. Ottomans, in lieu of chairs, and other Saracenic and Eastern properties, should be disposed about the hall.

THE SECOND APARTMENT.

The second apartment should be a well-furnished room, in the Eastern style, arranged with accommodations for washing, and containing a table, on which are a cross-hilted sword, and a Bible or Koran.

OFFICERS, AND THEIR DRESS WHEN IN THE CHAPTER.

1. VENERABLE GRAND MASTER.
2. SENIOR WARDEN.
3. JUNIOR WARDEN.
4. MASTER OF CEREMONIES.
5. SENIOR DEACON.
6. JUNIOR DEACON.
7. TREASURER.
8. SECRETARY.
9. CAPTAIN OF THE GUARD.
10. HOSPITALLER.
11. SENTINEL.

The Knights are all dressed in crimson robes, with a deep scarlet sash around the waist, a green collar edged with crimson about the neck, to which the Jewel is suspended, and a white silk sash worn from the left shoulder to the right hip, ornamented with gold fringe. On the left breast is the large white Cross of St. Andrew.

KNIGHT OF ST. ANDREW.

 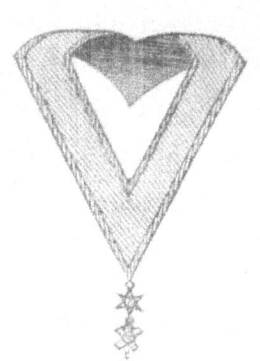 

The *Jewel* is two interlaced triangles, formed by arcs of large circles, with the concave outward, made of gold, and enclosing a pair of compasses open to twenty-five degrees. At the bottom, and to one of the points, is suspended a St. Andrew's Cross of gold, surmounted by a knight's helmet; on the centre of the cross is the letter י, enclosed in an equilateral triangle, and this again in a ring formed by a winged serpent; between the two lower arms of the cross may be suspended a key; on the corners of the cross the letters. נמיג

Assemblies of this degree are styled Chapters.

The *Battery* is nine, by • •—• •—• • • •

OFFICERS AND THEIR COSTUME, IN THE COURT OF SALADIN.

The throne is occupied by the Master of Ceremonies, who represents the Sultan, while the Grand Master represents Hugh of Tiberias, Lord of Galilee. The Senior Warden represents Malek Adhel, brother of the Sultan (Malek Adhel, Sayf-eddin—the just king and sword of religion). The Junior Warden, in the South, represents Malek Modaffer, Taki-edden—(the victorious king and devoted to religion)—Prince of Hamah and nephew of the Sultan. The Senior Deacon, seated or. the right of the throne, is Malek Daher—(triumphant king)—son of the Sultan and Prince of Aleppo; the Junior Deacon, on the left of the throne, Malek Afdel— (excellent king)—son of the Sultan and Prince of Damascus; and the Captain of the Guard—who accompanies the Grand Master, and, after introducing him, seats himself on the right of the Senior Warden, the Emir of Emessa.

The Knights all wear the Turkish costume—that is, the wide trowsers, vest and turban, all white, and a red sash around the waist, with a scimetar.

Behind the throne is a banner, in the shape of a shroud, white, on which, in black, are these words: *"Salah-eddin, king of kings—Salah-eddin, victor of victors—Salah-eddin must die."*

RECEPTION.

* * * * *

M∴ of C∴. Noble knight, since your forces entered this land of ours, I have learned something of your institution of knighthood, and would fain know more. I understand the sanctity of the knightly word, as you may see by the confidence I have placed in yours; and I have also heard from those who have been in your camps, as prisoners and otherwise, that there is among you a strange equality, so that a knight, though poor, may sit in the presence of a monarch. Tell me if that be so.

G∴ M∴ It is. Thou hast not been misinformed. The name of Knight, and gentle blood, entitle the possessor to place himself in the same rank with sovereigns of the first degree, so far as regards all but kingly authority and dominion. If the greatest king were to wound the honor of the poorest knight, he could not, by the law of chivalry, refuse satisfaction by single combat.

M∴ of C∴ And how may he aspire to mate in marriage?

G∴ M∴ With the noblest and proudest dame in Christendom. The poorest knight is free, in all honorable service, to devote his hand and sword, the fame of his exploits, and the deep devotion of his heart, to the fairest princess that ever wore a coronet.

*   *   *   *   *

G∴ M∴ Thou must profess thy belief in the one true and everliving God; and ye Saracens worship not the true God.

M∴ of C∴ Thou art mistaken, prince, for thou knowest not our faith. Doth not the Koran say, "There is no God but God—the living, the self-subsisting?" Your God is our God is our God; there is no God but he—the most merciful. To God belongeth the east and the west—therefore, whithersoever ye turn yourselves to pray, there is the face of God; for God is omnipresent and omniscient. We believe in God, and that which hath been sent down to us, and that which hath been sent unto Abraham and Ishmael, and Isaac and Jacob, and the tribes; and that which was delivered unto Moses and Jesus; and that which was delivered unto the prophets from their Lord. We make no distinction between any of them, and to God are we resigned. So speaketh the Koran everywhere.

G∴ M∴ Princely Saladin, didst thou ever think of the Lord Jesus Christ, or does thy faith allow thee to believe in him?

M∴ of C∴ Doth not the Koran say that whosoever believeth in God and the last day, and doeth that which is right, shall have their reward with their Lord? Doth it not say, "We formerly delivered the book of the law unto Moses, and caused apostles to succeed him, and gave evident miracles to Jesus, the Son of Mary, and strengthened him with the Holy Spirit? The angels said: O Mary, verily God hath chosen thee—verily God sendeth thee the good tidings, that thou shalt bear the Word, proceeding from himself; his name shall be Christ Jesus; God shall teach him the Scripture and wisdom, and the law and the gospel, and shall appoint him his apostle to the children of Israel. God took him up unto himself, and God is mighty and wise. And there shall not be one of those who have received the Scriptures who shall not believe in him before his death; and on the day of resurrection he shall be a witness against them?" These are the words of the Koran; and all the followers of the Prophet believe that Christ was an apostle from God, born of a Virgin and inspired, and did teach the truth.

*   *   *   *   *

You will now wash both hands and face, which, with the ceremonies performed, is a symbol of that baptismal rite observed among all Eastern nations, by way of purification—emblematical of that purity and innocence of soul, without which no one can enter into the order of knighthood nor into the pure abode of happiness above.

The candidate for knighthood not only serves a long apprenticeship in arms, and shows himself valiant and daring, and above all base apprehension of death, but should pass through a long and rigid probation, to prove himself, for his virtue, temperance, faith, constancy, and nobleness of heart, fit to be enrolled in the ranks of Chivalry. These, under circumstances, may be dispensed with, and the Order conferred even upon the field.

I do enjoin both of you, if you are not resolved to be henceforward virtuous, chaste, humble before God, merciful, tolerant, generous, and charitable, to proceed no further, lest hereafter you should be disgraced before the whole world as false and disloyal knights. Remember, your word must hereafter never be broken; you must never strike a prostrate foe, nor slay the prisoner that can no longer resist, nor refuse moderate ransom, nor defile yourselves with many women; and all true and loyal knights must be your brothers, and all distressed virgins your sisters, and all poor and destitute orphans your children.

* * * * *

PRAYER.

Our Father, who art in heaven—the God of Abraham, Isaac, and Jacob—the one only true God! look now upon these candidates, about to become knights and thy servants; aid them to perform punctually the vows they are about to assume; strengthen their good resolutions, and suffer not temptation to overcome them. Make them true knights, and teach them to exercise whatever powers they have with gentleness and moderation, and for the benefit of mankind and thy glory. Aid them to be true and loyal, frank and sincere; and may their knighthood here below be but preparatory to their final initiation into the mysteries of thy heaven of perfect happiness and perfect purity. Amen!

* * * * *

My brethren, I need not enlarge further to you on the duties of a knight. The Order of Knights Ecossais is a chivalric order, of great antiquity, and has numbered among its members many kings and princes; but its greatest boast is its intimate connection and alliance with an Order more ancient still.

*   *   *   *   *

In the name of God, St. Andrew, and St. Michael the Archangel, I dub thee Knight of the Ancient and Venerable Order of G∴ Scottish Knights of St. Andrew—known also as Patriarchs of the Crusades. Rise, good Knight and true Mason: be faithful, fearless, and merciful.

LECTURE.

Masonry is the handmaid of religion. The Brahmin, the Jew, the Mahometan, the Catholic, the Protestant—each professing his peculiar religion, sanctioned by the laws, by time, and by climate-may retain their faith, and yet may be Masons.

Masonry teaches, and has preserved in their purity, the cardinal tenets of the old primitive faith, which underlie and are the foundation of all religions. Masonry is the universal morality which is suitable to the inhabitants of every clime—to the man of every creed. It has taught no doctrines except those truths that tend directly to the well-being of man; and those who have attempted to direct it toward useless vengeance, political ends, the Kabala,

Hermeticism, Alchemy, Templarism, and Jesuitism, have merely perverted it to purposes foreign to its pure spirit and real nature.

The best, and, indeed, the only good Mason, is he who, with the power of labor, does the work of life—the upright mechanic, merchant, or farmer—the man who exercises the power of thought, of justice, or of love—whose whole life is one great act of performance of Masonic duty. The natural work of Masonry is practical life: the use of all the faculties in their proper spheres and for their natural functions. Love of truth, justice, and generosity, as attributes of God, must appear in a life marked by these qualities. The natural form of Masonry is goodness, morality, living a true, just, affectionate, self-faithful life, from the *motive* of a good man. It is loyal obedience to God's law. The good Mason does that which is good, which comes in his way, from a love of duty; and not merely because a law enacted by man or God commands his will to do it. Not in vain does the poor or oppressed look up to him. You find such men in all Christian sects, Protestant and Catholic; in all the great religious parties of the civilized world—among Buddhists, Mahometans, and Jews. They are kind fathers, generous citizens, and unimpeachable in their business: you see their Masonry in their works and in their play. The true Mason loves not only his kindred and his country, but all mankind; not only the good, but also the evil among his brethren. Though the ancient and the honorable of the earth bid him bow down to them, his stubborn knee bends only at the bidding of his manly soul. His Masonry is his freedom before God, not his bondage unto men.

The old theologies, the philosophies of religion of ancient times, will not suffice us now; there are errors to be made way with, and their places supplied with new truths, radiant with the glories of heaven. There are great wrongs and evils in Church and State, in domestic, social, and public life, to be righted and outgrown. Masonry cannot in our age forsake the broad way of life; she must journey on in the open street, appear in the crowded square, and teach men by her deeds—her life—more eloquent than any lips.

This degree is much devoted to Toleration, and it inculcates in the strongest manner that great leading idea of the Ancient Art—that a belief in the one true God, and a moral and virtuous life, constitute the only religious requisites needed to enable a man to be a Mason.

It has ever the most vivid remembrance of the terrible and artificial torments that were used to put down new forms of religion or extinguish the old. It sees with the eye of memory the ruthless extermination of all the people, of all sexes and ages—because it was their misfortune not to know the God of the Hebrews, or to worship him under the wrong name—by the savage troops of Moses and Joshua. It sees the thumbscrews and the racks; the whip, the gallows, and the stake; the victims of Diocletian and Claverhouse; the miserable covenanters; the non-conformists; Servetus bound, and the unoffending Quaker hung. It sees Cranmer hold his arm, now no longer erring, in the flame, until the hand drops off, in the consuming heat. It sees the persecutions of Peter and Paul, the martyrdom of Stephen, the trials of Ignatius, Polycarp, Justin, and Irenæus; and then, in turn, the sufferings of the wretched Pagans under the Christian emperors, as of the Papists in Ireland, and under Elizabeth and the besotted Henry; and all that in all ages have suffered by hunger and nakedness, peril and prison, the rack, the stake, and the sword—it sees them all, and shudders at the long roll of human atrocities.

Man never had the right to usurp the unexercised prerogative of God, and condemn and punish another for his belief. Born in a Protestant land, we are of that faith: if we had opened our eyes to the light under the shadows of St. Peter's at Rome, we should have been devout Romanists; born in the Jewish quarter of Aleppo, we should have contemned Christ as an impostor; in Constantinople, we should have cried, "Allah il Allah—God is great, and Mahomet is his Prophet." Birthplace and education give us our faith.

Few believe in any religion because they have examined the evidences of its authenticity, and made up a formal judgment, upon weighing the testimony. Not one in ten thousand knows anything about the proofs of his faith. We believe what we are taught; and those are most fanatical who know least of the evidences on which their creed is based.

What is truth to me is not truth to another. The same arguments and evidences that convince one mind, make no impression on another: this difference is in men at their birth. No man is entitled positively to assert that he is right, where other men, equally intelligent and equally well-informed, hold directly the opposite opinion. Each thinks it impossible for the other to be sincere; and each, as to that, is equally in error. "What is truth?" was a profound question—the most suggestive one ever put to man. Many beliefs of former and present times seem incomprehensible. They startle us with a new glimpse into the human soul—that mysterious thing, more mysterious the more we note its workings. Here is a man, superior to myself in intellect and learning, and yet he sincerely believes what seems to me too absurd to merit confutation; and I cannot conceive, and sincerely do not believe, that he is both sane and honest; and yet, he is both. His reason is as perfect as mine, and he is as honest as I am.

The fancies of a lunatic are realities to him. Our dreams are realities while they last; and in the past, no more unreal than what we have acted in our waking hours. No man can say that he hath as sure possession of a truth as of a chattel.

When men entertain opinions diametrically opposed

to each other, and each is honest, who shall decide which hath the truth, and how can either say with certainty that he hath it? We know not what is the truth. That we ourselves believe and feel absolutely certain that our own belief is true, is, in reality, not the slightest proof of the fact, seem it never so certain and incapable of doubt to us.

Therefore no man hath, or ever had, a right to persecute another for his belief; for there cannot be two antagonistic rights; and if one can persecute another because he himself is satisfied that the belief of that other is erroneous, the other has, for the same reason, equally as certain a right to persecute him.

The truth comes to us as the image of a rod comes to us through the water, bent and distorted: an argument sinks into and convinces the mind of one man, while from that of another it rebounds most quickly. It is no merit in a man to have a particular faith, excellent, and sound, and philosophic as it may be. It is no more a merit than his prejudices and his passions.

The sincere Moslem has as much right to persecute us, as we to persecute him; and therefore Masonry wisely requires no more than a belief in one great, all-powerful Deity, the Father and Preserver of the universe. Therefore she teaches her votaries that toleration is one of the chief duties of every good Mason. The Masonic system regards all the human race as members of one great family—as having the same origin and the same destination; all distinctions of rank, lineage, or nativity, are alike unknown. The whole tenor of the life of the benevolent Founder of the Christian religion was unremitting benevolence; his kind offices were extended alike to Gentiles and Jews, to publicans and sinners, as well as to his disciples.

Yet Masonry is eternally vigilant that no atheist or base libertine contaminates with his unhallowed tread the *sanctum sanctorum* of our temple; such can never gain admission there, without the grossest violation of vows the most sacred and solemn. It requires the acknowledgment of the existence of the Grand Master of the Universe, and to reverence his great and sacred name, irrespective of sectarian ideas; in a word, to practise every virtue which adorns and ennobles the human character, and fly every vice which sullies and degrades it. It inculcates a generous love for all mankind, it matters not of what religious creed.

No evil hath so afflicted the world as intolerance of religious opinion; the human beings it has slain in various ways, if once and together brought to life, would make a nation of people, which, left to live and increase, would have doubled the population of the civilized portion of the world; among which civilized portion it chiefly is that religious wars are waged.

No man truly obeys the Masonic law who merely tolerates those whose religious opinions are opposed to his own. Every man's opinions are his own private property, and the rights of all men to maintain each his own are perfectly equal. Merely to tolerate, to bear with an opposing opinion, is to assume it to be heretical, and assert the right to persecute, if we would, and claim our toleration as a merit.

The Mason's creed goes further than that; no man, it holds, has any right, in any way, to interfere with the religious belief of another. It holds that each man is absolutely sovereign as to his own belief, and that belief is a matter absolutely foreign to all who do not entertain the same belief; and that if there were any right of persecution at all, it would in all cases be a mutual right, because one party has the same right as the other to sit as judge in his own case—and God is the only magistrate that can rightfully decide between them.

To that Great Judge Masonry refers the matter; and, opening wide its portals, it invites to enter there, and live in peace and harmony, the Protestant, the Catholic, the Jew, the Moslem—every one who will lead a truly virtuous and moral life, love his brethren, minister to the sick and distressed, and believe in the One, All-Powerful, All-Wise, Everywhere-Present God—Architect, Creator, and Preserver of all things—by whose universal law of Harmony ever rolls on this universe: the great, vast, infinite circle of successive death and life; to whose ineffable name let all true Masons pay profoundest homage! for whose thousand blessings poured upon us let us feel the sincerest gratitude, now, henceforth, and forever. Amen.

SIXTH SERIES.

THE SIXTH SERIES OF THE ANCIENT AND ACCEPTED SCOTTISH RITE CONTAINS THREE DEGREES, KNOWN AS CHIVALRIC, AND WHICH ARE CONFERRED IN A CONSISTORY: THEY ARE THE KNIGHT OF KADOSH, GRAND INSPECTOR INQUISITOR COMMANDER, AND SUBLIME PRINCE OF THE ROYAL SECRET.

"I am all that has been, that is, and that will be, and no man hath ever lifted my veil."—*Temple of Neïtha.*

SEPHIROTH.

This division of the ten Sephiroth into three triads was arranged into a form called by the Kabbalists the Kabbalistic Tree, or the Tree of Life, as shown in the following diagram:

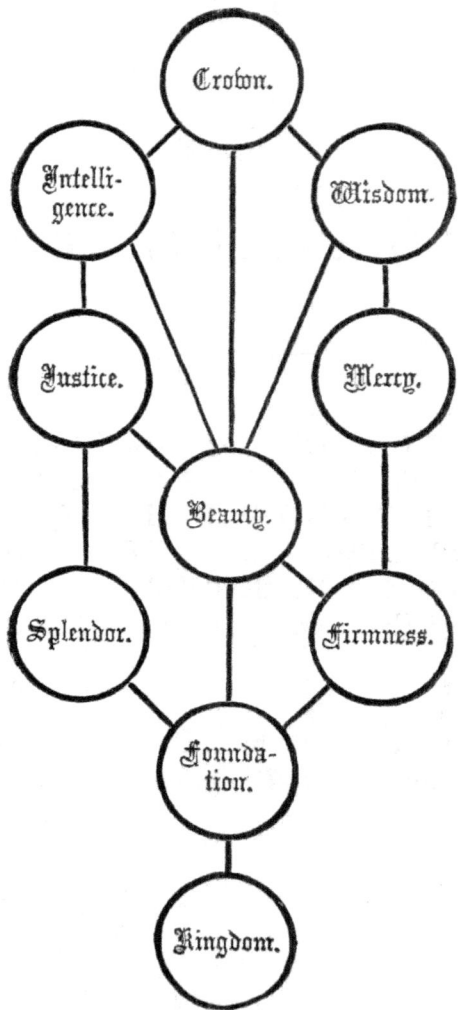

In this diagram the vertical arrangement of the Sephiroth is called "Pillars." Thus the four Sephiroth in the center are called the "Middle Pillar;" the three on the right, the "Pillar of Mercy;" and the three on the left, the "Pillar of Justice."

PREFATORY.

The three chivalric degrees of Knight Kadosh, Inquisitor Commander, and Prince of the Royal Secret are intimately connected, and form the Templar degrees of the Ancient and Accepted Scottish Rite.

The labors of Masonry are well-nigh ended, so far as instruction is concerned,—the virtues of the Order are rehearsed, and the reward for a due reverence of the obligations and a retention and observance of the vows and tenets of the Institution is accorded.

We now approach the *Holy Empire,* which signifies the attainment of the science and power of the Magi. The four words of the Magi are, To *Know,* to *Dare,* to *Will,* to be *Silent,* and are written in the four symbolic forms of the Sphynx.

The accomplishment of these degrees brings us to the completion of the third Temple; and the Royal Secret is solved, as to whether we have made this world a Temple fit for the abiding-place of the Grand Architect of the universe.

"IF it be asked, for what good are the Superior degrees cultivated? we might answer, that as to personal benefits, the opportunity to 'do good and communicate,' to practise all the Masonic virtues, as well as enjoy all the pleasures of fellowship and sociality—so far as these are considered within the sphere of the Masonic acquirements of any brother—the original working degrees of Ancient Craft Masonry will for him suffice. Only to one who wishes to attain a more extensive knowledge of, and become fully accomplished in, the religious, philosophic, and chivalric departments of our Order, as they were cultivated in the different ages of the world gone by, as well as at the present day, would we recommend initiation into the high degrees. He only will be competent to appreciate the honors and privileges attached to them, who possesses the disposition and ability to study the deeper and higher mysteries of our Kabala, and will not rest satisfied until he has discovered a satisfactory solution to every Masonic problem, and can, in every case, explain '*de quo fabulum narratur;*' who can thoroughly understand the *moral* mysteries, as well as those of art and science, which our legends unfold, and who has a laudable ambition to participate in the most exalted sphere, with congenial associates, in that subtle communion and fraternization which genuine 'Sublime Freemasonry' is peculiarly calculated to afford."

London Freemason's Quarterly Magazine.

THIRTIETH DEGREE.

Knight Kadosh

ARGUMENT.

A KNIGHT and Soldier of the Cross called Knight Kadosh proves himself practically a true defender of the Temple of the Most High God; and while armed with steel outwardly, he is inwardly armed with Faith and Love—Faith to God and Love to his fellow-man. It is his duty to defend the Order, to protect and assist all worthy pilgrims, the weak and the injured, the needy and the oppressed, with becoming humility and meekness, and yet with fidelity and prudence, as vowed on the Mystic Ladder.

This practical trial degree of the Knight Templar is replete with effective incident, and stands prominently forward as an interesting and exciting drama.

KNIGHT KADOSH.

THE THIRTIETH GRADE OF THE ANCIENT AND ACCEPTED SCOTTISH RITE, AND THE FIRST DEGREE OF THE CHIV. ALRIC SERIES.

APARTMENTS, FURNITURE, AND DECORATIONS.

Bodies in this degree are termed Chapters.
The main Hall is decorated with red and black columns.

The Throne in the East is surmounted by a double-headed Eagle, crowned, holding a poniard in his claws; over his neck is a black ribbon, to which is suspended the Cross of the Order; on his breast is an Equilateral

Triangle, around which are the words: "*Nec proditor Nec proditor, innocens feret.*"

There are 9 lights of yellow wax.

A drapery of white and black curtains, strewed with red crosses, descends between the wings of the Eagle, and forms a pavilion.

Behind the throne are two banners, one white with a green Teutonic cross upon it, and the motto "*Deus Vult;*" the other with a red cross on one side, and on the other a double-headed Eagle, holding a poniard, with the motto, in silver letters, "*Aut vincere, Aut mori.*"

JUDGES' HALL,

Black, lighted by a single lamp, of triangular or antique form, suspended from the ceiling. Everything in this apartment should be sombre.

There are five Judges, robed in black, and masked, each with a sword, at reception. The Judges are seated, Knights in attendance standing, who are also in black robes, and cowls over their heads, with their hands crossed over their breasts.

CAVE OR CHAMBER OF REFLECTION,

Is strewed with emblems of mortality, and is entered by descending a flight of stairs: but one light is used.

This chamber should be sombre in all its appointments, and is intended to represent the tomb of Jacques de Molay.

A rude altar, over which is placed a single lighted candle, a Bible, and a cup of wine; near the altar a gong.

MYSTERIOUS LADDER,

Is covered until the candidate is obligated. This Ladder has two supports and seven steps. The first support on the right is called O. E.; the second support on the left is called O. K.

The first Chamber is termed "Judges' Hall."
The second   "   "   "   "Chamber of Reflection."
The third   "   "   "   "Forum."
The fourth   "   "   "   "Senate Chamber."
The fifth   "   "   "   "The Road to the Holy Land."

Five Knights constitute a quorum, and should be dressed in black, with white gloves.

Kadosh signifies holy, consecrated, separated.

The *Jewel* is a Teutonic cross of gold, enamelled with red, in the centre of which are the letters J∴ B∴ M∴ On the reverse a skull transpierced by a poniard, and is hung to the sash.

Battery—•••••—•

OFFICERS OF THE COUNCIL:

GRAND COMMANDER, in the East;
GRAND CHANCELLOR, right of Grand Commander;
GRAND ARCHITECT, left of Grand Commander;
GRAND MASTER OF CEREMONIES, in the North;
GRAND TREASURER, right of Grand Commander in the North.
GRAND SECRETARY, left of Grand Commander in the South.
GRAND CAPTAIN OF THE GUARD, in the South;
SENTINELS, GUARDS, and KNIGHTS.

DRESS OF A KNIGHT KADOSH.

The regular costume of a Knight Kadosh, as prescribed by the Ancient Rituals, is as follows:

A white tunic of fine woollen stuff, in the shape of a Dalmatica, with large sleeves; reaching to the knees.

bordered with black, and having on the left breast a red Latin cross.

A mantle of black velvet, very full, and reaching midway between the knee and ankle, edged with red velvet, and having on the left breast a red Latin cross.

It is clasped in front of the throat with a plain Teutonic cross of gold.

A wide-brimmed hat of black felt, with a plume of red ostrich feathers, on the left side; and covering the lower end of the plume, a Teutonic cross of gold: on the front is a sun of gold, its rays extending the whole width of the front.

A knight's collarette, with points of linen cambric, with or without lace.

A black belt of leather with a true Teutonic cross in front, as a clasp, of jet and gold, on which are the letters J∴ B∴ M∴.

Closely-fitting pantaloons of white casimere; and worn over them yellow morocco boots, coming up halfway to the knee, bound around the top with narrow gold lace, and having tassels of white silk in front. Gold spurs.

A sword with straight silver guard, in a black scabbard, hangs from the belt; on the scabbard and hilt are the figures 30.

A collar of black watered silk ribbon, four inches wide, edged with narrow silver lace, and worn over the tunic and under the mantle. On the front part of the collar are embroidered in scarlet silk the letters

K-H, two Teutonic crosses, a double-headed Eagle, with wings extended, a crown resting on the two heads, holding a poniard in his claws.

The crown, both heads, and the blade of the poniard, are of gold; the handle of the poniard is oval, one-half black, and the other white.

At the end of the cordon, or when a collar is worn, then under the sash, is a poniard, its blade of steel, its handle oval, and one-half of it ivory, the other half ebony.

Round the body is a black sash, edged with silver.

Gloves are of white kid.

RECEPTION.

The reception commences by the introduction of the aspirant to the Judge's Hall, where he obtains permission to proceed to the Chamber of Reflection.

*   *   *   *   *

"Whoever shall be able to conquer the fear of death shall come safe out of the bowels of the earth, and have the right to be admitted into the 'Mysteries of the Order.'"

*   *   *   *   *

BOOK OF THE A. AND A. RITE.

Pending the following prayer and the remaining ceremonies in this chamber, the *"Miserere"* will be heard in the distance, on the organ.

MISERERE.

G∴ M∴ of C∴ You will then kneel with me, my brother, in the midst of these decaying relics of mortality, sad emblems of life and hope departed, and offer up with me prayers and supplications to the God of heaven.

"Our Father, who art in heaven," etc., etc.

*   *   *   *   *

He heapeth up riches and cannot tell who shall gather them. In the midst of life we are in death; yet to whom may we flee for succor, but to thee, O Lord! who, for our many sins, art justly displeased. O God most holy! O God most mighty! Ever and glorious Lord! save us from the pains of eternal death! Amen!

The following is the prayer of Jacques De Molay, just prior to his execution, and may very properly be introduced at this time:

"O God! permit us to meditate on the pains that Jesus suffered, that we might be redeemed; and enable us to imitate the example of endurance which he gave when he submitted, without a murmur, to the persecutions and torments which bigotry and injustice had prepared for him.

"Forgive, O God, those false accusers who have caused the entire destruction of the Order whereof thy Providence has made me the head. And if it please thee to accept the prayer which we now offer, grant that the day may come when the world, now deceived, may better know those who have sought to live for thee.

"We trust to thy goodness and mercy to compensate us for the tortures and death which we are now to suffer; and that we may enjoy thy divine presence in the mansions of happiness."

*   *   *   *   *

G∴ Com∴ It becomes my duty, at this time, to glance at the history of Masonry from its earliest date; but it would be impossible, within the limited time allowed me, to enter into a detailed account of the various incidents connected with this subject; I will, therefore, merely allude to some of the prominent points.

The incidents attending the erection of the Temple it is to be presumed you are already acquainted with. The conspiracy of the three assassins of the Grand Master, H∴ A∴, the incidents of his death so peculiarly reminding us of the death of the great exemplar Jacques De Molay; the zeal and energy of the brethren in the apprehension and punishment of the assassins; the wisdom of King Solomon in selecting a chosen few, and making them perfect in the arts and sciences; the elevation of the twelve Sublime Knights, elected to carry out the work of perfection; the great object and duty of the twelve, and their connection with our Grand Master, the builder of the third temple, in their completion of the first temple, and their partaking of a mystic oblation having reference to a portion of the body of their Grand Master, and vow to carry out his great designs; and our ancient Grand Master tasting of the bitter cup of death; the zeal and energy of our ancient brethren, Gibulum, Joabert, and Stolkin, in penetrating into the bowels of the earth and bringing thence the valuable treasures to enrich and adorn the temple of God; the rewards conferred on them by King Solomon in admitting them to perfection; the apostasy of Solomon; the destruction of the Temple; the finding of the sacred vault, and the dead body of Galaad at the entrance thereto, and the destruction of the Golden Delta; the captivity of seventy years, and return to Jerusalem under Zerubbabel; the incidents of the Knights of the East or Sword and Princes of Jerusalem; the establishment at Jerusalem of the Knights of the East and West; the Rose-Croix degree, and its connection with the building of the third temple; the Knights of Jerusalem and Knights of the Temple, called Knights Templars or Crusaders; the formation of the Order of Knights Templars; their devotion and heroism in the cause of Christianity.

You are now, my brother, about to be instructed in a portion of the secret mysteries. But before entering upon them, let us offer up our supplications to Heaven, as on all important occasions. You will kneel and join me in my appeal.

PRAYER.

O thou Eternal, beneficent, and all-glorious and gracious Grand Architect of the Universe! we, from the secret depths of our hearts, offer up to thee a living sacrifice. We pray thee to fill our hearts with thy love and the love we should feel for each other. We are brethren, journeying the rugged path of life to that bourne from which we cannot return. We humbly beseech thee, O Heavenly Father! to inspire our enemies with a just sense of the evils they have done, and a conviction of their wrong-doing: that they may make atonement for their manifold injuries and injustice to us; which do not belong to us, thy servants, to redress them ourselves; for thou hast said, O Lord! "Vengeance is mine, I will repay" that by their eyes being opened we might be reconciled, and by a hearty union take possession of those blessed lands, where the original temple was first established, and where thou hadst said, "I will dwell;" where we might be gathered together in one fold or band of brothers, there to celebrate thy great and holy name; and on the holy mountain, in whose bowels was deposited the ever-glorious and awful Name, celebrate thy praise. Amen!

All. So mote it be!

G∴ Com∴ You will now rise, my brother. I now charge you to make yourself familiar with the history of the Knights Templars; of their rise and progress; their great and glorious exploits; their numbers, wealth, and high standing in every kingdom of Europe; their persecution and fall, and the sufferings of the Grand Master, Jacques de Molay, and his brave Knights, by order of Pope Clement V.; the cruelty and barbarity of Philip the Fair and the potentates and governments of Europe; the actions of the Knights of Malta in the destruction of the Templars, and their receiving and holding many large possessions, the property of the Templars, as a reward for their treachery; the dispersion of the Templars, and their many sufferings and death. The facts and history, my brother, can be obtained from the sources I previously mentioned.

NE PLUS ULTRA.

THIRTY-FIRST DEGREE.

Grand Inspector Inquisitor Commander.

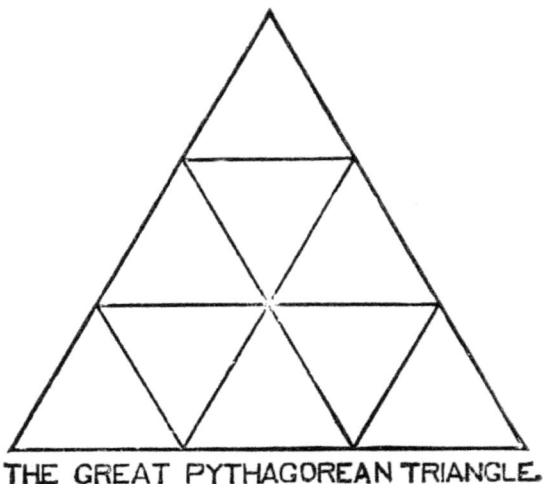
THE GREAT PYTHAGOREAN TRIANGLE.

ARGUMENT.

The practical test of the neophyte in the degree of Knights Kadosh, is in this degree of Inquisitor Commander changed to a thorough examination under charges against Masonic law and duty before the Order of the Five Brethren.

The wise sayings of sages and lawgivers are quoted for instruction, to remind the Knight of the serious vows that he has assumed, and how to preside in judgment and expound the law; to judge justly and punish sternly; but ever remembering the frailty and imperfection of human nature, to pardon and forgive while there yet remains hope of reformation.

To render judgment is a stern duty and an unwelcome task to be performed; for in this a man usurps, to some extent, the functions of God; he should therefore himself be just, upright, impartial, disregarding persons, influence, rank, and power.

GRAND INSPECTOR INQUISITOR COMMANDER.

THE THIRTY-FIRST GRADE OF THE ANCIENT AND ACCEPTED SCOTTISH RITE, AND THE SECOND DEGREE OF THE CHIVALRIC SERIES.

DECORATIONS.

The hangings are white. as also the canopy under which is the throne of the President.

There are ten gilded columns; one on each side of the President in the East; one on each side of the Counsellors in the West; three on the south side of the Tribunal, and three on the north; equidistant from each other.

Over the column on the right of the President is inscribed in large letters the word *Justitia*.

Over that upon his left, the word *Equitas*.

From these two columns springs a Gothic arch, from

the apex whereof is suspended over the head of the President the Tetractys of Pythagoras, thus:

$$\begin{matrix} & & \bullet & & \\ & \bullet & & \bullet & \\ \bullet & & \bullet & & \bullet \\ \bullet & \bullet & & \bullet & \bullet \end{matrix}$$

and under it a naked sword and the scales of justice.

Over the column on the right of the Counsellors is inscribed the word *Lenitas;* upon the left, the word *Misericordia.* From these two columns springs a Gothic arch, from the apex whereof is suspended in letters of gold the sacred word of the eighteenth degree.

On the three columns in the south, going from east to west, are the busts of Moses, Zoroaster, and Minos, with the name of each inscribed on his column.

On the columns on the north, also going from east to west, are the busts of Confucius, Socrates, and Alfred the Great, with the name of each inscribed on his column.

In front of the President is a table, on which are the Square and Compasses, the Plumb and Level, an hour-glass, a skull and cross-bones, a small pair of Scales, a naked Sword, and the Book of Constitutions.

In the centre of the room are ten lights, in the east, ten, and in the west ten; each ten being arranged in the form of the Tetractys.

The altar is covered with a black cloth; Judges' table covered with green cloth.

TITLES, OFFICERS, AND THEIR STATIONS.

The assembly is styled Supreme Tribunal.

The presiding officer is styled Most Perfect President and sits in the east.

GRAND INSPECTOR INQUISITOR COMMANDER.

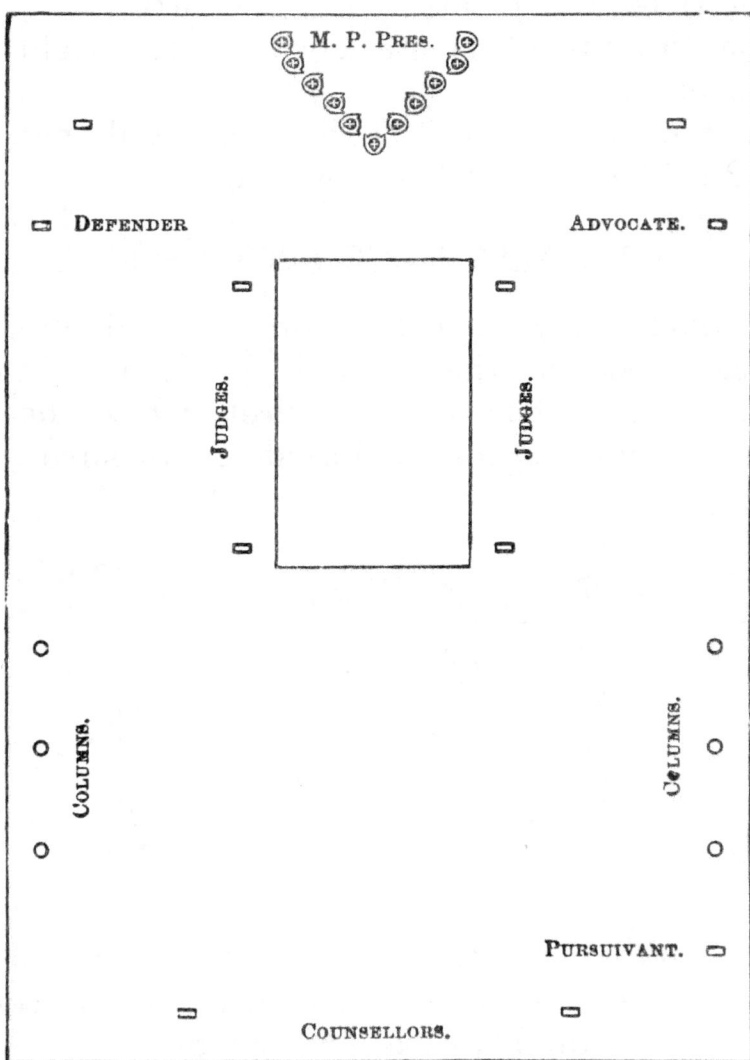

The Wardens are styled Counsellors, and sit in the west.

The Secretary (Keeper of the Seals and Archives) is styled Chancellor, and sits on the right of the President

The Treasurer sits on the left of the President.

The Advocate is stationed in the south.

The Defender is stationed in the north.

The Pursuivant is stationed on the right of the Counsellors.

All the members of the Supreme Tribunal, except the President, are styled Illustrious.

REGALIA, DECORATIONS, ETC.

No *apron* is worn in the Supreme Tribunal. In the inferior bodies the Grand Inspector Inquisitor Commanders wear one of entirely white sheep-skin, with a Teutonic cross, embroidered in silver, on the flap.

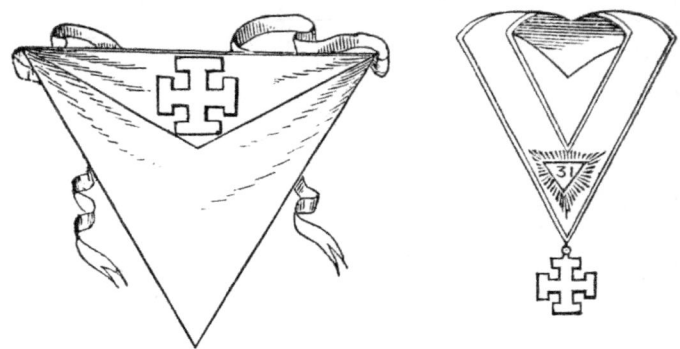

The *collar* is white; at the point is a triangle emitting rays, embroidered in gold, in the centre of which is the number 31 in Arabic figures.

In the inferior bodies, instead of a collar, a Grand Inspector Inquisitor Commander may wear around his neck a golden chain, from which hangs the cross of the Order; the links of the chain are formed of the interlaced attributes of the eight fundamental degrees of Masonry—viz., 1st, 2d, 3d, 4th, 14th, 16th, 18th, and 30th.

The *jewel* is a silver Teutonic cross.

The *hat,* same as Kadosh.

PREROGATIVES.

When a Grand Inspector Inquisitor Commander, wearing the proper insignia, visits a Lodge of an inferior degree, he announces himself as a Grand Inspector Inquisitor Commander. He is proved in the ordinary manner, and the report is made in the ear of the Master, who causes all the members to be placed around the altar; he then sends the two Wardens to receive him, by whom he is conducted to the altar. The Master then leaves his seat, and placing the three gavels upon the altar, he presents them to the visiting brother, who accepts, and returns them to the Master, and to each of the Wardens, after which he is conducted by the Master to the seat of honor.

"Lenitas .... Misericordia."

RECEPTION.

*   *   *   *   *

PRAYER.

Hear us with indulgence, O infinite Deity, whose attributes are infinite, and yet infinitely harmonious. Thou, of whose essence all justice, equity, and mercy, intermingled into one infinite excellence. Thou, to whom all thoughts and all actions of men are known and visible as thine own; to whom the infinite past and the infinite future are one now; and the infinitudes of space in all directions are here. Give us the wisdom and the will to judge justly, accurately, and mercifully; and when we come to be finally judged by thee, do not thou judge us as, in our feebleness and passion, we may have judged others; but forgive us and take us home to thee. Amen!

* * * * *

If the Knight Kadosh, when performing his pilgrimage, proves himself recreant of any obligation, he should here be accused of the same.

If deemed an unworthy Knight by the Judges on any accusation, he should be returned to the outer world for a probationary period; if not, the Most Perfect President proceeds, first taking a vote of the Judges.

* * * * *

M∴ P∴ Pres∴ Illustrious Knight, you desire to take upon yourself an arduous, responsible office. There is but one infallible, unerring Judge. All human judgment is, at best, uncertain; serious in its consequences, it must often, when time develops its errors, produce regret, and sometimes remorse. It is not wise to seek to judge our fellow-man; it is a stern duty, and an unwelcome task to be performed, and not a privilege to be coveted; and woe unto that man who assumes the prerogative of judgment, and, to some extent, usurps the functions of God, not being himself just, upright, impartial.

Subsequent to the dismissal of the Inquisition, and preparatory to the lessons and warnings being given, the following music will be played.

SONATA.

I was the just King Alfred of Saxon England, I framed wise laws, made upright judges, independent of my will and that of the people, and caused just and speedy judgment to be given. In all my realm, justice and right were sold to none; denied to none ; delayed to none. I slept little; I wrote much; I studied more. I reigned only to bless those over whom I had dominion. I have vanished into the thin past, and many ages have marched in solemn procession by my grave, yet I still live in the memory of men. They call me great king, wise lawgiver, just judge; follow, then, my example, or shudder to sit in judgment on thy fellows.

* * * * *

I was Socrates, the Athenian; I knew the holy mysteries, and reverenced God in nature. In the sacred groves of Athens, I taught to young and old that God was one, and the soul of man immortal. I taught obedience to the laws and decrees of the people of Athens, and the council of five hundred. When I sat in the court of the Areopagus, I swore by the paternal Apollo, by Ceres, and by Jupiter the King, that I would sentence uprightly and according to law—or, when the law was silent, to the best of my judgment; and that I would not receive gifts, nor should any other for me; nor receive bribes from any passion, prejudice, or affection; nor allow any other person to do the like by any means, whether direct or indirect, to prevent justice in the court. And when, by an unjust judgment, the same court condemned me to death, I refused to flee and escape, lest I should bring the laws into disrepute; holding the good citizen bound to submit to even the unjust judgment of the State. If thou wouldst fain become a judge of others, first prepare thyself by learning to obey the laws.

* * * * *

I was Confucius, who read and interpreted to the people of ancient China the great laws engraved by the finger of God, in everlasting letters, upon the pages of the many-leaved book of nature. I said to them, desire not for your country any other benefit than justice; the great law of duty is to be looked for in humanity. "Justice is Equity," to render to every man that to which he is entitled. He who would stand above the ordinary level of man must be exempt from prejudices and self-conceit and obstinacy, and be governed by the mandates of justice alone. Hear much, reflect much, and say nothing superfluous. Let doubt of guilt be acquitted; and presumption of innocence be solid proof. "That is the noblest recompense of human virtue!" Do thou strive so to live and act, to obey and govern, and thou, too, mayest live in the good opinion of men, after thou art dead, and thine influences may make thee, too, a king over the minds of men.

* * * * *

I was Minos, the lawgiver of Crete. I taught the Cretans that the laws which I enacted were dictated by Zeus, the Father; for all true and righteous laws, and all human justice, are but developments of that eternal and infinite justice, that is of the essence of the Deity. He who assumes to judge his brethren clothes himself with the prerogative of God. "Woe unto thee," if, being thyself vicious or criminal, thou dost assume to judge others; and still more, if thou givest corrupt judgment; for then will thy memory be execrated, and in all time it shall be the bitterest reproach to an unjust judge to call him by thy name.

* * * * *

I was Zoroaster, whose words became law to the Persians. I said he is the best servant of God, whose heart is upright, who is liberal, with due regard to what is just to all men; who turns not his eyes toward riches, and whose heart wishes well to everything that lives. He alone is just who is charitable, and merciful in his judgments; and he alone is wise who thinks well, and not evil, of other men. Satisfy thine own conscience, and fear neither the outrages of fortune nor the injuries of enemies. Crime is not to be measured by the issue of events, but by the bad intentions of the doer. Study, therefore, the dominion of thyself, and quiet thine own commotions, and hold it the noblest ovation to triumph over thy passions.

* * * * *

I was Moses, the leader and lawgiver of the Israelites. I was initiated into the mysteries and wisdom of Ancient Egypt; and that wisdom dictated the statutes by which Israel was governed. Thou shalt take no gift; for the gift blindeth the wise and perverteth the words of the righteous. Ye shall do no unrighteousness in judgment. Thou shalt not respect the person of the poor, nor honor the person of the mighty. Ye shall hear the small as well as the great. Ye shall not fear the face of man; for judgment is of God.

   *   *   *   *   *

Sen∴ Couns∴ Thou hast heard the words of the great sages, lawgivers, and philosophers of antiquity. Behold! the monogram of the greatest lawgiver that has ever come among men, and listen reverentially to his teachings. If ye forgive not men their trespasses, neither will your heavenly Father forgive your trespasses. But if ye forgive men their trespasses, your heavenly Father will also forgive you. With what judgment ye judge, ye shall be judged. And with what measure ye mete, it shall be measured to you again. If thy brother trespass against thee, go and tell him his fault between thee and him alone. If he shall hear thee, thou hast gained thy brother. Judge not according to the appearance, but judge righteous judgment. If thy brother trespass against thee, rebuke him, and if he repent, forgive him; and if he trespass against thee seven times in a day, and seven times in a day turn again to thee, saying, "I repent," thou shalt forgive him. Blessed are the merciful; for they shall obtain mercy.

*   *   *   *   *

You have heard the lessons of immortal wisdom, once uttered by mortal lips that have long since mouldered into dust. Through those lips God spake unto men; for of him alone cometh all wisdom.

*   *   *   *   *

M∴ P∴ Pres∴ I invest you with the white collar and jewel of this degree; see that the purity of the former and the lustre of the latter be never sullied or dimmed by injustice, inhumanity, or impurity.

THIRTY-SECOND DEGREE.

Sublime Prince of the Royal Secret.

ARGUMENT.

This is the third and last of the Kadosh degrees, and consummates the Templarism of Masonry. The degree was originally a Christian degree of knighthood; its object was, for a long time, to reconquer the Holy Land and plant the Banner of the Cross once more on the ruined walls of Jerusalem. Many of the Knights of the Crusades were Masons, and thus became acquainted with the legend which Masonry had preserved.

The Knights Kadosh are the legitimate successors of the Templars.

None but earnest and sincere men, unselfish, and whose philanthropy is not a mere name, but a practical reality, should enter here—such as will do Masonry good service in the war which she is waging against the ancient enemies of the human race—a lover of wisdom and an apostle of Liberty, Equality, and Fraternity.

"No virtue is acquired in an instant, but step by step."—BARROW.

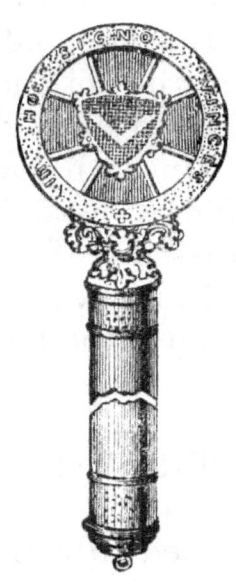

SUBLIME PRINCE OF THE ROYAL SECRET.

THE THIRTY-SECOND GRADE OF THE ANCIENT AND AO CEPTED SCOTTISH RITE, AND THE THIRD DEGREE OF THE CHIVALRIC SERIES.

DECORATIONS.

Bodies of this degree are styled Consistories. The hangings are black, strewed with tears of silver, skeletons, human skulls, and cross-bones.

In the East is a throne, to which you ascend by seven steps, draped with black satin, like the hangings, but strewed with flames without tears. Before the throne is an altar covered with black satin, strewed with tears; on it are painted or embroidered a death's-head and two cross-bones; over the death's-head is the letter J, and under the cross-bones the letter M. On this altar are the Book of Constitutions and Statutes of the Order, a naked sword, a sceptre, and a balance. In the West are the two Wardens. In front of each is a table, covered with crimson cloth, lined and edged with black, and strewed with tears. On each cover, in front, are the four letters N-K&8756; M-K&8756; On each table are two naked swords crossed.

The Hall is divided into two parts by a balustrade. In the West is the camp of the Princes.

OFFICERS AND TITLES.

The Master is styled Illustrious Commander-in-Chief; the two Wardens, Lieutenant Commanders; and the Orator, Minister of State. Beside these officers, there are a Grand Chancellor, Grand Secretary and Keeper of the Seals and Archives, Grand Treasurer, Grand Engineer and Architect, Grand Hospitaller, Grand Master of Ceremonies, Grand Captain of the Guard, Grand Standard-Bearer, and Grand Sentinel.

There are also in the Hall, west of the officers, on the right and left, fourteen members, clothed in red, with out aprons, and each having on his breast, suspended from a black ribbon worn as a collar, the jewel of one of the degrees—viz.: numbering these members from one to fourteen, they wear respectively the jewels of the 30th, 28th, 25th, 21st, 19th, 18th, 16th, 14th, 13th, 10th, 8th, 7th, 5th, and 3d degrees.

The first five are the Standard-Bearers of the Corps that encamp around the pentagon, and the last nine are Commanders of the Corps that encamp around the nonagon; the camp is as shown in the following illustration:

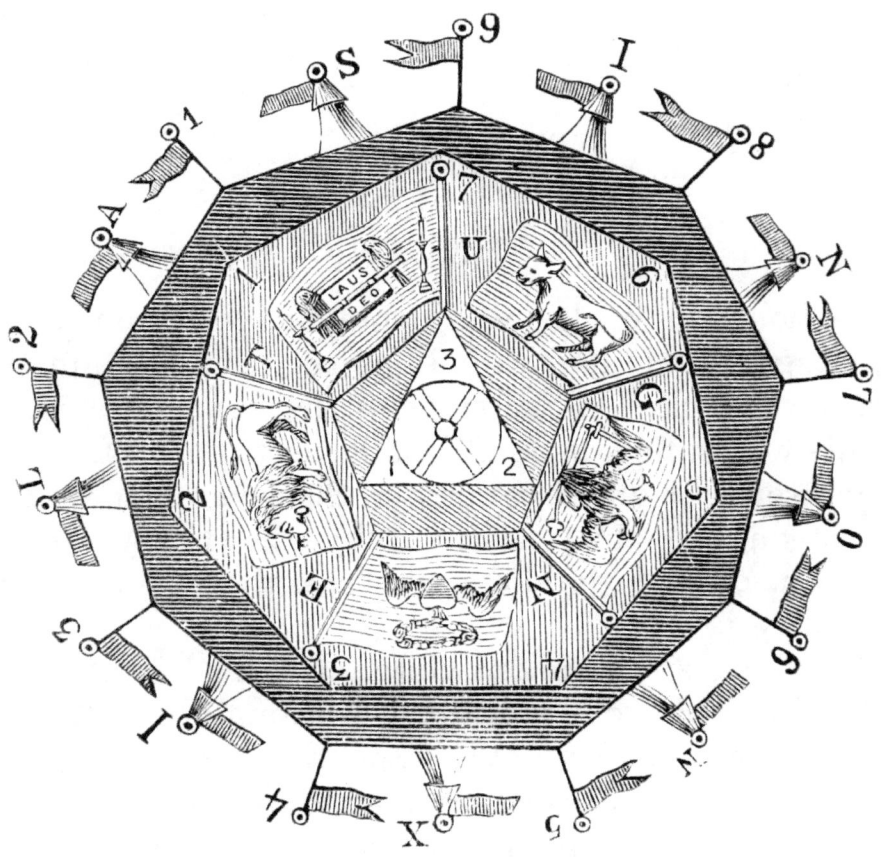

The names of the first five are as follows:

    1st.   Bezaleel........for the Standard.......T
    2d.   Aholiab.........   "   "   ......E
    3d.   Mah-Shim...... "   "   ......N
    4th.   Garimont....... "   "   ......G
    5th.   Amariah.......   "   "   ......U

The names of the others are:

    1st.   Malachi............for the Tent..........S
    2d.   Zerubbabel....... "   "   ....A
    3d.   Nehemiah........ "   " L
    4th.   Joabert............ "   " I
    5th.   Paleg...............   "   " X

6th. Jehoiada.........for the Tent...........N
7th. Aholiab..........   "   "   ....O
8th. Joshua..........   "   "   ....N
9th. Ezra..............   "   " I

THE CAMP

Is a nonagon, enclosing a heptagon, which encloses a pentagon, and that an equilateral triangle, and that again a circle. On the sides of the nonagon are nine tents with a flag, pennon, and letter to each. Each tent represents an entire camp, and the several sides of the nonagon are thus assigned by the rituals to the Masons of the several degrees from the 1st to the 18th, as follows:

S∴ Flag and pennon white, sprinkled lightly with crimson. That tent indicates the camp of the Knights Rose-Croix and Knights of the East and West, 18th and 17th degrees. The Commander, Malachi.

A∴ Flag and pennon light green. That tent indicates the camp of the Knights of the East or Sword and Princes of Jerusalem, 15th and 16th degrees. The Commander, Zerubbabel.

L∴ Flag and pennon red. That tent indicates the camp of the Grand, Elect, Perfect and Sublime Masons, 14th degree. The Commander, Nehemiah.

I∴ Flag and pennon black and red. That tent indicates the camp of the Knights of the Royal Arch and Grand Master Architects, 13th and 12th degrees. The Commander, Joabert.

X∴ Flag and pennon black. That tent indicates the camp of the Sublime Knights Elected, Elect of Fifteen and Knights Elect of Nine, 11th, 10th, and 9th degrees The Commander, Paleg.

N∴ Flag and pennon red and black, in diamonds. That tent indicates the camp of the Intendants of the Building, 8th degree. The Commander, Jehoiada.

O∴ Flag and pennon red and green. That tent indicates the camp of the Provost and Judges and Intimate Secretaries, 7th and 6th degrees. The Commander, Aholiab.

N∴ Flag and pennon green. That tent indicates the camp of Perfect Masters and Secret Masters, 5th and 4th degrees. The Commander Joshua.

I∴ Flag and pennon blue. That tent indicates the camp of the Masters, the Fellow-Crafts and Apprentices of Symbolic Masonry and Volunteers, 3d, 2d, and 1st degrees. The Commander, Ezra.

On each of the external sides of the pentagon is a standard, each designated by a letter, and each supposed to indicate the camp of a corps of Masons, occupying a side of the pentagon, viz.:

T∴ Field purple; on it the Ark of the Covenant in gold, between two green palm-trees, or two lighted candlesticks of gold. Motto at the base, "*Laus Deo.*" Around this standard are stationed the Knights Kadosh and the Grand Scottish Knights of Saint Andrew, 30th and 29th degrees. Standard Bearer, Bezaleel.

E∴ Field blue; on it is a golden lion, holding in his mouth a key of gold, and a gold collar around his neck, with the figures 525 on the collar. Motto at the base, "*Custos Arcani,*" and in some rituals, "*Ad Majorem Dei Gloriam*"—the latter is the motto of the Jesuits. Around this standard are stationed the Knights of the Sun, the Commanders of the Temple, and the Princes of Mercy, 28th, 27th, and 26th degrees. Standard Bearer, Aholiab.

N∴ Field white; on it is a flaming heart, with black

wings, crowned with a green laurel wreath. Motto at the base, "*Ardens Gloria Surgit.*" Around this standard are stationed the Knights of the Brazen Serpent, the Princes of the Tabernacle, and the Chiefs of the Tabernacle, 25th, 24th, and 23d degrees. Standard Bearer, Mah-Shim.

G∴ Field green; on it is a black eagle, with two heads, with an imperial crown of gold resting on both heads; holding in his dexter claw a sword, point in base; and in his sinister claw a bloody heart. Motto at the base, "*Corde Gladio Potens.*" Around this standard are stationed the Princes of Libanus and the Knights Noachite or Prussian Knights, 22d and 21st degrees. Standard Bearer, Garimont.

U∴ Field gold; on it is a black ox. Motto at the base, "*Omnia Tempus Alit.*" Around this standard are stationed the Masters Ad Vitam and the Grand Pontiffs, 20th and 19th degrees. Standard Bearer, Amariah.

At the angles of and inside the triangle are supposed to be encamped the Princes of the Royal Secret and the Grand Inspector Inquisitor Commanders, with such Knights of Malta as, having proved themselves true and faithful, may have been received among us.

CLOTHING.

The Illustrious Commander in Chief is clothed in the modern costume of royalty, of crimson; he is armed with a sword and shield. On the table, in front of him, lie his *Abacus* and balance. The Lieutenant Commanders are also armed with a sword and shield, with heads covered.

Neither the officers nor members when in costume

wear any apron, but only the collar, to which is suspended the jewel of the Order.

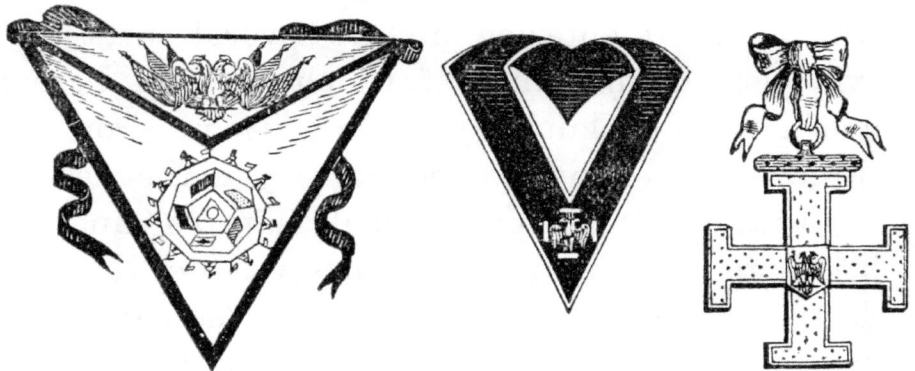

The *collar* is black, edged with silver; on the point is embroidered, in red, a Teutonic cross, and in the centre of the cross a double-headed silver eagle. The collar is lined with scarlet, and on the lining is embroidered a Teutonic cross, in black.*

The *girdle* is black, with silver fringe, and on the front is embroidered a red Teutonic cross.

The *jewel* is a double-headed white and black eagle, resting on a Teutonic cross, of gold.

The *apron* is white, satin or velvet, lined, and edged with black; on the flap is embroidered a double-headed eagle and flags of three colors on either side thereof. In the middle of the apron is embroidered the plan of the camp of the Princes.*

Kadosh hat—feathers white and crimson.

Battery—•–• • •

RECEPTION.

* * * * *

G∴ M∴ of C∴ My brother, the 32d degree of the Ancient and Accepted Rite, which we are now conferring

---

* Collar and Apron are dispensed with, and The Order substituted, see p. 186. *Proc. Sup∴ Council*, p. 71 of 1877.

on you is the military organization, as the 31st degree is the judicial organization of the Order. The camp which you are entering, and its several parts, are all symbols, the meaning of which we will hereafter endeavor to explain to you. As you pass around and through this camp, we will give you the necessary explanation as to its external features, and recall briefly to your mind the characteristics of the several degrees whose standards float over the camp, to aid you in hereafter understanding the esoteric meaning of the whole. The external lines of the camp form a nonagon, or a figure of geometry with nine equal sides. You perceive that on each side of the nonagon is a tent with a flag and pennon; that each flag and its pennon are of a different color from the others, and that each tent is designated by a letter. Each represents a camp, and the several sides of the nonagon are assigned by our rituals to the Masons of the different degrees from the 1st to the 18th.

*   *   *   *   *

At the 9th tent were encamped the Apprentices, Fellow-Crafts and Masters of the Blue or Symbolic Degrees, and the volunteers. The commanding officer represents Ezra.

The 1st degree shows you man, such as nature has made him, with no other resources than his physical strength.

The 2d degree teaches the necessity and holiness of labor, and consequently of knowledge.

The 3d degree teaches us that our unavoidable destiny is death; but at the same time, in the ceremony and in the very name of Hiram, it shadows forth the great doctrine of another life, and the immortality of the soul.

* * * * *

At the 8th tent were encamped the Secret Masters and Perfect Masters, or the Masons of the 4th and 5th degrees. The commanding officer represents Joshua.

* * * * *

At the 7th tent were encamped the Intimate Secretaries and Provosts and Judges, or the Masons of the 6th and 7th degrees. The commanding officer represents Aholiab.

* * * * *

At the 6th tent were encamped the Intendants of the Buildings, or the Masons of the 8th degree. The commanding officer represents Jehoiada.

* * * * *

At the 5th tent were encamped the Knights Elect of Nine, the Illustrious Elect of Fifteen, and the Sublime Knights Elected, or the Masons of the 9th, 10th, and 11th degrees. The commanding officer represents Paleg.

* * * * *

At the 4th tent were encamped the Grand Master

Architects and the Knights of the Royal Arch, of the Masons of the 12th and 13th degrees. The commanding officer represents Joabert.

* * * * *

At the 3d tent were encamped the Grand, Elect, Perfect and Sublime Masons of the 14th degree. The commanding officer represents Nehemiah.

* * * * *

At the 2d tent were encamped the Knights of the East or Sword and Princes of Jerusalem, or the Masons of the 15th and 16th degrees. The commanding officer represents Zerubbabel.

* * * * *

At the 1st tent were encamped the Knights of the East and West and the Knights Rose Croix of H-r-d-m, or the Masons of the 17th and 18th degrees. The commanding officer represents Malachi.

* * * * *

G∴ M∴ of C∴ Sir Knight, you have now passed round the nonagon, and a full explanation has been given you of each tent by its commander. Within this nonagon you perceive is traced a heptagon, or a figure of geometry with seven equal sides; and within that a pentagon, or one with five equal sides. On each of the external angles of the pentagon you perceive a standard, designated by a letter, which indicates the camp of a corps of Masons occupying externally a side of the pentagon.

* * * * *

At the 5th standard were encamped the Grand Pontiffs and Masters Ad-vitam, or the Masons of the 19th and 20th degrees. The commanding officer represents Amariah.

* * * * *

At the 4th standard were encamped the Noachites or Prussian Knights, and the Knights of the Royal Axe or Princes of Libanus, or the Masons of the 21st and 22d degrees. The commanding officer represents Garimont.

* * * * *

At the 3d standard were encamped the Chiefs of the Tabernacle, the Princes of the Tabernacle, and the Knights of the Brazen Serpent, or the Masons of the 23d, 24th, and 25th degrees. The commanding officer represents Mah-Shim.

* * * * *

At the 2d standard were encamped the Princes of Mercy or Scottish Trinitarians, the Grand Commanders of the Temple, and the Princes Adept or the Knights of the Sun, or the Masons of the 26th, 27th, and 28th degrees. The commanding officer represents Aholiab.

* * * * *

At the 1st standard were encamped the Grand Scottish Knights of St. Andrew or Patriarch of the Crusades, and the Knights Kadosh, or the Masons

ADMISSION OF A NOVICE TO THE VOWS OF THE ORDER OF THE TEMPLE

of the 29th and 30th degrees. The commanding officer represents Bezaleel.

   *   *   *   *   *

G∴ M∴ of C∴ Sir Knight, enclosed in this pentagon you observe an equilateral triangle; at its angles are said to be encamped the Princes of the Royal Secret, the Grand Inspector Inquisitor Commanders, and such Knights of Malta as, having proved themselves true and faithful, have been accepted and received among us. Within the triangle is a circle, in which are said to be the quarters of the Sovereign Grand Inspectors General of the 33d degree, who serve as Lieutenant Commanders under the Most Puissant Sovereign Grand Commander. In most of the engraved tracing-boards of this degree, within the circle is a cross with five arms of equal length, which were to be the quarters of the five Princes who, as Lieutenant Commanders, were in turn to be second in command, and whose standards float at the five angles of the pentagon.

   *   *   *   *   *

C∴ in C∴ Sir Knight, if you have in good faith assumed the obligations of the preceding degrees, the general features of which have now been summarily recited to you, and if you have studied and understood the doctrines which they teach and the principles which they inculcate, you are entitled to our regard and esteem, and are fitted to do the duties of a good Mason; for you have bound yourself to do all that virtue, honor, and manhood can require, and you have learned all that ancient and modern philosophy can teach in regard to the great mysteries of God and the universe.

* * * * *

PRAYER.

Kind and indulgent Father of the great family of men! Supreme Intelligence, author of Life and Light! aid us in our efforts to make this world more worthy of thee, and bless with thy favor our brother who marches to restore to light those who have forgotten thee and thy truth! For the infinite love thou bearest to thy suffering children, aid him and us in our warfare against ignorance, and against those who mislead, impose upon, and deceive thy people; and make the light of thy knowledge shine in all the corners of the earth. Amen!

SUBLIME PRINCE OF THE ROYAL SECRET.

While the armor is being buckled on the novice, the following will be heard in an adjoining apartment:

HYMN.

SPANISH CHANT.

1. Un-to thee, great God, belong Mys-tic rites and sa-cred song; Low-ly bend-ing at thy shrine, Hail, thou Ma-jes-ty Di-vine.

Glorious Architect above—
Source of light and source of love,
Here thy light and love prevail:
Hail! Almighty Master, hail!

The Knightly Armor of the Templar should be complete in every respect, and should be fully explained to the novitiate as it is piece by piece buckled upon him.

  *   *   *   *   *

Sir Knight, thou art now in form and semblance, and by declaration of principle, and, we trust, in spirit, a true Knight Templar: as such, it is your sworn duty to aid us in endeavoring to make this world a Temple fit for the abiding-place of the G∴ A∴ of the U∴

  *   *   *   *   *

C∴ in C∴ Receive this sash; its color is an emblem of sorrow and mourning for the miseries and sufferings of humanity. Receive, also, and wear this Teutonic cross of gold, the jewel of the Order; deserve it by the services you shall hereafter render to the good cause in which you now claim to be a chief and leader.

  *   *   *   *   *

INVOCATION.

This beautiful prayer should be intonated with organ accompaniment.

Com∴ in C∴. O thou Immutable, thou Immaculate and Immortal.

Choir Chant. Holy, holy, holy, Lord God of Sabaoth, we implore thee.

C∴ in C∴. By whose will we are born and by whose will we die, thou never-ending, thou great eternal, by whose beneficence we call thee Father.

Choir Chant. Holy, etc.

C∴ in C∴. Thou infinite Spirit of Light and Life, be with us. Let thine outstretching wings, expansive as the eagle's, give us shelter

Choir Chant. Holy, etc.

C∴ in C∴. Be thou to us like the night-dew's cooling balm upon earth's fevered brow. Teach us to know and dread thy wrath. Fill our hearts with love, and, when the end of life draws near, waft us with gentle winds to thy blest abode, where thy myriads chant.

Choir Chant. Holy, etc.

C∴ in C∴. Aid us, O Lord! to make this world a Temple of Peace and Love, fit for thy great abode.

Choir Chant. Holy, etc.

Choir. Amen! Amen! Amen!

C∴ in C∴. (*natural voice*) and Amen!

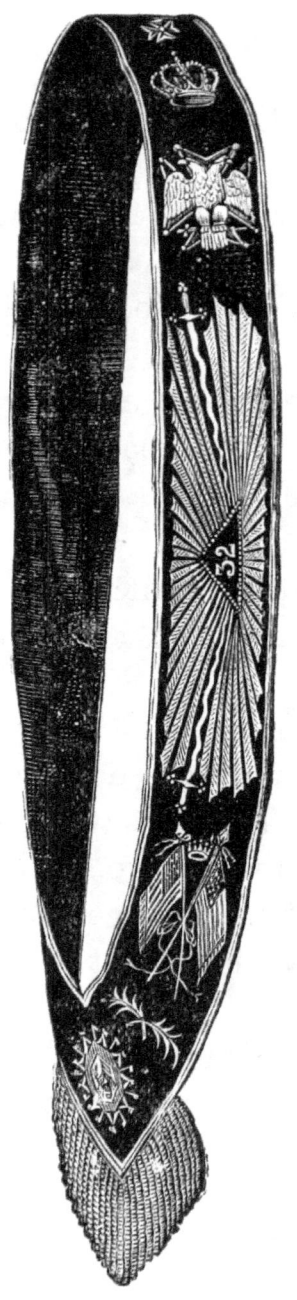
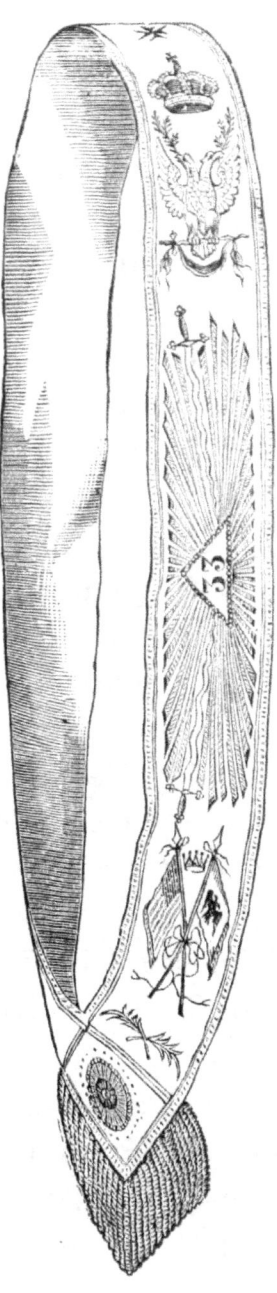

THE ORDER FOR THE 32d DEGREE.

BLACK moire antique ribbon, four inches wide, lined with red, and trimmed with silver lace, worn from the left shoulder to the right hip. Where it crosses the breast is a delta with rays, in the center, the figures 32 in Arabic characters: a waving sword on each side pointing toward the figures ; above this a large red Teutonic cross, and upon it, and covering it. except the extremities or points, a double-headed silver eagle, wings extended, grasping a two-edged naked sword in its talons, over the heads of the eagle a crown ; above this at the point which rests upon the left shoulder, a small red Maltese cross ; below the delta two American flags, with staffs crossed, above and between the staffs a ducal crown. All is embroidery of gold, silver, etc.: at the extremity which rests upon the left hip is the tracing-board of the camp painted or embroidered. The lower point of the Order is trimmed with silver bullion fringe three inches long.

THE ORDER FOR THE 33d DEGREE.

The Regalia of the officers of the Supreme Council is a collar of white moire antique with "*Royal purple*" trimming. Active Members wear the white Baldric with "*Royal purple*" trimming. Honorary Members the Baldric as above with crimson trimming.

486B

THIRTY-THIRD DEGREE.

Sovereign Grand Inspector-General.

PREFATORY.

It may not be improper, in connection with this, the last degree of the Ancient and Accepted Scottish Rite, although but a casual allusion is made to the ritual of the grade, to premise that Masonry is not of itself a Religion.

Like the Sun, it disseminates light and is the source of light; but, unlike that great luminary, which illuminates but one-half the globe at one and the same time, Masonry with its effulgence lights perpetually the entire Universe, and sends its rays of healing, consolation, and good cheer, dispelling ignorance, superstition, and error.

Every good Mason respects the religion of his brother, though differing, perhaps, from his own, and hopes that all may be true in those respects where differences arise, and that each may be sufficiently near the truth to solve for himself the great problem of life and death;

and surely no one who has looked thoughtfully on the checkered road through the wilderness of this life, or who has stood, even for a moment, near the brink of the cold river of death, would be otherwise than reverential in the presence of any shrine to which a fellow creature may kneel for aid or consolation;—

> "For we are doomed our native dust
> To wet with many a fruitless shower;
> And ill it suits us to disdain
> The Altar, to deride the fane
> Where simple sufferers bend in trust
> To win a happier hour."

To those who seek in this work a knowledge of the tenets and inculcations of the Rite, who may peruse the instructions and formula herein contained, the hand of sympathetic fellowship is extended, believing that the result of a careful study, combined with the ambition of the Enthusiast, will convince each and all that the Rite of which we essay to teach is replete in all its parts with the highest morality and fraternal devotion, leading man to sublimest thoughts and appreciation of the Present and a Hereafter; ever realizing in its surroundings and adornments the truth of that happy thought of England's youthful poet:

> "A thing of beauty is a joy forever:
> Its loveliness increases; it will never
> Pass to nothingness."   *   *   *

SOVEREIGN GRAND INSPECTOR-GENERAL.

THE THIRTY-THIRD AND LAST DEGREE OF THE ANCIENT AND ACCEPTED SCOTTISH RITE.

The assembly is styled a Supreme Council, only one of which is allowed in any country except the United States, where there are two.

DECORATIONS.

Hangings, purple; with skeletons, death's heads, crossbones, etc., painted or embroidered thereon. In the East a magnificent throne ; over it a purple canopy trimmed with gold. Beneath the canopy is a transparency representing a delta, in the centre of which are seen the ineffable characters. Near the centre of the room is a quadrangular pedestal covered with scarlet cloth, on which rests a naked sword. On the north side of the council chamber is a skeleton erect, holding the white banner of the Order, opposite which, in the South, is the flag of the country. Over the interior portion of the entrance is a blue scarf bearing the device DEUS MEUMQUE JUS. In the East is a candelabra with five branches; in the West, one with three branches; in the North, one with a single branch; and in the South, another with two branches; 5 + 3 + 1 + 2 (11) lights. The *hat* of a S∴ P∴ R∴ S∴ may appropriately be worn.

INSPECTOR-GENERAL.

The Thirty-third degree, or Inspector-General, being mainly executive in its character, and but seldom conferred, it is not deemed essential or for the benefit of the brethren generally to introduce any portion of its lectures here. It is conferred as an honorarium on those who for great merit and long and arduous services have deserved well of the Order.

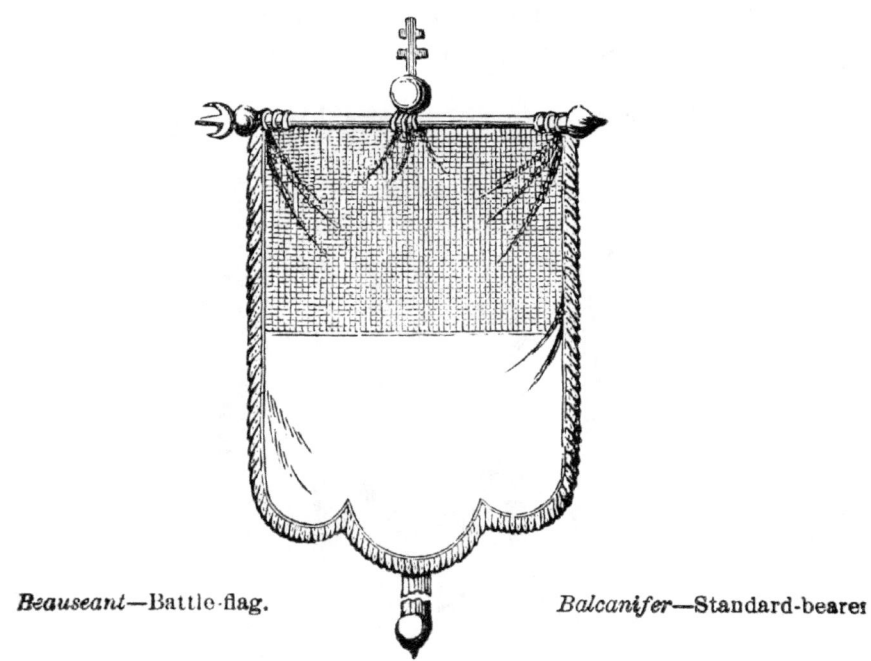

Beauseant—Battle-flag.   *Balcanifer*—Standard-bearer

APPENDIX
TO
THE FUNDAMENTAL STATUTES AND GRAND CONSTITUTIONS OF THE SUPREME COUNCIL OF THE THIRTY-THIRD DEGREE.
1786.

ARTICLE I.

The Banner of the Order is white, bordered with a fringe of gold, and having in the centre a double-headed black eagle, its wings displayed, beak and legs gold, holding with one claw the hilt, gold, and with the other the blade, *steel,* of a sword placed horizontally, hilt to the right and point to the left. From the sword hangs, lettered, gold, the motto, in Latin, "DEUS MEUMQUE

Jus." The eagle is crowned with a triangle of gold and a purple fillet fringed and starred with gold.

ARTICLE II.

The distinctive insignia of Sovereign Grand Inspectors General are:

1. A Teutonic Cross worn on the left breast.

THE GRAND DECORATION OF THE ORDER.

2. A broad white watered ribbon bordered with gold, and having on the front a golden triangle glittering with rays of gold, in the centre whereof is the number 33; and on each side of the upper angle of the triangle is a sword of silver pointing towards its centre. This ribbon, worn from the left shoulder to the right ands in a point, with gold fringe, and has at the junction a rosette of crimson and leek-green ribbon, whereon is the general jewel of the Order.

3. The Jewel is an eagle like that on the banner, wearing the golden diadem of Prussia.

4. The Grand Decorations of the Order rest on a Teutonic Cross. They are a nine-pointed star, formed by three triangles of gold, one upon the other, and interlaced. From the lower part of the left side toward the upper part of the right extends a sword, and, in the opposite direction, a hand of *Justice.* In the middle is the shield of the Order, blue; upon the shield is an eagle like that on the banner; on the dexter side of the shield is a golden balance, and on the sinister a golden compass resting on a golden square. Around the whole shield runs a stripe of blue, lettered in gold with the Latin words "Ordo ab Chao;" and this stripe is enclosed by a double circle formed by two serpents of gold, each holding his tail in his mouth. Of the smaller triangles formed by the intersection of the principal ones, those nine that are nearest the blue stripe are colored red, and on each is one of the letters that constitute the word S. A. P. I. E. N. T. I. A.

5. The first three officers of the Supreme Council wear also a white scarf or sash, fringed with gold, hanging from the right side.

ARTICLE III.

The Great Seal of the Order is a silver shield bearing a double-headed eagle, like that upon the banner of the Order, crowned with the golden diadem of Prussia, and over that a triangle of gold emitting rays, and in its centre the number 33. The eagle may, however, be surmounted by either the crown or triangle alone.

At the base of the shield, under the wings and claws of the eagle, are thirty-three golden stars in a semicircle. Around the whole is this inscription:

"SUPREME COUNCIL OF THE 33D DEGREE FOR....."

POWERS AND DUTIES OF DEPUTIES OF THE SUPREME COUNCIL.

CONSTITUTION.

ART. **36.**—1. There shall be a DEPUTY OF THE SUPREME COUNCIL for each State and Territory, who shall represent the SUPREME COUNCIL in his district, with power to visit and preside over any body of the Rite therein, and to do any act he may deem necessary in order fully to represent the Supreme Council.

2. He shall perform any duty specially assigned to him by the SUPREME COUNCIL, or the Most Puissant Sovereign Grand Commander.

3. He shall inspect all works of the Rite therein, correct irregularities, see that the Constitutions and the Regulations of the SUPREME COUNCIL and the General Laws of the Rite are respected and obeyed ; and he may suspend the charter or the functions of any officer of any subordinate body until the next Annual Session of the SUPREME COUNCIL, when he shall present the matter to it for such action as it may deem necessary ; *provided, however,* that such officer, or any member or members of such body, may appeal from his order to the Most Puissant Sovereign Grand Commander for his decision ; but the pendency of such appeal shall not vacate such order. If, in consequence of the suspension of

any officer or officers, there is no one remaining who succeeds to the chair under the Constitutions and Ritual, the Illustrious Deputy may appoint an officer with full powers to preside during such suspension, or until the vacancy is regularly filled. Such suspension of the charter shall not of itself affect the Masonic standing of the members of the body.

4. He may transmit and present directly to the SUPREME COUNCIL, or the Most Puissant Sovereign Grand Commander, the petitions for dispensations, charters and letters patent preferred to him by Consistories, Chapters, Councils, Lodges, or individuals under his jurisdiction, having first obtained the recommendation of the Council of Deliberation when such recommendation is required.

5. He shall collect all dues from the various Bodies of the Ancient Accepted Scottish Rite in his jurisdiction, and on or before the fifteenth day of July in each year forward the same, with a detailed statement thereof, to the Grand Secretary-General.

6. He shall lay before his Council of Deliberation a full report of the work in his jurisdiction, calling attention to such things as demand its special consideration.

7. He may, when unavoidably necessary, specially deputize in writing another member of the Thirty-third Degree, resident of the State, to perform for him, in his name, any specially enumerated official act, and shall be responsible for the acts of such substitute. In all such cases he shall send a copy of such deputization to the Most Puissant Sovereign Grand Commander.

8. Should he be obliged to leave his State on temporary business for an uncertain period of time, he may, with the consent of the Most Puissant Sovereign Grand Commander, appoint an Active Member as Deputy to act for him in his absence.

9. Any Brother or Body aggrieved by an act or decision of an Illustrious Deputy, may appeal therefrom to the SUPREME COUNCIL at its next Annual Session; but such an appeal shall not be suspensive. In such case it shall be the duty of the Illustrious Deputy to present such appeal and a copy of all papers relating thereto to the SUPREME COUNCIL as soon as practicable after the opening of its next Annual Session.

CEREMONIAL

OF

Inauguration, Constitution, and Installation

OF THE

VARIOUS SUBORDINATE BODIES OF THE ANCIENT
AND ACCEPTED SCOTTISH RITE

OF

MASONRY.

RIGHT HAND—CEREMONIAL—PERFECTION.

"WITHOUT reprieve condemned to death,
For want of well pronouncing 'Shibboleth.'"

MILTON

CEREMONY

OF

INAUGURATION AND CONSTITUTION

OF A

LODGE OF PERFECTION.

THE Lodge-room is arranged as for a ceremony of reception; the interlaced triangle over the throne is not lighted, and the pedestal is covered. In front of the East, seats are placed sufficient to accommodate the officers of the Consistory, and not less than twelve in number.

CEREMONY.

A Lodge of Perfection is opened in full form.

The Grand Captain of the Guard will form the Consistory in a procession in an adjoining room, in the following order:

GRAND TYLER,
GRAND MASTER OF CEREMONIES, GRAND HOSPITALLER,
GRAND TREASURER, GRAND SECRETARY,
GRAND KEEPER OF SEALS, GRAND CHANCELLOR,
GRAND MINISTER OF STATE, SECOND LIEUTENANT COMMANDER,
ILLUSTRIOUS DEPUTY COMMANDER, FIRST LIEUTENANT COMMANDER,
GRAND STANDARD BEARER,
ILLUSTRIOUS COMMANDER-IN-CHIEF.

*   *   *   *   *

T. P. G. M. Illustrious Commander-in-Chief, in the name of this Lodge of Perfection, I welcome you and those who attend you among us; more especially as you bring Letters of Constitution, authorizing us to continue our labors as a Lodge of Perfection, and at the same time to inaugurate and install its officers, whose zeal for the interests of the order has gained us that favor.

Com.-in-Chief. Thrice Potent Grand Master, permit me to return thanks for this fraternal reception. The Consistory, knowing your zeal and devotion for our Ancient and Accepted rite, have favorably considered your request, and have caused Letters of Constitution to issue, empowering you to assemble as a legal Lodge, and to discharge the duties of our rite in a regular and constitutional manner, according to the original forms of the order and the regulations of the Supreme Council, and now propose to inaugurate your Lodge and to install its officers.

* * * * *

Com.-in-C. The officers of the Consistory will approach the East and be seated. Illustrious Grand Master of Ceremonies, you will now conduct to their appropriate stations in the Lodge the officers of the Consistory, and let the officers of the Lodge (commencing with the Captain of the Guard) yield up their stations respectively, and place their regalia upon the Altar of Incense; after which, you will conduct them to their seats in front of the East, vacated by their superior officers.

* * * * *

Com.-in-C. Illustrious Grand Master of Ceremonies, conduct now the Thrice Potent Grand Master (after he shall have laid aside his regalia) to his proper seat among his officers.

Com.-in-C. Illustrious Grand Chancellor, you will now read the Letters of Constitution.

Grand Chancellor reads.

Com.-in-C. Perfect and Sublime Brethren of .... Lodge of Perfection, No....., you have heard read your Letters of Constitution; do you accept them, and do you now desire that your Lodge shall be inaugurated?

Omnes. We do.

Com.-in-C. Perfect and sublime Brethren, the step which you now take is a serious and important one; heretofore you were only temporarily organized, but when you shall have been inaugurated and installed under these Letters of Constitution, you become a permanent body; and if you should so conduct yourselves as to cause them to be taken away, you will incur great reproach, and prove yourselves unworthy Masons. It will become the duty of each and every member of the Lodge to labor unceasingly for its success.

The work of the Lodge must not be confined to the mere ceremony of opening and closing and conferring of degrees, but should be devoted to mutual instruction, to the cultivation of the social feelings, and of brotherly kindness, and to the practice of earnest beneficence and charity.

Morally, the work of a Lodge of Perfection extends far beyond mutual relief and assistance: the field of its exertions is not included within the four walls of a Lodge, nor limited by the circle of the brethren; it is society, the country, the world.

Intellectually, its work is not confined to dry and lifeless formulas or trivial interpretations, but includes the profoundest philosophical instructions in regard to the great mysteries of God and nature.

If these, my brethren, are your views of the works and purposes of Masonry, kneel with us, and let us beseech our Father who is in Heaven, to prosper this work and bless all our labors with success.

* * * * *

PRAYER.

Great Architect of the Universe, Creator, and Preserver of the world, teach us our duties as Masons and as men! Incline our hearts and strengthen our hands to perform them, and make our work, faithfully done, effectual to the benefit of our order, of society, of our country, and of universal humanity.

Give us wisdom to judge what is proper and becoming for us to do, and may this Lodge which we are now about to inaugurate and consecrate, be and continue an active and efficient instrument in relieving human suffering, dispelling ignorance, eradicating error, and promoting the happiness of men. *Amen.*

Omnes. So mote it be.

All rise and are seated.

Com.-in-C. Illustrious Grand Master of Ceremonies, you will cause the members of the Lodge of Perfection to assemble round the Altar of Incense to take the general oath of fealty and allegiance.

The members assemble in due form.

The Commander-in-Chief descends from the throne, passes inside the triangle to the altar, lights the incense, and says:

Brethren of the Lodge of Perfection will now kneel on the right knee and repeat after me the vow of

FEALTY AND ALLEGIANCE.

In the presence of our Heavenly Father, by this holy altar erected to Him, by the incense which now ascends therefrom, in token of our gratitude and adoration, and calling on these Illustrious Brethren now present, as witnesses, I do solemnly vow to be faithful and loyal to the Ancient and Accepted Scottish rite to ever maintain its honor and independence, support its regular and constituted authorities, and zealously endeavor to propagate its principles, enlarge its borders, and increase its influence.

That I will be loyal and faithful to my country and its government and laws, and to the great cause of oppressed and suffering humanity.

That I will labor to disseminate truth and knowledge among men, to eradicate error and dispel ignorance, and to make Masonry efficient to enlighten and enfranchise men.

That I will be loyal and faithful, and bear true fealty and allegiance to the Supreme Council and Sovereign Chiefs of Exalted Masonry.

That I will hold no Masonic communication whatever, as a Mason of said rite, with any Masonic body or Mason pretending to be subject to any Masonic authority of said rite in said jurisdiction, other than said Supreme Council, of which the Illustrious Brother .... is now the Sovereign Grand Commander. So help me God!

Second Lieut. * * * In the name of our Father which art in Heaven, I consecrate this Lodge of Perfection to peace, harmony, and union; may it ever pour oil on the waters of strife, and persuade men no longer to hate their brethren!

First Lieut. * * * In the name of the order of Freemasonry and of our Ancient and Accepted Scottish rite, I consecrate this Lodge of Perfection to charity, beneficence, and good deeds; may it ever labor to assist the needy, console the suffering, and cheer with the wine of contentment the disconsolate.

Com.-in-C. * * * In the name of the Ancient and Accepted Scottish Rite of Freemasonry, I consecrate this Lodge of Perfection to truth and the diffusion of knowledge among men; may it ever labor unweariedly in the great cause; and may every seed it sows, generate like the wheat, and produce fruit in one season.

PROCLAMATION.

To the glory of the Grand Architect of the Universe, in the name and under the auspices of the Supreme Council of the Ancient and Accepted rite, and by virtue of the powers in me vested as [*position of installing officer*], I do constitute and form these brethren into a regular Lodge of Perfection of said rite, to be known and distinguished as.......Lodge of Perfection, No...

I do hereby empower it, henceforward, to meet as a regular Lodge of Perfection, duly constituted and inaugurated in conformity to the laws and usages of the Ancient and Accepted Scottish rite. And may the Great Architect of the Universe prosper direct, and counsel it in all its doings. *Amen.*

Omnes. So mote it be.

Com.-in-C. •.

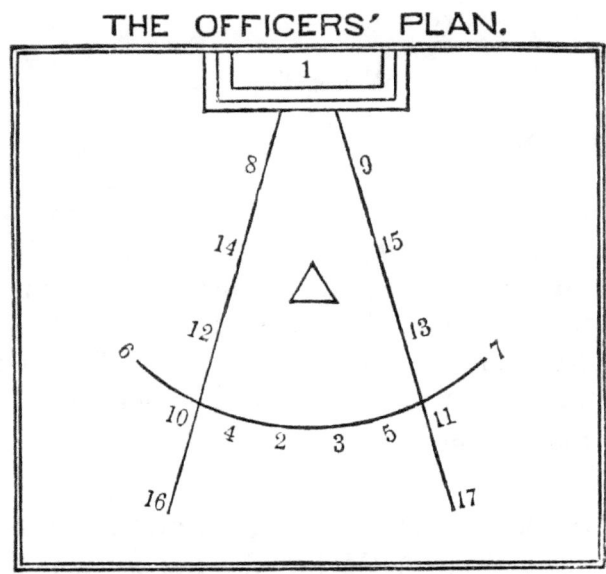

THE OFFICERS' PLAN.

CEREMONIAL DEGREE

AT THE

INSTALLATION OF OFFICERS

OF THE

LODGE OF PERFECTION.

INTRODUCTORY.

It is the prerogative of Princes of Jerusalem to invest the Officers of Lodges of Perfection with the secrets appertaining to their respective offices.

The Thrice Potent Grand Master, Senior and Junior Grand Wardens, and the Grand Master of Ceremonies, are the only officers entitled to the *Secret Directory*. On the production of a certificate of their election, duly signed and sealed, the following ceremonies are observed.

RECEPTION.

A Council of Princes of Jerusalem being opened:

The Grand Master of Ceremonies retires to the anteroom, and prepares the candidate by divesting him of his hat, shoes, etcetera; hoodwinks him, and conducts him to the door of the Council Chamber, where the Guard announces his approach by the sound of a trumpet, which is answered from within by the Grand Master of Entrances. The door is opened from within by the Grand High Priest.

* * * * *

M∴ E∴ S∴ P∴ This is the legend and fable of this degree, chronologically arranged. During the life of King Solomon, the Secret Directory for the Ineffable degrees was drawn up under his direction, and deposited in the pedestal of the Pillar of Beauty

CEREMONIAL DEGREE OF PERFECTION.

on which he ordered this inscription, in hieroglyphics, to be engraved, "* * *" It was known to the brethren that on his signet the inscription, "Solomon, King of Israel, son of David and Bathsheba" was engraved in the same hieroglyphics.

* * * * *

After his death, in consequence of the disorders and civil commotions which prevailed in the kingdom of Judah, Masonry was much neglected until the time of Hezekiah.

In the first year of his reign the brethren assembled by order of that king, for the purpose of reorganizing the Lodge of Perfection, but being unable to discover the Secret Directory, they could not fully effect their purpose. They therefore passed a decree that the next candidate for an office in the Lodge of Perfection, before he took his seat as such, should make diligent search for the same. This decree was carried into effect on the admission of the next candidate, who discovered the Secret Directory in the manner you have represented; and in consequence of this discovery the secrets of Ineffable Masonry were again communicated to worthy brethren from generation to generation.

M. E. S. P.; ●—when the G∴ H∴ P∴ says:

G∴ H∴ P∴: "If I have seen any perish for want of clothing, or any poor without covering; if his loins have not blessed me, and if he were not warmed with the fleece of my sheep; if I have lifted up my hand against the fatherless, when I saw my help in the gate; then let mine arm fall from my shoulder-blade, and mine arm be broken from the bone."

"Behold! happy is the man whom God correcteth, therefore despise not thou the chastening of the Almighty; he shall deliver thee in six troubles, yea, in seven there shall no evil touch thee; when thou walkest through the fire, thou shalt not be burned, neither shall the flame be kindled upon thee; when thou passest through the waters they shall not overflow thee;" for the Lord God of Israel shall be thy defender and preserver; he will be thy rock and thy shield; blessed be his holy name, forever and ever *Amen.*

> The newly-installed officers retire, unless they are Princes of Jerusalem; and none but Princes of Jerusalem being present, the Council is closed in due form.

CEREMONY

OF

INSTALLATION

OF A

LODGE OF PERFECTION

Com.-in-C. Brethren of the Lodge, these are the officers whom you have elected! Look upon them, and do you, Illustrious Brethren, officers of the Consistory, the same! and if any one present has any objection to offer, why any one of them shall not be installed, let him now prefer it, or else forever after hold his peace.

No objection being made:

Brother Grand Master of Ceremonies, present the Thrice Potent Grand Master elect.

My brother, your brethren have been pleased to elect you to the office of Thrice Potent Grand Master of this Lodge of Perfection. Before your investiture it is necessary you should signify your assent to these ancient charges and regulations which define the duty of a Grand Master of a Lodge of Perfection! Listen, therefore, and respond.

I. You agree to be impartial and upright, and to obey in every point the moral laws of the Ancient and Accepted Scottish rite.

You promise not to engage in any plot or conspiracy against government; and to submit peacefully to the will of the majority; and to act with honor and generosity toward all men.

II. You agree to hold in veneration the ancient landmarks and great principles of our order; to respect and obey the authorities of the Ancient and Accepted Scottish rite, supreme and subordinate, according to their stations; and to submit to the decision and awards of your brethren in any case where the constitution or principles of the order require it.

III. You promise to avoid disputes and quarrels; to be modest in your behavior and carriage; courteous to all men, and faithful to your Lodge and brethren, and carefully to refrain from intemperance and excess.

IV. You promise hospitably to treat and courteously to receive all brethren, and to discountenance impostors and all who seek to disturb the Ancient and Accepted Scottish rite.

V. You agree to diffuse and disseminate the principles of our order; to pay due homage to the Supreme Council, and strictly to conform to all edicts emanating therefrom that are not subversive of the principles and ground-work of the Ancient and Accepted Scottish rite.

VI. You admit that it is not in the power of any man or body of men to make innovations in the essential and fundamental principles of the Ancient and Accepted Scottish rite.

VII. You promise to attend regularly the meetings of your Lodge, and to instruct and counsel the brethren; that you will faithfully and punctually perform all your duties as Grand Master, and that you will never open or close your Lodge without giving a lecture, or some portion thereof, for the instruction of the brethren.

VIII. You admit that no new Lodge of Perfection can be formed without permission of the Supreme Council, or a Deputy Inspector-General in a country where there is no Consistory, and that no countenance should be given to an irregular Lodge, or to any person initiated therein.

IX. You admit that no person can be regularly allowed to receive any degree in a Lodge of Perfection, or admitted a member of the same, without previous notice and due inquiry into his character, nor unless he be a Master Mason, in good standing.

X. You agree that no visitor shall be received into your Lodge without due examination and proof of his title to be so, unless he is personally known as a Grand Elect, Perfect, and Sublime Mason, to some member of your body.

These are the regulations of the Ancient and Accepted Scottish rite. Do you submit to these charges and promise to support these regulations, as Ineffable Masons have done in all ages before you?

T. P. G. M. I do.

CHARGE.

Com.-in-C. My brother, your ready assent to the charges and regulations of the order, justifies the confidence which your brethren have reposed in you, and authorizes me to proceed with your installation. You cannot have advanced to the degree which you have attained in our rite without becoming acquainted with the requisites necessary to constitute an efficient Master of a Lodge of Perfection, with the duties that devolve upon the position, and of the serious responsibility which he incurs.

The honor, reputation, and usefulness of your Lodge will chiefly depend upon the mode in which you discharge the duties of your office. If you should be satisfied with merely knowing by rote the formulas, the phrases, and ceremonies of the work, and end with that, you may maintain good order and conduct the work with regularity, but you will soon see indifference succeed to zeal, inattention to punctuality, lassitude to interest, and stagnant immobility to activity.

You cannot satisfy your promise never to open and close your Lodge without giving a lecture, or some portion thereof, for the instruction of the brethren, by asking a few trivial questions of routine. It would be absurd to require of you to take a solemn obligation to do that; and a sad matter if Masonry would so cheapen its oaths.

Whenever your Lodge is closed, and an evening has passed away without your having given the brethren some new and useful information, *you will have failed to do your duty.*

Think not that the field of Masonic learning has been so often reaped and gleaned that there is nothing left for you to gather. Its history has never yet been written. Its symbols are only in part understood. Its philosophy is a vast region almost wholly unexplored. You are to arouse the indolent, encourage the desponding, and incite the unreflecting brethren to do something the influences whereof shall be felt beyond the limits of the Lodge— something for society, something for humanity. Admonish them of the duty that rests upon them—so to act and behave as to bring no discredit or reproach upon the order. Charge them to practise out of the Lodge the duties taught in it, and by their forbearance, frankness, discretion, equity, and profound regard for truth and honor, to convince all who know them of the excellence of our institution.

I hope your example will remain as the best and brightest of lessons for your successors, to show them in what way to walk, and how to act; to deserve well of the order, to be entitled to its gratitude, and to win for themselves honor and reputation.

Brother Grand Master of Ceremonies, present the deputy Grand Master elect.

Charge to the Deputy Grand Master.

My brother, your brethren have been pleased to elect you Deputy Grand Master of this Lodge of Perfection, to take the place of the Thrice Potent, in case of his absence. The duties which, in that case, you are to perform are known to you, and need not be repeated. When he is present, you are to assist him with your counsel and advice in maintaining the dignity and authority of his office, and the peace and harmony of the Lodge, and perform such other duties as are laid down in the ritual. I congratulate you on being thought worthy by your brethren of this honorable station, and earnestly hope that you may give them no reason to regret the choice they have made.

Brother Grand Master of Ceremonies, present the Senior Grand Warden elect.

Charge to the Senior Grand Warden.

My brother, your brethren have been pleased to elect you as Senior Grand Warden of this Lodge of Perfection. In the absence of the Thrice Potent and his Deputy, you are to govern the Lodge and perform the duties of his office: and in that case you are bound by all the pledges and promises he has made; and you will consider all that has been said to him as addressed equally to you. When he is present, you are to assist him and second all his efforts. Your acquaintance with the history, symbols, and philosophy of our rite, should be as extensive as his; therefore you should prepare yourself, so as never to be taken unawares when called to the performance of any duty.

I firmly rely on your knowledge, your zeal for the order, and your attachment for your Lodge, for the faithful discharge of the duties of this important trust.

Brother Grand Master of Ceremonies, present the Junior Grand Warden elect.

Charge to the Junior Grand Warden.

My brother, you have been elected to the office of Junior Grand Warden of this Lodge of Perfection.

You may be called upon to fill the place of the Senior Grand Warden, or even that of the Grand Master or his Deputy, and in such case the promises they have respectively made become yours. You should therefore be as fully instructed, and your office demands of you the same diligent study and thoughtful care.

Your regular and punctual attendance is required by our laws, and it is expected you will faithfully discharge the duties attached to that responsible office.

Brother Grand Master of Ceremonies, present the Grand Orator elect.

Charge to the Grand Orator.

My brother, you have been elected Grand Orator of this Lodge of Perfection. It will be your duty to pronounce a discourse to the neophyte at every reception, and to the Lodge if required. It may also of right call upon you to read an essay or lecture upon the history, philosophy, doctrine, or symbolism of the rite. It is therefore indispensable that you should make yourself familiar with those subjects, so that you may be able to instruct and enlighten the brethren. I trust that the duties of your office will be so performed that your name will be hereafter identified with the prosperity of the Lodge, and mentioned with honor and respect by all who love our order.

Brother Grand Master of Ceremonies, present the Grand Treasurer elect.

Charge to the Grand Treasurer.

My brother, you have been elected Grand Treasurer of this Lodge of Perfection. It is your duty to receive all moneys from the Secretary, make due entry of the same, and pay them out on the order of the Lodge, rendering account thereof at the proper season. These duties are responsible and important, and your faithful performance of them will entitle you to the good opinion and gratitude of your brethren.

Brother Grand Master of Ceremonies, present the Grand Secretary elect.

Charge to the Grand Secretary.

My brother, you have been elected Grand Secretary of this Lodge of Perfection. It is your duty to record the proceedings of the Lodge, to receive all moneys due the same, and to pay them over to the Grand Treasurer, taking his receipt therefor.

I earnestly hope that you will so perform its duties as to merit the esteem and applause of your brethren.

Brother Grand Master of Ceremonies, present the Grand Master of Ceremonies elect.

Charge to the Grand Master of Ceremonies.

My brother, you have been elected the Grand Master of Ceremonies of this Lodge of Perfection. It will be your duty to examine and introduce all visiting brethren; to examine, prepare, introduce, and accompany all candidates; to arrange all processions, and act as Marshal thereof.

I trust you will perform them to the entire satisfaction of the Grand Master and the Lodge.

Brother Grand Master of Ceremonies, present the Grand Captain of the Guard elect.

Charge to the Grand Captain of the Guard.

My brother, you have been elected Grand Captain of the Guard of this Lodge of Perfection. You are to guard well the entrance of the same, to cause all summonses to be served, and to obey such orders of the Grand Master as he may communicate to you; and I do not doubt but that you will perform your duties faithfully, and keep due watch over our entrance into the Sanctuary.

Brother Grand Master of Ceremonies, present the Grand Hospitaller elect.

Charge to the Grand Hospitaller.

My brother, you have been elected Grand Hospitaller of this Lodge of Perfection. It is our earnest wish that you may so administer the affairs of your office, that when you lay it down, the exchequer of the Lodge may overflow with the thanks of the widows and the gratitude of orphans.

Brother Grand Master of Ceremonies, present the Grand Tyler.

Charge to the Grand Tyler.

My brother, you have been elected Grand Tyler of this Lodge of Perfection. Receive this sword, and after you shall have taken the oath of office, you will repair to your station, and guard well the approach to the entrance to the Lodge, that no cowan overhear us and no impostor intrude himself among us.

Illustrious Grand Master of Ceremonies, you will now place the officers of the Lodge of Perfection at the Altar in due form to take the oath of office.

> G∴ M∴ of C∴ places them in a semicircle, facing the E., M. in the centre.

Com.-in-C. [* * * *all rise.*] Attention, brethren of the Grand Consistory and Lodge, and witness this oath of office.

OATH.

You and each of you, in the presence of the Great Architect of the Universe, and with these brethren as witnesses, do solemnly and sincerely swear, that you will support the Constitutions, Regulations, Statutes, and Institutes of the Ancient and Accepted Scottish rite, and the Regulations and Constitution of the Supreme Council, as the fundamental law of the Ancient and Accepted Scottish Rite. That you will faithfully and impartially perform, each to the best and utmost of his skill and ability, the duties of the office to which he has been elected in this Lodge of Perfection. So help you God.

•

Illustrious Grand Master of Ceremonies, you will now invest the officers of the Lodge with their appropriate regalia and conduct them (excepting the Thrice Potent Grand Master) to their stations (commencing with the Grand Tyler), and let the officers occupying the stations yield them up.

The officers being so placed:

Thrice Potent, your officers are at their respective stations, and nothing remains but for you to assume yours: be pleased to do so.

Receive, my brother, the warrant of your Lodge [*presenting it*]; may it continue and prosper, and may its name be ever honored among men.

Receive now this mallet, symbol of authority; assume the government of your Lodge, and rule it with urbanity, impartiality, and firmness.

PROCLAMATION.

To the glory of the Great Architect of the Universe, in the name and under the auspices of the Supreme Council, I proclaim .... Lodge of Perfection, No. ....., to be consecrated and inaugurated, its officers duly installed, and the Lodge legally organized and prepared to enter upon its labors.

Brethren of the Consistory, unite with me in congratulating the Thrice Potent Grand Master and his Lodge.

Omnes. 3, 5, 7, 9.

Com.-in-C. or *T∴ P∴* [●—*all are seated.*]

CONSTITUTION AND INSTALLATION

OF A

COUNCIL OF PRINCES OF JERUSALEM.

The Princes and brethren being convened at some convenient place adjacent to the Council Chamber of the Princes of Jerusalem, the procession is formed, and moves in the following order:

1. Tyler, with drawn sword.
2. Masters of Ceremonies, with insignia.
3. Entered Apprentices, Fellow Crafts, and Master Masons.
4. Four brethren, carrying the Ark of the Covenant.
5. First Light, carried by a Brother.
6. Three Master Masons.
7. Second Light, carried by a Brother.
8. Three Master Masons.
9. Third Light, carried by a Brother.
10. Three Master Masons.
11. A Key, borne by a Secret Master
12. Six Secret Masters, as Levites.
13. Perfect Master, carrying the Cubic Stone; two Perfect Masters, and one Perfect Master, carrying an Urn;—all marching abreast.
14. An Intimate Secretary.
15. Seven Provosts and Judges.
16. Five Intendants of the Building.
17. Nine Elect of Nine.
18. Fifteen Elect of Fifteen.
19. Twelve Sublime Knights Elected.
20. Three Grand Master Architects.
21. Nine Royal Arch of Enoch.
22. Twenty-six Grand Elect, Perfect, and Sublime Masons.
23. Fourth Light, carried by a G.: E.: P.: and S.: Mason.

INSTALLATION OF PRINCES OF JERUSALEM. 517

24. Seven Knights of the East or Sword.
25. Five Princes of Jerusalem.
26. Members of Lodges of Perfection.
27. Officers of Council of Princes of Jerusalem to be installed.
28. Installing and Constituting officers

In the above order the procession arrives at ...., where the following anthem is sung, until the procession has gradually walked three times round the hall:

ANTHEM.

1. Let there be light, the Al-migh-ty spoke, Re-ful-gent streams from cha-os broke, To il-lume the ris-ing earth. (........OMIT........) And gave the plan-ets birth.

Well-pleased the great Je - - ho-vah stood, The power su-preme pronounced it good. (.....OMIT....

518   BOOK OF THE A. AND A. RITE.

In choral numbers Masons join, To bless and praise this Light divine.

    Parent of Light, accept our praise,
    Who shed'st on us thy brightest rays,
       The Light that fills our mind.
    By choice selected, lo! we stand
    By friendship joined a social band,
       That love, that aid mankind.
       In choral numbers Masons join
       To bless and praise this Light divine.

  The altar is then placed in the centre of the hall, and on it are deposited the four great Lights, and on proper pedestals are placed the insignia, implements, and symbols, borne in procession, and the furniture for investiture.

  The brethren then join in the following

ANTHEM.

To Heaven's high Architect all praise, all

INSTALLATION OF PRINCES OF JERUSALEM.

The following may very judiciously be embodied in the

ADDRESS.

Every good, Ineffable, and Sublime Mason uses, as he is solemnly bound to do, the utmost caution to prevent the secrets of this important branch of Masonry from being unlawfully obtained; and all the checks and restrictions which wisdom and experience have suggested, are used to prevent these degrees from falling into improper hands, and being conferred without the sanction of lawful and constitutional authority.

In respect to this, as well as in all other moral and social duties, sublime Freemasonry has its rewards and punishments, its obligations and vows, as well as its fundamental laws and regulations, which every honest and true brother is willing to be governed and abide by; and neither in this regard, nor in any other, can they be broken with impunity.

The mystic mysteries of religion and science which formed the foundation upon which the superstructure of Ineffable Masonry has been erected, covered so large a field of investigation and study, and involved so many abstruse and critical points, that unless they were set forth in technical and orthodox phraseology, or at least that certain of the more abstruse portions of the Secret Directory were preserved in some character, hieroglyphic or otherwise, their vitality and truthfulness would be destroyed, and in a few generations no trace or resemblance of their original character would remain.

Our society is maintained upon the broad principles of rendering mutual aid and of exercising mutual love and friendship, as well as to preserve our adoration of the Almighty Artist, and to improve our minds with the principles of science.

The history of Masonry, as contained in the higher degrees, gives an account of events only to be found in the archives of our sublime institution, which could not be committed to memory without constant application for a lifetime; therefore, had the same course been adopted in the perpetuation of these degrees as that prescribed for the symbolic Lodge, they would long ere this have been lost to the world and have been buried in oblivion.

But as Numa pronounced his sacred writings lifeless, so, be it remembered, anything which you may find indited, and without the spirit of ceremonial action, and the soul of exposition diffused through it, from the breathing, burning voice of the living man and brother, and the reciprocating thoughts and feelings of the instructor and the instructed, will be but an inert mass of senseless matter, and wholly unproductive of any useful or happy results and consequences.

The following short ceremony then ensues, of

CONSTITUTION AND INSTALLATION.

The Heralds sound the trumpets.

The Grand Master of Ceremonies rises, and says:

I announce to the Illustrious Brethren here assembled, that the Council of Princes of Jerusalem, for the city of ...., State of ...., is now about to be constituted, and its officers installed and proclaimed.

Puissant Commander-in-Chief, is it your will and pleasure that the ceremony of Constitution and Installation shall now proceed?

Com.-in-Chief. It is. Let the Warrant of Constitution be now read.

Warrant read by Deputy Grand Commander.

Com.-in-Chief. Illustrious Grand Master of Ceremonies, you will place the Princes of the Council at the altar in proper form for the purpose of taking the oath of fealty and allegiance.

Illustrious Grand Standard Bearer, you will advance the banner of the order to the altar.

> The Master of Ceremonies forms the Princes around the banner and altar, in the form of a triangle: the Princes kneeling on the left knee, repeat the following. (*vide* page 504.)
>
> (The general oath of fealty and allegiance is then administered.

Com.-in-Chief. Let the Princes named in the warrant rise and approach the East.

S. P. Grand Master in the centre.

In the name of the Supreme and Sovereign Grand Master of the Universe, by whom princes rule and to whom be all honor and glory, in my character, and by virtue of my prerogatives as presiding officer (representing) the Supreme Council, from whom the charter just read has emanated through its Sovereign Consistory, I hereby constitute you, valorous Princes, into a Council of Princes of Jerusalem, under the distinctive title of .... for the city of .... in the State of ....; and you henceforth have full power and authority to assemble legally, to elect and install your officers, to elevate to the degrees of Knight of the

East or sword, and Prince of Jerusalem, Grand, Elect, Perfect and Sublime Freemasons, lawfully and constitutionally entitled thereto, and may the blessing of Heaven be upon you.

The Heralds again sound the trumpets, and the ceremony of Installation follows.

INSTALLATION.

Com.-in-Chief. Most Illustrious Lieutenant Commander, have you examined the Most Equitable Sovereign Prince, Grand Master, named in the warrant (or elected), and can you vouch for his skill and capacity for the Most Illustrious Order of Ancient, Sublime, Free, and Accepted Masonry?

Lieut. Commander answers.

Then let the Most Equitable Sovereign Prince Grand Master be presented for installation.

Lieut. Commander presents him, saying.

L. Com. Most Puissant Commander-in-Chief, I present my worthy and valorous Brother ...., to be installed Sovereign Prince Grand Master of this new Council of Princes of Jerusalem. I have witnessed his fervor, zeal, and constancy, his good conduct and morals, and find him possessed of the requisite skill and capacity for the duties of his station.

Com.-in-Chief. Do you, my brother, promise strictly to observe the rules enforcing justice and good order, and to strive to lead an irreproachable life?

II. That you will be just and equitable in all your ministrations?

III. That you will put away every kind of party spirit, hatred and envy towards your brethren, and never combat with them, or give to or accept a challenge from one of them?

IV. That you will never swerve from, nor permit any of your brethren to swerve from or violate the general or particular laws of Sublime, Ancient, Free, and Accepted Masonry; and that you will never advise or direct any brother in anything that relates to our illustrious order, except in conformity with said rules and the truth?

V. That you will advocate the principles and sustain the glory of our illustrious order in its fullest extent, whenever it becomes necessary?

VI. That you will acknowledge the authority and submit to the ordinances and decrees of the Supreme Council, by whom the Council in which you have been chosen to act, has been constituted?

VII. Do you submit to these charges, and promise, on the faith and honor of a Knight and Prince of Masonry, to observe them?

  * * * * *

Most Equitable Prince, with the greatest pleasure I now salute you as Sovereign Prince Grand Master of this Council, placing the most implicit reliance in your zeal, fidelity, skill, and capacity for the exalted station to which the partiality of your brethren has elevated you.

I confide to your charge the warrant of the Council over which you are to preside, also the book of ordinances and decrees of the Supreme Council, for your guidance. You are, my brother, the representative of an ancient member of the Craft, denominated in the old Constitutions, as the Prince and General Master Mason of the Jews. Emulate his virtues. Receive this hand of Justice in token of that justice you, as a Prince, are bound to exercise. As presiding officer of your Council, the mallet is also committed to your hands.

  * * * * *

High Priest is presented.

Com.-in-Chief. In the remote ages of antiquity, as indeed in more modern times, learned men, devoted to ecclesiastical matters, participated in the councils of nations; and when it is considered that the ancient mysteries, now known by the name of Free Masonic, were sustained and protected by civil government, we can readily account for the religious character of the ritual that obtained in those mysteries which were indubitably improved by religious ceremonials and obligations. You, my brother, are the representative of an ancient Israelitish Pontiff of Jehovah. May the zeal, fervor, constancy, and success which characterized his labors, attend you in the discharge of your functions. Among other things, it will be your duty to perform all religious solemnities in this Council, and on all public occasions, when required

Receive the insignia of your office, and worthily preside in the absence of the Sovereign Prince Grand Master.

Your official badge (a circle enclosing a delta), which I now present to you, it is needless to remind you, symbolizes the Eternal, whose we are, and whom we are bound to serve.

Senior Grand Warden is presented.

Com.-in-Chief. To you, as a brother well versed in the usages of Masonry, your duties as first or Senior Warden are well known I doubt not your willingness and ability to discharge them with honor and fidelity. You occupy the place of strength and power. As Prince of Judah, receive this column of strength, the badge of your office.

Junior Grand Warden is presented.

Com.-in-Chief. As second or Junior Grand Warden, you are the assistant and supporter of your senior. With your counsel and labors and those of your senior, you are to aid in the working and ordinary business of your Council. In the symbolic yet glorious work of re-edification, be the stanch coadjutor of your senior companion. Accept this badge of your office, and may He who stood upon the circle of the earth and set a compass on the face of the deep, be with thee and bless thee.

Secretary or Keeper of Seals is presented.

Com.-in-Chief. Most valorous brother, by virtue of your office, the duties of corresponding and recording secretary devolve upon you. You are also to receive all petitions, and take charge of the seals of this Council and of its minutes of proceedings. As Prince of the Law, receive this balance.

Grand Treasurer is presented.

Com.-in-Chief. It is your duty to keep in trust all the funds, securities, and vouchers of this Council. Our secret treasures are also committed to your charge. As Prince of the Temple, receive this badge, the symbol of our mystic edifice.

Grand Master of Ceremonies is presented.

Com.-in-Chief. It is your province to attend your associate officers in the works and labors of this Council, and to perform such

INSTALLATION OF PRINCES OF JERUSALEM.   525

other services as Masonic custom has prescribed. As Prince of the workmen, I invest you with this badge of your office.

Grand Master of E∴ is presented.

Com.-in-Chief. Your appropriate station is near the inner door of the Council Chamber, to receive reports from the guards with out, announce all applicants for admission, and to discharge the other duties Masonic usage requires from a Prince of the Guards. Receive the implement of your office.

Grand Tyler is presented.

Com.-in-Chief. Valorous brother, immemorial usage has fixed your duties, which relate to the admission of members and visitors. They are well known to you. We rely upon your fidelity and discretion to discharge them properly. Receive the implement of your office.

The grand honors of a Prince of Jerusalem are then given.

At every succeeding installation of officers of a Council of Princes of Jerusalem, a Past Most Equitable Master may install the new Sovereign Prince Grand Master, and the new Grand Master installs the other officers.

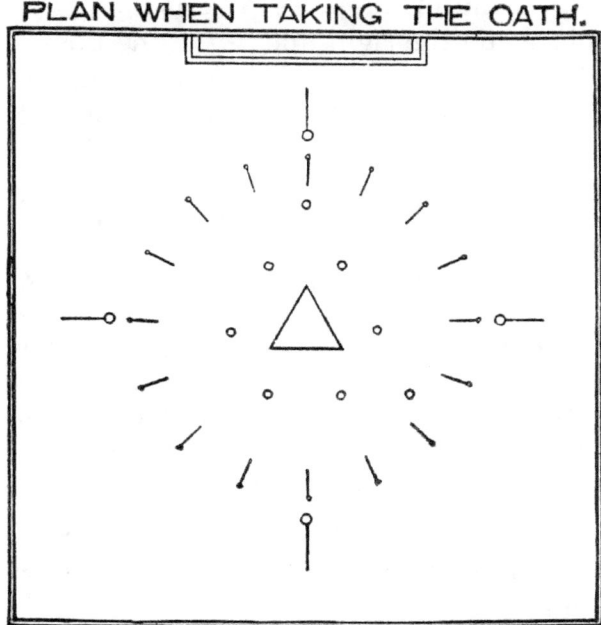

INSTALLATION OF OFFICERS

OF A

SOVEREIGN CHAPTER ROSE CROIX.

The hall must be fitted up in the most brilliant style, the floor strewed with flowers, and the walls hung with garlands.

The three columns, Faith, Hope, and Charity, are placed as in the second apartment in case of reception. At the beginning of the ceremony, the hall must be in the most profound obscurity. The officers and members of the Chapter occupy their ordinary seats, and wear their collars, the black outside, and the jewels veiled.

Between the altar and the throne, in the East, a certain number of chairs are prepared for the Most Wise and the officers of the Chapter. That of the Most Wise is near the altar, and the others are placed on the right and left of the East.

Nine brethren, with stars* and swords, are in readiness to wait upon the Consistory; also a sufficient number of members with swords.

All being in readiness, the Consistory is formed in procession by the Grand Marshal in an adjoining room, as follows:

GRAND MASTER OF CEREMONIES.

SENTINEL.

GRAND TREASURER,	GRAND MINISTER OF STATE,
GRAND SECRETARY,	SECOND LIEUT. COMMANDER,
DEPUTY ILL. COMMANDER-IN-CHIEF,	FIRST LIEUT. COMMANDER,
GRAND STANDARD BEARER,	GRAND CAPTAIN OF THE GUARDS,

COMMANDER-IN-CHIEF.

---

* In visitations, torches are termed stars.

Com.-in-C. Sublime Prince, Grand Master of Ceremonies, you will inform the Most Wise of the Sovereign Chapter that the Grand Consistory is now ready to proceed with the installation.

* * * * *

Most Wise. Illustrious Commander-in-Chief, it is not in our power to continue our labors. Confusion and consternation prevail among us. Darkness covers our Temple; all our implements are shattered. We have not the word. We beg, therefore, Illustrious Commander-in-Chief, to take into consideration our zeal and good intentions; lend us your assistance for the purpose of continuing the labors of this Chapter, which, under the auspices of the Illustrious body over which you preside, hopes to fulfil its duties to God and man.

Com.-in-C. Most Wise and brethren, it is our duty and pleasure to grant you the assistance you demand at our hands; but the word cannot be recovered without proper labor. Follow me, Sir Knights, and, with the aid of God our Father, we will recover the "word."

* * * * *

Most Wise. Ill Commander-in-Chief, we have seen the names of the three fundamental laws of our Order, "Charity," "Hope," and "Faith."

Com.-in-C. True, my brother, "Charity" is love to God and man; "Hope," a feeling next to, and the consequence of, Charity, and which cheers us in all our toils for the ultimate result of our Grand Master's Doctrine; "Faith" is a feeling which naturally proceeds from "Charity" and "Hope," and which causes us firmly to believe that our Father will never forsake those who labor faithfully for a noble and just cause. Such, my brethren, are the noble thoughts which must guide you; and if you are faithful to your mission, you will soon recover the "word."

* * * * *

PRAYER.

Almighty and ever-glorious and gracious Lord God, creator of all things, and governor of everything thou hast made, mercifully look upon thy children, now assembled in thy name, and in thy presence, and bless and prosper all our works begun, continued, and ended in thee. Graciously bestow upon us wisdom, in all our doings; strength of mind in all our difficulties; and the beauty of harmony and holiness in all our communications and work. Let "Charity" be the fruit of our obedience to thy holy will, and "Hope" the foundation of our "Faith."

O thou preserver of men! graciously enable us now to consecrate this Chapter, which we have erected to the honor and glory of thy name, and mercifully be pleased to accept this service at our hands.

May all the proper work of our institution, that may be done in this Chapter, be such as thy wisdom may approve, and thy goodness prosper. And finally, graciously be pleased, O thou Sovereign Architect of the Universe, to bless the Craft wheresoever dispersed, and make them true and faithful to thee, to their neighbor, and to themselves. And when the time of our labor is drawing near to an end, and the pillar of our strength is declining to the ground, graciously enable us to pass through the "valley of the shadow of death," supported by "Charity, Hope, and Faith," to those mansions beyond the skies, where love, and peace, and happiness forever reign before thy throne! *Amen.*

Com.-in-C. In the name of the supreme and eternal God, the Grand Architect of heaven and earth, to whom be all honor and Glory, I dedicate this Chapter of Rose Croix. May universal toleration and love dwell therein forever and ever!

* * * * *

Com.-in-C. Most Wise, officers, and members of .... Sovereign Chapter of Rose Croix, No. ...., do you solemnly promise,

I. To be good and true, and strictly to observe and propagate the rational principles of the Ancient and Accepted rite?

II. To bear and forbear, to be just and equitable towards all men?

III. To discountenance intolerance and religious and political persecution?

IV. Never to be guided by animosity, by your political or religious opinions, in all questions relating to the members of your Chapter, or to such brethren who may apply for initiation into the same, and to your neighbors at large?

V. To promote the general welfare of society, and to cultivate all social virtues?

VI. To avoid carefully all piques and quarrels, to be cautious in your behavior, courteous to your brethren, and faithful to all the oaths and obligations which you have taken in our order, and to the letters capitular which the Supreme Council has granted to your Chapter?

*   *   *   *   *

In the presence of Almighty God our Father, and of my brethren, I, ..., Most Wise, of .... Sovereign Chapter of Rose Croix, No. ...., do hereby and hereon solemnly vow and swear, to perform to the best of my ability the duties imposed upon me in my aforesaid capacity, to obey and enforce the General Statutes of the Ancient and Accepted rite; the laws and edicts of the Supreme Council; and also the rules and regulations of .... Sovereign Chapter of Rose Croix, No. ....

I furthermore solemnly vow and swear, to do all in my power to maintain peace, harmony, and union among the members of this Sovereign Chapter, and to conduct the labors thereof with justice, impartiality, and forbearance. So help me God!

*   *   *   *   *

I constitute and form you into a regular Chapter of Sovereign Princes of Rose Croix, eighteenth degree of the Ancient and Accepted rite; and I hereby grant unto you full power and authority to act as a regular Chapter, according to the constitution and statutes of the Order, and may the Grand Architect of the Universe bless all your lawful labors!

Ill∴ Grand Master of Ceremonies, conduct the Most Wise of this Sovereign Chapter to his seat, on my left, and all the officers of the same to their respective places.

*   *   *   *   *

Most Wise, after the discourse with which we have been favored, and in which the Orator has expounded the sublime doctrines of Scottish Masonry in such language as only conviction and sincerity can dictate, and especially after the obligations which you have taken as a Knight of the Rose Croix, and as the Most Wise of this Sovereign Chapter, your duties are known to you, my brother, and I have now but to express to you the confidence which the order places in you, in your worthy officers, and in the Chapter over which you have the honor to preside.

*　　　　*　　　　*　　　　*　　　　*

(He then invites the members to make their observations, cause, the box of fraternal assistance to be passed, and finally calls the Chapter from labor to refreshment.)

INAUGURATION AND INSTALLATION

OF A

CONSISTORY

OF

SUBLIME PRINCES

AND

COMMANDERS OF THE ROYAL SECRET.

THE ANCIENT TEMPLAR'S PENNANT.

"YET LET US PONDER BOLDLY: 'TIS A BASE
BANDONMENT OF REASON TO RESIGN
OUR RIGHT OF THOUGHT—OUR LAST AND ONLY
PLACE OF REFUGE."

INAUGURATION OF THE TEMPLE.

DECORATIONS.

A square table will be placed in the centre of the Lodge-room and on it a vase for burning perfumes. On this table there will be no light. Between it and the throne will be placed the altar of obligation, on which is the book of constitutions, two naked swords crossed, and a Kadosh dagger in its scabbard, upon the book of constitutions. Between the swords is a lamp with a large globe shade, which must be filled with pure olive-oil.

In front of the seat of the Ill∴ Com∴-in-Chief will be five lights in the form of a square, the fifth one in the centre; three on the table of the First Lieut. Commander, and two on that of the Second Lieut. Commander,—all to be very large and long, and of yellow wax. Other lights may be used by the Secretary and Treasurer, and elsewhere in the hall, so that it shall be well lighted.

The altars are covered with white, and hung with garlands of flowers and leaves.

CEREMONY OF CONSECRATION.

At the appointed hour the Princes will seat themselves, in no particular place or order.

The Most Powerful Sovereign Gr∴ Com∴ will sit in front of the table of perfumes, and the Secretary General will sit at the head of the column of the South: before him, a triangular table. The Temple will not be lighted until after the benediction of the new fire.

Gr∴ Com∴ Ill∴ Grand Sec'y. Gen'l∴, what brings us together here?

Sec'y∴ Gen'l∴ M∴ P∴ Sov∴ Grand Commander, we have come

hither to inaugurate this Temple, which the Supreme Council desires to dedicate to the God of Beneficence.

Gr∴ Com∴ (rising). Is it your pleasure, Sublime Princes and Commanders, that this Temple shall be inaugurated?

All. It is.

Gr∴ Com∴ Sublime Princes, the world is filled with the ruins of temples, erected by the ancients to their imaginary deities. In Egypt, India, Ethiopia, and Chaldea, the lover of antiquity and the eager student gaze enraptured on the huge remains of mighty edifices sorely stricken by the relentless hand of time, in which, when they stood in all their splendor and glory in that East, teeming with the hosts of its mighty population, ATHOMON and AMMON, BRAHMA and BUDDAH, TOTH and BAEL were worshipped. The great cavern temples of Elephanta, Salsette, Carnac, Luxor, and Thebes, still remain to astound us with their vastness. The sculptured columns of an hundred fanes builded to the gods of Olympus, and enriched with all that was rare and wondrous in architecture, painting, and statuary, still remain, some standing and some fallen and broken on the classic soil of Greece. The artist is familiar with the great temples reared to the gods in Rome; and the ruins of Etruscan sanctuaries still tempt the antiquarian.

While Hiram worshipped in the Temple of Belus, builded by his ancestors in his royal city of Tyre, Solomon, whom masonry claims for its Grand Master, erected the first Temple at Jerusalem, believing that the infinite and omnipotent God would come down and dwell therein, and utter his oracles from between the extended wings of the cherubim on the mercy-seat; whither the priests repaired to consult the Shekina, or oracle of God.

The Mahometan rears his mosques, the children of Israel their synagogues, and the Christian his churches, devoted to the worship and disputes of an hundred sects. To adorn the cathedrals of the great Catholic world, the arts contributed their most glorious works; and there the great productions, of the genius of Angelo and Raphael, and many other immortal painters and sculptors, yet remain unapproachable in beauty and sublimity, to be imitated and copied, but never to be equalled.

If the shattered columns and mouldering walls of pagan temples, if the arches and vaults of mosque and church and cathedral could speak, what lessons could they not teach to the human race! what a history could they not give of the atrocities of which man is capable when enslaved by his fear of the angry and murderous gods, or changed to a wild beast by a savage fanaticism! How have the shrieks of human victims echoed within the walls of those pagan fanes, and the blood of human sacrifice flowed over their altars down the sides of the pyramids of Mexico!

How often has the mosque heard Paradise and the houri promised as a reward for the slaughter! how often the church and cathedral rung with the thunder of interdict and excommunication, and the frenzied shouts that responded to the fanatical apostles of the Crusades!

Sublime Princes, you propose to erect here a Masonic Temple, and dedicate it to the God of Beneficence and Love. The cardinal principles of Free Masonry are Charity and Toleration. According to its principles, ambition, rivalry, ill-will, and the jealousies and disputes of sects, cannot cross the threshold of its sanctuaries and enter within their sacred walls; and yet such are the frailties and imperfections of man, that they do find entrance there; sect denounces sect, and even borrows of an intolerant church its weapons to smite down heresies withal.

Into this temple, my brethren, which we are now about to inaugurate, into this Consistorial Chamber of our beautiful and beloved Ancient and Accepted rite, let no such unholy visitors ever intrude; let ambition and rivalries, jealousies and heartburnings, never effect an entrance within its portals! Let its sacred walls never resound with the accents of hatred, intolerance, uncharitableness! Let it be truly a temple of peace and concord, and not of Pharisaical self-righteousness. Let charity and loving-kindness be ever enthroned between its columns; and let its members, recognizing every Mason as a brother, hold out to him the hand of amity and fraternity, and practise here and everywhere, to their utmost extent, the great, tolerant, generous, liberal doctrines of our Ancient and Accepted rite.

Persuaded, my brethren, that these are your views and feelings, that your only desire is to advance the prosperity and fortunes of Masonry, and to inform and improve yourselves, and that it is to this end you seek to establish a point of union, where you may the more effectually labor for the good of the craft and art to which we are all loyal; where you may offer up your loving and grateful homage to our beneficent and infinitely loving Father who is in heaven, I have, by virtue of the power with which I am invested as the M∴ P∴ Sov∴ Gr∴ Commander of the Supreme Council of Sov∴ Gr∴ Ins∴ Gen∴ of the thirty-third degree, convoked you this day in this asylum for the purpose of dedicating and consecrating the same as the Hall and Consistorial Chamber of the Consistory of Sublime Princes and Commanders of the Royal Secret thirty-second degree of the Ancient and Accepted rite in and for the ...., of dedicating and consecrating it to the Supreme and Sovereign Author and Preserver of all things, by devoting it to virtue and good works, as a house wherein lessons of wisdom and philosophy, beneficence and harmony shall ever be taught as they are ordained and prescribed by the universal constitutions of Free Masonry. After which we shall proceed to inaugurate the Consistory, and to invoke for it health, prosperity, and continuance, and to install its officers, that it may commence its labors.

Be pleased, Illustrious brethren, to unite with me, and aid me in commencing the labors of this day.

Gr∴ Com∴: My brethren, as the world is darkened with ignorance and error, and lies in the twilight of superstition and routine, so in this Temple the dim light struggles with the darkness, and does not prevail. Let us kneel here, before our Father who is in heaven, and acknowledge our faults and errors; implore him to give us light, a spark of that divine fire, which in his exhaustless munificence ever flows from the sun to bless the grateful earth, and which our ancient brethren imagined to be the substance of Deity; that we may therewith illumine this Temple, accepting it as an omen and assurance that the light of wisdom and knowledge will some day illumine the whole world, and make it a fit Temple for a God of infinite love.

PRAYER.

Our Father who art in heaven, the heavy shadows of barbarism yet lie gloomy and motionless on much of this fair earth, which thou hast made and given unto thy children for a dwelling-place; and even where the dawn of civilization has come, the mass of the people are yet in the twilight of ignorance, error, and superstition. Illumine this our Temple with a spark of thy celestial fire—that Temple now in darkness,

INAUGURATION OF THE TEMPLE. 537

as a type and symbol of the moral darkness of the world. And as the shadows flee away and disappear from between our columns, when our lamps kindled at the exhaustless fountain of light, blaze in the Masonic Temple, so may that moral darkness disappear in thy good time, before the light of truth and knowledge. Amen.

All.: So mote it be.

* * * * *

I consecrate this Temple to the dissemination of truth and knowledge in philosophy, and morals among men, and may our Father who is in heaven deign to accept this homage of our hearts, and smile upon our efforts to enlighten and instruct his children, our feeble attempts to imitate his unbounded munificence, and to make of this world a real temple in which our great family of brotherhood shall worship him in spirit and in truth!

* * * * *

Gr.: Com.: And may those who shall instruct in this temple so practise the virtues which Masonry inculcates, and be so animated by the spirit of peace and concord, so love, assist, and instruct one another, and may their conduct and demeanor be in every respect so upright, honorable, and courteous, as to secure the Royal Art that consideration which alone can assure and perpetuate its stability, progress, and glory. Amen!

* * * * *

Gr.: Com.: In the name and by the authority of the Supreme Council of Sovereign Grand Inspectors-General of the thirty-third degree of the Ancient and Accepted rite, for ...., I do declare this temple for the occupation of the Consistory of Sublime Princes and Commanders of the Royal Secret thirty-second degree, in and for ...., to be inaugurated and consecrated in due form; and I do hereby dedicate it to the God of infinite beneficence and love, and to the cause of humanity, now and henceforward, invoking for it his protection and favor!

* * * * *

INSTALLATION.

Gr. Com. Ill∴ Brethren, your temple is duly inaugurated and prepared for the reception of the Consistory of Sublime Princes of the Royal Secret, in and for ...., which therefore, with your consent, I now propose to install. Is it your pleasure that I now proceed?

All. It is.

Gr. Com. Ill∴ Brothers, this moment is one of great gratification to myself, and of much interest to all Masons of the Ancient and Accepted rite. A new Consistory is about to be received into the sisterhood of those eminent bodies, and your Masonic virtues, your intelligence, ardor, and zeal, give us reason to hope that its career will be one of great prosperity and good fortune.

The propagation of the Ancient and Accepted rite has heretofore been slow. This has been owing in part to the prejudices entertained against it, in part to the inertness of those who have been at its head, and in part to the fact that it is meant to be an exclusive and not a popular rite, that it selects the best and the most eminent Masons for its members, desires no others, and is better content to remain stationary than to open its doors to any one that asks admission, and is able to pay the fee.

In the name and by the direction of the Supreme Council, I charge it upon you, my brethren, that you will adhere to, and be governed by this rule; that you select none but eminent, enlightened, and well-informed Masons of irreproachable character, and respectable standing in society, to become members of your body; and that you earnestly and urgently impress the same rule upon your subordinates. For the strength of our order consists far more in the quality than in the number of its initiates, and all its objects and purposes are defeated and itself denaturalized, when its portals are open indiscriminately to every comer.

But we see with the highest satisfaction our ranks filled with

INSTALLATION.

learned and virtuous Masons, who can appreciate its excellencies, and whose lives and conduct will gain for it consideration and esteem.

We rejoice to see new temples reared, in their modest and harmonious proportions, to a Deity of beneficence and love, and new altars erected to send up to him the sweet incense of grateful and affectionate hearts.

Be pleased to give us your attention, illustrious brethren and princes, while we read the letters patent of constitution for the Consistory of the Sublime Princes and Commanders of the Royal Secret, in and for ...., granted by the Supreme Council.

Ill∴ Grand Secretary General, be pleased to read aloud the letters patent of the constitution.

Secretary General reads aloud the letters patent of the constitution.

Gr. Com. Ill∴ brethren, having heard your letters patent of constitution, do you now accept and receive them?

All. We do.

Gr. Com. And do you freely consent and agree to abide by all their conditions and reservations?

All. We do.

Gr. Com. Ill∴ Grand Master of Cer∴, you will now assemble in due form around the altar of obligation the officers of the Consistory in and for ...., to take the proper vow of fidelity and allegiance.

All the officers repeat after the Grand Commander the following

OATH OF FEALTY AND ALLEGIANCE.

I, the undersigned, do hereby promise on my word of honor, and swear true Faith, Allegiance, and Fealty to the SUPREME COUNCIL OF SOVEREIGN GRAND INSPECTORS-GENERAL of the Thirty-third and last Degree for the Northern Masonic Jurisdiction of the United States of America, sitting at its Grand East in the City of Boston, Massachusetts, of which the ILLUSTRIOUS HENRY L. PALMER (or the M. P. Sovereign Grand Commander for the time) is the Most Puissant Sovereign Grand Commander, and will support and abide by its Constitution, Statutes, Orders, and Decrees.

That I will hold allegiance to the said Supreme Council and be loyal thereto, as the SUPREME AUTHORITY OF THE RITE so long as I may continue to reside within its Jurisdiction; will hold ILLEGAL and SPURIOUS every other Body that may be established within its Jurisdiction, claiming to be a Supreme Council; and every other Body of said Rite within the same Jurisdiction that does not hold its powers mediately or immediately from said Supreme Council, and will hold no communication whatever in Scottish Rite Masonry with any member of the same nor allow them to visit any Body of the Rite of which I may be a member; and I will dispense justice to my brethren, according the laws of equity and honor.

And should I violate this, my solemn Vow and Pledge, I consent to be expelled from Masonry, and all rights therein, and in any Body of the Rite, and to be denounced to every Body of the Ancient Accepted Scottish Rite in the world as a traitor and forsworn.

And may God aid me to keep and perform the same. Amen.

Gr∴ Com∴ In the name and under the auspices of the Supreme Council of Sov∴ Gr∴ Ins∴ Gen'l∴ of the thirty-third degree, for ...., and by virtue of the authority with which I am invested by the Supreme Council, I do proclaim the Consistory of Sublime Princes and Commanders of the Royal Secret, thirty-second degree of the rite aforesaid, in and for ...., to be duly inaugurated and a legitimate body of said rite for ...., and its works to be in full force and vigor. With me, my brethren!

    *   *   *   *   *

Gr. Com. Receive, Ill∴ Brother, the letters patent of constitution of this Consistory and the Book of Gold, in which these letters patent are to be copied, attested, and signed by all the Princes of the Consistory, and in which Book of Gold, also, the minutes of this inauguration and installation are to be entered, and the future deliberations and proceedings of the Consistory to be recorded. And do you deliver them to the Gr∴ Secretary, when he shall have been installed.

Gr∴ Com. Ill∴ Gr∴ Sec'y∴ Gen'l∴, you will now proceed to elect the officers of this Consistory, commencing with the Ill∴ Commander-in-Chief; you will receive their ballots, and let the First and Second Lieut. Commanders (for the time being) count and report the votes.

Gr∴ Sec∴ Ill∴ Brothers, you will now proceed to elect the officers of this Consistory, commencing with the Ill∴ Commander-in-Chief.

*   *   *   *   *

Gr∴ Com. Ill∴ Brother, the office and dignity of Commander-in-Chief of this Consistory, of which your brethren have thought you worthy, and upon your election to which by their unsolicited suffrages I congratulate you, is not only one of great honor, but of labor and responsibility. It imposes upon you very important duties.

Presiding in the Consistory, your first duty is impartiality; and your second, to maintain that equality among the brethren which should always exist among Masons. It is the necessary basis of our order, and to it we owe the glory and prosperity of Masonry. Wealth, rank, and social position, distinguish no one Mason from another.

The officers and dignitaries are but agents, intrusted by the order with authority for the exclusive good of the mass of Masons: every member of the Consistory is your peer, and is entitled to equal consideration; and every Mason, however humble in degree or station, if worthy, is your equal. The possession of degrees indicates no superiority, unless accompanied by superior knowledge, and greater capacity for doing good.

That only which one learns and does in Masonry makes him superior to his brethren, and that superiority is one of intellect and moral character alone.

I congratulate you on your accession to the high office which you now hold, and most earnestly hope that you may so worthily fill it, that it shall be found to have been fortunate for the Consistory and the order that you were elected its first Commander-in-Chief.

*   *   *   *   *

Special Charge to the First Lieutenant.

Gr∴ Com∴ Ill∴ Brother, the members of this Consistory have selected you to take the place of the Ill∴ Commander-in-Chief in case of his absence, and to succeed him for the residue of the term, in case of his death.

The duties which you are in that case to perform are known to you, and need not be repeated. When he is present you are to assist him with your counsel and advice, and aid him in maintaining the dignity and authority of his office, and the peace and harmony of the Consistory. I congratulate you on being thought worthy by your brethren of this honorable station, and earnestly hope that you may give them no reason to regret the choice they have made.

Charge to the First Lieutenant.

Gr∴ Com. Ill∴ Brother, the office to which you have been elected, though in rank and power below that of Commander-in-Chief, is of great importance. As his First Lieutenant, you will receive from him his orders, communicate them, and see that they are obeyed; and in his absence and that of his illustrious Deputy, you will perform the duties of his office. The efficiency of the Commander depends on that of his Lieutenants; and if they are indifferent and incompetent, his labor, besides being largely and improperly increased, will to a great extent prove unavailing.

Often, indeed, more depends upon the subordinate than upon the Chief; and it is not uncommon for the latter to reap and wear the laurels that in justice belong to the former.

Will you promptly obey him and faithfully second his exertions? You are especially charged with the supervision within and without the Consistory of your column.

You are peculiarly the conservator of the peace of the Consistory and it is your especial duty to settle all difficulties and unveil all dissensions that may arise among the brethren. You will to that end carefully watch all approaches to misunderstanding, and discountenance all censorious or sarcastic remarks in debate or elsewhere, and especially keep a careful watch over your own temper, never suffering yourself to utter a harsh or bitter word to a brother. Teach every brother by your wise example to bear with the infirmities of another; and beware particularly of obstinacy and pride of opinion, out of which most difficulties in Masonry grow.

Ill∴ Grand Master of Ceremonies, you will please conduct the Ill∴ First Lieutenant Commander to the West, and seat him on the right of the Ill∴ Brother who for the time occupies that station.

Charge to the Second Lieutenant.

Gr∴ Com∴ Ill∴ Brother, your office is equal in importance and responsibility to that of First Lieutenant of the Commander-in-Chief; you receive from him the orders of that Chief, and are to see them duly executed. You are to have in charge your column, and keep careful watch over the conduct of those thus under your supervision, as well as over yourself. It is your especial duty to see that the members regularly attend the meetings of the Consistory, an office not likely to prove a sinecure. It would be folly to expect that none of the brethren will become indifferent and lose their interest in the work. Some will become disinterested at fancied slight or injury, some dissatisfied because measures proposed by them are not approved by the majority; and more will weary of your labors, when the first gloss of novelty is worn off. Business will interfere with some, and pleasure or indolence with that of others. Against all this it will be your peculiar duty to struggle, to arouse the flagging zeal of some, and excite the sluggish resolution of others; to heal the wounded pride of one, and show another the unreasonableness of his pique and discontent. Be especially careful that in the exercise of your authority, you yourself give just cause of offence to none; and strive to justify the good opinion of your brethren, so signally displayed by your election to the office which you hold.

Ill∴ Grand Master of Ceremonies, you will please conduct the Illustrious Second Lieutenant Commander to the West, and seat him on the right of the Ill∴ Brother who for the time occupies that station.

*   *   *   *   *

Gr∴ Com∴ By virtue of the powers with which I am invested in the name and by the authority of the Supreme Council of Sovereign Grand Inspector General of the thirty-third and last degree of the Ancient and Accepted Rite for ...., I do now install you, Illustrious Brother and Prince ...., in and invest you with the office and dignity of Illustrious Commander-in-Chief. You, Illustrious Brother and Prince ...., I do install in and invest with the office and dignity of Illustrious Deputy Commander-in-Chief.

You, Illustrious Brother and Prince ...., I do install in and invest with the office and dignity of First Lieutenant Commander; and you, Illustrious Brother and Prince ......, I do install in and invest with the office and dignity of Second Lieutenant Commander of the Consistory of Sublime Princes and Commanders of the Royal Secret thirty-second degree, Ancient and Accepted rite of Freemasonry, in and for ....; and each of you hereafter shall possess and enjoy all the powers, honors, privileges, and prerogatives to his said proper office belonging and appertaining.

* * * * *

Gr∴ Com∴: Illustrious Second Lieutenant Commander, with you is the bright constellation composed of the two stars, Justice and Equity, which to a Mason should be as inseparable as the Dioscuri, whose appearance in the heavens was deemed by the mariners of Samothrace as indicative of fair weather; and I commend them to your especial charge, and hope that, enforcing them among the brethren, you will ever regulate by them your own official and private conduct. Be seated, Illustrious Second Lieutenant Commander!

Gr∴ Com∴: Illustrious First Lieutenant Commander, with you is the bright constellation composed of the three stars, LIBERTY, EQUALITY, and BROTHERHOOD; they will govern in this Grand Consistory, as they govern everywhere else in Masonry. LIBERTY and constitutional law, EQUALITY with order and subordination, BROTHERHOOD of the virtuous and good, making the strong protectors of the weak, the rich the sympathizers of the poor! I commit the three lights to your charge: never forget or fail to remind your brethren, that these three sublime words contain a whole creed of which every Mason ought to be an apostle. Be seated, my brother.

* * * * *

Gr∴ Com∴: Illustrious Commander-in-Chief, I invest you with this collar and jewel of your office, to be worn in your absence by your Illustrious Deputy. I am sure that each of you will wear them worthily and well. You are to occupy the East, the place of light, and I need not tell you that it will be your duty to instruct your brethren, and consequently to inform yourself in all that it concerns them to know.

With you, as the sweet constellation of the five stars, FAITH, HOPE, CHARITY, HONOR, and DUTY, I commit them to your charge. Look well to them, and let them never cease to burn in your Consistory; for whenever one of them disappears and is seen no more among you, Masonry also will have left you, to seek some more congenial region.

Illustrious Commander-in-Chief, Officers, and Brethren, in your midst in........your columns, and in every corner of your Consistory, shines the great central sun of Truth. Receive it in charge, and let its light never be obscured. Study and reflect, my brethren, and gain wisdom and knowledge, and attain unto the truth, and with zeal apply your knowledge to the benefit of your followers, and may light and peace and joy ever remain and abide with you.

Illustrious Brethren and Princes, members of the Consistory, unite with me in applauding the installation of our Illustrious Brother........, in the high office of Illustrious Commander-in-Chief; * * * With me, my brethren!

    *   *   *   *   *

Gr∴ Com∴: Illustrious Commander-in-Chief, I surrender into your hands the government of your Consistory, and place under your charge the Book of Gold and Letters Patent of Constitution, now in the hands of our Secretary General, and may success attend your exertions, and order and peace ever prevail among you.

Com∴-in-Chief∴: Attention, Sublime Princes. Join me in returning our thanks and doing honor to our Ill∴ Bro∴ the Grand Commander.

    *   *   *   *   *

Com∴-in-Chief∴: The officers elect will please approach the East.

> They approach and form a line in front of the throne, in the order in which they have been elected, when the Grand Commander administers the oath of office, as follows:

OATH OF OFFICE.

I,........., in the presence of the Great Creator and Preserver of the Universe, do solemnly swear that I will support the Constitution, Regulations, Statutes, and Institutes of the Ancient and Accepted rite, the Laws and Statutes of the Supreme Council of Sovereign Grand Inspector General of the thirty-third degree for ...., and the Statutes of this Consistory not contrary thereto.

That I will faithfully, and to the best of my skill and ability, perform and discharge the duties to which I have been elected or appointed.

That I will use every exertion in my power to advance the interest, increase the usefulness, and augment the splendor of the Ancient and Accepted rite. So help me God.

To the Grand Minister of State.

Sublime Prince........, you have been elected to the office of Grand Minister of State of this Consistory, in which office is included that of Grand Orator. The office is one of labor and responsibility. He who accepts it should be capable of edifying and instructing his brethren. He must address the Consistory on proper occasions, pronounce discourses to candidates, give his opinion, when required by the Commander-in-Chief, upon questions of Masonic Law, and read essays and lectures upon Masonic subjects, when requested by the Consistory. He must therefore make himself familiar with the constitutions, regulations, institutes and statutes, with Masonic law and philosophy, with the doctrines of the rite, and the history of the order. I need not tell you that all this requires intellect and study, and no one can do a graver injury to Masonry, than he who occupies a high and important office, and then neglects its duties. It is when little or no real instruction is given in symbolic Lodges, no essays are read there, and all the learning and doctrine of the order are neglected, that their meetings become uninteresting, tiresome, and unprofitable.

The field before you is vast, my brother, and will afford ample scope for your intellect and learning, and I trust that your brethren will have cause to rejoice that they have selected you to labor in it. You will now take your station at the right of the Illustrious Deputy Commander-in-Chief.

To the Grand Chancellor.

Sublime Prince........, you have been elected to the office of Grand Chancellor of this Consistory. You are the constitutional and legal adviser of the Commander-in-Chief, and to you he looks for counsel. It is your duty to prepare all accusations against Masons charged with the commission of offences against our laws. You will inspect and sign all diplomas, briefs, patents, letters of constitution, and certificates, and see that they are in due form and contain the necessary conditions. It is therefore indispensable that you should be familiar with the constitution, regulations, laws, statutes, institutes, and forms of the order. In the absence of the Grand Minister of State you will perform his duties, and you must therefore acquaint yourself with the history, doctrine, and philosophy of Masonry, that you may be prepared to do so. And finally, it is your duty to conduct all proper correspondence with other Consistories and foreign Masonic bodies. I hope you may so perform these varied and important duties as to earn for yourself honor, and benefit this Consistory and the order. You will please be seated at my left.

To the Grand Secretary.

Sublime Prince,........, you have been elected to the office of Grand Secretary of this Consistory. It will be your duty to take charge of all papers and proceedings to be laid before the Consistory, and present them in due time; to turn over to the Grand Keeper of the Seals such as are proper to be kept among the archives; to enter and record in the Book of Gold all the proceedings, deliberations, decisions, and decretals of the Consistory; to conduct all correspondence with the Bodies and individual Masons under its jurisdiction; to prepare and sign all diplomas, briefs, patents, letters of constitution and certificates, submitting them to the Grand Chancellor for examination, and procuring them to be sealed by the Grand Keeper of the Seals, and signed by the necessary officers; to receive all moneys due the Consistory from all sources whatever, and give duplicate receipts therefor, and to pay the same over to the Grand Treasurer; to keep regular account of all such receipts and payments, with such other duties as of right and by prescription to the office of Grand Secretary do belong. These varied and important duties require for their proper and faithful discharge honesty, accuracy, and punctuality. Upon you the prosperity of the Consistory will to a great extent depend; and I earnestly hope that when you retire from office, you will do so with the general regret of the brethren.

To the Grand Treasurer.

Sublime Prince........, you have been elected to the office of Grand Treasurer of this Consistory; it is your duty to receive from the Grand Secretary all the funds and moneys of this Consistory, to pay them out upon its order, and to keep a just and correct account of the same. I need not say how necessary it is that those duties should be performed with punctuality and accuracy. The confidence in you displayed by your brethren, assures me that you will be faithful to the trust thus imposed upon you. You will please assume your station.

To the Grand Keeper of the Seals.

Sublime Prince........, you have been elected to the office of Grand Keeper of the Seals of this Consistory. It will be your duty to keep in charge the seals and letters patent of constitution of this Consistory; you will affix the Great Seal to all diplomas, briefs, patents, letters of constitution and certificates, prepared by the Consistory and approved by the Grand Chancellor, and to all exemplifications and copies of proceedings, statutes, decretals, and papers in like manner prepared and approved. You will also be the Keeper of the Archives, and Librarian of this Consistory, and will take charge of everything proper to be preserved in the archives and library, and will endeavor, by correspondence with other Masonic bodies, as far as possible, to increase and enrich the same, reporting upon their condition from time to time, and suggesting such measures as may be necessary for their preservation. Receive now from the Grand Secretary the seals of this Consistory and the letters patent of constitution thereof. (*In the Northern Jurisdiction this office is abolished.*)

To the Grand Engineer.

Sublime Prince ...., you have been elected to the office of Grand Engineer of this Consistory. It will be your duty to see that its hall is supplied with the proper furniture and decorations, properly arranged to prepare it for the reception of candidates and for its ordinary sessions; to assist in examining visiting brethren; to arrange the camp; and to act as First Grand Expert at receptions. The good opinion of your brethren warrants us in believing that you will perform those duties with zeal and fidelity. You will please assume your station.

To the Grand Hospitaller.

Sublime Prince ...., you have been elected to the office of Grand Hospitaller of this Consistory. You will be its Almoner, not only to dispense its charities, but to seek out and make known to it meritorious cases of distress and want, to be relieved. The most deserving cases of need and destitution are often those that do not obtrude themselves upon the world, or seek the light of day. To visit the homes of the wretched, to seek out the sick and the suffering, and to dispense to them blessings, concealing with scrupulous care the source from whence they flow, to pour the balm of consolation upon the bruised and wounded heart, to sympathize with the unfortunate, and to minister to the wants of the helpless—these are deeds truly worthy of one who claims to be a child of the duty of infinite beneficence and love of God, who allows suffering, and misery, and destitution to exist in the world, in fact, that this may give opportunity for the exercise of that beneficence by which man resembles him; and, in fact, that his children may feel that most exquisite of pleasures which we enjoy when comforting and helping our brethren. You will please assume your station.

To the Grand Master of Ceremonies.

Sublime Prince ...., you have been elected to the office of Grand Master of Ceremonies of this Consistory. It will be your duty to precede and attend the Commander-in-Chief, to receive, examine, and introduce all visitors, and to receive, prepare, introduce, and conduct all candidates. Upon the faithful and intelligent performance by you of these duties the regularity of the labors of the Consistory will in a great measure depend: the impression made upon the candidates by their reception, and the pleasure of the brethren in their labors, and upon your politeness and courtesy, will also depend the gratification and comfort of those illustrious brethren who do us the honor to visit and encourage us.

You will now assume your station, and enter on the discharge of your duties.

To the Grand Captain of the Guards.

Sublime Prince ...., you have been elected to the office of Grand Captain of the Guards of this Consistory. It is your duty to guard the entrance of the chamber of the Senate, to receive and communicate the pass-words, and to perform such other duties as by prescription and custom appertain to your office. Your punctual attendance at our meetings is important; and our knowledge of your worth assures us that the duties of your office will be always faithfully performed. Receive this sword, the weapon of a knight, the emblem of your authority, and the symbol of honor, and repair to your station.

To the Grand Standard Bearer.

Sublime Prince ...., you have been appointed Grand Standard Bearer of this Consistory. It is your duty to carry and defend the Standard of the order. The Banner represents its holy and noble principles, which none of us can yield up but with our lives; and no emergency of danger will excuse him who bears the Standard for its loss or dishonor. You will please assume your station.

To the Grand Tyler.

Sublime Prince ...., you have been appointed Grand Tyler of this Consistory, during the pleasure of the Commander-in-Chief. You know the duties of your office. Receive this sword, in all time the peculiar weapon of the Tyler of every Masonic body. Repair to your post, and guard well the approach to the chamber of the Consistory, that no cowan overhear us, and no impostor intrude himself among us!

   *   *   *   *   *

Attention, Sublime Princes! Your officers are now duly installed, and this Consistory is completely organized and prepared to proceed with its labors. Let us applaud, my brethren!

INSTALLATION. 551

* * * * *

HYMN.

6s & 4s.

1. Praise ye Jehovah's name, Praise thro' his courts proclaim; Rise and adore; High o'er the heavens above, Sound his great acts of love; While his rich grace we prove, Vast as his power

Now let our voices raise
Triumphant sounds of praise,
  Wide as his fame:
There let the harps be found:
Organs with solemn sound,
Roll your deep notes around,
  Filled with his name.

While his high praise ye sing,
Strike every sounding string;
  Sweet the accord!
He vital breath bestows—
Let every breath that flows,
His noblest fame disclose:
  Praise ye the Lord.

The installing officer will make the following endorsement on the Letters Patent of Constitution before delivering them to the Grand Secretary.

To the Glory of the Grand Architect of the Universe.

We,........, thirty-third, and ...., the Supreme Council of Sovereign Grand Inspectors General, thirty-third degree of the Ancient and Accepted Scottish Rite for ...., do hereby declare and make known, that on the .... day of the Hebrew month called ...., of the year of true light ......, answering to the .... day of ...., V∴ E∴....., by virtue of the powers with which we are invested .... aforesaid, we did convoke and assemble in general conclave, at the city of ...., in the State of ...., the Sublime Princes and Commanders of the Royal Secret, mentioned in the within Letters Patent of Constitution, and did then and there, in the name and by authority of the Supreme Council, congregate the said Sublime Princes and Commanders into, and did constitute and inaugurate the Consistory of Sublime Princes and Commanders of the Royal Secret in, the sacred asylum of the same; and did then and there duly install the Sublime Prince .... as the Illustrious Commander-in-Chief, the Sublime Prince .... as the Illustrious Deputy Commander-in-Chief, the Sublime

INSTALLATION. 553

Prince .... as the First Lieutenant Commander, and the Sublime Prince .... as the Second Lieutenant Commander thereof.

........33d.

Before delivering the Book of Gold, the installing officer will write on the first page as follows:

We, the undersigned ...., thirty-third, and ...., the Supreme Council of the Sovereign Grand Inspectors General, thirty-third degree, for ...., do declare that we have delivered this Book of Gold to the Consistory of Sublime Princes and Commanders of the Royal Secret thirty-second degree of the Ancient and Accepted Scottish rite, at the time of its installation, to be used as a record of its proceedings, the same containing .... pages, this included. In witness whereof, I do now set my hand to this endorsement, and affix hereto the Seal of my Arms, in the said State of ...., this, &c., &c..........

........33d.

The Secretary General and the Lieutenant Commanders appointed *pro tem.*, will sign the record of proceedings of the Session of Installation, in the character of Installing Officers.

PROTOCOL FOR THE INSTALLATION SESSION.

To the Glory of the Grand Architect of the Universe.

DEUS MEUMQUE JUS.

At the Orient of the Supreme Council of Sovereign Grand Inspectors General of the thirty-third degree of the Ancient and Accepted Rite, for ...., under the C∴ C∴, near the B∴ B∴, answering to .... N∴ L∴, the .... day of the ...... Hebrew month, called........

HEALTH, STABILITY, POWER.

We, ..., thirty-third, and ......, the Supreme Council of Sov∴ Gr∴ Ins∴ General, thirty-third degree, for ......, and the Sublime Princes and Commanders of the Royal Secret, ..., being met and assembled under the order of the said ......, and the Illustrious Brother ...... acting as First Lieutenant Commander; the Illustrious Brother ......, as Second Lieutenant Commander; and the Illustrious Brother ......, as Secretary General *pro tem.;* and also the Sublime Princes of the Royal Secret, ..., at the city of ......, in the State of ......, on the .... day of ......, the said Illustrious Brother ...... presiding, did announce that he had the letters patent of constitution, granted upon ......, said Supreme Council to the Sublime Princes above named, constituting them the Consistory of Sublime Princes and Commanders of the Royal Secret thirty-second degree of the Ancient and Accepted Rite, in and for ..... And this being the day set and appointed for inaugurating the said Consistory, and for the election and installation of the officers thereof, and the said Illustrious Brother ...... aforesaid, being invested with full power thereto. Thereupon the ...... aforesaid, seated near the altar of perfumes, announces that he is about to commence the labors of the day, by inaugurating the temple, and dedicating it to the Deity of infinite beneficence.

The ......, &c., &c.

> Everything done by the installing officer on the occasion should be stated in the minutes—*i. e.,* his calling the brethren to assemble around the altar, the oath administered, etc., mentioning all the material points of the work; and the same with the other work that follows, up to the time when he yields the chair to the Commander-in-Chief.
>
> There being no further business, the minutes are read and approved; all the members of the Consistory sign the copy of the Letters Patent of Constitution in the Book of Gold, and the proceedings of the Consistory after installation.
>
> Then the box of fraternal assistance is passed around, and the Consistory is closed in due form.

CEREMONY OF BAPTISM

IN THE

ANCIENT AND ACCEPTED SCOTTISH RITE.

The following ceremony, called MASONIC BAPTISM, is frequently performed in Europe, but has not been generally adopted in the United States. It is inserted here as an interesting subject of information, and for use, when required.

This ceremony can be conferred only by a Lodge of Perfection or Symbolic Lodge; and when by the former, it works in the Entered Apprentice degree.

A child of either sex may be baptized by this ceremony alone, until it has attained the age of twelve years if a boy, and of eighteen if a girl. A boy over the age of twelve years can be baptized only when received a *Louveteau,* or adopted; and a girl over eighteen only when adopted.

The ceremony is particularly intended for infants. It secures to either boy or girl the protection and assistance of the Lodge and the brethren; and, in the case of a boy, the right to be received a *Louveteau* at the age of twelve years.

In any case, the father of the child must be a Mason, or its mother the daughter of a Mason. In the latter case, the child may be baptized, but, though a boy, cannot become a *Louveteau.* The father or grandfather, as the case may be, must be, if living, or must have been, if dead, at the time of his death an affiliated Mason, unless his non-affiliation is, or was, not attributable to his own fault, indifference, or neglect; and this rule, also, is relaxed where the mother is a ward or adopted child of the Lodge.

PRELIMINARIES.

It needs no vote of the Lodge to consent to the baptism of a child. Every one that comes within the conditions is entitled to it as of right. If inquiry is necessary, however, to ascertain the facts, a committee may be appointed; and in case of doubt whether non-affiliation of the father or grandfather is or has been, under the circumstances, excusable, the Lodge will decide by a majority of votes.

When a child is to be baptized, the Lodge will proceed to select a brother of the Lodge to be its godfather, and the wife or sister of a brother of the Lodge to be its godmother.

Vacancies in these offices will be filled by the Lodge, from time to time, as they occur, until the child, if a boy, reaches the age of twelve years; and if a girl, of twenty-one, or until she marries.

The Lodge will then appoint a delegation of three members to communicate with the parent or parents of the child—or, if he have none living or competent to act, then with its nearest relatives—to obtain their consent to the baptism, and secure their presence at the ceremony. If the child be of such age as that it is proper for itself to be consulted, the delegation will do that also.

If it have no father, or if he be unable, unfit, or unwilling to assist at the ceremony, the delegation will, if possible, arrange with one of its nearest relatives, male, to act as its father in the ceremony. If they cannot, they will select a Past Master of the Lodge, or, if there be none, some other past officer, to act in the place of its father.

So, if it have no mother or other near female relative, able, fit, and willing to assist at the ceremony, they will select the wife, sister, or daughter of some brother of the Lodge, to act in the place of its mother.

They will procure white garments for the child, and, if they be unable to procure them for themselves, garments of black for the father, and of white for the mother.

They will also procure a locket for the child, if it be a girl under ten years of age, or a bracelet if over that age; and if it be a boy, a ring, and make whatever other arrangements that are necessary.

The ceremony being a public one, public notice may be given

CEREMONY OF BAPTISM.

ARRANGEMENT OF THE HALL OR LODGE.

The arrangement of the hall is brilliant, hung with garlands and strewed with flowers.

CEREMONIAL.

When the spectators have taken their seats, the Lodge is opened in the degree of Entered Apprentice or Perfection, in a room adjacent to the hall, and proceeds thither in procession, the members and visiting brethren together, and in due order.

Instead of opening in E. A., the Lodge will be opened in the degree of Perfection.

The procession will be formed in the following order:
1. Captain of Guard.
2. Members by two's.
3. Officers in reverse order of rank.
4. Celebrant.
5. Sovereign Grand Inspectors General.

Every member in the procession must be in regalia.

On entering the Lodge, the procession will proceed up the middle aisle, and then file right and left to their seats. The organ will play a march, until all are seated.

The greatest decorum will be observed.

Then the Master • *which is answered by each of the Wardens in turn, rises and says:*

W. M. The solemnity which calls us to meet together to-day is one which most eminently accords with the purposes and spirit of our institution.

It is not a mere idle and showy ceremonial, designed to obtrude ourselves upon the notice of the world, or to give an empty title to those who are as yet too young to appreciate and understand. Masonic Baptism was instituted far more for the parents than for the children, while it affords each father an occasion for renewing his own obligations. He, also, by concurring in an act which impresses upon his child of his own sex, in advance, the character of Mason, and which gives it, of either sex, a right to the protection and careful guardianship of the Lodge, obliges himself of necessity to rear it in the principles of Freemasonry; to teach it generosity, charity, and beneficence; to mould it, as it were, from its earliest years in such fashion that virtue shall be its habit, and love of its fellow-creatures its instinct.

In our ceremony of Baptism we neither imitate nor have it in view to supply the place of any religious rite of any church. For baptism is not the exclusive property of religion. As the natural symbol of purification of the soul, it was used in the ancient mysteries and solemnities of India, Egypt, and Greece. When the aspirant to a knowledge of these old mysteries cleansed his body with water, he did so as a pledge that he would in like manner cleanse his soul and spirit from vice and immorality. It was not imagined that the ceremony itself had any healing virtue, or conferred holiness upon the recipient. From these mysteries, from Eleusis and Samothrace, and from the Essenes, this rite has come to us by legitimate transmission, and we use it in no spirit of irreverence, but in the simple sense in which it was used in the land watered by the Nile, before the building of the Pyramids. The candidate at Eleusis, purifying himself, before entering into the mysterious temple, by washing his hands in holy water, was admonished to present himself with a mind pure and undefiled, without which the external cleanliness of the body would by no means be accepted. Such only is the sense of our Baptism.

For Masonry is no religion, nor does it assume to take the place of any religion, but only to inculcate those principles of pure morality which Reason reads on the pages of the great Book of Nature, and to teach those great primary truths on which all religions repose. What edifice of faith and creed each brother builds upon that foundation we have no *right* to inquire, and therefore do not seek to inquire. It is enough for us to know that each believes in the existence of a Supreme Intellect, Creator and Preserver of all things, a Deity of infinite tenderness, pity, and love; and that we are not mere successive phenomena, proceeding from combination and organization, but living souls, distinct from matter, and destined to survive after our bodies are dissolved. To one who did not thus believe, our symbols would have no meaning.

We therefore venture to hope that, in the simple ceremonial

CEREMONY OF BAPTISM.

about to be performed, you may be interested, and perhaps may even hear somewhat that may lead to profitable reflection, that fruitful mother of wise and upright action.

The Master again seats himself.

An interlude of music of eight bars

When the music ceases, an alarm is given at the door by several raps.

J. D. Brother Senior Warden, there is an alarm at the door of our Temple.

S. W. Worshipful Master, there is an alarm at the door of our Temple.

W. M. Cause inquiry to be made, Brother Senior Warden, by whom the alarm is given, and what it is that he desires.

S. W. Inquire, Brother Junior Deacon, by whom, &c.

The Junior Deacon goes to the door, opens it, and inquires:

J. D. Who is it gives the alarm here, and what does he desire?

Tyler. I give the alarm. There are here, in waiting, the child of a Mason [or .... children of Masons], and its [or their] parents, the parents desiring that their children should be baptized.

The Junior Deacon closes the door, returns to his seat, faces the Senior Warden, salutes with his hand, and says:

J. D. Brother Senior Warden, the alarm is given by the Tyler, who reports that there are in waiting, &c.

S. W. Worshipful Master, the alarm is given by the Tyler, who reports, &c.

W. M. Brother Master of Ceremonies, give this child [or these children] and its [or their] parents admission, taking with you the necessary assistance.

The residue of this ceremony is given as for more than one child. The Master and officers can readily make the necessary changes, if there be but one.

The Master of Ceremonies, knowing how many of the children are too young to walk, takes with him the same number of brethren, and one more, and repairs to the ante-room. When he is ready to enter, be gives any ordinary alarm.

J. D. Brother Senior Warden, there is an alarm at the door of the Temple.

S. W. Worshipful Master, there is an alarm at the door of the Temple.

W. M. Cause inquiry to be made, Brother Senior Warden, who it is that gives the alarm, and what is his desire.

S. W. Brother Junior Deacon, inquire who it is, &c.

The Junior Deacon goes to the door, opens it, and asks:

J. D. Who is it, &c.?

M. C. It is the Master of Ceremonies, accompanying the children for whom baptism is desired, and their parents.

The Junior Deacon returns to his place, faces the Senior Warden, salutes, and reports:

J. D. Brother Senior Warden, the Master of Ceremonies desires to enter, accompanied by the children for whom baptism is desired, and their parents.

S. W. Worshipful Master, the Master of Ceremonies, &c.

W. M. Throw open the doors, and let them enter.

S. W. Throw open the doors, and let them enter.

The Master gives ● ● ● and all the brethren rise. The Junior Deacon goes to the door and opens it. The Master of Ceremonies enters first, with drawn sword, followed closely by a brother bearing a candlestick with three branches, in which are three lighted candles of equal sizes, and different colors, white, black, and rose-color, forming a triangle. After him come, two by two, as many brethren as there are children too young to walk, each carrying a child upon a cushion covered with light-blue silk; and behind these come in procession, two by two, the other children, and then the fathers and mothers of all.

As the head of the procession enters, the trumpets will sound a flourish of eight bars. The Master of Ceremonies will halt in the West until the music ceases: then conduct the procession up the middle aisle to the East, turn to the right and make the three circuits, graduating the time to the lesson and music.

As soon as the Master of Ceremonies commences the movement up the middle aisle, the Junior Warden will commence the lesson.

Between the lesson said by J. W., S. W.. and Master, there will be a chant.

The procession is conducted by the Master of Ceremonies three times slowly around the Lodge-room, with the sun, while the officers repeat as follows:

CEREMONY OF BAPTISM.

S. W. Young children are an heritage of the Lord. As arrows are in the hand of a mighty man, so are young children. Happy is the man that hath his quiver full of them; he shall not be ashamed, but will speak with the enemies in the gate.

Chant.

S. W. If his children forsake my law and walk not in my judgments, if they break my statutes and keep not my commandments, then will I visit their transgressions with the rod, and their wrong-doing with stripes. Nevertheless, my loving-kindness will I not utterly take from them, nor permit my pledge to fail.

Chant.

W. M. Suffer little children to come unto me, and forbid them not: for of such is the kingdom of God. Whosoever shall not receive the kingdom of God as a little child, he shall not enter therein. Whosoever shall receive one such child in my name, receiveth me: and whosoever shall receive me, receiveth not me, but him that sent me.

Chant.

At the end of the three circuits, the procession halts in front of the Senior Warden in the West, the Master of Ceremonies placing the brethren who bear the infants in front, the other children on each side of them, and the fathers and mothers in the rear, in a line. On the right hand stands the brother bearing the candlestick.

W. M. Brethren and sisters, you have brought these young children to receive at our hands Masonic Baptism. We are prepared to accept the duties which the administration of that rite will impose upon us. This Lodge is always proud and happy thus to receive under its protection the children of the brethren Each of us with joy accepts the new obligations created by such reception, for in the performance of duty the true Mason finds the only real happiness. Are you, on your part, prepared to renew, those of you who are brethren, your obligations to the order, to the Lodge, and to the children of your brethren of the Mystic Tie; and those of you whom we hail with a new and exquisite pleasure as our sisters, to promise to spare no exertion in making these children such as every true-hearted mother desires her children to be? And do you accept us individually and this Lodge, as your seconds and assistants in this holy work!

<ul style="list-style:none"><li>One of the fathers, answering for all, makes such response as he deems appropriate; or he may use the following at his option:</li></ul>

Father. Worshipful Master, the fathers and mothers of these children ask me to say, in their names, that it is because they so profoundly feel the immense responsibility which God has imposed upon them in intrusting to them the education of these young immortals, and because of their intense desire well and faithfully to perform that duty, that they have been willing to place them under the protection of this Lodge, in the hope of insuring to them that purity of heart, and stainlessness of soul, which are symbolized by Masonic Baptism. Well, indeed, do these trembling, agitated mothers, and these anxious fathers, know how numerous and how dangerous are the snares and pitfalls which youth must encounter in the intricate paths of life.

They know that very shortly some of these little ones may be left fatherless and motherless, helpless as young birds with broken wings that trail upon the earth; and they feel that they can pass away more contentedly if they know that over their orphans will be extended the care and affection of this Lodge, to ward off destitution and the enemies that will be eager to assail their innocence and virtue.

These fathers are prepared gladly to renew their obligations. What occasion more appropriate than this, upon which you are faithfully fulfilling yours?

These mothers gladly, most gladly, and gratefully accept for their children your proffered protection, and pray you to appreciate a thankfulness in them for which words have no adequate expression.

<ul style="list-style:none"><li>When the father concludes, the Master says:</li></ul>

W. M. Brother Master of Ceremonies, conduct these children and their parents to the places provided for them.

<ul style="list-style:none"><li>The Master of Ceremonies conducts the procession to the platform in the rear of the altar. The other children are seated in front, the fathers and mothers in the rear, and the brethren who bear the infants hand them to their mothers, who place them, still upon the cushions,</li></ul>

CEREMONY OF BAPTISM. 563

on their knees. The brother who bore the candlestick sets it on the south of the altar, and he and the other brethren who formed part of the procession, find seats among the other brethren. The Master gives one rap, and all the brethren are seated.

W. M. We have been early taught in Masonry that, before engaging in any important undertaking, we ought to implore the assistance of Deity. Let us do so, my brethren, with Humility and trustfulness.

PRAYER.

O Eternal God, and merciful and loving Father, enable us to perform the duties which we now propose to take upon us in regard to these children. May we be enabled to help their parents to lead them in the way that they should go, and to persuade them to return to it if they err or stray therefrom. Help us to teach them their duties to themselves, to others, to their country, and to thee. Help their parents to train them up in virtue, truth, and honor, obedient to thy laws, generous, forgiving, and tolerant. Let thy fatherly hand, we beseech thee, be ever over them. Give them the spirit of wisdom and understanding, of knowledge and of true and virtuous uprightness, that they may continually serve, honor, and obey thee, their heavenly Father; and may this ancient ceremony which we are now about to perform, be indeed the symbol to them of purity of heart, of innocence, and of blameless life. Let them grow up as young plants, and with their age and stature increase in wisdom and virtue and in favor with thyself, and with all whose excellence makes their good opinion of any worth. Preserve among them and among us, peace, friendship, and tenderness; and may we all, being steadfast in Faith, joyful through Hope, and rooted in Charity, so pass the waves of this troublesome world, that finally we may come to the land of everlasting life, there to advance ever nearer to thee, world without end: *Amen!*

All. So mote it be.

The brethren, having knelt during the prayer, now rise, and the following hymn is sung:

HYMN.

{ Re - joice, rejoice, fond mothers, That ye have given birth }
{ To these im-mor-tal be-ings, These children dear of earth. }

{ Oh! fond and anx - ious moth - ers, Look up with joy - ful eyes, For a boundless wealth of love and power, In each young spi - rit lies. }
{ Bless God both night and morn - ing, Each with a joy - ful heart, For the child of mor - tal pa - rent hath With the E - ter - nal part. }

CEREMONY OF BAPTISM.

> The stars shall lose their brightness,
>   And like a parched scroll
> The earth shall fade; but ne'er shall fade
>   The undying human soul.
>
> Oh then rejoice, fond mothers,
>   That ye have given birth
> To these immortal beings,
>   These children fair of earth.

(•)

W. M. Who offer to take upon themselves the offices of godfathers and godmothers of these children? Let those who do so approach, and be seated near them.

<small>Those previously selected to act as such rise, repair to the platform, and are seated by the Master of Ceremonies in the rear of the parents. Then the Masters says:</small>

W. M. Brethren and sisters, by accepting the offices of godfathers and godmothers of these children, you consent to become the special instruments through which the Lodge shall watch over and protect them,—its eyes to see, and its ears to hear, all dangers and hazards, all trials and temptations that may approach, and menace to entice them; its voice to warn them, to encourage them, to cheer them, and persuade them, and its hands to repel and ward off from them all harm and all evil influences. Informed that such shall be your offices and your duty, do you still consent to assume, and promise to perform them?

A Godfather. We do.

W. M. It is well. Remember that to their parents and yourselves will, in great measure, be committed the destiny of these young immortals, and that you must answer to our heavenly Father for the fidelity with which you fulfil the duties that you now voluntarily assume.

Fathers and mothers, we do not presume to instruct you in regard to your duties to your children. Of those duties, however negligently they may perform them, no father or mother of ordinary intelligence is ignorant. In the Lodge we remind each other of our duties, not because we do not know what they are but that we may incite each other to perform them, and to over come the obstacles to faithful and punctual performance interposed by our indolence, our frailties, our passions, and the enthralments of business, pleasure, or ambition.

Be not offended, therefore, if we detain you for a few moments, while we enumerate some of those duties, for the purpose of enabling you to see that we understand in what manner we are to assist you if you continue to live, and in what manner to endeavor to fill your places if you should be taken away from these children before they attain such age as no longer to need our counsel and protection.

* * * * *

Orator. Teach your sons and daughters that one may be clothed in rags, may be occupied in the lowest business, may make no show, be scarcely known to exist, and yet may be more truly great than those who are more commonly so called; for greatness consists in force of soul, that is, in force of thought, of moral principle, and love, and this may be found in the humblest condition. For the greatest man or woman is that one who chooses right with the most invincible resolution, who resists the sorest temptations from within and without, who bears the heaviest burdens cheerfully, who is calmest in storms, and most fearless under menaces and frowns, whose reliance on truth, virtue, and God is most unfaltering.

* * * * *

J. W. Teach them, first of all, to love, honor, and obey their parents, for that not to do so is ungrateful, unnatural, and hateful. Teach them to respect those older than themselves, and to listen patiently to their counsel, and even to their reproofs, because, if they are just, they ought to profit by them; and if they are unjust, they ought to be too glad, knowing them so, to be angry.

* * * * *

S. W. That the love which we bear to the country that gave us birth is not unreasoning nor absurd, but is an instinct of our nature, implanted by God in mankind for the preservation and prosperity of nations; that it is not artificial nor fictitious, but as natural and genuine as the love of a child for its mother; that indeed, our country *is* our mother; and when her honor and interests require it, she may justly call on us to peril fortune and life in her service; that patriotism is with reason accounted the most illustrious of virtues, and the patriot the most eminent of men; and with equal reason the traitor has in all ages been deemed execrable.

* * * * *

W. M. The child, owing to the great Architect of the Universe its existence, its senses that make it to enjoy, its intellect that enables it to acquire knowledge, surrounded everywhere by his blessings, ought to be taught in its earliest years to revere and love him, as the author of all the goodness, affection, generosity, and loving-kindness that display themselves in his creatures. Teach it that it is in loving those qualities in others, it loves God; and that, loving him, it should try to do that only of which he will approve. It is his love for it that is reflected in the bosom of its mother. It is his affection for it, his pity when it suffers. that speak in the eyes of its playmates.

PRAYER.

Almighty and Incomprehensible Intelligence, of the perfection of whose nature and the plenitude of whose love and tenderness we in vain endeavor to conceive by the ideal which each fashions for himself of the Absolutely Perfect, the Absolute Good, the Absolute and Perfect Mercy, Pity, and Love, and whose unimaginable and immeasurable perfections in that infinitely lower Ideal we devoutly worship and love, enable us to read, though imperfectly, yet not wrongly, and in a mistaken sense contrary to thy truth, the lessons of duty which thou hast written in thy magnificent hieroglyphics, expressions of thy will, thy thought, and thy affections, on the great pages of the wondrous book of the universe; to these children, to our own, and to all whom the law of duty has placed, or may in any wise place, under our charge, give to all of us who are here present, resolution to fulfil all the duties which by thy law that character and relation create and impose upon us. Amen!

All. So mote it be.

(•)

W. M. Brother Master of Ceremonies, let these children

that are to be baptized be now brought to the altar of baptism.

> The Master of Ceremonies conducts the children, their parents, godfathers, and godmothers to the East, and places them in front of the pedestal, or table, on which are the water, oil, and salt. In front are the mothers and fathers, bearing or leading the children, according to their age, and behind them the godfathers and godmothers. If there are several children, they should be arranged in a semicircle facing the pedestal or table.
>
> The Master comes down from the throne, stands upon its steps, and says: • • •

W. M. My brethren, the most glowing words are inadequate to express the love and admiration which we ought to feel toward our Father in heaven.

> He lights the three vessels of incense on the three small triangular tables in front of the East, and then proceeds to the pedestal or table, and says:

W. M. Before the young initiate could enter into the Temples of the Mysteries, our ancient brethren required him to wash his hands in pure water, as a symbol and pledge of his innocence, of the sincerity of his intentions, and of the present and future purity of his soul. From them it has come down to us, a custom venerable by its antiquity, the legacy of the remote past, known and practised in the Orient centuries before John the Baptist came preaching in the wilderness, or even before Solomon laid the foundation of the Temple of God. *Let none here mistake it for a religious ceremony, or accuse us of irreverence.*

> Beginning on the left of the line, he learns the name of each child, takes it in his arms, if it be an infant, and with the right hand, if it be able to walk, carries or leads it to the pedestal, and lifts its left hand into a basin of perfumed water, saying, as he does so:

W. M. C. E., I wash thee with this pure water. May God give thee, and maintain thee in, that innocence and purity of heart of which this cleansing is a symbol.

> He then returns the child to its parents, and proceeds in the same manner with the next, until all are baptized. Then, he takes in his hand the vessel of perfumed oil, goes to each in turn, beginning as before on the left, and dipping the little finger of his right hand in the oil, marks on the forehead of each a Delta, saying, as he does so:

CEREMONY OF BAPTISM.

W. M. With this oil of anointment, emblem of fruitfulness and plenty, I set upon thy forehead the Delta, the symbol of the wisdom, might, and love of the Deity. May he be pleased to make thee fruitful of all good works.

When he has thus anointed all, he replaces the vessel of oil on the table or pedestal, and then, standing in front of it and facing the children, stretches out his hands toward them, and says:

W. M. May the blessing of our Father in heaven rest upon you, my children. May you never know the bitterness of want, or the remorse that follows crime; the loneliness of a life without love; the midnight agonies of bruised and suffering hearts; the miser's dream of gold; ambition's hungering for greatness; the quenched light of a broken spirit; the sense of deadly and undeserved wrong; affection trusting and betrayed; or the abiding curse of weariness of life. And may our heavenly Father comfort, encourage, and uphold you amid the disappointments, the sufferings, and the trials of life; amid its fevered cares and sad diseases; in all losses of friends by death or unworthiness; in all dangers and temptations. And may he in his great love and mercy pardon and forgive all your frailties or errors, temper the wind to the shorn lamb, and gather you into his fold of heaven. Amen.

All. So mote it be.

W. M. Brother Master of Ceremonies, reconduct these children, with their parents, to their seats.

The children are reconducted, with their parents, to their seats on the platform; the godfathers and godmothers take their seats among the audience. As soon as they are seated, the following ode is sung:

ODE.

A lit - tle spring had lost its way, A -

CEREMONY OF BAPTISM.   571

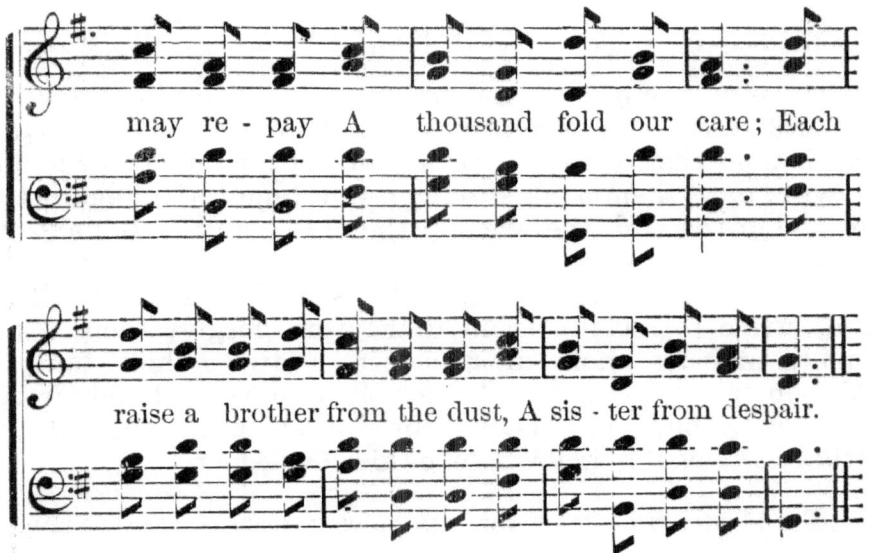

may re-pay A thousand fold our care; Each raise a brother from the dust, A sis-ter from despair.

The act we do to-day is small,
  The issues may be great;
We know not on these little ones
  What destinies may wait:

To one, perhaps, its country owe
  Its safety or its fame;
The world not willingly let die
  This or the other's name.

When the ode is concluded, the Master rises and says:

W. M. Brother Master of Ceremonies, invite the godmothers of these children to place them at the altar, that we may there vow to watch over and protect them.

Music.

Each godmother takes her godchild, and carries it to the altar of obligation; they place them around and close to it—the infants upon their cushions on the floor, and the older children standing, hand in hand; then the brethren leave their places, the Master comes down from the East, and they form a circle around the children, and kneel on one knee, each with his left hand upon his heart, and his right hand raised toward heaven, and the Master says:

W. M. My brethren, repeat after me:

VOW.

All. We solemnly vow and promise that we will watch over and protect these children until they become men and women, or so long as they or we live, or it continues in our power to do so. We will guard them against danger and temptation; against the violence of the bad, the wiles of the crafty and malignant, and the lures of those who love to corrupt youth and to ruin innocence. We will help, aid, and assist them if they fall into need, strive to reclaim them if they err, forgive them if they repent, instruct their inexperience, reprove their faults of omission or commission, and teach them to be good and virtuous, not only by our precepts, but by our example: and may our Father in heaven help us to keep this vow. Amen.

The Master rises, takes the vessel of salt, returns, kneels again, and says:

W. M. When the wild Arab of the desert has tasted salt with his guest, that guest is sacred to him, even if his hands are red with the blood of the father or son of his host. Let us, by the same pledge, seal our vow of fidelity to these children that we have now taken under our protection, and let our promise be as inviolable as that of the rude Bedouin.

He places a little of the salt on his tongue, and says:

W. M. With this salt I confirm my vow.

Then he passes the salt to his brother on the right, who also places some on his tongue, saying the same, and so it passes around the circle. When it returns to the Master, he takes it and all rise; then he puts a little of the salt on the lips of each of the children, and afterwards says:

W. M. And whenever any one of these children, who have now tasted this salt of inviolable faith, or any one in their behalf, shall call upon us to aid them in need, distress, or danger, this solemn pledge shall be redeemed. To your seats, my brethren, but let the godfathers of these children remain with their parents

Except the godfathers and the fathers of the children, the brethren repair to their seats. Then the Master gives to each godfather a small apron, perfectly triangular, of white lamb-skin, with a triangular flap permanently turned up, and the flap and apron edged with narrow blue

CEREMONY OF BAPTISM. 573

ribbon, with a cord of blue silk, tasselled, but with no ornaments or devices on it whatever, and says to them:

W. M. My brethren, invest now these young children with the apron, emblem of that labor to which man is destined by our Father in heaven; and in doing so we pledge ourselves diligently to remind them, whenever occasion offers, that every Mason, and indeed every man, should lead an active and laborious life. And now every one, no matter of what sex, rank, condition, or fortune, is bound to contribute his or her contingent toward the accomplishment of the great work, and to supply at least one ashlar toward the rebuilding of the Temple.

The godfathers invest the children with the aprons, and immediately the following verses are sung:

SONG.

Stand-ing still is child-ish fol-ly,
Go-ing back-ward is a crime;
None should pa-tient-ly en-dure....

While oppression lifts a finger
To affront us by his might;
While an error clouds the reason
  Of the universal heart,
Or a nation longs for freedom,
  Action is the wise man's part.

When these verses have been sung, the Master hands each godfather a jewel for his godchild—a Delta of silver or gold, each side of which measures an inch, with the letter Yod on one side, engraved in the centre, and round it the Pentacle of Solomon, and on the other side a five-pointed star, and in the centre a Tau Cross.

The jewels are suspended to a narrow blue ribbon by a small ring at one apex of the Delta. Each godfather hangs the jewel on the breast of his godchild, passing the ribbon over its neck, the Master saying, as he hands them the jewels:

CEREMONY OF BAPTISM.

W. M. Invest your godchildren, my brethren, with these jewels, the gift of the Lodge. The Delta is the symbol of the Deity, its three sides reminding us of his all-knowing wisdom, his almighty power, and his all-embracing love. The letter in the centre on one side is the initial of his ineffable name, and the symbol of his unity. The Tau Cross is the Egyptian symbol of immortality. The mysterious meanings of the interlaced triangles on the Pentacle of Solomon, and of the five-pointed star or the Pentalpha of Pythagoras, are known to us as Masons. Teach them in due time that this jewel ever reminds them of their duty to God and their fellow-creatures.

As soon as the children are invested with the jewels, the following verses are intoned:

>Onward!—there are ills to conquer;
>Daily wickedness is wrought;
>Tyranny is served with pride,
>Bigotry is deified,
>Error intertwined with thought;
>Vice and misery ramp and crawl:
> Root them out! their day is past,
>Goodness is alone immortal,
> Evil was not made to last.
>
>Onward! and all earth shall aid us,
> Ere our peaceful flag be furled;
>Masonry at last shall conquer,
> And its altar be the world.

After these verses are sung, the Master gives each godmother the locket, bracelet, or ring, as the case may be, for her godson or goddaughter, and says:

W. M. Accept, my sisters, for your godchildren, these little presents from the Lodge. Let them wear them as tokens of our affection; and whenever they need the protection or assistance of the Lodge, let them send to it the gift we now make, and the appeal will never be ineffectual.

The godmothers put the ornaments in the proper place on their godchildren. • • •

W. M. In the name and under the auspices of the Supreme Council of Sovereign Grand Inspectors-General of the thirty-third and last degree, I proclaim these children to be purified by Masonic Baptism, and anointed with the Oil of Consecration to Masonic duty. Proclaim it along your columns, brethren Senior and Junior Wardens, and charge all Free and Accepted Masons (or all Grand, Elect, Perfect and Sublime Freemasons, Ancient and Modern) over the surface of the two hemispheres, to know and acknowledge them as such!

S. W. Brethren of my column, hear ye! I proclaim these children to be purified by Masonic baptism, and anointed with the Oil of Consecration to Masonic duty, and I charge all, &c.

J. W. Brethren of my column, &c.

W. M. Brother Master of Ceremonies, conduct these, and those in whose charge they are, to their seats.

This being done:

W. M. Join me in the plaudit, my brethren.

The brethren, with the Master, rap three times three, and cry three times, *"Huzza!" "Huzza!" "Huzza!"* each time striking the left shoulder in front with the palm of the right hand; then the Master raps once, and all seat themselves. He then says:

W. M. Brother Orator, the floor is yours.

The Orator pronounces a discourse suitable to the occasion.

The Master then requests the godfathers to address the assembly.

Address of a godfather.

After which he may request any distinguished brother present to do so.

After the address, the Master requests two young ladies, if any are present, to pass the box of fraternal assistance. He counts and declares the amount contributed, and sends it by the Master of Ceremonies to the Treasurer, with the proper directions, unless some brother moves that it be given to some particular brother who is in need; n which case the Lodge determines.

This done, the Master says:

W. M. The labors of the day are concluded. May they be profitable unto us all! Go in peace! and may our Father in heaven bless and prosper us in all our laudable undertakings! Amen.

W. M. I declare this Lodge at refreshment. Brother Junior Warden, it remains in your charge.

GRAND VISITATIONS—HONORS DUE, ETC.

The *ruling* body of each series of degrees of the Ancient and Accepted Scottish Rite should have, under the supervision of the Keeper of the Seals and Archives, a *Visitors' Register,* for names, titles, &c.,—which should be accessible in the ante-room whenever communications are being held. The names of all visitors should be registered, and sent into the body for its consideration, and also that future reference may be had thereto.

A Knight Rose-Croix may be received in a body of the Ancient and Accepted Rite, subordinate to his grade, with two stars and two swords.

A Knight Kadosh is received, in any body below the thirtieth degree, with three stars and three swords.

The actual Commander of a Council of Kadosh, with five stars and five swords, and arch of steel.

A Prince of the Royal Secret, in any body below the thirty-second degree, with five stars and five swords, and arch of steel.

The Commander-in-Chief of a Consistory, other than that of the jurisdiction, with six stars and six swords, and arch of steel.

The Commander-in-Chief of a Consistory, within whose jurisdiction the inferior body is holden, and all Deputy Inspectors General of the thirty-third degree, regularly commissioned by the Supreme Council, and all Sovereign Grand Inspectors General of the thirty-third degree, other than those hereinafter mentioned, with seven stars, and seven swords, and arch of steel.

All active and emeriti members, and deputies of the Supreme Council, and active members of other Supreme Councils in alliance, with nine lights and nine swords, steel arch, swords clashing and gavels beating.

A Sovereign Grand Commander of another jurisdiction, or a Past Sovereign Grand Commander of *any* jurisdiction, with ten stars and ten swords, steel arch, swords clashing and gavels beating.

The Sovereign Grand Commander of the Supreme Council, or his Special Delegate and Proxy, with eleven stars and eleven swords, steel arch, swords clashing and gavels beating.

But no honors are to be rendered to any Mason whose dignity or rank in the Ancient and Accepted Rite shall be inferior to that in which the Presiding Officer is clothed; or when the Commander-in-Chief of the Consistory shall, in any inferior body, have been already received and be present: except, in *any* case, when the visitor is an *active* member of the Supreme Council, or its Deputy, or a Sovereign, or Past Sovereign Grand Commander, or the Special Delegate or Proxy of the Sovereign Grand Commander. In the Consistory no honors are paid to any one not possessing the thirty-third degree, except Commanders-in-Chief of other Consistories, and Past Commanders-in-Chief of the Consistory itself. These have six stars and six swords.

FORMS OF REFECTIONS,

COMMONLY TERMED FEASTS OR BANQUETS.

ARRANGEMENT.

The regalia of office should be worn, and the hall hung with garlands, banners, and emblems. The table should be in the form of a *semicircle*. If in that form, the Master sits in the middle of the convex side; the Senior Warden, at the extremity on his right; the Junior Warden, at the extremity on his left; the Deputy Master, at the Master's right hand; the Secretary, on the right of the Senior Warden; the Treasurer, on the left of the Junior Warden; the Hospitaller, on the right of the Deputy Master; the Orator, on the left of the Master; the Master of Ceremonies, in front of the Master; the Keeper of the Seals, on the left of the Senior Warden; the Captain of the Guard on the right of the Junior Warden.

FORMS OF REFECTIONS.

At a *straight* table the Master sits at the head, with the Deputy on his right; the Senior Warden, at the foot; the Junior Warden, about midway between them, on the south side, taking the Master's seat for the East; the Secretary, on the right, and the Treasurer, on the left of the Senior Warden; the Hospitaller, on the right of the Deputy Master; the Orator, on the left of the Master; the Master of Ceremonies, opposite the Junior Warden; the Keeper of the Seals, on the left of the Treasurer; the Captain of the Guard, on the right of the Secretary.

At a table of the form of a *cross* the Master sits at the head with the Deputy on his right; the Senior Warden, at the foot; the Junior Warden, at the left end of the transverse bar; the Master of Ceremonies, at the right end of the same; the Secretary, on the right, and the Treasurer, on the left of the Senior Warden; the Hospitaller, on the right of the Deputy Master; the Orator, on the left of the Master; the Keeper of the Seals, on the left of the Treasurer; the Captain of the Guard, on the right of the Secretary.

Visitors of high rank are stationed right and left of the Master in the East, other visitors indiscriminately.

Refections in the A∴ and A∴ Scottish Rite should be held, if convenient, with the Lodge open in the Symbolic Degrees, otherwise in Perfection.

Orders from the Master should be promulgated through the Wardens.

During the Ceremonial portion of the Refection and until the completion of the Toasts all should be orderly, and conducted with the utmost decorum; the *entree* to the Banquet Hall should be by two's, and the officers and brethren should file right and left to their respective positions, without confusion. All standing and at order, the Master announces the opening of the Banquet, and is followed by a short invocation from the Orator to the G∴ A∴ of the U∴, supplicating his benediction on all.

TOASTS OF OBLIGATION AT REFECTIONS.

These are given by the Master, and repeated by the Senior Warden and the Junior Warden in succession. They are sacramental—i. e., they can never be omitted. They are as follows:

1. To the Chief Magistrate of the country, by his proper title
2. To the Supreme Council.
3. To the Sovereign Grand Commander, by name.
4. To the Grand Consistory, if there be one.
5. To the Grand Lodge and Grand Master of Masons of the State.
6. To the Grand Chapter, and other grand bodies of the jurisdiction.
7. To the memory of the brethren of these degrees, whose labors here below have ceased during the present Masonic year.
8. To all Masons and Masonic bodies, of all rites and degrees, over the surface of the earth! Honors and laurels to the worthy, health to the sick, comfort to the needy, and succor to the oppressed everywhere.

If there are visiting brethren or guests, they are toasted as such after the seventh; and if any *special* toast is presented, as peculiar to the particular degree in which the refection is had, it is given after the fourth.

The mode in which the toast is drunk, and the drinking acclamation given, is prescribed hereafter.

All the toasts of obligation are drunk standing.

All toasts of obligation are ordered by the Master, except that of *The Master* himself, which is ordered by the Senior Warden.

In the preparation of the table, all articles must be placed in parallel lines. For the better accomplishment of this, four lines of different colors are frequently drawn: on the innermost one are placed all dishes and articles of food; on the second are the decanters and bottles; on the third, the glasses; and on the fourth, the plates.

Immediately prior to the toasts of obligation being ordered, the Master, giving a battery of one, says: "Brothers Senior and Junior Wardens, announce on your respective columns that the works which have been temporarily suspended, are again resumed with full force and rigor." The Wardens having made the announcement, and the Guard being set, the brethren cease eating and prepare for the toasts.

Toasts are given in the following form, the Master saying: "Brothers Senior and Junior Wardens, invite the brethren on your respective columns to prepare to charge, in order that we may give the (first) toast of obligation." Which being announced by the Wardens, the Master continues: "Charge, and in Order;" when each brother will stretch out his right hand to the bottle or decanter in front of him, and fill his glass. All replace in line the glasses and decanters. Presently, all the brethren having Charged and being in Order, the Wardens announce the same to the Master.

The Master, giving a battery of one, says: "Arise, and to Order," which as usual is repeated by the Wardens. If there is sufficient room at the table, there are no brethren seated inside the semicircle. If brethren, however, are within the circle when the last order is given, they may remain seated, at the option of the Master. The brethren on the outer side of the table having risen with uniformity, all the *Entered Apprentices* and *Fellow-Crafts* at the table, will place the left hand on it, fingers together and thumbs extended. The Master Masons will take the sword in the left hand, and place the banner on the left fore-arm; brethren of the Superior Degrees will place the banner on the left shoulder, the sword being in the left hand.

The first toast is then ordered.

DIRECTIONS IN DRINKING TOASTS OF OBLIGATION

The Master directs as follows:
    Right hand to the sword.
    Raise the sword.
    Salute with the sword.
    Sword to the left hand.
    Right hand to the cannon.
    Draw the cannon.
    Fire in three times, 1, 2, 3.
    Lower the cannon.
    Cannon to the front.
    Salute with the cannon.

The salute is given by placing the right hand near the right shoulder and lowering it perpendicularly. The Master then says, "One, two, three." At *one*, pass the cannon to near the left shoulder; at *two*, draw the cannon to the right shoulder; at *three*, lower the cannon. This movement should be repeated three times quickly—then resume the original position, the right hand near the right shoulder.

The Master further directs:

"Deposit the cannon—1, 2, 3." At the word *"three,"* all the cannon are placed on the table with the greatest uniformity and at the same instant.

The following orders are then given:

    Sword to the right hand.
    Raise the sword.
    Salute with the sword.
    Return the sword (which is done without noise).

The battery of the Degree is then given.

Recreation is generally announced between the toasts, that the brethren may have more freedom, but the Master's gavel must produce instant silence and order.

After the last toast of obligation it is usual to sing a Masonic song.

Brethren are not permitted to leave the table or banquet-room pending the ceremonies without permission from the Master, for the Lodge is virtually at work.

Moderation, order, and temperance are essential requisites.

MASONIC GLOSSARY.

Barrel,	Decanter or bottle.	Red powder,	Wine.
Black powder,	Coffee.	Red flour,	Pepper, red.
Black flour,	Pepper, black.	Recreation,	Suspension of work of the table.
Banner,	Napkin.		
Battery,	A blow.	Rough ashlar,	Bread.
Cannon,	Glass or cup.	Sand,	Salt.
Cement,	Mustard.	Shovel,	Spoon.
Charge,	To fill the glass.	Strong powder.	Spirituous liquor.
Fulminating powder,	Beer, Ale etc	Sword,	Knife.
		Stars,	Lights.
Fire,	To drink	Tile,	Trenchard.
Masticate,	To eat.	Trident,	Fork.
Material,	Food.	Trowel,	Spoon.
Order,	Place in a line.	Veil,	Tablecloth.
Pencil,	The pen.	White powder,	Water.
Platform,	Plate.	Workshop,	Table.
Powder,	Any liquid.		

FORMS OF REFECTIONS. 583
AULD LANG SYNE.

Then here's a hand, my trusty frien',
    And gie's a hand o' thine,
We'll take a right gude willie waught
    For auld lang syne.
For auld lang syne, my dear,
    For auld lang syne,
We'll take a cup of kindness yet,
    For auld lang syne.

EXTRACTS FROM CONSTITUTIONS.
DISCIPLINE.

ART. **101.**—1. The several Bodies of the Rite have jurisdiction in cases of discipline over their own members, unaffiliated Masons of the Rite within their territorial jurisdiction, and sojourners for offences committed within the territorial jurisdiction of such Bodies.

2. The trial shall be conducted according to the usual rules in Masonic trials; but the Council of Deliberation may adopt a Code of Procedure, except so far as one may be prescribed by the SUPREME COUNCIL.

3. Charges and specifications may be amended at any stage of the proceedings.

4. If the sentence be suspension or expulsion from all Masonic rights, it shall not take full effect until confirmed by the Council of Deliberation or the SUPREME COUNCIL, but shall operate as a temporary suspension until thus confirmed or reversed.

5. In all such cases when there is no appeal, a full transcript of the record and the evidence shall be laid before the Council of Deliberation at its next session, or if the time before such next session shall, in the judgment of the Illustrious Deputy, be too short, it may be presented at the next succeeding session.

6. In all cases an appeal lies by any Mason of the Rite aggrieved, to the stated session of the Council of Deliberation to be held next after thirty days from the close of the trial, or if an annual session of the SUPREME COUNCIL intervenes, to the SUPREME COUNCIL, if the appellant so elects: during the pendency of the appeal a judgment of suspension or expulsion is not vacated, but operates as a temporary suspension.

7. A full transcript of the record and evidence shall accompany the appeal, and the case shall be determined upon such transcript; but the Council of Deliberation, or the SUPREME COUNCIL, may grant a new trial for reasons not appearing in the transcript, if in its judgment justice requires it.

8. The Council of Deliberation shall consider the matter while open on the highest degree to which the accused has attained ; and it may modify, sustain or reverse the judgment of the subordinate Body, and send the case back for a new trial, or enter such judgment as it deems that justice and the good of the Rite require.

9. The judgment of the Council of Deliberation shall take effect without reference to which of the subordinate Bodies rendered the original judgment.

10. From the judgment of the Council of Deliberation an appeal lies to the Supreme Council ; the causes of appeal shall be specified and no other causes than those specified shall be considered by the SUPREME COUNCIL, which may render such judgment, or give such direction to the case as it deems just.

11. When complaint is made or information given to an Illustrious Deputy, of the commission of an offence of a grave character by any member of the Rite in his jurisdiction, he may cause charges to be filed with him, to be tried by the Council of Deliberation at its next session, or at a session to be specially called by him for the purpose, with original jurisdiction. The Deputy shall cause all necessary notice to be given, and may appoint a commissioner to take testimony from either party in the nature of deposition ; or, after notice to the accused and an opportunity to be heard thereon, he may appoint commissioners, who must be members of the Council of Deliberation, to take all the testimony, and report the same and their conclusions thereon to the Council of Deliberation : the Council shall hear the case and render its judgment, which shall be final and subject to the appeal hereinbefore provided. The Illustrious Minister of State shall act as prosecutor in such cases, and may have the assistance of any brother of the Rite. If the accused is an officer, the Illustrious Deputy may suspend his official functions pending the trial.

12. This article shall not apply to Sovereign Grand-Inspectors-General, who are amenable to the SUPREME COUNCIL only.

COUNCILS OF DELIBERATION.

HOW COMPOSED.

ART. 53.—The Active, *Emeritus,* Past-Active, and Honorary members of SUPREME COUNCIL resident in each State ; the Past-Commanders-in-Chief of Consistories ; the first three officers of Consistories and Chapters of Rose Croix ; and the first four officers of Councils of Princes of Jerusalem, and Lodges of Perfection in each State, constitute a COUNCIL OF DELIBERATION for that State, of which the Illustrious Deputy for that district is *ex-officio* Most Illustrious Commander-in-Chief.

MEETINGS.

ART. 54.—Such Council shall meet at least triennially in the year next preceding the triennial election of the Officers of the SUPREME COUNCIL, and may hold stated annual meetings. Special meetings thereof may be called by the Illustrious Deputy. It may fix the place of all meetings except such as may be specially called by the Illustrious Deputy.

QUORUM.

ART. 55.—Nine Members shall constitute a quorum for the transaction of business.

OFFICERS.

ART. 56.—The Council may elect the following officers to hold office until their successors shall be chosen.
1. The Illustrious First Lieutenant-Commander.
2. The Illustrious Second Lieutenant-Commander.
3. The Illustrious Minister of State and Grand Orator.
4. The Illustrious Grand Prior.

COUNCILS OF DELIBERATION.

5. The Illustrious Grand Chancellor.
6. The Illustrious Grand Treasurer.
7. The Illustrious Grand Secretary.
8. The Illustrious Grand Engineer and Architect.
9. The Illustrious Grand Hospitaler.
10. The Illustrious Grand Master of Ceremonies.
11. The Illustrious Grand Standard-bearer.
12. The Illustrious Grand Captain of the Guard.
13. The Illustrious Grand Sentinel.

In cases of vacancy in any office, or failure to elect officers, the Illustrious DEPUTY may make appointments to be in force until the next election.

If the DEPUTY of the SUPREME COUNCIL should fail to be present at any meeting of a Council of Deliberation. the Illustrious First Lieutenant-Commander, or in his absence the Illustrious Second Lieutenant-Commander, shall preside.

JURISDICTION AND POWERS.

ART. 57.—1. The Council has, in its District, legislative and judicial power not herein reserved to the SUPREME COUNCIL and not inconsistent with the Constitutions and Regulations, and subject to the rights of appeal herein provided.

2. The Council may open on the Fourteenth, Sixteenth, Eighteenth, or Thirty-second Degree for the transaction of business relating to the Bodies or Brethren of those degrees respectively ; but business not relating specifically to the higher degrees shall be transacted by the Council while open on the Fourteenth Degree, when all the members may be present.

3. It shall have power to levy such taxes upon the Bodies within its District as it may deem necessary for its proper support, but not to include expenses of, nor compensation to, any officer or member of the Council, for attendance thereupon. Funds now held by any Council shall continue to be held for the purposes for which they were created, and all taxes heretofore levied by any Council are hereby confirmed.

4. All applications for charters shall be presented to the Council for its approval ; and no charter shall be granted by the SUPREME COUNCIL without the recommendation of the Council of Deliberation, except by a two-third vote.

APPEALS.

ART. 58.—Any person aggrieved by the action of the Council of Deliberation, may appeal therefrom to the SUPREME COUNCIL at its next annual session, *provided* any provision of the Constitutions or Regulations of the SUPREME COUNCIL is involved. The appeal shall be filed with the Illustrious Deputy, and shall specify wherein any provision of the Constitutions or Regulations has been violated by the action of the Council of Deliberation. The Illustrious Deputy shall cause a duly certified copy of so much of the record as shows the action appealed from, to accompany the appeals.

CEREMONIAL

FOR A

LODGE OF SORROW.

ANCIENT AND ACCEPTED SCOTTISH RITE.

THE walls of the place where the ☐ is to be held should be covered with black, and, if practicable, be sprinkled with silver tears.

In the centre of the room is a coffin, or sarcophagus.

The regalia of the highest degree conferred on the deceased will be placed on the coffin. The head of the coffin toward the East.

After the ☐ is properly prepared, no one should enter it except those having charge of the decorations, and the organist, until the hour for the ceremonies to take place. The members, in the mean time, convening in an outer room, guarded by a Sentinel who will permit no one to enter under the grade of Perfect Master.

When the hour arrives, a procession will be formed of all the brethren, under the direction of the Captain of the Guard, in two ranks, in reverse order of grade, and will enter the ☐, the organ playing a solemn march. The members remain standing, and the R∴ W∴ proceeds to open a ☐ of P∴ M∴ in due form. Previous to declaring the ☐ opened. the following Hymn will be sung, followed by a Prayer.

HYMN.

GREENVILLE.

Come, ye sighing sons of sorrow,
   View with me your brother's tomb;
Learn from it your fate—to-morrow
   Death perhaps may seal your doom.
Sad and silent flow our numbers,
   While disconsolate we mourn
Loss of him who sweetly slumbers,
   Mould'ring 'neath the silent urn.
Once, when full of life, he never
   Proved unfaithful to our laws;
We'll, like him, be zealous ever
   To promote the glorious cause.

R∴ W∴ Let us pray.

PRAYER.

Omnipresent and Heavenly Father, it hath pleased thee in thy wise dispensation to call from the frail body that was its earthly habitation the immortal spirit of our deceased friend. May time, while it heals the wounds thus inflicted, still more indelibly imprint upon our saddened hearts the salutary teachings of this mournful occasion; and may the consoling reflection, that afflictive sorrow is not the visitation of thy wrath, but rather the illustration of that harmonious law, which, by thine omniscient fruition, conducts to good and perfect issue in all the fulness of thine appointed season. Let loss of friends and brethren increase affection and earnest solicitude for those yet spared, and stimulate the performance of all obligations that friendship, love or honor demand; and when the last hour shall shadow forth our departure from the scenes of this life, may a firm and abiding faith in Thy merciful and forgiving goodness dispel the dread of final dissolution.

Response. So mote it be.

The R∴ W∴ now declares the ☐ opened. After which he will rise in his place and address the Lodge as follows, concluding by such remarks as he may deem necessary and appropriate, and subsequently presenting to the ☐ the orator for the occasion. The R∴ W∴ can omit the following, and substitute his own language and views if he so desires:

R∴ W∴ Brethren, in the midst of life we are in death, and none know what a day may bring forth. We live but to see those we love pass away into the silent land before us. The arrows of the insatiable archer passing us continually, smite the bosoms of our friends and brethren, teaching us the impressive lesson constantly repeated, yet soon forgotten, that every one of us must before long yield up his body to be the inheritance of worms, in a house of darkness and dishonor. Death and the dead are ever with us, teaching us the uncertainty and brevity of life, and the instability of human fortune, and demanding of us the performance of the last sad offices of charity and brotherhood.

But "thy brother shall live again"—not some undefined spirituality, some new and strange being, but our brother himself, in that same character, affections, and spiritual identity: what noble and consoling words sent to us from Heaven, uttered from the great realm of invisible life!

There is life for us somewhere; and we ask not where. We can wait God's good time for that. Somewhere in this great universe we shall find our brothers and our lost ones, and be with them evermore. The Mason believes that there is that within us which shall never die; that the soul is essentially immortal, and immortally blessed; that one law alone shall govern God's whole universe, and that law the law of Love.

To magnify this law of brotherly love, Masonry opens wide its portals, and invites to enter there, and live in peace and harmony, every man, of whatever nation or tribe, who will lead a truly virtuous and moral life, love his brethren, minister to the sick and distressed, and believe in the one All-powerful, All-wise, every-where-present God, Architect, Creator, and Preserver of all things, by whose universal law of harmony ever rolls on this universe, the great, vast, infinite circle of successive death and life; to whose ineffable name let all true Masons pay profoundest homage; for whose thousand blessings poured upon us, let us feel the sincerest gratitude, now, henceforth, and forever.

Death has some time since entered our ☐, and called from its labors our———Brother——— ——— and now we, obeying the demands of duty, pay these last honors to his memory.

Our Illustrious brother——— ———, having been selected by ———, to deliver an oration on the life, character, and public virtues of our departed brother, I now have the honor to present him to the ☐.

ORATION.

At the conclusion of the oration. by permission of the R. W. any brother present may deliver a short address, touching the character of any of the deceased brethren for whom the ☐ of sorrow is held.• • •.

R. W. What man is he that liveth and shall not see death? Shall he deliver his soul from the hands of the grave?

Organ response and chant, after each paragraph of the lesson:

Glory be to thee, O Lord.

S. W. Man walketh in a vain shadow. He heapeth up riches, and cannot tell who shall gather them.

R. W. We go whence we shall not return, even to the land of darkness and of the valley of the shadow of death, without any order, and where the light is as darkness.

S. W. There the wicked cease from troubling, and there the weary be at rest.

* * * * *

R. W. Man dieth and wasteth away. Yea, man giveth up the ghost, and where is he?

* * * * *

S. W. As the waters fail from the sea, and the flood decayeth and drieth up; so man lieth down and riseth not up, till the heavens shall be no more.

* * * * *

R. W. It is better to go to the house of mourning, than to the house of feasting, for that is the end of all men, and the living will lay it to his heart.

592   BOOK OF THE A. AND A. RITE.

   *   *   *   *   *

R. W. The Lord gave, and the Lord hath taken away. Blessed be the name of the Lord. [*A pause.*] Let us enter into silence.

While the foregoing lessons are being recited, twenty-eight members, including the representative of Adoniram and Master of Ceremonies, will retire to an outer room and prepare for what is to follow.

   *   *   *   *   *

Adon. Behold, O Lord, we are in distress! our hearts are turned within us; there is none to comfort us, mourning and lamentation are heard among us.

M. of C. God is our God forever. He will be our guide even unto death.

Adon. Thou hast cut off the life of our brother, and the waters of affliction flow over our heads. The joy of our heart has ceased, and our gladness is turned into mourning.

M. of C. Let us die the death of the righteous.

The following will now be sung:

HYMN.

CEREMONIAL FOR A LODGE OF SORROW.

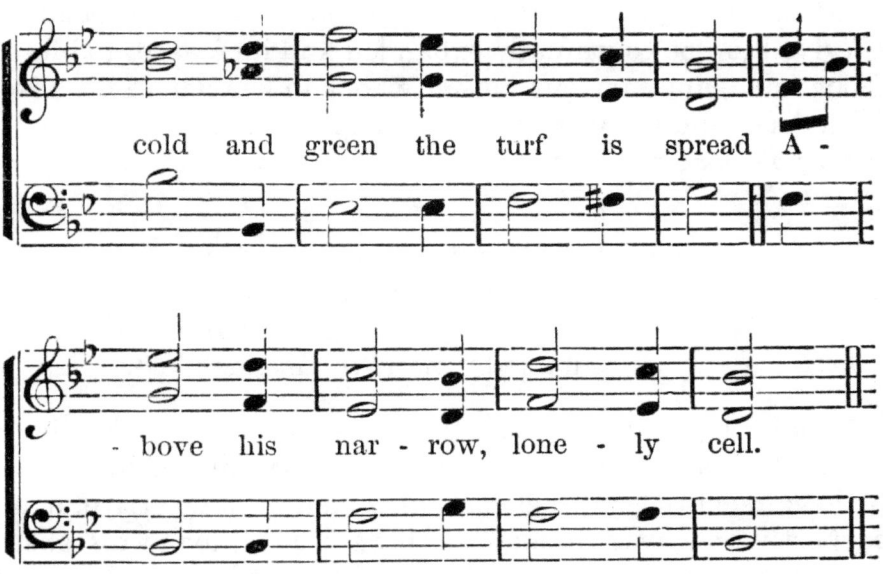

cold and green the turf is spread A-bove his narrow, lonely cell.

Adon. Let us pray.

PRAYER.

O almighty and eternal God, there is no number of thy days or of thy mercies. Thou hast sent us into this world to serve thee, but we wander far away into the path of error. Our life is but a span in length, and yet tedious because of the calamities that enclose us on every side. The days of our pilgrimage are few and evil; our bodies frail, our passions violent and distempered, our understandings weak, our wills perverse. We adore thy majesty, and trust like little children to thy tender mercies. Give us patience to live well, and firmness to resist evil. Bless us, O God, bless our beloved fraternity throughout the world. May we live and emulate the example of our departed brother; and, finally, may we in this world attain a knowledge of thy truth, and in the world to come, life everlasting. Amen.

Response. So mote it be.

* * * * *

His name is graven on the stone
   That friendship's tears have often wet,
But this great Order's heart upon
   That name is stamped more deeply yet

Adon. May all the influences of our brother for good, that survive him, be continually expanded and increased, to bless his fellow-men, and may our Father who is in heaven, in his wisdom, counteract and annul all those that tend to evil.

Response. So mote it be.

* * * * *

> As Hiram slept, the widow's son,
>   E'en so our brother takes his rest;
> His battles fought, his duties done,
>   His name by many thousands blest.

Adon. May we not forget the lessons taught us by our brother's death; but remember the uncertainty of life, and the little value of those things for which men most do strive: may we earnestly endeavor to obey the laws of God, avoid dissensions, hatred, and revenge. May we be truthful, and live and die loving our brethren.

Response. So mote it be.

* * * * *

> So let him sleep that dreamless sleep,
>   His glories clustering round his head:
> Be comforted, ye loved, who weep
>   The true, the frank, the fearless dead.

Adon. May the relatives of our brother be consoled in their great affliction, and sustained in all the trials and hardships they may have to encounter in this world; and loving God and trusting in his infinite beneficence, may they and we, in his good time, be gathered in peace unto our fathers and again meet our friend and brother in another world.

Response. So mote it be.

* * * * *

Adon. Let us pray.

PRAYER BY A BROTHER.

O merciful and loving Father, who hast made our present life but temporary, and thus by the admirable providence of thy designs hast decreed that the pangs and sorrows of suffering virtue, the misery of the oppressed, and the tyranny of the wicked, should not be perpetual, encourage to perseverance all who labor in the cause of truth and virtue, and who are weary and faint-hearted, assuring them that none so labor without result, nor even at last are unrewarded. Extend thy right hand of graciousness over this our beloved country. Plant obedience to thy will in the hearts of its inhabitants, that they may ever regard thee as the dispenser of all good. Impress upon the hearts of all, that good government and pure religion walk hand in hand. We beseech thee to exalt our Order, and to illuminate it with the rays of thy divine light. Preserve it in all its beauty from the attack of its adversaries, the imprudences of its members, and the innovations of time. Persuade its disciples, like him whose death we this day commemorate, to set forth everywhere in our land its holy principles of toleration, brotherly love, and truth. Amen.

Response. So mote it be.

Adon. My brethren, in the various degrees of Masonry through which we have passed, our travels around the Lodge were to remind us of the journey of human life, in which Freemasonry is an enlightened and beautiful path; but our present march will be gloomy and funereal. Our ———— is no more. Death is among us. Our Lodge is in mourning. The great calamity has fallen upon us. The great destroyer hath summoned away our brother in the midst of his days and usefulness. We beheld his sun at meridian, and rejoiced at its brightness, but alas! it has now set, and the evening shades of existence have closed around him forever.

All the succession of time, all the changes of nature, all the varieties of light and darkness, and every contingency to every man and every creature doth preach our funeral sermon, and leads us to see how time digs the grave in which we must sooner or later lay our sins and our sorrows, and our mortal bodies moulder away and again become in atoms a part of the material world. Every day's necessity calls for a reparation of that which Death fed on all night as we lay and slept in his outer chambers. While we think a thought, we die; the clock strikes, and reckons on our portion of eternity.

Death reigns in all our time, and is the fate of every man and woman, the heritage of worms and serpents, of rottenness and cold dishonor.

Death regards not those sweet engagements and improving joys so well know to Freemasons, for this day is mine and yours, but who shall say what shall be on the morrow? For let our life be never so long, if our strength were as great as the Titans, and our sinews as strong as the cordage of the foot of an oak, yet still the period shall be, that all this shall end in death; and people will talk of us awhile, good or bad, as we deserve, or as they please, and once it shall be told in the neighborhood that we are dead. And all this is the law and constitution of nature—the unalterable event of Providence—the decree of Heaven. The chains that bind us to this condition are as strong as destiny, and as immutable as the eternal laws of God.

Let us then, my brethren, endeavor to emulate the example of the great and good of our beloved Order who have gone before us. The noble career and virtuous life of our ——— brother, which has been recited to you this evening in such able and eloquent terms, it is to be hoped will have the desired effect; and may we, like our departed brother, endeavor to lead a wise and virtuous life, the better to prepare ourselves for a peaceful death.

* * * * *

Darkness, death, and the grave are reserved for all men.

* * * * *

One fate comes alike to all—the night of death after the short day of life.

* * * * *

After death and the grave come the resurrection, and light and life eternal

* * * * *

Adon. Remember now thy Creator in the days of thy youth, and ere the silver cord be loosed, or the golden bowl be broken, or the wheel broken at the cistern. Then shall the dust return to the earth as it was, and the spirit return to the God who gave it.

* * * * *

Adon. Blessed be their rest, and ever fragrant the acacia o'er the sacred sod that covers them.

Let us kneel, and in the presence of these emblematic symbols of our sorrow and regret, under these funereal arches, before these palpable evidences of the nothingness of our own nature and the immensity of God, let every selfish and sinful thought be forever buried. Let us renew the oath of forgetfulness of all wrongs and injuries that may have been inflicted upon us. May peace and concord imbue the heart of every brother of our beloved rite, and may all controversies and inimical sentiments be banished now and forever. May hope, joy, and unity be proclaimed throughout all our temples, and before the cycle of another year shall come, let perfect peace and union be, and abide with us continually.

May we, as Masons, never be estranged in vain and empty differences, and henceforward be inspired by an ardent devotion to the interest of our country, Masonry, and universal humanity.

All. So mote it be.

* * * * *

Adon. The seed dies, and out of its death springs the seed of the new wheat. Farewell, my brother.

* * * * *

Adon. Behold, I will show you a mystery. We shall not all sleep, but we shall all be changed, in a moment, in the twinkling of an eye, at the last trump; so when this corruption shall put on incorruption, and this mortal shall put on immortality, then shall be brought to pass the saying that is written: "Death is swallowed up in victory. O death, where is thy sting? O grave, where is thy victory?"

The will of God is accomplished. Let us now return to our labors and brighter scenes. Our duty is here completed. Let us now rejoice that our brother has been raised from his prostrate state and admitted to the Perfect Lodge above.

* * * * *

Weep no more! He is not dead.
On the earth he rests his head
But his spirit everywhere,
Like the sunlight, fills the air.

R. W. May the blessing of our Father who is in Heaven rest upon us all, now and forevermore.

R∴ W∴ now closes Lodge of P∴ M∴

LUTHER'S "JUDGMENT HYMN."

1. Great God, what do I see and hear, The end of things cre - a - ted,
The Judge of man I see ap - pear, On clouds of glo - ry seat - ed;
The trumpet sounds, the graves restore The dead which they contained before,
Pre - pare, my soul, to meet him.

The dead in God shall first arise
  At the last trumpet's sounding;
Caught up to meet him in the skies,
  With joy the Lord surrounding:
No gloomy fears their souls dismay,
  His presence sheds eternal day
On those prepared to meet him.

  But sinners, filled with guilty fears,
Behold his wrath prevailing;
  For they shall rise, and find their tears
And sighs are unavailing.
  The day of grace is past and gone:
Trembling they stand before the throne
  All unprepared to meet him.

Great God, what do I see and hear!
  The end of things created!
The Judge of man I see appear,
  On clouds of glory seated!
Beneath his cross I view the day
  When heaven and earth shall pass away
And thus prepare to meet him.

FORMS

OF APPLICATION FOR DEGREES IN ALL BODIES OF THE ANCIENT AND ACCEPTED SCOTTISH RITE, AND PETITION FOR DISPENSATION OR CHARTER.

FORM OF APPLICATION

To the officers and members of   , sitting in the Valley of   . The undersigned hereof humbly shows that he is desirous of being admitted as a member of   , and humbly requests that he may be received among you, and he will ever pray for the prosperity and glory of the Order and the welfare of the brethren.   [Signed]

When born, .
Occupation,
Resides at,
Place of birth,
Member of (here state what Symbolic Lodge, Lodge of Perfection, Council, Chapter, or Consistory.)
Refers to

FORM OF PETITION FOR DISPENSATION OR CHARTER.

Your petitioners being (here insert their titles by the degrees they have taken) and members of (insert the body to which they belong), in the State of   , and Valley of   , being anxious to increase the knowledge of, and the true interest of, the Ancient Accepted Scottish Rite by the cultivation of the sublime and superior degrees, would respectfully solicit your Supreme Body to grant them a Charter or Dispensation to open a (here insert the name of the body), and confer the degrees thereunto belonging, and transact such other business as may appertain to this particular body, in the State of   , and Valley of   ; and if the prayer of your petitioners be granted, they pledge themselves to conform in all things to the Rules, and Regulations, and General Laws made for the Government of (here insert the name of the body), and to abide by and conform to the Constitutions of the Rite.

CHARACTERISTICS

THAT MAY BE ADOPTED BY ROSE-CROIX KNIGHTS.

The Rose-Croix Knight selects his name, taking, if possible, one not already assumed by any member of the Chapter; to ascertain which, reference is had to the "Register of Characteristics," which each Chapter must keep, and in which the Secretary registers the name and Characteristics of the candidate, as soon as he selects the latter. If he desires to select a name which some other Knight already bears, an *adjective* should be added to distinguish him; as, if there be already a brother styled *Eques â Sinceritate,* or, *ab Excellentiâ,* the new Knight should be called *Eques â Sinceritate verâ,* or, *ab Excellentiâ eximiâ,* &c.

Eques â (or *ab,* when the noun that follows begins with a vowel) *Toleratione,* &c.

SUBSTANTIVES.

Ab Honestate,	Honesty.	A Firmitate,	Firmness.
A Verecundia,	Modesty.	A Vigore,	Vigor.
A Comitate,	Amity.	A Severitate,	Severity.
A Veneratione,	Veneration.	A Hospitalitate,	Hospitality.
A Virtute,	Virtue.	A Luctu,	Mourning.
A Magnanimitate,	Magnanimity.	A Moestitia,	Sadness.
A Lenitate,	Mildness.	A Candore,	Candor.
A Prudentia,	Prudence.	Ab Æmulatione,	Emulation.
A Sapientia,	Wisdom.	A Zelo,	Zeal.
A Justitia,	Justice.	A Decoro,	Decorum.
Ab Æquitate,	Equity.	A Civilitate,	Civility.
A Liberalitate,	Liberality.	A Hilaritate,	Joyousness.
A Sinceritate,	Sincerity.	Ab Austeritate,	Austerity.
A Fraternitate,	Fraternity.	Ab Obedientia,	Obedience.
A Habilitate,	Dexterity.	A Docilitate,	Docility.
A Benevolentia,	Benevolence.	A Fervore,	Terror.
A Gratia,	Grace.	Ab Amicitia,	Friendship.
Ab Honore,	Honor.	Ab Indulgentia,	Forbearance
A Veritate,	Truth.	A Suavitate,	Suavity.

A Caritate,	Affection.	A Tristitia,	Sadness.
A Spe,	Hope.	A Castitate,	Chastity.
A Fiducia,	Confidence.	A Sobrietate,	Sobriety.
A Fide,	Faith.	Ab Æquanimitate,	Equanimity.
A Bonitate,	Goodness.	Ab Integritate,	Integrity.
Ab Amore,	Love.	A Puritate,	Purity.
A Modestia,	Modesty.	Accurata,	Punctuality.
A Moderatione,	Moderation.	A Generositate,	Generosity.
A Temperantia,	Temperance.	Ab Affabilitate,	Affability.
A Silentio,	Silence.	A Misericordia,	Mercy.
A Taciturnitate,	Taciturnity.	A Commiseratione,	Commiseration
A Reticencia,	Reticence.	A Clementia,	Clemency.
A Fortitudine,	Fortitude.	A Toleratione,	Toleration.
A Constantia,	Constancy.	A Reveratione,	Reverence.
A Humilitate,	Humility.	Ab Amore Patriæ,	Patriotism.
A Pietate,	Piety.	A Gratitudine,	Gratitude.
A Robore,	Strength.		

ADJECTIVES.

Magnus,	Great.	Firmus,	Firm.
Major,	Greater.	Sublimus,	Sublime.
Maximus,	Greatest.	Excelsus,	Lofty.
Summus,	High.	Excelsior,	Loftier.
Grandis,	Large.	Superbus,	Proud.
Optimus,	Best.	Strenuus,	Energetic.
Fortis,	Strong.	Candidus,	Candid.
Bonus,	Good.	Ingenuus,	Ingenuous.
Melior,	Better.	Fulgens,	Shining.
Sincerus,	Sincere.	Lucidus,	Bright.
Novus,	New.	Decorus,	Decorous.
Insignis,	Excellent.	Purus,	Pure.
Verus,	True.	Indulgens,	Indulgent.
Exactus,	Exact.	Suavis,	Courteous.
Ardens,	Ardent.	Sanctus,	Secret.
Constans,	Constant.	Liberalis,	Liberal.

The following in red should be prefixed to the signature of a brother of the Ancient and Accepted Rite, when signing any document relating to the Order:

If a Rose-Croix Knight, ⚜

If an Inspector General, ⚜

If a Sov∴ G∴ Commander, or
    Past—the Cross of Salem, ⚜

Commence at the Beak and finish by the Tail, but do not touch the Body
Secret constitutions.

"My task is done—   *   *   *
       *   *   *; it is fit
The spell should break of this protracted dream;
The torch shall be extinguished which hath lit
My midnight lamp—and what is writ is writ;
Would it were worthier! *   *   *"

"Ye! who have traced the Pilgrim to the scene
Which is his last, if in your memories dwell
A thought which once was his, if on ye swell
A single recollection, not in vain
He wore his sandal-shoon and scallop shell:
Farewell! with *him* alone may rest the pain —
If such there were—with *you*, the moral of his strain!"
Childe Harold.

TABLEAU

OF

ACTIVE MEMBERS OF THE SUPREME COUNCIL

FOR THE

NORTHERN MASONIC JURISDICTION OF THE U. S. OF A.

GRAND EAST, BOSTON, MASSACHUSETTS.

OFFICERS.

HENRY L. PALMER, M∴ P∴ Sov∴ Gr∴ Commander.

CHARLES LEVI WOODBURY, P∴ Gr∴ Lt.-Commander.

SAMUEL CROCKER LAWRENCE, Gr∴ Minister of State.

MARQUIS F. KING	Deputy for Maine.
GEORGE W. CURRIER	" New Hampshire.
MARSH O. PERKINS	" Vermont.
SAMUEL WELLS	" "Massachusetts.
GEORGE M. CARPENTER.................	" Rhode Island.
CHARLES WILLIAM CARTER	" Connecticut.
JOHN HODGE	" New York.
ANDREW B. FRAZEE........................	" New Jersey.
ANTHONY E. STOCKER	" Pennsylvania.
HUGH MCCURDY	" Michigan.
ENOCH TERRY CARSON	" Ohio.
NICHOLAS R. RUCKLE	" Indiana.
JOHN CORSON SMITH	" Illinois.
——————	" Wisconsin.

NEWTON D. ARNOLD, Gr∴ Treasurer-General.

CLINTON FREEMAN PAIGE, Gr∴ Secretary-General.

LUCIUS R. PAIGE, Gr∴ Keeper of Archives.

TABLEAU.

Charles T. McClenachan, Gr∴ Master-Gen∴ of C∴

Robert Emmett Patterson, Gr∴ Marshal-General.

William R. Higby, Gr∴ Standard-Bearer.

George Otis Tyler, Gr∴ Capt∴ of Guard.

Joseph P. Abel, Assistant Gr∴ Sec∴ Gen∴

SUBORDINATE OFFICERS.

Josiah Lafayette Seward, Gr∴ Prior.

J. H. Hobart Ward, Gr∴ Marshal of the Camp.

Amos Pettibone, Gr∴ Marshal of the Camp.

Andrew Nembach, Gr∴ Organist.

Charles H. Heyzer, Gr∴ Seneschal.

TRUSTEES OF PERMANENT FUND.

Charles L. Woodbury, Term expires	....	1895
Henry L. Palmer,	" "	1896
Benjamin Dean,	" "	1897
John L. Stettinius,	" "	1898
Samuel C. Lawrence,	" "	1899
George M. Carpenter,	" "	1900
Clinton F. Paige,	" "	1901

ACTIVE MEMBERS.

Daniel Sickels	Brooklyn, N. Y.
Lucius Robinson Paige	Cambridgeport, Mass.
Anthony Eugene Stocker	Philadelphia, Pa.
Charles Thomson McClenachan	New York, N. Y.
Henry Chapman Banks	" "
David Burnham Tracy	Detroit, Mich.
Josiah Hayden Drummond	Portland, Me.
Benjamin Dean	Boston, Mass.
Enoch Terry Carson	Cincinnati, O.
William Riley Higby	Bridgeport, Conn.
Clinton Freeman Paige	Binghamton, N. Y.
George Whitfield Bentley	New London, Conn.
Henry L. Palmer	Milwaukee, Wis
Charles William Carter	Norwich, Conn.
John Caven	Indianapolis, Ind.

SAMUEL CROCKER LAWRENCE	Boston, Mass.
WALTER AUGUSTUS STEVENS	Chicago, Ill.
ABRAHAM TOLLES METCALF	Kalamazoo, Mich.
CHARLES LEVI WOODBURY	Boston, Mass.
VINCENT LOMBARD HURLBUT	Chicago, Ill.
GEORGE OTIS TYLER	Burlington, Vt.
BRENTON DANIEL BABCOCK	Cleveland, O.
JOHN LONGWORTH STETTINIUS	Cincinnati, O.
ROBERT EMMETT PATTERSON	Philadelphia, Pa.
NEWTON DARLING ARNOLD	Providence, R. I.
FRANK ALBERT MCKEAN	Nashua, N. H.
EDWARD PAYSON BURNHAM	Saco, Me.
JOHN CORSON SMITH	Chicago, Ill.
ANDREW BLAIR FRAZEE	Camden, N. J.
HUGH MCCURDY	Corunna, Mich.
NICHOLAS R. RUCKLE	Indianapolis, Ind.
CHARLES M. COTTRILL	Milwaukee, Wis.
MARQUIS FAYETTE KING	Portland, Me.
PHINEAS GEORGE CANNING HUNT	Indianapolis, Ind.
GEORGE MOULTON CARPENTER	Providence, R. I.
JOHN HODGE	Lockport, N. Y.
GEORGE W. CURRIER	Nashua, N. H.
JAMES ISAAC BUCHANAN	Pittsburg, Pa.
ALBERT P. MORIARTY	New York. N. Y.
GILBERT W. BARNARD	Chicago, Ill.
MARSH O. PERKINS	Windsor, Vt.
ANDREW BUNTON	Manchester, N. H.
SAMUEL WELLS	Boston, Mass.
JAMES A. HAWLEY	Dixon, Ill.
JAMES H. CODDING	Towanda, Pa.
BARTON SMITH	Toledo, O.

EMERITI MEMBERS.

ATHANASIUS COLO VELONI	Brooklyn, N. Y.
FRANCIS A. BLADES	Detroit, Mich.

PAST ACTIVE MEMBERS.

THOMAS EVANS BALDING	Milwaukee, Wis.
WILLIAM PITT PREBLE	Portland, Me.

TABLEAU. 607

HONORARY MEMBERS, RESIDENTS OF OTHER JURISDICTIONS.

NATHANIEL GEORGE PHILIPS, P∴ Sov∴ Gr∴ Com∴ Supreme Council for England, Wales, etc.

JOHN MCCOLL, Member of the Supreme Council, Uruguay.

WILLIAM HENRY HUTTON, P∴ Sov∴ Gr∴ Com∴ Supreme Council, Canada.

JOHN VALENTINE ELLIS, P∴ Sov∴ Gr∴ Com∴ Supreme Council, Canada.

JOHN WALTER MURTON, Sov∴ Gr∴ Com∴ Supreme Council, Canada.

NON-RESIDENT HONORARY MEMBERS.

JAMES C. L. WADSWORTH	San Francisco, Cal.
WILLIAM FILMER	San Francisco, Cal.
ENOCH B. STEVENS	Southport, N. C.
FREDERICK A. WHEELER	Baltimore, Md.
ALDEN C. MILLARD	Independence, Mo.
EDWARD H. BROWN	Grass Valley, Cal.
LLOYD D. RICHARDSON	Hot Springs, Ark.

SUPREME COUNCILS

RECOGNIZED BY AND

IN RELATIONS OF AMITY WITH THE SUPREME COUNCIL, NORTHERN JURISDICTION.

SUPREME COUNCIL FOR THE SOUTHERN JURISDICTION OF THE UNITED STATES OF AMERICA.

THOMAS H. CASWELL, San Francisco, Cal., Acting Gr∴ Com∴

FREDERICK WEBBER, 433 Third Street, N. W., Washington, D. C., Gr∴ Sec∴ Gen∴

MARTIN COLLINS, St. Louis, Mo., Representative of this Supreme Council.

SAMUEL C. LAWRENCE, 28 Lancaster Street, Boston, Mass., Representative near this Supreme Council.

SUPREME COUNCIL FOR FRANCE AND DEPENDENCIES.

LOUIS PROAL, Paris, M∴ P∴ Sov∴ Gr∴ Commander.

JULES IRIBE, Gr∴ Sec∴ Gen∴, Rue Rochechouart, 42, Paris.
C. GOUNARD, 33 Rue de Berry, Paris, Representative of this Supreme Council.
ANTHONY EUGENE STOCKER, M.D., 2212 Fitzwater Street, Philadelphia, Pa., Representative near this Supreme Council.

SUPREME COUNCIL FOR ENGLAND, WALES, AND DEPENDENCIES OF THE BRITISH CROWN.

H. R. H. ALBERT EDWARD, PRINCE OF WALES, K∴ G∴, 33°, GRAND PATRON.
The Right Hon. The EARL OF LATHOM, 33 Golden Square, London, Sov∴ Gr∴ Commander.
HUGH DAVID SANDEMAN, 33 Golden Square, Gr∴ Sec∴ Gen∴.
CAPT. NATHANIEL GEORGE PHILIPS, 33 Golden Square, London, Representative of this Supreme Council.
CLINTON FREEMAN PAIGE, 104 Stewart Building, New York City, Representative near this Supreme Council.

SUPREME COUNCIL FOR SCOTLAND.

The Right Hon. The EARL OF KINTORE, Sov∴ Gr∴ Commander.
LINDSAY MACKERSY, Freemasons' Hall, 74 Queen Street, Edinburgh, Gr∴ Sec∴ Gen∴.
CHARLES LEVI WOODBURY, Boston, Mass., Representative near this Supreme Council.

SUPREME COUNCIL FOR IRELAND.

The Right Hon. H. E. CHATTERTON. Sov∴ Gr∴ Commander.
GEORGE HILL MAJOR, Gr∴ Sec∴ Gen∴, Freemasons' Hall, Moseworth Street, Dublin.
E. W. MAUNSELL, Nyanza, Black Rock Co., Dublin, Representative of this Supreme Council.
BENJAMIN DEAN, Boston, Mass., Representative near this Supreme Council.

SUPREME COUNCIL FOR BELGIUM.

EMILE DEMOT, Bruxelles, Sov∴ Gr∴ Commander.
GUSTAV JOTTRAUD. Rue du Marché aux Poulets, 20, Bruxelles, Gr∴ Sec∴ Gen∴.
GUSTAV WASHER, Bruxelles, Representative of this Supreme Council.
LUCIUS R. PAIGE, Cambridgeport, Mass., Representative near this Supreme Council.

TABLEAU.

SUPREME COUNCIL FOR BRAZIL, VALLEY OF LAVRADIO.

Antonio J. de M. Soares, Sov∴ Gr∴ Commander.
Rodrigo A. M. Reis, Gr∴ Sec∴ Gen∴, Rua do Lavradio, 81, Rio Janeiro.
Dr. Francisco José Cardoza, Jr., Representative of this Supreme Council.

SUPREME COUNCIL FOR THE ARGENTINE REPUBLIC.

José J. Montero, Buenos Ayres, Sov∴ Gr∴ Commander.
Estevan Guabello, Gr∴ Sec∴ Gen∴, Cangallo, 1232, Buenos Ayres.
Pedro Mallo, M. D., Representative of this Supreme Council.

SUPREME COUNCIL FOR URUGUAY.

Dr. Carlos de Castro, Montevideo, Sov∴ Gr∴ Commander.
Col. Nicholas Bardas, Calle Queguay, No. 227, Montevideo, Gr∴ Sec∴ Gen∴.
John McColl, Montevideo, Representative of this Supreme Council.

SUPREME COUNCIL FOR PERU.

Gen. Manuel Beingolea, Lima, Sov∴ Gr∴ Commander.
Pedro Marzo, Gr∴ Sec∴ Gen∴, Apartado, 85, Lima.
Ricardo H. Hartley, Lima, Representative of this Supreme Council.

GRANDE ORIENT LUSITANO UNIDO SUPREMO CONSELHO, DE MACONARIA PORTUGUEZA.

Augusto Sebastiao de Castro Guedes, Lisbon, Sov∴ Gr∴ Commander.
Guillierme A. F. Gomes, Travessa do Guarda, 35, Lisbon, Gr∴ Sec∴ Gen∴.
Dr. Antonio M. Da Cunha Bellem, Lisbon, Representative of this Supreme Council.

SUPREME COUNCIL FOR ITALY, ORIENT AT ROME.

Dr. Timoteo Riboli, Rome, Sov∴ Gr∴ Commander.
Adriano Lemmi, M∴ P∴ Del∴ Gr∴ Commander.
Dr. Teofilo Gay, Palazo Poli, 42, Rome, G∴ Sec∴ Gen∴ and Representative of this Supreme Council.
Samuel C. Lawrence, Boston, Mass., Representative near this Supreme Council.

SUPREME COUNCIL FOR MEXICO.

Ignacio Pombo, Apartado 52, City of Mexico, Sov∴ Gr∴ Commander.

Juan N. Castellanos, City of Mexico, Gr∴ Sec∴ Gen∴

Ignacio Mariscal, City of Mexico, Representative of this Supreme Council.

Address of Gr∴ Sec∴ Gen∴, Sr. Dn. Juan N. Castellanos, Plazuela de Santo Domingo, ex-Aduana Apartado Postal Núm 734, México.

SUPREME COUNCIL FOR NEW GRENADA.
(NOW UNITED STATES OF COLOMBIA.)

Fulgencio Segrera, Cartajena, Sov∴ Gr∴ Commander.

Octavia Baena, Cartajena, Gr∴ Sec∴ Gen∴

Rafael Hernandez, Cartajena, Representative of this Supreme Council.

Clinton F. Paige, 104 Stewart Building, N. Y., Representative near this Supreme Council.

SUPREME COUNCIL FOR CHILI.

J. De M. Beneventé, Valparaiso, Sov∴ Gr∴ Commander.

H. Plunket Bouchier, Valparaiso, Gr∴ Sec∴ Gen∴

George H. Kendall, Valparaiso, Representative of this Supreme Council.

Charles W. Carter, Norwich, Conn., Representative near this Supreme Council.

SUPREME COUNCIL FOR CENTRAL AMERICA.

Guillermo Nanne, Guatemala, Sov∴ Gr∴ Commander.

Felix Matos, Gr∴ Sec∴ Gen∴, 8a Calle Or, 20, Guatemala.

Juan Padilla, Guatemala, Representative of this Supreme Council.

Thomas R. Lombard, 160 Broadway, New York, Representative near this Supreme Council.

SUPREME COUNCIL FOR GREECE.

Prince D. Rhodocanakis, Athens, Sov∴ Gr∴ Commander.

Nikolaos Damaskinos, Athens, P∴ Gr∴ Lieut∴ Com∴

Em. Galani, Dr. Ph., Gr∴ Sec∴ Gen∴, Athens.

Andreás Kalyvas, Athens, Representative of this Supreme Council.

TABLEAU.

SUPREME COUNCIL FOR THE DOMINION OF CANADA.

JOHN WALTER MURTON, Hamilton, Ont., Sov∴ Gr∴ Commander.
HUGH MURRAY, Hamilton, Ont., Gr∴ Sec∴ Gen∴.
HUGH A. MACKAY, Hamilton, Ont., Representative of this Supreme Council.
ENOCH T. CARSON, Cincinnati, O., Representative near this Supreme Council.

SUPREME COUNCIL OF COLON, FOR CUBA AND THE WEST INDIES.

PRUDENCIO RABELL Y PUBILL, Habana, 55 Altos, Cuba, Sov∴ Gr∴ Commander.
JOSÉ GARCIA PADRÓN, Lagunas 76, Habana, Gr∴ Sec∴ Gen∴ and Representative of this Supreme Council.
ALBERT P. MORIARTY, 104 Stewart Building, New York, Representative near this Supreme Council.

SUPREME COUNCIL FOR SWITZERLAND.

JULES BESANCON, Sov∴ Gr∴ Commander, Lausanne.
FRED RAMUZ, Gr∴ Sec∴ Gen∴, Rue Holdimand, 10, Lausanne.
REV. TH. REDARD, Representative of this Supreme Council.

SUPREME COUNCIL FOR EGYPT.

TITO FIGARI, Cairo, Sov∴ Gr∴ Commander.
S. A. ZOLA, Gr∴ Sec∴ Gen∴ H. B. M. Consul, Cairo, and Representative of this Supreme Council.
DANIEL SICKELS, 104 Stewart Building, New York, Representative near this Supreme Council.

SUPREME COUNCIL FOR TUNIS.

GUSTAV DESMONS, Sov∴ Gr∴ Commander.
NICOLO S. CASSANELLO, Gr∴ Sec∴ Gen∴.
NICOLO S. CASSANELLO, Representative of this Supreme Council.

SUPREME COUNCIL FOR SPAIN.

JOSÉ MARIA PANTOGA, Sov∴ Gr∴ Commander.
EDUARDO C. DE PUGA, Gr∴ Sec∴ Gen∴, Libertard, 27, Madrid.
JUAN UTOR Y FERNANDEZ, Representative of this Supreme Council.
ENOCH T. CARSON, Cincinnati, O., Representative near this Supreme Council.

HEBREW CALENDAR.

INEFFABLE Freemasons have been accustomed to date all their acts and instruments relating to the Ancient Accepted Scottish Rite after the manner of the Jews, according to the Hebrew calendar. The Judaic year is luni-solar; being governed in its length as nearly as possible by the time taken by the earth in its revolution round the sun, and in its division into lunar months, which accord as well as they can with the time that the moon requires in passing around the earth. A lunation occupies about 29 days, 12 hours, and 44 minutes; therefore, as each day and consequently each month commences and terminates at midnight, some months must have 29 days only, and others 30 days. And again; as twelve lunar months do not fill the whole space of time of a solar year by about eleven days, some years must have thirteen months. The Jews commenced the year at two different periods. The ecclesiastical year began in the month Nisan, on or immediately after the new moon following the vernal equinox, and regulated the time of their religious fasts and festivals; the civil year began in the month Tisri, as near as possible to the occurrence of the new moon after the autumnal equinox, and was used in all their civil, legal, and historical matters, and is the year used in the calendar adopted by ineffable Freemasons.

The intercallary month Veadar (second Adar) occurs only in years having thirteen months. Owing to the difference in the length of some of the months (Marchesvan, Chisleu, and Elul), a year of twelve months may contain 353, 354, or 355 days; and a year of thirteen months, 383, 384, or 385 days.

To find the Jewish year corresponding with a given year of our Lord, add 3760 to the portion of the year preceding the first day of the month Tisri, and 3761 to the remainder of the year.

HEBREW CALENDAR.

In a cycle of nineteen years, the 3d, 6th, 8th, 11th, 14th, 17th, and 19th have thirteen months, and the remaining twelve have twelve months each. The year of this cycle is determined by the remainder, after dividing the year A∴ M∴ by 19.

The months, with the number of days in each, are:

1. Tishri .... 30 days.
2. Marchesvan, Khesvan, or Bul .... 29 or 30 "
3. Kislev .... 29 or 30 "
4. Tebeth .... 29 "
5. Shebat .... 30 "
6. Adar .... 29 "
(Veadar .... 29 ")

7. Nisan or Abib .... 30 days.
8. Ijar, Iyar, or Zif .... 29 "
9. Sivan .... 30 "
10. Tamuz .... 29 "
11. Ab .... 30 "
12. Elul .... 29 "
and in intercallary years, 30"

HEBREW ALMANAC:

From 1885 to 1898, indicating the first days of the Hebrew month with the corresponding dates of the vulgar or common era, together with the Feast days to be observed by Chapters of Rose-Croix.

1st Shebat, 5645 .... 17th Jan., 1885.
" Adar, " .... 16th Feb., "

Ash Wednesday ... 18th Feb., "
Holy Thursday .... 2d April, "
Good Friday .... 3d " "
Easter Sunday .... 5th " "
Ascension .... 14th May "
Pentecost .... 24th " "

1st Nisan, 5645 .... 17th March, "
" Ijar " .... 16th April, "
" Sivan, " .... 15th May, "
" Tamuz, " .... 14th June, "
" Ab, " .... 13th July, "
" Elul, " .... 12th August, "
" Tishri, 5646 .... 10th Sept., "
" Khesvan " .... 10th Oct., "
" Kislev, " .... 9th Nov., "
" Tebeth, " .... 9th Dec., "
" Shebat, " .... 7th Jan., 1886.
" Adar, " .... 6th Feb., "
" Ve-Adar, " .... 8th March, "

Ash Wednesday . 10th March, 1886.
Holy Thursday ..... 22d April, "
Good Friday .... 23d " "
Easter Sunday ... 25th " "
Ascension .... 3d June, "
Pentecost .... 13th " "

1st Nisan, 5646 ... 6th April, "
" Ijar, " .... 6th May, "
" Sivan, " .... 4th June, "
" Tamuz, " .... 4th July, "
" Ab, " .... 2d August, "
" Elul, " .... 31st " "
" Tishri, 5647 ..... 30th Sept., "
" Khesvan, " .... 30th Oct., "
" Kislev, " .... 28th Nov., "
" Tebeth, " .... 28th Dec., "
" Shebat, " .... 26th Jan., 1887
" Adar, " .... 25th Feb., "

Ash Wedneaday,..23d Feb., "
Holy Thursday ..... 7th April, "
Good Friday .... 8th " "
Easter Sunday ... 10th " "

Ascension	19th	May, 1887	1st Ab, 5649	29th	July, 1889
Pentecost	29th	" "	" Elul, "	28th	August, "
			" Tishri, 5650	26th	Sept., "
1st Nisan, 5647	26th	March, "	" Khesvan,"	26th	Oct., "
" Ijar, "	25th	April, "	" Kislev, "	24th	Nov., "
" Sivan, "	24th	May, "	" Tebeth, "	24th	Dec., "
" Tamuz, "	23d	June, "	" Shebat, "	22d	Jan., 1890
" Ab, "	22d	July, "	" Adar, "	21st	Feb., "
" Elul, "	21st	August, "	Ash Wednesday	19th	Feb., "
" Tishri, 5648	19th	Sept., "	Holy Thursday	3d	April, "
" Khesvan "	19th	Oct., "	Good Friday	4th	" "
" Kislev, "	17th	Nov., "	Easter Sunday	6th	" "
" Tebeth, "	16th	Dec., "	Ascension	15th	May, "
" Shebat, "	14th	Jan., 1888	Pentecost	25th	" "
" Adar, "	13th	Feb., "			
			1st Nisan, 5650	22d	March, "
Ash Wednesday	15th	Feb., "	" Ijar, "	21st	April, "
Holy Thursday	29th	March, "	" Sivan, "	20th	May, "
Good Friday	30th	March, "	" Tamuz, "	19th	June, "
Easter Sunday	1st	April, "	" Ab, "	18th	July, "
Ascension	10th	May, "	" Elul, "	17th	August, "
Pentecost	20th	" "	" Tishri, 5651	15th	Sept., "
			" Khesvan,"	15th	Oct., "
1st Nisan, 5648	13th	March, "	" Kislev "	13th	Nov., "
" Ijar, "	12th	April, "	" Tebeth, "	12th	Dec., "
" Sivan, "	11th	May, "	" Shebat, "	10th	Jan., 1891
" Tamuz, "	10th	June, "	" Adar, "	9th	Feb., "
" Ab, "	9th	July, "	"Ve-Adar, "	11th	March, "
" Elul, "	8th	August, "	Ash Wednesday	11th	Feb., "
" Tishri, 5649	6th	Sept., "	Holy Thursday	26th	March, "
" Khesvan,"	6th	Oct. "	Good Friday	27th	" "
" Kislev, "	5th	Nov., "	Easter Sunday	29th	" "
" Tebeth, "	5th	Dec., "	Ascension	7th	May, "
" Shebat "	3d	Jan.. 1889	Pentecost	17th	" "
" Adar, "	2d	Feb. "			
" Ve-Adar, "	4th	March, "	1st Nisan, 5651	9th	April, "
			" Ijar, "	9th	May, "
Ash Wednesday	6th	March, "	" Sivan, "	7th	June, "
Holy Thursday	18th	April, "	" Tamuz, "	7th	July, "
Good Friday	19th	" "	" Ab, "	5th	August,"
Easter Sunday	21st	" "	" Elul, "	4th	Sept., "
Ascension	30th	May, "	" Tishri, 5652	3d	Oct., "
Pentecost	9th	June, "	" Khesvan,"	2d	Nov., "
			" Kislev, "	2d	Dec., "
1st Nisan 5649	2d	April, "	" Tebeth, "	31st	Dec., "
" Ijar, "	2d	May, "	" Shebat, "	30th	Jan., 1892
" Sivan, "	31st	" "	" Adar, "	29th	Feb., "
" Tamuz, "	30th	June, "			

HEBREW CALENDAR.

Ash Wednesday 2d	March,	1892.
Holy Thursday.... 14th	April,	"
Good Friday 15th	"	"
Easter Sunday 17th	"	"
Ascension 26th	May,	"
Pentecost 5th	June,	"
1st Nisan, 5652... 29th	March,	"
" Ijar, "...... 28th	April,	"
" Sivan, "...... 27th	May,	"
" Tamuz, "...... 26th	June,	"
" Ab, "...... 25th	July,	"
" Elul, "...... 24th	August,	"
" Tishri, 5653 ....22d	Sept.	"
" Khesvan,"............22d	Oct.,	"
" Kislev, " 20th	Nov.,	"
" Tebeth, " 20th	Dec.,	"
" Shebat, " 18th	Jan.,1893.	
" Adar, " 17th	Feb.,	"
Ash Wednesday .. 15th	Feb.,	"
Holy Thursday.... 30th	March,	"
Good Friday 31st	March,	"
Easter Sunday 2d	Aprll,	"
Ascension 11th	May,	"
Pentecost...............21st	"	"
1st Nisan, 5653... 18th	March,	"
" Ijar, "...... 17th	April,	"
" Sivan, "...... 16th	May,	"
" Tamuz, "...... 15th	June,	"
" Ab, "...... 14th	July,	"
" Elul, "...... 13th	August,	"
" Tishri, 5654 ...... 11th	Sept.,	"
" Khesvan,"........... 11th	Oct.,	"
" Kislev, " 10th	Nov.,	"
" Tebeth, " 10th	Dec.,	"
" Shebat, "............. 8th	Jan.,	1894.
" Adar, " 7th	Feb.,	"
"Ve-Adar, " 9th	March,	"
Ash Wednesday 7th	Feb.,	"
Holy Thursday......22d	March,	"
Good Friday 23d	"	"
Easter Sunday 25th	"	"
Ascension 3d	May,	"
Pentecost............. 13th	"	"

1st Nisan, 5654 ......7th	April,	1894.
" Ijar, "............7th	May,	"
" Sivan, "............5th	June,	"
" Tamuz, "............5th	July,	"
" Ab, " 3d	August,	"
" Elul, " 2d	Sept.,	"
" Tishri, 5655............ 1st	Oct.,	"
" Khesvan,"............31st	Oct,,	"
" Kislev, "............29th	Nov.,	"
" Tebeth, " 28th	Dec.,	"
" Shebat, " 26th	Jan.,	1895.
" Adar, " 25th	Feb.,	"
Ash Wednesday......27th	Feb.,	"
Holy Thursday........ 11th	April,	"
Good Friday............ 12th	April,	"
Easter Sunday........ 14th	April,	"
Ascension 23d	May,	"
Pentecost.................. 2d	June,	"
1st Nisan, 5655 ......26th	March,	"
" Ijar, "..........25th	April,	"
" Sivan, "..........24th	May,	"
" Tamuz, " ········23d	June,	"
" Ab, "..........22d	July,	"
" Elul, "..........21st	August,	"
" Tirshri, 5656 .... 19th	Sept.,	"
" Khesvan,".............19th	Oct.,	"
" Kislev, "............. 18th	Nov,	"
" Tebeth, "............. 18th	Dec.,	"
" Shebat, "............. 16th	Jan.,	1896
" Adar, " 15th	Feb.,	"
Ash Wednesday......19th	Feb.,	"
Holy Thursday.......... 2d	April,	"
Good Friday 3d	April,	"
Easter Sunday..........5th	"	"
Ascension................ 14th	May,	"
Pentecost.................24th	May,	"
1st Nisan, 5656 ......15th	March,	"
" Ijar, "..........14th	April,	"
" Sivan, "..........13th	May,	"
" Tamuz, "..........12th	June,	"
" Ab, "..........11th	July,	"
" Elul, "..........10th	August,	"
" Tirshri, 5657 ....8th	Sept.,	"
" Khesvan, "...............8th	Oct.,	"

1st Kislev, 5657 .... 6th Nov., 1896.	1st Tamuz, 5657 .... 30th June, 1897.
" Tebeth, " .... 6th Dec., "	" Ab, " .... 30th July, "
" Shebat, " .... 4th Jan., 1897.	" Elul, " .... 29th August, "
" Adar, " .... 3d Feb. "	" Tishri, 5658 .... 27th Sept., "
" Ve-Adar " .... 5th March, "	" Khesvan, " .... 27th Oct., "
	" Kislev, ..." .... 26th Nov., "
Ash Wednesday .... 3d March, "	" Tebeth, " .... 26th Dec., "
Holy Thursday .... 15th April, "	" Shebat, " .... 24th Jan., 1898.
Good Friday .... 16th April, "	" Adar, " .... 23d Feb., "
Easter Sunday .... 18th April, "	
Ascension .... 27th May, "	Ash Wednesday .... 23d Feb., "
Pentecost .... 6th June, "	Holy Thursday .... 7th April, "
	Good Friday .... 8th April, "
1st Nisan, 5657 .... 3d April, "	Easter Sunday .... 10th April, "
" Ijar, " .... 3d May, "	Ascension .... 19th May, "
" Sivan, " .... 1st June, "	Pentecost .... 29th May, "

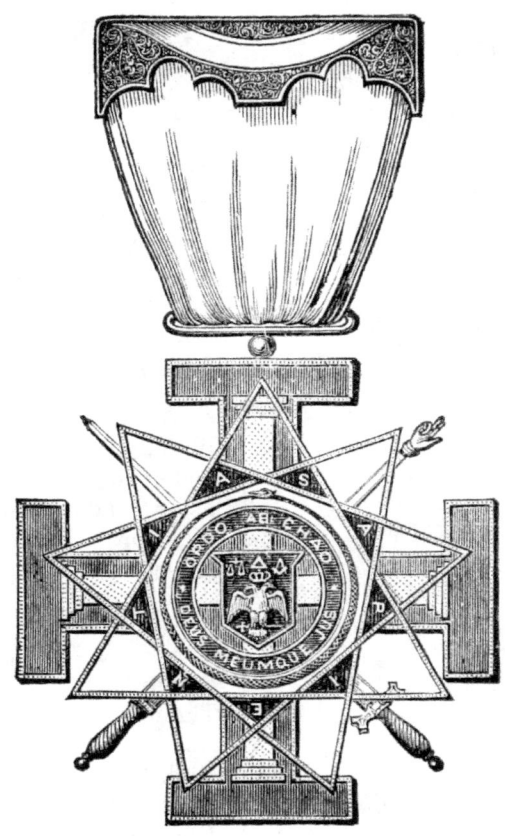

INDEX.

	Page.
Anthems	518, 517, 261
Appendix to Grand Constitutions, 1786	493
Articles for government of Rose-Croix Knights	215
Banner of the Order	494
Banquets, Masonic	578
Baptism, Masonic—By whom conferred, etc.	555
Who are entitled to	556
Arrangement of Hall	557
Ceremonial	557
Procession	560
Hymn	564
Ode	569
Vow	572
Song	573
Jewels	574
Beauseant	493
Calendar, Hebrew	613
Charter, form of application for	600
Characteristics of Rose-Croix Knights	601
Childe Harold, extract from	603
Chant	233
Chapter Rose-Croix—Constitution and Installation	526
See Knight of the Rose-Croix.	
CHIEF OF THE TABERNACLE—23d Degree	331
Argument	332
The Lodge, its decorations, etc.	333
Reception	343
Invocation	343
Lecture	344
Classification of Degrees	9
Colors of the various series of Degrees	330
Covering for the head, description of	180
Consistory of Sublime Princes	532
Inauguration of the Temple	533
Ceremony of Consecration	533
Installation	538
General oath of Fealty and Allegiance	539
" " Office	546
Hymn	552
Endorsement of Letters Patent	552
" Book of Gold	553
Protocol of Installation	553
Signing of Record obligatory	554
See Sublime Prince of the Royal Secret.	
Council of Princes of Jerusalem—Constitution and Installation	516
Procession	516
Anthem	518, 517
Address	519

618 BOOK OF THE A. AND A. RITE.

	Page.
Ceremony of Constitution	521
" Installation	522
Power of a Past Most Equitable Master to Install	525
See Prince of Jerusalem.	
Decorations, 33d Degree	491, 469
Dedication	3
Degrees, form of application for	600
Dispensation, form of application for	600
Directory, Secret—who entitled to hold	506
Dirge	391
Feasts, forms of	578
First Series—Symbolic Degrees	26
Fifth Series	285
Fourth Series	213
Freemasonry, definitions of	302, 212
Glossary, Masonic	582
Grand Decorations	495
GRAND, ELECT, PERFECT AND SUBLIME MASON—14th Degree	149
Representation of Jewels	150
Scenic view of form of Lodge and Decorations	151
Argument	152
Form of Lodge and Decorations	153
Clothing and Decorations	156
Lesson for Opening and Closing	158
Reception	161
Investment	167
Charge	176
History	170
Closing	174
See Lodge of Perfection.	
GRAND INSPECTOR INQUISITOR COMMANDER—31st Degree	453
Argument	454
Decorations of Court	455
Officers, Titles, etc	456
Regalia, Decorations, etc	458
Prerogatives, Reception	459
GRAND MASTER ARCHITECT—12th Degree	125
Argument	126
The Chapter, its Decorations	127
Officers, Titles, etc	128
Clothing, Ornaments, Jewels, etc	128
Opening 130	
Reception	130
Lecture	133
Investment	134
History	135
Clothing	136
GRAND MASTER OF ALL SYMBOLIC LODGES—20th Degree	303
Argument	304
Apartment and Decorations	305
Officers, etc	306
Reception	307
Lecture	309
GRAND PONTIFF—19th Degree	289
Argument	290
Apartments	291
Officers and Decorations	292
Reception	293
Investiture	299
Lecture	300
Grand Visitations	577

INDEX.

	Page.
Hebrew Calendar	618
History of the Ancient and Accepted Scottish Rite	11
Honors due at Grand Visitations	577
Hymns....598, 592, 589, 564, 552, 297, 293, 282, 280, 273, 264, 258, 235, 231, 226,	73
INSPECTOR-GENERAL—33d Degree	492
Introduction to Ineffable and Sublime Degrees	23
INTENDANT OF THE BUILDINGS—8th Degree	83
Argument	84
Apartment and its Decorations	85
Officers, Titles, etc	85
Regalia, Jewels, etc	86
Reception	87
Lesson	89
Investiture	90
History	91
INTIMATE SECRETARY—6th Degree	61
Argument	62
Apartments and Decorations	63
Officers and their Costumes	63
Reception	64
Investment	65
History	66
KNIGHT OF THE BRAZEN SERPENT—25th Degree	357
Argument	358
The Lodge, its Decorations	359
Reception	362
KNIGHT COMMANDER OF THE TEMPLE—27th Degree	385
Argument	386
Lodge, Furniture, etc	387
Officers and Titles	388
Dress, Decorations, etc	389
Reception	391
History	394
KNIGHTS ELECT OF NINE—9th Degree	95
Argument	96
Scenic view of Hall	98
Decorations, etc	99
Officers, Titles	99
Clothing	100
Opening	101
Reception	102
History	103
KNIGHTS ELECT OF FIFTEEN—10th Degree	105
Argument	106
The Chapter, its Decorations	107
Officers, Titles, etc	107
Ornaments, Jewels, etc	108
Opening	109
Reception	111
History	112
KNIGHT OF THE ROYAL AXE—22d Degree	323
Argument	324
Lodge, Officers, Decorations, etc	325
Opening	327
Reception and History	327
KNIGHT OF THE EAST OR SWORD—15th Degree	183
Argument	184
Apartments of the Council	185
Officers	186
Opening and Reception	188
KNIGHTS OF THE EAST AND WEST—17th Degree	219
Argument	220
Apartments and Decorations	221

	Page.
Officers	224
Clothing and Regalia	224
Opening	225
Reception	229
Investiture	234
Lecture	236
History	240
KNIGHT KADOSH—30th Degree	439
Argument	440
Apartments, Furniture, Decorations	441
Officers of the Council	443
Dress of Knight Kadosh	443
Reception	445
Mystic Ladder	451
KNIGHT OF THE ROSE-CROIX—18th Degree	243
Argument	244
Apartments	247
Officers and their Jewels	251
Clothing and Decorations	251
Reception	254
Charge and Lecture	259
Ceremony of the Table	263
Holy Thursday	265
" " Ceremony	267
" " Address	268
Ceremony of Extinguishing the Lights	270
Easter Sunday	272
" " Ceremony	273
Ceremony of relighting on Easter Sunday	275
Funeral Ceremony	276
KNIGHT OF THE SUN—28th Degree	399
Argument	400
Council-Chamber, its Furniture, etc	401
Officers, their Stations, Clothing, etc	404
Opening	407
Reception	409
Scenic View of Egyptian Mysteries	414
KNIGHT OF ST. ANDREW—29th Degree	417
Argument	418
Apartments and their Decorations	419
Officers and Costumes	420
Reception	422
Lecture	427
Lodge of Perfection—Inauguration and Constitution of	501
Oath of Fealty and Allegiance	504
Ceremonial Degree at Installation	506
Installation of Officers of	508
General Oath	514
See Grand, Elect, Perfect and Sublime Mason.	
Masonic Glossary, for Toasts	582
Miserere	446
NOACHITE, OR PRUSSIAN KNIGHT—21st Degree	315
Argument	316
The Chapter, its Decorations	317
Reception	319
History	320
Odes..572, 175, 166, 87,	53
Ode to Masonry	288
Perfection—*See* Lodge of Perfection.	
PERFECT MASTER—5th Degree	47
Argument	48

INDEX. 621

Page.

Scenic view at Reception	49
Decorations	51
Officers, Titles	52
Clothing	52
Reception	53
Scenic view at Tomb	58
History	59
Prefatory 489, 437, 287, 215, 181,	26
PRINCE OF JERUSALEM—16th Degree	195
Argument	196
Apartments of the Council	197
Officers, 1st Apartment	198
Jewels	198
Costumes and Regalia	199
Officers, 3d Apartment	201
Costumes	201
Reception	203
Decree	207
History	209
PRINCE OF MERCY—26th Degree	367
Argument	368
Decorations of Chapter	369
Reception	372
PRINCE OF THE TABERNACLE—24th Degree	347
Argument	348
The Court, its Decorations, etc.	349
Officers and Clothing	350
Reception	352
Proem	7
PROVOST AND JUDGE—7th Degree	69
Argument	70
Apartment and its Decorations	71
Officers, Titles, etc	72
Regalia, Jewels, etc	72
Reception	73
Investiture	77
History	78
Red Letter	487
Refections, forms of	578
Regulations as to Decorations of the Order	488, 496
ROYAL ARCH OF ENOCH—13th Degree	137
Argument	138
Decorations of Chapter	139
Officers, Regalia	139
Opening	141
Reception	144
History	145
Right Arm, Ceremonial, Lodge of Perfection	500
Secret Directory, who entitled to	506
Second Series—Ineffable Degrees—Prefatory	26
SECRET MASTER—4th Degree	29
Argument	30
Scenic view of Holy Place	31
The Lodge and its Decorations	33
Officers of Lodge	35
Clothing and Regalia of	35
Opening of Lodge of	37
Reception	38
Signature, Official—Prefix to	602
Sonata	461
Songs	583, 573
Statutes relating to Discipline and Councils of Deliberation	584
Sublime Freemasonry-Opinion of London Freemason's Quar. Ma	438

SUBLIME KNIGHTS ELECTED—11th Degree	115
Argument	116
The Lodge, its Decorations	117
Officers, Titles, etc	117
Clothing, Ornaments and Jewels	117
Opening	119
Reception	120
History	122
Closing	124
SUBLIME PRINCE OF THE ROYAL SECRET—32d Degree	467
Argument	468
Decorations	469
Officers, Titles	470
The Camp	472
Clothing	474
Reception	475
Scenic view of Admission of Novice	480
Invocation	485
Symbolic Degrees	26
Toasts of Obligation	579
" How drank	580
" Directions in drinking	581
" Masonic Glossary	582
" Song—Auld Lang Syne	583
Third Series	179
Triple Triangle, Emblematic	22
Visitations, Grand—Honors due. etc	577

Look for these and other great titles at:
http://www.stoneguildpublishing.com

Book of Ancient and Accepted Scottish Rite Freemasonry by Charles T. McClenachan

The Book of the Holy Graal by A. E. Waite

The Book of the Lodge by George Oliver

The Builders by Joseph Fort Newton

The Chymical Marriage of Christian Rosencreutz translated by A. E. Waite

The Doctrine and Literature of the Kabalah by A. E. Waite

Fama Fraternitatis and Confession of the Rosicrucian Fraternity by A. E. Waite

Freemasonry in the Holy Land by Robert Morris

The Freemason's Manual by Jeremiah How

The Freemason's Monitor by Daniel Sickels

The History of Freemasonry and Concordant Orders

The History of Initiation by George Oliver

Illustrations of the Symbols of Freemasonry by Jacob Ernst

The Kybalion by The Three Initiates

Low Twelve by Edward S. Ellis

The New Masonic Trestleboard by Charles W. Moore

Opinions on Speculative Masonry by James C. Odiorne

The Perfect Ceremonies of Craft Masonry

The Poetry of Freemasonry by Rob Morris

Real History of the Rosicrucians by A. E. Waite

The Symbolism of Freemasonry by Albert G. Mackey

Symbolism of the Three Degrees by Oliver Day Street

Taylor's Monitor by William M. Taylor

Taylor-Hamilton Monitor of Symbolic Masonry by Sam R. Hamilton

Three Hundred Masonic Odes and Poems by Rob Morris

True Masonic Chart or Hieroglyphic Monitor by Jeremy Cross

www.ingramcontent.com/pod-product-compliance
Lightning Source LLC
Chambersburg PA
CBHW060307240426
43661CB00059B/2680